T0319912

Revolution in Development

Revolution in Development

MEXICO AND THE GOVERNANCE OF THE GLOBAL ECONOMY

Christy Thornton

UNIVERSITY OF CALIFORNIA PRESS

University of California Press
Oakland, California

Library of Congress Cataloging-in-Publication Data

Names: Thornton, Christy, author.
Title: Revolution in development : Mexico and the governance of the global
    economy / Christy Thornton.
Description: Oakland, California : University of California Press, [2021] |
    Includes bibliographical references and index.
Identifiers: LCCN 2020021294 (print) | LCCN 2020021295 (ebook) |
    ISBN 9780520297159 (cloth) | ISBN 9780520297166 (paperback) |
    ISBN 9780520969636 (epub)
Subjects: LCSH: International economic relations. | Mexico—Economic
    policy—History—20th century.
Classification: LCC HC135 .T535 2021 (print) | LCC HC135 (ebook) |
    DDC 337—dc23
LC record available at https://lccn.loc.gov/2020021294
LC ebook record available at https://lccn.loc.gov/2020021295

29 28 27 26 25 24 23 22 21 20
10 9 8 7 6 5 4 3 2 1

For Gail

CONTENTS

Introduction

HOW COULD MEXICO MATTER?

WHO GOVERNS THE GLOBAL ECONOMY? Who establishes the agenda, makes the decisions, and structures the institutions that set the rules of the game? According to the conventional wisdom, such governance has been largely the purview of the most powerful nations and empires in the world. Rich countries set the rules, and the poorer and weaker ones are compelled to follow them. In this story, the idea that a country like Mexico could influence the governance of the global economy seems a dubious proposition. Wracked by devaluations and debt crises, Mexico experienced a thorough reorientation of its economy in the last decades of the twentieth century, as the United States and international financial institutions prescribed privatization, liberalization, and austerity as conditions for debt relief. At the other end of the twentieth century, Mexico endured more than a decade of fractious and bloody social revolution, in which property was destroyed or expropriated and debt ignored or repudiated. In the decades in between these extremes, Mexico pursued an inward-looking development strategy based on import-substitution industrialization, with high tariffs and state subsidies providing protection from the outside world. What role could such a country play on the world stage?

Against the conventional narrative, this book presents the little-known history of how officials in Mexico seized moments of profound international change during the twentieth century to assume a leadership role in the struggle for a different kind of world economic order. The Mexican vision for global economic governance was one that afforded *representation* to the countries of what would become the Global South and enabled *redistribution* of the surplus capital of the Global North.[1] As they looked to reconstruct their war-torn country in the aftermath of the twentieth century's first social revolution, Mexican leaders quickly came to understand that their national economic

I

progress was deeply dependent on the rules and institutions that governed global capitalism, and they therefore set out to change those rules to favor their country and others like it. In so doing, they advanced early demands for institutions to promote international economic development—and compelled the powerful countries of the world to respond. They argued for new multilateral agreements, outlined innovative new international institutions, and fought during crucial global negotiations for both the rights of the poorer states and the duties of the richer ones. This fight, waged over more than five decades, was Mexico's revolution in development. In important ways, these Mexican officials won key victories: while some of their more radical proposals were rejected or deflected, many were in some form co-opted into Northern plans for international institutions and agreements, as US officials came to recognize the utility of, for example, multilateral development lending. Even when their more radical proposals were stymied by the interests of Northern bankers and industrialists, Mexican officials and their allies won important concessions from the world powers, using a politics of immanent critique to hold the United States accountable to the promises of multilateral liberalism.

Mexico's revolution in development was, I argue, a vision that transcended the boundaries of the national developmentalist project, seeking not just to transform the domestic economy but to devise new rules and institutions for managing the *global* economic systems into which Mexico was increasingly integrated. It is a dream that still echoes to this day: that the global capitalist economy, managed under the proper institutions and rules, could allow the poorer, weaker, indebted countries of the world to overcome their structural disadvantages and enjoy a share of the returns of capitalist progress.[2] As debates about reforming international financial institutions continue today, however, the unintended consequences of Mexico's vision need to be underscored, as the pursuit of this dream ultimately led its leaders to defend precisely the institutions that would be used to dismantle the country's state-led developmentalist project during the crisis of the 1980s. This history, then, should serve as a cautionary tale for today's dreamers.

THE SOUTH IN INTERNATIONAL POLITICAL ECONOMY

Under what circumstances could a country like Mexico have an impact on the creation of international institutions and the reform of global governance? Such a question can't be adequately answered with ahistorical theoretical abstraction, but rather requires paying careful attention to the specific historical circumstances in which Mexican actors and their allies sought to change, or to reinforce, the prevailing system.[3] The conditions of possibility for the formulation and reformulation of theoretical perspectives have, of course, been deeply shaped by the way that history has itself been understood; theorizing what *could* happen is a function of how we understand what *did* happen. Rather than positing general conditions under which weak states can influence strong ones, therefore, the chapters that follow demonstrate that disputes over the shape of the international economic system helped to define how strength might be exercised and how weakness would be understood. Mexico's advocacy of a fairer system of governing the global capitalist economy, undertaken in an often uneasy alliance with others from throughout Latin America and the rest of the Third World, defined important contours of legitimacy within which the United States managed its rise to power and conditioned US responses to the decline of that power.

In many prevailing historical and theoretical explanations for the development of the twentieth-century international order, however, the actions of countries like Mexico matter little. In the conventional historical narrative of the creation of the Bretton Woods institutions, for example, visionaries in the United States and Great Britain imagined a world order through a North Atlantic lens and conjured innovative new institutions—the International Monetary Fund (IMF) and the World Bank—to realize their vision. Given that this narrative was written from the archives of state power in the Global North, it is perhaps unsurprising that it often reflected the attitudes of actors for whom the interests, ideas, and demands of the poorer and weaker states were an afterthought, at best, if they were considered at all.[4] During the negotiations in the lead-up to the Bretton Woods Conference in early 1944, for example, a British Treasury official, incensed at the inclusion of so many Latin American delegates in the planning process, expressed a view often echoed in most of the subsequent historiography: it was "silly to make the pretense that the Mexicans . . . and the Brazilians would discuss 'at the expert level' a document which the American Treasury was endorsing." They were there, he argued, "to sign in the place for the signature," nothing more.[5]

Although few scholars would embrace such explicit paternalism today, some important theoretical perspectives have nevertheless precluded the possibility of the story in these pages, based on their understandings of the US rise to power. Some world-systems theorists, for example, have argued that the United States arrived on the world stage in 1945 able to "impose on the world an order of its own choice," with the result that "U.S. hegemony was built from the top down" through the creation of new multilateral organizations.[6] The varied institutions of the United Nations were thus established, in Immanuel Wallerstein's words, as a mere "fig-leaf" for US power.[7] In these narratives, the rising United States had to contend with other great powers, the interests of capital, and the struggles of labor and social movements, but much less with the demands or aspirations of the weaker and poorer states.[8] A similar story has been told in some Gramscian and historicist theories of international political economy; in Craig Murphy's conception, for example, the "liberal learning" that US leaders accomplished in the interwar period came largely from the teachings of European theorists and Northern business interests, whose lessons shaped the establishment of the "free world order."[9] The result, Robert Cox similarly argued, was the creation of a "consensual, homogenous, hegemonic" US-led world order, the "Pax Americana."[10] In this world order, "Third World elites do not participate with the same effective status as top-level elites in the formation of the consensus."[11] Under conditions of hegemonic consensus, then, representatives of less-powerful states could act, but not under conditions of their own choosing—and not usually in ways that could be consequential for the larger system.[12]

If these frameworks precluded the possibility that Global South actors could have been influential in the *creation* of the postwar systems of global economic governance, however, the forceful demands of the Third World in response to the crisis of the 1970s demonstrated that the apparent hegemonic consensus was fraying. The "revolt against the West" begged new theoretical explanations.[13] Following the struggle for the New International Economic Order (NIEO), for example, Steven Krasner adapted the concept of "metapower behavior" in the early 1980s to argue that it was not *despite* massive relational power asymmetries but *because* of those asymmetries that Third World states sought to "alter the principles, norms, rules and decision-making procedures that condition international transactions"—to change the rules of the game.[14] The conditions under which Third World states could have some leverage in changing global governance systems, Krasner argued, were first, when US power was in relative decline; second, when Third World states had high levels of access within international institutions; and third, when those states were able to construct a coherent ideological program, overcoming disparate interests and goals. But these explanations were less general theoretical conditions than they were a perceptive description of the particular historical conjuncture of the 1970s. As such, Krasner joined other scholars who have identified the 1970s as the moment when the Third World "learned to aggregate their voting power," as Cox put it: when decolonization created the possibility of influence, which, these theories implied, had not existed previously.[15]

Despite this newfound aggregating power, however, what followed was not increased Third-Worldist agitation but the "lost decade" of structural adjustment at the behest of the international financial institutions (IFIs), followed by the founding of the World Trade Organization (WTO) as a new forum for implementing the so-called Washington Consensus of liberalizing, market-oriented reforms. In this era, the ability of the Global South to resist Northern imperatives, let alone change them, seemed further diminished. Scholars and policy makers began therefore to theorize the nature of global governance itself, initially concerned more with the eclipse of the state by new global forces than with the role of the poorer and weaker states in managing the institutions of the global economy.[16] But especially after the streets of Seattle exploded with protestors angry at the exclusionary nature of the IFIs—joining a social movement wave of Zapatistas, *piqueteros*, water warriors, and others fighting against programs backed by the World Bank, the IMF, and the US government—scholars began to posit a "democratic deficit" within international institutions, arguing that their undemocratic nature was undermining their very legitimacy.[17] Concern that global organizations were "stifling the voice of the South" became widespread, and calls for reform became perennial.[18] Subsequently, when the "pink tide" of leftist leaders in Latin America began to reject the oversight of the IFIs, and when leaders in Brazil, India, China, and then South Africa began to self-consciously organize together as the BRICS consortium, theorists began to explore the possibilities for "South-South cooperation," asking how rising powers might build new institutions and linkages that would bypass Northern-dominated institutions altogether.[19] That the countries of the South could matter no longer seemed in dispute.

Renewed contention from the Global South has therefore opened new space for scholars to return to the historical record on which our theoretical perspectives have been built—looking back, for example, to the Bandung moment to trace antecedent lessons for contemporary South-South cooperation.[20] In doing so, however, scholars have found that they have to contend with the enormous condescension of Northern historical actors themselves. Tracing North-South contention within the United Nations back to the late

1940s, for example, John Toye and Richard Toye noted the need to counter the arrogance, bias, and paternalism that pervades the US and European archival record, making an explicit methodological case for "treating seriously the developing countries' view that differences in the level of economic development are relevant to the obligations that countries should be asked to assume in international trade and financial relations."[21] They clearly anticipated skeptical readers, however, assuring their audience that "in principle, this is a perfectly respectable argument," thereby demonstrating the tenacity of theoretical understandings to the contrary. Taking up the methodological challenge posed by Toye and Toye, Eric Helleiner went even further back to uncover the "forgotten foundations" of the Bretton Woods institutions in the ideas and demands that actors from the Global South, and from Latin America in particular, brought before US and European officials.[22] Helleiner's work rereads the US archival record on which so much previous scholarship had been based to demonstrate that in fact, Global South concerns had not only been present at the creation of the post-1945 world order, but they had anticipated and shaped it in profound ways—not least by introducing a demand for development.

Despite these advances, however, relatively few scholars have written the history of international institutions and the order they sustain "from the outside in," using sources from and centering perspectives beyond those of the United States and Europe.[23] Reacting to histories of "governing the world" that continue to exclude the South, Amitav Archaya has recently argued against the persistence of a "parochial and one-sided view [that] ignores the extent to which foundational ideas of what we know today as 'global governance' were far from an American or Western monopoly."[24] As Adom Getachew has recently demonstrated, actors from Africa, the Caribbean, and the worldwide Black diaspora could be "worldmakers" in their own right.[25] Against theories that posit unidirectional North-South norm diffusion or that limit Third World ideas about development and progress to the purely domestic, inward-looking sphere, Getachew reminds us that leaders in the Global South have long imagined new ways of ordering the world and have organized to bring them into being.

Following the insights of this interdisciplinary range of thinkers, the chapters that follow revise the historical narrative and reveal the role that Mexico played in the creation and reform of the institutions, agreements, and organizations that together comprise our system of global economic governance. Methodologically, this requires returning to the archive and reading

Mexican sources—state records from the office of the presidency; the Secretaría de Relaciones Exteriores (SRE), Mexico's foreign ministry; and the Secretaría de Hacienda y Crédito Público, Mexico's finance ministry; as well as the personal papers of Mexican economists, diplomats, and political figures, and the Mexican press—along with and against the grain of US and European archival sources. Bringing these sources together often reveals contention that has been hidden by the exclusive reliance on Northern records, uncovering multidirectional influences disavowed by powerful actors seeking to legitimate that power. What emerges from this methodology is less an intellectual history of Mexican economic thought than a reconstruction of theorizing in practice, as Mexican officials tested precocious ideas about the global economy and their place within it during active negotiations about treaties, trade agreements, and international institutions.

Theoretically, in working from the outside in, my analysis departs from perspectives that seek to explain the rise of US hegemony as a *consensus* project. Instead, following William Roseberry, I understand the construction of US hegemony as characterized by "contention, struggle, and argument."[26] Antonio Gramsci argued that understanding hegemony required not simply explaining the actions of the dominant classes but also uncovering the actions of the subaltern classes, "their active or passive affiliation to the dominant political formations, their attempts to influence the programmes of these formations in order to press claims of their own, and the consequences of these attempts in determining processes of decomposition, renovation, or neo-formation."[27] Using such a perspective to understand global economic governance requires a conception of the US rise to power as structured by what Julian Go and George Lawson call the dynamics of "interactive multiplicity," in which the mechanisms for the projection of US power were "formed and reformed through interactions with actors assumed to be external to or subordinate to them."[28] This book looks through a Mexican lens to demonstrate that US hegemony—rather than being "built from the top down"—has in fact been shaped by iterative, repeated struggle from subordinate states, *themselves* shaped by internal social struggles over property, access, and representation. Paying close attention to these processes requires using the concept of hegemony, as Roseberry implored, "not to understand consent but to understand struggle."[29] Such an understanding is important to illuminate not only the alternative possible futures that were imagined by actors in the Global South, but to reveal precisely how those alternative paths were foreclosed—and therefore to serve as a lesson for contemporary efforts at reform. Mexico's historical struggle, therefore, and its complicated, contradictory, and surprising consequences are the subject of this book.

THE MEXICAN CASE

Having established a broad framework for approaching the study of interventions by Global South actors in international political economy, the question remains: Why Mexico? A country defined by its "revolutionary nationalism," Mexico might seem to be a strange candidate for *internationalist* leadership.[30] Given that there was no Mexican equivalent to the Comintern or to the programs of Fidel Castro's Cuba seeking to export Mexico's brand of revolution abroad, historians have argued that the Mexican revolutionary process was not internationalist as such.[31] But an exclusive focus on Mexican nationalism in the postrevolutionary period has obscured the ways in which nationalism and internationalism frequently represent two sides of the same coin—or two aspects of a single, integrated process.[32] In the Mexican case, the world's reactions to the policies pursued in the name of economic nationalism made an internationalist project necessary. As one scholar has argued, in the twentieth century, "The Mexican revolution was the first important challenge to the world order of the industrial-creditor, and capitalistic, nations made by an underdeveloped nation trying to assert control over its economy and reform its internal system."[33] Mexico's challenge to the world order, however, was more than simply an attempt to more effectively control what happened *inside* its borders. It was also, this book shows, a struggle to redraw the economic and financial map within which those borders were delineated. For the postrevolutionary Mexican state, therefore, "the common front was to be an internationalism of the underdeveloped countries based on a vital nationalism which articulated common aspirations for development and independence."[34]

This common front meant that Mexican leaders were not alone, of course, in their advocacy, and in fact they needed to cultivate allies from the rest of Latin America and the Third World and to actively build coalitions among like-minded states to advance their vision. If the ideas and policies that Mexican officials pursued in these pages were shared, what is distinctive about the Mexican case? Three factors make Mexico's interventions particularly important. First, the physical proximity with the United States not only facilitated close exchange between Mexican and US representatives over long periods, creating deep working relationships that would be drawn upon as US officials formulated policy, but also made Mexico of particular importance to many US geopolitical goals. Mexican officials would repeatedly use this fact in their favor, leveraging their position between the United States and others in Latin America and the Third World to extract concessions. Second, the revolutionary process itself provided an important ideological justification for Mexican advocacy. Mexican economic ideas were rooted in the juridical force and ideological weight of Mexico's 1917 constitution, which redefined property and subsoil rights as vested not in the individual but in the nation. Of course, putting the constitution's lofty provisions into practice domestically was a long and contested process, subject to the same social struggles that had marked the constitutional convention itself, as workers and campesinos on the one hand and industrialists and landholders on the other pressed their claims upon the state. Nevertheless, a rhetoric of historical duty deriving from the revolution pervaded Mexican internationalist advocacy; having overseen the process of crafting the "world's first fully conceived social-democratic charter," Mexican leaders repeatedly argued that their country had a responsibility to carry that vision to the world stage.[35] Such rhetoric could serve as merely a justification for some other interest, material or political, but it was one that, as the chapters that follow show, was repeatedly invoked.

Finally, and perhaps most important, the interventions of Mexican leaders traced in these pages were profoundly shaped by Mexico's access to—and exclusion from—the international financial system. In 1914 Mexico defaulted on existing debt from before and during the revolutionary struggle, and the postrevolutionary state spent the next three decades negotiating Mexico's reinsertion into the system of international finance, public and private. Intense pressure from US and European bankers and bondholders, who organized into collective associations and allied with the more powerful states, established real constraints on postrevolutionary state building, and therefore shaped Mexican ideas about the nature of sovereignty itself. Isolated from international capital markets even as other countries experienced a lending boom, Mexican officials began to theorize the insufficiencies of *political* sovereignty in the absence of *economic* sovereignty. As the dust settled on the revolutionary struggle, Mexican political figures recognized that their economy did not exist asynchronously at a different and unrelated developmental stage from that of the United States or Europe, but rather came to understand that Mexico's development prospects were deeply constrained by a rapidly globalizing economic interdependence. Decades before either modernization or dependency became codified bodies of theory to explain Mexico's place in the world, Mexican officials grappled with such ideas in practice, in negotiations over Mexico's access to capital and markets. Mexican leaders therefore actively sought to create an international framework—and not just an inward-focused, national policy—conducive to reinserting Mexico into the global financial system on equitable terms. As the chapters that follow make clear, it was precisely the struggle over access to capital—over the legal structures that might govern it and the institutions that might provide it—that shaped the patterns of how Mexico intervened in debates over global economic governance.

Revolution in Development uncovers these patterns in Mexican advocacy, which began at the close of the First World War, as world leaders debated the purview of the new League of Nations, and culminated in the late 1970s, when Mexican president Luis Echeverría spearheaded the writing of the Charter of Economic Rights and Duties of States, the agreement that would underpin the creation of the NIEO. Across these six decades, Mexican representatives repeatedly intervened in international negotiations to call for the creation of new institutions or the reform of existing ones, insisting on not only the rights of what were variously called the small, poor, weak, or debtor states, but on the responsibilities of the rich and powerful ones as well. Throughout the period, they sought not only *representation* in multilateral institutions—foreseeing and attempting to forestall the "democratic deficit" that would come to be criticized later—but also *redistribution* of productive capital from North to South, especially through long-term, concessional lending.

This is not, however, a story of unbroken continuity over six decades, but rather one of a dialectical evolution over time. Each instance in which Mexican ideas and proposals were rejected, deflected, or co-opted into international governance structures shaped how Mexican actors approached subsequent moments. Excluded from international financial markets, Mexican leaders in the 1920s and 1930s called for the wholesale revision of the system of international debt and credit. As Mexico slowly regained access to international lending in the 1940s, Mexican proposals sought to reshape the rules of new commercial and financial institutions being proposed by the United States and its Northern allies, to make sure they would benefit debtors as well as creditors. As credit finally started to flow to the country in the 1950s and 1960s, Mexican actors reversed their critical course, defending existing institutions from the insurgent demands of other Third World states still excluded from the new development regime. Finally, in the 1970s, as the United States sought to unilaterally redefine the rules for international trade and finance, Mexican leaders fashioned themselves as intermediaries. Even as they ramped up their reliance on international lending, Mexican officials attempted to negotiate a reformed world order that would stave off revolutionary upheaval by meeting the economic demands put forward by Global South leaders. While any one of the individual moments traced in the chapters that follow might appear to be of only minimal consequence, taken together, they reveal broader patterns of Mexican influence in global economic governance.

To trace these patterns, this book provides a new interpretation of the history of Mexican foreign policy, situating Mexican relations with the United States within a larger set of first hemispheric and then global negotiations.[36] It therefore requires two shifts in periodization. The first pushes the conventional understanding of Global South political mobilization as a post-1945 phenomenon backward in time, in order to read Latin American contention with the United States alongside later struggles over the end of the European empires. This requires crossing what I have called elsewhere the "decolonization divide," centering the analysis not simply on struggles over political or territorial sovereignty, but rather on the long fight for *economic sovereignty* that defined so much of the twentieth century.[37] The second shift in periodization concerns how scholars have long understood the turning points in the history of the postrevolutionary Mexican state. The book begins as the military phase of the Mexican revolution is drawing to a close in the late 1910s and follows the rise of the postrevolutionary developmental state to the cusp of the neoliberal transition in the early 1980s. As such, it crosses the traditional historiographical boundary marked by the end of the Cárdenas presidency in 1940, which a broad consensus has long understood as a transition between the revolutionary period and the corporatist, developmental state.[38] As the chapters that follow make clear, adequately explaining the evolution of Mexico's internationalist advocacy requires crossing this temporal border, paying close attention to patterns that could be ignored or disavowed by historical actors themselves.

Who were the actors who carried out this advocacy? They were largely state representatives, drawn mostly from Mexico's educated middle classes and elites; they were almost entirely men, and most worked largely within the confines of the party apparatus that would come to be the Partido

Revolucionario Institucional (PRI). The PRI governed Mexico as a single-party state for more than seven decades and not only produced an official nationalist mythology based on the legacy of the revolution, but also oversaw a complex corporatist project that sought industrial modernization while containing conflict between capital, labor, and the peasantry—sometimes through force.[39] While the Mexican political system was highly presidentialist, and a few presidents played particularly active roles in Mexico's international negotiations, most of the actors under study here comprised a middle stratum of the Mexican state, within the bureaucracies of state power in the offices of the foreign ministry; the finance ministry; the Banco de México, Mexico's central bank; and Nacional Financiera, the state development bank, among others. As these bureaucracies solidified, the *políticos* of earlier eras, assigned their positions in the bureaucracy because of personal connections and partisan loyalties, gave way to *técnicos* who had credentialed expertise in fields like economics, statistics, and finance.[40] Nevertheless, these state actors were not autonomous from larger social forces within Mexico, and their decisions were frequently shaped by ongoing domestic social struggle, as the state pursued its own legitimating project at home. Accordingly, the chapters that follow strive to put Mexico's foreign policy decisions in their domestic political-economic context.

From the perspective of Mexican history, the actors under study here were in no sense subalterns.[41] In international fora, however—even though the individuals who pursued the international projects traced in these pages came largely from the county's relatively wealthy and connected families; frequently were educated in foreign universities in the United States and Europe; and served in Mexico's diplomatic, governmental, and scholarly echelons of power—these Mexican officials frequently experienced profound instances of subordination, dismissal, and exclusion. On the global stage, even elite, highly educated, light-skinned Mexicans who spoke fluent French or English were often regarded as inferior by their counterparts in the United States and Europe, as the quote previously cited from the British Treasury official about who could discuss financial topics "at the expert level" makes clear.[42] These exclusions often took racialized and gendered forms, in which Mexican advocacy could be dismissed by someone like John Maynard Keynes as irrational because of its embodied source.[43] While the chapters that follow analyze these exclusions, they also explain the circumstances in which they could be overcome, highlighting instances in which Mexican actors used either their country's geopolitical position or their personal connections to make inroads with those in power in the North. While this book tells a story of elites, it is one in which they operate in uneven, hierarchical systems of international power.

Grappling with both the social position of the actors under study here as well as the contours of their political project to advance Mexico's capitalist development requires us to recognize that an "outside-in" reading of the history of international institutions and agreements does not automatically produce a straightforward story of heroic resistance by the Global South against a domineering Global North. Further, highlighting these Mexican interventions should not be read as a simple reclamation of the agency of Mexicans or the Mexican state in the world economy, affirming Mexican fitness or belonging—or a simple assertion that, despite being written out of the historical record, Mexico was there.[44] Rather, although this book details Mexican proposals for reforming an exclusionary and unequal global economic system, it also uncovers how such reforms could be incorporated into that system as it changed over time. By arguing for mechanisms for international economic development and fighting for greater access to global financial resources, Mexican advocacy paradoxically helped sharpen the tools that would be used to dismantle its long-standing developmental project in the neoliberal period. Thus, Mexico's revolution in development—a phrase chosen precisely for its productive ambiguity—encompasses not only the transition from revolutionary social goals to state developmentalism over the course of the twentieth century, but also Mexico's articulation of and demand for a concerted program of *international* development. But Mexico's fight to change the structures of the global economy in which its national development program was situated, even when successful at achieving its aims, had unintended consequences. This revolution in development, therefore, like others before it, may have paradoxically "perfected [the] machine instead of breaking it."[45]

STRUCTURE OF THE WORK

The chapters that follow proceed chronologically, detailing successive historical moments in which Mexican officials intervened—or, importantly, chose not to intervene—in debates over the governance of international institutions. Over the period under study here, Mexican officials sought to shape an international system predicated on the sovereign equality of states (arguing over issues of *representation*) that would create conditions conducive to the economic development of the poorer countries (arguing over issues of *redistribution*). How they approached these negotiations varied. Some interventions were overtly political in nature, based on broad claims about the moral economy in which Mexico was embedded, while others were more strictly technical, seeking to rewrite specific institutional rules. Some were meant to create entirely new organizations, while others attempted to reform existing or proposed institutions and frameworks. Most important, some were transformative, while some were essentially conservative: while Mexico's early interventions largely fought to overturn or at least significantly alter the status quo, once some gains had been realized, Mexican officials could be found arguing *for* the status quo, hedging against the more radical interventions of other Third World countries. As previously outlined, the strategies that Mexican state actors pursued in each moment were structured by both the domestic and international political-economic conditions under which they took place.

The book begins in Paris in 1919, with the creation of the first major multilateral organization, the League of Nations. Chapter 1 argues that Mexico used the Paris negotiations to stake a claim not just to the formal equality of states in international institutions, but also to a substantive understanding of economic sovereignty, rooted in the 1917 constitution's redefinition of property rights. While the Mexican representative at Paris did not set out to make a strident political intervention regarding representation that would question the very legitimacy of the new institution, events forced such a strategy on Mexican president Venustiano Carranza. That intervention then set an agenda that was followed a few years later, at the Inter-American Conference in Santiago, Chile, in 1923. There, Mexican officials made a more technical intervention regarding representation, intended to reform the rules governing the one general multilateral organization to which the United States belonged, the Pan-American Union, to ensure a more democratic structure for international politics.

Chapters 2 and 3 trace a shift from struggles over representation to those over redistribution, as Mexican officials reacted to the dislocations engendered by the Great Depression. As detailed in chapter 2, in 1933 the Mexican foreign minister made a political intervention couched as a technical reform in the agenda of the Inter-American Conference at Montevideo. The proposal called for a wholesale reconsideration of the structure of international debt and credit, casting it as a social relation between rich and poor countries.

Over the years that followed, Mexican officials refined this call into a technical proposal for an entirely new institution that would have been the world's first international development bank. The Inter-American Bank (IAB) project, the subject of chapter 3, was then co-opted by US planners, who oversaw the process of creating a charter and bylaws for the institution, only to see it scuttled by the interests of private capital within the United States. In the process, however, US planners came to understand the usefulness of a multilateral lending institution for the consolidation of their hegemonic project.

Lessons learned in the fight over the IAB then informed the negotiations in which Mexican officials intervened in the 1940s. Chapter 4 examines Mexico's technical reform efforts in 1944 to fight for both representation and redistribution within the proposed new global financial institutions, the International Bank for Reconstruction and Development (IBRD, or World Bank) and the IMF. Mexico not only intervened decisively to put development issues on the agenda of the new institutions; it also advocated for better representation and more democratic decision-making, prefiguring the criticisms that would be leveled at these institutions beginning in the 1990s. Chapter 5 examines Mexico's interventions over representation within the broader creation of the United Nations and details the technical campaign Mexico waged to secure redistribution through development assistance from the United States at the Chapultepec Conference in 1945. Chapter 6 examines Mexico's interventions to reform the proposed International Trade Organization (ITO), and shows how, as was the case with the IAB, Mexican success in securing concessions from the US delegation resulted in US capital blocking the project altogether.

Despite the failure to create the IAB or the ITO, however, one cumulative result of the demands made by Mexico and its allies in the 1930s and 1940s was the extension of increased credit to countries like Mexico through institutions such as the World Bank and the Export-Import Bank (Ex-Im Bank). When in the 1950s and 1960s foreign capital began to pour into Mexico, the country's officials abruptly changed tactics, as chapter 7 demonstrates. In this period, Mexico made a few political interventions that allowed it to maintain plausible distance from its largest creditor, while at the same time seeking technical reforms that were actually meant to *defend* the international financial status quo. In a period when myriad new political and economic institutions were being created in the burgeoning Third World, Mexico largely retreated from its leadership role and even played a key role in arguing down a Third World proposal to circumvent the IMF. Instead, when unilateral US economic policy changes began to have an impact on Mexican finance and trade, Mexican officials decided to pursue a new broader framework for global economic governance. As chapter 8 shows, Mexican president Luis Echeverría and his advisers proposed the Charter of Economic Rights and Duties of States, a detailed political and technical document meant to create a new framework for global economic governance that would address questions of both representation and redistribution. The negotiations with both the Global North and the rest of the Global South, however, revealed the contradictions of Mexico's position as an intermediary, attempting to stay in the good graces of Mexico's most important source of credit—the United States—while correcting the most egregious imbalances of international power. As Mexican officials would discover, this was a difficult balance to strike.

By the 1970s, of course, not only was Mexico receiving hundreds of millions of dollars in official development loans, but the petrodollar lending bonanza meant that loans from private banks also poured into the country. Echeverría seemed finally poised to fulfill the vision that Mexican officials had long advocated, using the country's increased access to credit to direct industrial investment and ramp up social spending while also championing the economic rights of the Global South. But if Echeverría's debt-driven, Third-Worldist populism represented the realization of Mexico's revolution in development, it was also its last gasp, as the conclusion argues. Papering over the contradictions of the country's economy, Echeverría and his successor, José López Portillo, oversaw an unprecedented expansion in public and private foreign debt. When, in August 1982, Mexico's finance minister Jesús Silva Herzog announced that Mexico could no longer pay its debts, it was precisely those international institutions that Mexico had argued for, benefited from, and then defended from more radical Third-Worldist criticism that emerged as key instruments in dismantling Mexico's state-led developmental project.

Today, with the global economy once again in crisis, and as debates recur about the reform of the IFIs and the role of the Global South within them, the chapters that follow make clear that many of the key criticisms of global economic governance in the twenty-first century were, in fact, anticipated by Mexican planners in earlier eras.[46] During the Bretton Woods negotiations in the summer of 1944, for example, Mexico's Antonio Espinosa de los Monteros had charged that, the way the US plans were written, the IMF might be able to make debtor countries "change their laws and perhaps even their constitutions at a minutes notice, regardless of political, social or economic difficulties."[47] It was a prescient worry, anticipating the conditionality of structural adjustment by decades. In the moment, however, Espinosa was assuaged with a technical reform introduced by a US official, which would allow countries like Mexico to opt out of the currency-valuation provision he was protesting. While Mexican officials harbored few illusions about the asymmetries of power within the institutions they advocated and fought to reform, they nonetheless sought to rewrite the rules and create a fairer framework for governing the world economy. This fight echoes to this day. Its consequences should, as well.

ONE

———

Recognition and Representation

THE MEXICAN REVOLUTION AND
MULTILATERAL GOVERNANCE

WHEN MEXICAN PRESIDENT VENUSTIANO CARRANZA stood before congress in 1918 to outline his vision of the role that the revolutionary government should play in the world—a set of principles that would come to be known as the Carranza Doctrine—he was presiding over an uneasy peace. In Europe, the First World War was in its final days, while in Mexico, the armed phase of the revolution seemed to finally be drawing to a close. Mexico's revolutionary struggle had been a protracted, internecine battle not only to oust longtime dictator Porfirio Díaz from power but also to define the political and economic terms for what might come next. Peasant insurgencies led by leaders like Pancho Villa and Emiliano Zapata clamored for the redistribution of land; radicalized workers, steeped in the anarcho-syndicalist ideas of the Flores Magón brothers, fought for better conditions in the mines, railroads, and factories where they toiled; and liberal intellectuals and political figures argued over and then took up arms for the ideals of democracy, demanding effective suffrage and an end to the continuous reelection that had kept Díaz in power for decades. Even after the aging dictator was finally ousted in 1911, fighting continued for years among various factions; the best estimates are that nearly 1.5 million people died as a result of war and disease, with hundreds of thousands more living in exile outside the country.[1] With its population devastated, infrastructure destroyed, foreign investments overrun, and debts in default, what role could poor and fractious Mexico possibly play on the world stage?

Despite the inauspicious domestic context, however, in the half decade between 1918 and 1923, Mexican officials inaugurated a campaign to rewrite the rules of international politics. In so doing, Carranza and his allies launched Mexico's postrevolutionary struggle for representation in multilateral institutions, based on a forceful defense of the sovereign equality of states. Though this struggle was largely waged over questions of how countries like Mexico would participate in international institutions, first concerning Mexican membership in the League of Nations and then the Pan-American Union, it was also driven by concerns about the imbalance of global economic power. The administrations of Carranza and his successor, Álvaro Obregón, intervened in international debates to defend Mexico's economic sovereignty as a key aspect of its global political standing. If states were to be truly equal, Mexican officials asserted, they should enjoy the freedom to structure their economies according to their national principles and priorities, without interference from foreign capital or its government protectors. Carranza's vision for the world, and the tactics of Mexican officials who organized collective action to defend it on the international stage, defined important principles and strategies that would structure Mexican interventions for decades to come.

THE CONSTITUTION AND THE POLITICAL ECONOMY
OF THE CARRANZA DOCTRINE

By 1915, Carranza's Constitutionalist army had defeated its revolutionary rivals for power, and the landowning former senator from the northern state of Coahuila was named head of the provisional government that would rewrite Mexico's constitution. While the draft constitution that Carranza introduced at the Querétaro convention was fairly conservative and proposed mainly political reforms, representatives of the still powerful labor and agrarian factions of the revolutionary struggle—labeled by their critics as *jacobinos*—fought for over two months to obtain more sweeping changes to Mexico's governing charter.[2] The resulting constitution of 1917 went far beyond Carranza's liberal proposal and emerged as "the world's first fully conceived social-democratic charter," codifying labor rights such as a minimum wage, an eight-hour workday, and the right to organize and bargain collectively, as well as rights to secular universal education, health care, and welfare.[3] In addition, and most consequential internationally, the new constitution radically redefined property rights in Mexico. Article 27 declared that "private property is a privilege created by the Nation," and granted the state the right to impose limitations on ownership in order "to ensure a more equitable distribution of public wealth."[4] The provisions of Article 27 meant that large estates could be broken up and their land redistributed, foreign ownership of property could be restricted, and the ownership of subsoil resources—the minerals and petroleum that had been extracted by US and European companies granted extensive concessions by the previous regime— was to be vested not in individual or corporate owners, but in the nation as a whole. A profound challenge to the liberal conception of property, Article 27 caused immediate concern in foreign capitals, where investors and land- holders began to lobby their governments to defend their existing concerns.[5] Following the promulgation of the new constitution, Carranza easily won election to the presidency, making him the chief defender of a much broader and deeper charter than the one he had proposed—particularly in the face of those who attacked it from abroad.

As the attacks on Mexico's new property regime intensified, not least by US and British oil interests, Carranza came before congress in late 1918 to link the principles of the constitution to Mexico's foreign policy and the country's place in the world. He seized a moment of profound international change— the armistice in Europe would be signed just two months later—to lay out the tenets of the Carranza Doctrine.[6] Arguing that Europe's descent into war had proven that region's inadequacy for the task of shaping international politics going forward, Carranza outlined an alternative international vision. His influences were varied, and he drew from a long-standing Porfirian rhetoric of nationalism and defense of Mexico's sovereignty—a rhetoric to which the aging dictator had repeatedly turned to legitimate the "national honor" of a regime that was making massive concessions to foreign capital.[7] But Carranza mixed this Porfirian official nationalism with an echo of Wilson's Fourteen Points as well as an emphasis on the historical import of the revolution, which, he argued, had imparted to Mexico a duty to exercise international leadership.[8] The doctrine that he outlined to the Mexican congress and the international press in September 1918 demanded the formal equality of for- eigners and nationals before the law; diplomatic equality among nations and mutual respect for their sovereignty; and absolute nonintervention in the internal affairs of other nations. A particularly important aspect of these principles, Carranza argued, was that states should no longer use their diplo- matic representatives to protect private interests—a practice he identified not only as a cause of war but also as a serious problem his own government faced with regard to the implementation of the new constitution.

The Carranza Doctrine therefore articulated a definition of sovereignty that turned on the relationship of the state to property—on Mexico's defense of its sovereign right to determine its own economic policy—and emphasized an understanding of economic sovereignty as every bit as inviolable as territorial sovereignty. After outlining the principles of his doctrine to congress, Carranza ensured his ideas were publicized to the foreign press through interviews, speeches, pamphlets, and books. Carranza partisans Antonio Manero and Hermila Galindo published volumes defending the Carranza Doctrine and traveled extensively to promote it in Latin America, Europe, and the United States.[9] Then, only a few months after Carranza elaborated his country's new foreign policy, the doctrine that bore his name was tested on an international stage, as the world debated the establishment of a new, multilateral organization in Paris. In theory, the Carranza Doctrine should be compatible with Wilson's plans for the new League of Nations, as Carranza had conceived his doctrine not as a rejection of Wilsonian liberalism but as its extension into economic and social realms—a fulfillment of the Wilsonian promise. In practice, however, Carranza's foreign policy and the constitution it was based on were seen in many quarters as a mortal threat to the liberal capitalist order. When the great powers convened to chart out a future for that order, therefore, Mexico's challenge became a central concern.

MEXICO IN PARIS

Countless intellectuals and activists from around the world looked to and descended upon Paris in 1919, hoping that the birth of a new world order might bring recognition of their national struggles for self-determination—and Mexican officials were no exception.[10] The talks at Versailles were the first global negotiation about representation in a multilateral institution, and while Mexico had remained neutral during the war and was therefore not party to the peace talks, Carranza did not intend for Mexico to sit out the discussion about the proposed League of Nations. In December 1918 he sent to Paris his longtime collaborator and emissary, Minister of Industry, Labor, and Commerce Alberto J. Pani. Pani was given the official charge of acting as a "suitable observer for the negotiations for the elaboration of a Peace Treaty that would without doubt plan the basis for the future geographic, economic and political structure of the world."[11] Immediately upon his arrival, Pani's presence in Paris began to provoke concern. The *New York Times* reported that the Mexican diplomat would not only seek official status as a representative of a neutral country at the conference, but would "endeavor to have the ideas of the new Mexican constitution incorporated as a principle of international law."[12] While Pani's correspondence with Carranza betrays no such project, the very existence of the new Mexican constitution and the presence of an official representing Carranza's government were seen as a dire threat.[13]

Indeed, for a diverse array of actors, the consequences of Wilson's project to establish a League of Nations turned on what was called the "Mexico question," that is, the legitimacy of the 1917 constitution's redefinition of the relationship of the state to property. Would the League codify Mexico's right to its economic sovereignty under the rubric of self-determination? Would it prevent the US government or foreign corporations from seeking redress for the loss of property? Or would it force Mexico to change its governing principles? A pitched battle began over the place of Mexico both at the Versailles conference and in the new international order. From the moment he arrived in Paris, Pani was besieged by European holders of Mexican bonds, whose investments had been delayed or destroyed in the course of the revolutionary fighting.[14] What's more, the Catholic Church sent Monsignor Francis Kelley from Chicago to make his case against the anticlericalism of Mexico's new constitution.[15] In addition, Pani had to deal with the presence in Paris of Francisco León de la Barra, a renowned international lawyer who had briefly become Mexico's provisional president after Díaz had been deposed—and who was now actively organizing anti-Carranza exiles around the world to oppose not only the new government but the new constitution.[16] León de la Barra met repeatedly with members of the US delegation in Paris to press his case for a return to the constitution of 1857; Pani struggled to get an audience and met only once with a US representative.[17] Further, there were also powerful opponents of the Mexican revolution in both the US and British delegations. One British foreign office staffer, for instance, argued that the Mexico question would have to be addressed at the conference, as Mexico was "at present [a] plague spot comparable only to Russia."[18] Perhaps most consequentially, foreign capitalists had also been organizing against the new Mexican constitution. The National Association for the Protection of American Rights in Mexico, an organization made up of the most powerful US interests in mining, petroleum, banking, and other business sectors, sent a formidable envoy to Paris: Edward Doheny, the chairman of Mexican Petroleum. Doheny was the most prominent US oilman in Mexico, controlling one and a half million acres of land, and in Paris he argued forcefully to anyone who would listen against allowing Mexico to set the dangerous precedent of new constitutional provisions on property.[19] The forces arrayed against Carranza's envoy were many.

Even while these varied groups fought to advance their interests in the Mexico question at Paris, however, back in the United States, Republican intransigence over the Mexican constitution, and what the League might mean for it, was also growing. President Woodrow Wilson knew he had to address growing opposition to the League at home, so he returned to Washington in February 1919 to advocate for the organization and negotiate with congressional critics. The question of US freedom of action in Latin America, and in Mexico in particular, came up so often during Wilson's tour that he returned to Paris convinced that the only way to get the new institution ratified by congress was to include a reservation for the Monroe Doctrine, which would theoretically protect US prerogatives in the Western Hemisphere, in the Covenant of the League of Nations itself.[20] Late in the negotiations, therefore, Wilson introduced an amendment to the Covenant that ensured the League would not affect the validity of "regional understandings such as the Monroe Doctrine," telling the other members of the commission that he was introducing the language "by way of concession" to his critics at home.[21]

Mexican government officials had been closely watching the debate over the Monroe Doctrine clause in both Paris and Washington. Noting that Wilson himself had called the Monroe Doctrine "one of the difficulties of our relationship with Latin America" in a speech to Mexican newspaper editors in 1918, Carranza argued to the press that his eponymous foreign affairs doctrine, in enshrining the principles of equality between nations and absolute nonintervention, rendered the Monroe Doctrine moot.[22] When word arrived from Pani that the text of the Covenant with the Monroe Doctrine reservation would be published in the coming days, Carranza dropped a bombshell, declaring to the Mexican press that "the Mexican Government has not recognized and will not recognize the Monroe Doctrine or any other doctrine that attacks the sovereignty and independence of Mexico."[23] Soon after releasing the declaration, Carranza gave an interview the *New York World*'s Robert F. Murray. In the widely published interview, Carranza described the Monroe Doctrine as an anachronistic imposition and took Wilson to task directly; the Doctrine, he argued, "seeks to impose and does impose upon independent nations a protectorate which they do not ask for and they do not require."[24] Regarding the League of Nations, he would declare, "The Mexican Government has not made nor will it make any effort to enter that international society, inasmuch as the bases upon which it is founded do not establish, as regards either its organization or its operation, a perfect equality for all nations and races, and the Mexican government has proclaimed as fundamental principles of its international policy, that all the states of the globe should have the same rights and the same obligations."[25] For Carranza and the doctrine to which he had attached his name, the central principle of international relations had to be the equality of sovereign nations. In his interview with Murray, he was clear: "There is no Monroe Doctrine for strong nations and there would be no necessity for such doctrine for [the] benefit of weak ones if [the] principle of equality is adhered to."[26] Carranza reiterated this in September in his next annual message to congress, arguing that including the Monroe Doctrine in the new international organization would create a "forced tutelage" of Latin America at the hands of the United States.[27]

Of course in the end, the inclusion of the Monroe Doctrine reservation wasn't enough to mollify Wilson's critics in the Senate, and the United States didn't join the League; Mexico didn't either, until it received an explicit invitation to do so more than a decade later, in 1931. But the contradiction in Wilson's attempt to reconcile unilateral prerogative with multilateral legitimacy provided an opening for Carranza to define Mexico's position on multilateral governance, one that insisted on equal representation of sovereign states on the world stage. Rooted in the roiling battle over Mexican property rights, Carranza's insistence that "weak" and "strong" states be subject to the same rules in global governance established a fundamental principle that would guide Mexican interventions going forward. Just a few years later, at the Fifth Inter-American Conference in Santiago, Chile, in 1923, Mexican officials would work to turn Carranza's broad principles into concrete rules for international governance.

REDEFINING REPRESENTATION

Given the US failure to ratify the League Covenant and join the new organization, debate raged in the early 1920s about whether the Pan-American Union—an interstate organization created in the late 1880s to promote commercial ties among the American republics—represented a threat or an opportunity for the United States. There were those, like international legal expert Phillip Marshall Brown, who thought that the Pan-American Union could represent a kind of American corollary to the League, and that by expanding its mandate the United States could realize its ideals without surrendering its power.[28] But this view was tempered by those who recognized the potential threats of multilateralism. Dana G. Munro of the State Department's Latin America Division, for example, pointed out the disjuncture between the idea of expanding the role of the Pan-American Union and continuing the military action and dollar diplomacy that the United States was pursuing in Central America and the Caribbean. He feared that the Latin American countries, "distrusting our motives and failing to appreciate the benefits which our intervention is conferring about some of our weaker neighbors, would see to make the [Union] an instrument for obstructing our whole Caribbean policy."[29] Though an obviously paternal understanding of the "benefits" of intervention, Munro's warning was nonetheless a prescient recognition of the dangers the United States might face in committing itself to multilateralism.

This debate set up the context for what would become a central fight at the Inter-American Conference at Santiago in 1923 over how the Pan-American Union should be governed. Despite the fact that Mexico would not have an official representative at the conference, Mexican representatives played an outsized role. According to the existing rules of the Pan-American Union, because Washington had refused to recognize the new government of Álvaro Obregón—who led a revolt against Carranza and was subsequently elected president in 1920—Mexico could not officially participate as a member of the Union's Governing Board and was therefore shut out of the conference planning. The question of recognition once again linked the issues of property and sovereignty. After having recognized the Carranza government, the Wilson administration subsequently refused to extend diplomatic recognition to the governments that followed, unless they met a series of conditions, centered mainly on whether the provisions 1917 constitution concerning property rights would be retroactively implemented.[30] Despite having argued in the campaign against retroactivity, when Obregón assumed the presidency on December 1, he still lacked US recognition—and he was now facing the incoming presidency of the Republican Warren G. Harding. Harding counted among his closest confidants Senator Albert Fall, who had just concluded his lengthy Senate investigations into the political and economic threat represented by the Mexican revolution.[31] But even for those who took a less hard line against Mexico within the Harding administration than Fall did, the Mexico question on property rights was key—and not just vis-à-vis the interests of oil companies, but also regarding other property claims resulting from the revolution, as well as the settlement of external debts. Given these interests, the Harding administration insisted that, as a precondition for recognition, Obregón must sign a "treaty of friendship and commerce" that would delineate Mexico's responsibilities with regard to foreign ownership of property.[32] The Mexican government, however, refused this as contrary to the constitution and an affront to Mexican sovereignty. Negotiations over settling the economic claims would drag on over the years, and indeed decades, to come.

Nevertheless, despite the fact that Obregón's government was not recognized in Washington and therefore didn't have a representative on the Pan-American Union's Governing Board as it planned the Santiago conference, Mexico's role would be turn out to be key. Samuel Guy Inman, the journalist and activist who was both a participant in and chronicler of Pan-Americanism, later recalled a conversation with Chile's president Arturo Alessandri that made clear the importance of Mexico to the proceedings: the Mexican chargé d'affaires in Santiago was the "most important person at the conference," Alessandri told Inman, because the other delegates were essentially taking their marching orders from him.[33] In fact, the Mexican diplomat, Carlos Trejo y Lerdo de Tejada, used the convening of the Santiago conference to push a technical agenda from behind the scenes to institute a permanent reform of the statutes of the Pan-American Union. The intention was to counter the rules that allowed the Union to function as what some observers called "the colonial division of the Department of State," and therefore to counteract what the growing power of the United States portended for the democratic possibilities of the Union.[34]

THE POLITICS OF PLANNING FOR SANTIAGO

It was in this dual context—the ongoing debate about the utility of international organizations and the US refusal to recognize the Mexican government—that the Inter-American Conference, the first to be held since before the First World War, was planned.[35] The meeting was to be of great importance, the Pan-American Union's former director, John Bassett Moore, wrote in the *New York Times*, because it would take up what he called "practical Pan-Americanism"—that is, not just high-minded statements, but the question of how the Union should be permanently governed, to settle how disputes would be handled and economic and political cooperation strengthened.[36] Up to that point, the structure of the Pan-American Union had been organized on a somewhat ad hoc basis, with each of the previous conferences recommending the creation of bodies and commissions based on the pressing issues of the time. A previous conference had established provisions for the organization of the Governing Board, the body that was essentially the executive committee of the Union. The board was composed of the diplomatic representatives of the Latin American countries in Washington, and chaired, always, by the US secretary of state. That meant that those countries whose governments weren't recognized—and therefore didn't have official diplomatic representation in Washington—did not have a seat at the Governing Board's table.

As the Santiago conference approached, the role of Mexico raised an important question: If Mexico remained unrecognized by the United States, would Mexican representatives be invited to the forthcoming conference? By October 1922 the clamor about Mexico's participation had grown very loud in the press, both in Washington and in capitals all over Latin America; it was an issue that, reported one US paper, even "the president is taking a deep interest in."[37] In response, the new director general of the Pan-American Union, Leo S. Rowe, felt compelled to address publicly what he saw as a "widespread misconception."[38] Rowe circulated to the press a statement that affirmed that Mexico could expect to be invited to the conference by the host country, Chile. Further, he argued, that because the Governing Board had consulted with all of the governments of the member countries of the Union to ask for suggestions for the program of the upcoming conference, "the subjects to be included in the program were submitted to the Mexican Government in exactly the same way as to the other governments of the American continent."[39] Despite this assurance, however, the Mexican representatives at the now-unrecognized embassy in Washington were unconvinced, and the chargé d'affaires, Manuel Tellez, argued in a note to the Mexican minister of foreign relations—none other than Alberto J. Pani—that Rowe had sidestepped the most important question. The fact that Mexico would be invited was never in doubt, Tellez argued; the real issue, he stressed, was the representation on the Governing Board itself, the lack of which, he said "puts our government in an unjust and disadvantageous situation as a member of that institution."[40]

Thus, despite the fact that Mexico would be "allowed" to attend, Pani decided to use Mexico's exclusion from the Governing Board to force a larger debate on the structure of the Union and the equality of its members.[41] Pani formally declined the Chilean invitation in January 1923, arguing that "involuntary abstention" from the conference stemmed not from the Mexican government's will, but from US refusal to grant recognition without a treaty.[42] He circulated Mexico's statement to the rest of the Latin American governments, arguing that "the sovereignty of the Mexican nation has never been questioned in the 100 years of independence and it cannot be questioned now."[43] The responsibility to stand against the US-led violations of Mexican sovereignty, Pani wrote, was not just a national one, but an international one: given US interventionism in the past, Mexico would shoulder the Pan-American responsibility of preventing possibility of further interventions in the future. In Santiago, Trejo made sure that the Mexican position would be widely circulated in the press and gave a long interview to Chile's *La Nación* in which he elaborated Mexico's position with regard to the recognition rule for the Governing Board and called for a collective effort by the Latin American governments to change it.[44] In fact, he was already planning such an effort.

A VERY PRESENT ABSENCE: MEXICO AND THE REFORM AGENDA

To open the conference, Chilean president Arturo Alessandri gave a welcome address in which he heralded the "new international democracy that we are at present constructing," which he said would be built "on the basis of the respect to the sovereign power of the states and of absolute equality before the infinite majesty of justice and law."[45] He emphasized the rights of small states as equal to those of large ones, deploying the words of former US secretary of state Elihu Root, who had argued in 1906, "We deem the independence and equal rights of the smallest and weakest member of the family of nations entitled to as much respect as those of the greatest empire."[46] The irony was not lost on those assembled; while Alessandri's conclusion was followed by a chorus of applause for Chile and for the United States, the gallery broke out in a chorus of "vivas" for Mexico, as well. Trejo was present in the hall and reported receiving "frank manifestations of sympathy" for himself and his country.[47] Indeed, Samuel Guy Inman reported to US newspapers that Trejo's presence was "greeted with cheers."[48]

While he made explicit reference to only a few of the agenda topics before the delegates, Alessandri's opening address demonstrated the importance of the need for reform of the statutes of the Pan-American Union. An editorial in Mexico City's *Excélsior* put it bluntly: "in order that the Pan-American Congresses should be something more than a diplomatic comedy," a permanent reform of how the Union was organized would be necessary.[49] The question was therefore taken up by the conference's political committee. Argentina's Manuel Montes de Oca was appointed to head the committee, and the United States appointed Rowe as its delegate. The expectation was that the consideration of organization would be fairly straightforward. But in the first few days of the conference, Rowe caught wind that the Costa Rican delegate, Alejandro Alvarado Quirós, might be planning to submit a radical proposal: to allow the countries of the Union to substitute special representatives to the Governing Board, in the place of their accredited diplomatic representatives in Washington. He reported to Henry Fletcher, the head of the US delegation, that he thought the Costa Rican proposal was ill-advised for two reasons, both of which reflected his position as director general of the Pan-American Union itself. First, he said, there wasn't enough work undertaken by the Governing Board to warrant the expense of special representatives, and second, there would inevitably arise tension between the special representative to the Union and the diplomatic representatives in Washington. He concluded, "I have been hoping that he [will] refrain from presenting this amendment."[50]

By this time, however, Mexico's Trejo had undertaken considerable behind-the-scenes work to shape the debate. This was in keeping with the preliminary memos drawn up at Mexico's foreign relations ministry regarding the conference, which had counseled that it would be wise to "wait to see if another nation initiates an attack, and then second it." It could be dangerous, the memo warned to "assume a theatrical attitude" and make public propaganda.[51] Instead, Trejo opened numerous unofficial channels of communication with the delegates that he thought would be amenable to Mexico's goals.[52] He had initially intended to hold nightly official dinners for delegates, but accusations from the United States that Mexico sought to influence the proceedings made him realize that informal daily lunches with small groups would best allow him to "know even the intimate details of the commissions and do my work of helping [the delegations] in an efficient way," but to do so "without enemy press making any mentions that might prejudice the situation." From then on, he worked constantly, he reported, with César Zumeta of Venezuela, Manuel Márquez Sterling of Cuba, Alejandro Alvarado Quirós of Costa Rica, and a series of others.[53] Alvarado Quirós had given no indication in conversations in Costa Rica before the conference that such reform was on his agenda; it was clearly in consultation with the Cuban and Mexican representatives that he developed his proposal.[54] Before they presented it publicly, however, knowing that they would face the opposition of the United States, Trejo, Márquez Sterling, and Alvarado Quirós needed to secure broad support for the proposal, so they convened private meetings with representatives from almost a dozen countries at which they worked out the bloc that would vote in favor.

On April 9, Alvarado Quirós made his proposal to reform the governance of the Pan-American Union public, submitting it to the political committee and then, as Fletcher later reported, giving it immediately to the press, who were otherwise shut out of the session. A newspaper reported that in introducing his proposal, Alvarado Quirós's primary reference was to the exclusion of Mexico: "We are incomplete," the paper quoted him as saying. "This assembly is missing the most forceful nation of América; missing the most gallant of our sister nations; missing Mexico."[55] In view of the situation vis-à-vis the nonrecognition of Mexico, reform must be implemented, he argued. Such meetings should not be "subject to capricious recognitions, but gatherings of genuine representatives of the peoples of the continent." To address the underlying problem, the Costa Rican proposal made a radical change: the representatives to the Governing Board, Alvarado Quirós argued, should be accredited not to the US government, but to the Pan-American Union itself. In addition, the proposal argued that in cases where there was not an accredited representative, either that country's diplomat in Washington or another member of the board could enter a vote for the absent representative.[56] Moreover, the proposal outlined that the US secretary of state could remain the chair of the board, but in his absence, the vice-chair, appointed by rotation, would take over his duties.[57] While the document as presented was dry and procedural, the plan was described by the committee chair, Argentina's Manuel Montes de Oca, as "transcendental," and was reported in US newspapers as having "created a sensation."[58]

The fact that Alvarado Quirós had mentioned Mexico specifically in introducing his proposal turned attention to Trejo, who reported back to Pani in Mexico City that there was a "perceptible influence and sympathy for Mexico among the delegations."[59] A confidential report of the Cuban delegation to its government argued that while the reform of the governing structures of the Pan-American Union had long been discussed, "it was the 'case of Mexico' that was the blow that inspired the spirits," and further noted that there was not only highly vocal support for Mexico in gatherings in the halls of the conference but also "spontaneous demonstrations" in the streets of Santiago.[60] The adulation from various Latin American quarters, of course, also drew the suspicion of the US representatives, to which Trejo felt compelled to respond. He gave a long interview to the Santiago paper *La Nación* in which he attempted to clarify Mexico's intentions. Mexico was not seeking special advantage, he insisted; rather, "its thesis is for collective benefit; its only desire is that the sovereignty of all the countries of the continent will be—as equals—always whole and complete, as behooves a congress of nations."[61] He was even more straightforward in writing to Pani in Mexico City: the proposal was "a tactical declaration that the current organization of the Union does not correspond to the unselfish purposes that should preside over it."[62] Here, as had been the case in Paris, the Mexican representative was using an international forum not only to emphasize the internal contradictions of US multilateral liberalism but also to try to overcome them in the interest of the smaller and weaker states.

THE US RESPONSE TO REFORM

In the United States, the stakes of the reform effort were quite clear; even the *New York Times* reported that the Costa Rican proposal brought up "the question of North American control" of the Pan-American Union.[63] "It was evident," wrote Trejo later, "that the Achilles heel of the Pan-American Union, the United States, had been wounded."[64] Suggesting a recess to study the proposal, Rowe argued that it was clearly a clandestine Mexican effort to seek representation on the Governing Board, but he noted that the desire for reform on the part of the Latin Americans "was difficult to combat owing to the inability to set before the Conference the particular and special reasons of objection."[65] In other words, the United States could not flat out argue that it opposed the measure because it might confer some modicum of recognition to Mexico. Fletcher wrote to Secretary of State Charles Evans Hughes to argue that while he didn't think that the Costa Rican proposal would pass, it was receiving support from other countries that had faced their own issues with regard to recognition by the United States in the past.[66] Fletcher worried that the proposed reorganization might, by forcing the US secretary of state to deal with a representative of a nonrecognized government, "put him in the very embarrassing position of having to leave the

Governing Board or else take the stand in defense of United States policies."[67] In other words, it might open up a breach between the US national
interest and freedom of action to pursue it and the multilateral commitments that the United States had made within the Union. Awaiting further
instructions from Hughes, Fletcher reported that the US delegation would
seek to prevent the current governing structures from being substantially
changed.[68] In Washington, Secretary of State Hughes decided to go over the
heads of the representatives in Santiago and communicate directly with
their home governments; he hoped to pressure the governments of Costa
Rica and Cuba to withdraw the proposals their delegates had made.[69]
Fletcher hoped to use this kind of pressure to break the bloc of support that
seemed to back up the reform.

There was dissent, however, within the US delegation. While Fletcher
intended to circumvent to the extent possible the implications of the reorganization, George Vincent, president of the Rockefeller Foundation,
introduced a vigorous objection to resisting the Costa Rican proposal by
procedural means. Vincent argued that "if the Pan-American Union is to
be a living organization, it must not be ruled by the wishes of a single country," and therefore "it seemed proper and fitting for all participating countries to have representation."[70] Such a view represented a current of broader
internationalist sentiment in the United States, including the arguments
that the international lawyer Phillip Marshall Brown had put forward
before the conference convened. Samuel Guy Inman also shared this sentiment, and he told Trejo that he had cabled the State Department arguing
that the US should take advantage of the moment presented by the Costa
Rican proposal to rectify its wrongheaded Pan-American policy and recu-
perate its weakened moral strength.[71] Within the US delegation, these
arguments held some water, and Fletcher admitted in a cable to Hughes
that "it would be unwise to oppose the spirit" of the proposal.[72] Ack-
nowledging this, another delegate, former senator Willard Saulsbury Jr.,
suggested that in order to defeat the Costa Rican proposal but still recognize that the majority of the Latin American nations would probably support such a reform, the US delegation should submit a counterproposal:
those countries that did not have diplomatic representation in Washington
could, "with the consent of the majority of the Governing Board of the
Pan-American Union," have a representative there.[73] The group agreed to
write up something akin to Saulsbury's position and cabled the proposed
text to the State Department.

A particular emphasis of the US campaign to defeat the Costa Rican proposal was the idea that radical reform of the governance of the Union would cause the entire institution to implode, and that, as Rowe put it, "without the Secretary of State as presiding officer, the organization would run great danger of falling to pieces."[74] Delegates from the United States began to spread back-channel rumors that the country might even withdraw from the Union if the reform was passed.[75] The United States was not alone in its countercampaign; Chile's Augustín Edwards, for example, was particularly vigorous in his defense of the status quo. Edwards, the founder and owner of the *El Mercurio* newspaper in Santiago, was the leader of Chile's conservative party and his country's longtime ambassador in London. He had also recently been elected president of the General Assembly of the League of Nations in Geneva. Trejo reported that together Edwards and Fletcher "actively worked and schemed to break up our group, to produce desertions, etc., up to the point of employing with certain delegates coarse attitudes and threats."[76] Edwards exhibited a suspicious profile in the eyes of a number of the Latin American representatives; having resided in Europe for decades, he was regarded in some circles as an inexcusable anglophile. (At one point while Edwards was talking in an early session of the conference, Trejo reported that a Chilean intellectual seated near him said, loudly enough to be heard by those nearby, "For being an Englishman, Edwards' Spanish is not half bad!"[77]) Edwards also took up the argument that the reform presented a danger to the institution, arguing to other delegates that, for example, if the US secretary of state was no longer the head of the Governing Board, the Union would suffer an irreparable loss in prestige, rendering it ineffectual. When Edwards tried to insist to Cuba's Carlos Agüero that the Pan-American Union's stability rested on the leadership being vested in the United States and not being turned over to a Latin American, however, Agüero replied, "Tell me, Mr. Edwards, how is it, then, that League of Nations did not collapse with you as president?"[78]

Given all of the behind-the-scenes maneuvering, there was a moment when it seemed the US pressure campaign would prevail, and Trejo reported that he and Márquez Sterling had, in a moment of despair, begun to draft a statement that the Cuban representative would release to the press upon the defeat of the Costa Rican proposal, which would attempt to salvage the honor of Cuba and the Central American countries by highlighting their moral rectitude in defending the rights of small states.[79] In the end, however, it was a statement they would not need.

On April 18, after more than a week's recess, the political committee again took up Costa Rica's proposal. In the session, Fletcher presented the US counterproposal: a country that didn't have diplomatic recognition in Washington could confer its representation on another member of the board, thereby deputizing a country that did have recognition to register the votes of the unrecognized country.[80] In rejecting this counterproposal, Alvarado Quirós insisted that Costa Rica's proposal was not specific to the case of Mexico, but was instead intended to prevent any future problems arising from these sorts of conflicts, and therefore to give both the Governing Board and the Pan-American Union itself more legitimacy and strength.[81] As he said in an interview with Samuel Guy Inman published in US papers, Costa Rica's proposal was "not against the United States or for Mexico, but to found a real basis for Pan-American progress."[82] In other words, Costa Rica's proposal was not a temporary fix, but a permanent reform, one that had the strong support of Venezuela, Colombia, and Panama during the committee session.[83] The Colombian delegate, Carlos Uribe Echeverri, also used the session to add a further proposal: that the presidency of the Governing Board should be rotating, rather than always assigned to the US secretary of state, "as a manifestation of the equality that should govern the American peoples."[84] Delegates from the United States had feared this proposal, but it would be very difficult to oppose without lending credence to the argument that the Union and its Governing Board were simply instruments for perpetuating US supremacy.

Fletcher, sensing defeat, tried another tactic: he argued in the political committee session that Costa Rica's proposal was too radical to be approved at the conference itself, and that it should instead be sent to member governments for consideration. Alvarado Quirós was insistent, however, and his support from other delegates was clear. To break the impasse, a subcommittee was proposed, with the mandate of finding a compromise position.[85] The subcommittee was headed by Argentina's Montes de Oca and comprised representatives from Costa Rica, Cuba, Colombia, Brazil, Uruguay, and the United States. It had been announced in the press that Brazil would support the United States, in addition to the vehement support already offered by the Chileans.[86] What's more, some representatives from the larger and richer countries were clearly becoming irritated at the insurgency of their circum-Caribbean counterparts. The famous Chilean jurist Alejandro Álvarez chastised Cuba's Agüero, telling him that the South American countries were not prepared to have the Pan-American Union put in danger "by the intransigence of the smaller and less important countries."[87]

Nevertheless, the representatives of the "smaller and less important countries" refused to let themselves be intimidated. Márquez Sterling and Trejo redoubled their efforts, and about the representatives whose support was in doubt, Trejo reported back to Pani, "We are working to acquire them."[88] They set up private meetings with representatives who had been targeted by US pressure, arguing that the fear of breaking the Union was unfounded. The US delegates would never withdraw, they said, because doing so would hurt the United States more than anyone—especially, they contended, because US prestige in Europe hinged on the perception of influence in Latin America. Further, they argued, it would be unacceptable to put off the topic for further study; the conference itself, with the presence of so many countries standing together, was the best hope for the Latin American group to realize their goals collectively.[89] In the course of this organizing, the Cuban delegation managed to convene a special secret meeting of all eleven countries that they thought would support the Costa Rican proposal: the five Central American countries plus Cuba, Haiti, the Dominican Republic, Panama, Colombia, and Venezuela.[90] At the secret meeting, the group, which Trejo took to calling the *bando latinoamericano*, developed the exact text of the proposal that they would present as a bloc to the subcommittee. The proposal had three main principles, on which the group would accept no compromises: that attendance at the Pan-American conferences was a right enjoyed by all members of the Union; that countries could delegate special representatives to the Governing Board in case of nonrecognition by another state; and that the president and vice president of the Governing Board would be elected by the member states.[91]

In the subcommittee meetings, Fletcher again raised the idea of postponing a decision, but he also accepted a series of compromises. While the original Costa Rican proposal was that representatives be accredited directly to the Union and not to the United States, the compromise language argued for keeping accredited diplomats as the core of the body but appointing a special representative in cases of nonrecognition. This was accepted by both the United States and the *bando latinoamericano*. Further, "in order to break deadlock," Fletcher conceded another point: the United States would not insist on the inclusion of language that made clear that special representation in no way implied recognition, as long as this was the understanding of the subcommittee.[92] In addition, Fletcher stated, if the Latin Americans felt there was "inequality" in the secretary of state being the permanent chair of the Governing Board, and there was some move to change that, the United States would raise no opposition. So the compromise was reached; with the acceptance of new language allowing for the appointment of special representatives, the original Costa Rican proposal on direct accreditation would be referred to the countries for further study. This secured the postponement that Fletcher had wanted, allowing him to claim that as victory—but the reforms proposed in its place had effectively secured the goals of the original proposal. The proposal approved by the subcommittee was now identical to that drafted by the *bando latinoamericano* in the secret meeting. Fletcher's defeat was palpable when he cabled to Hughes: "After a week of protracted negotiation I believe this is the best possible solution and that any further attempt at mediation would be unwise and unsuccessful."[93] The small countries had won; the new proposal, reported Trejo, was a triumph of the Latin American and the Mexican position.[94]

The proposal was then presented to the full political committee by Argentina's Montes de Oca, who, in a clear reference to Mexico, declared, "I am pleased to state that, in finding conciliatory formulas for conflicting ideas, there were consulted, always with the same spirit, the special situations of the all of the countries of the Americas, even those that are found to be absent from this meeting of sister democracies."[95] In the next meeting, the modification of the Costa Rican proposal was approved by the political committee and it was later approved unanimously in the full plenary session of the conference on April 30, securing a victory in what Trejo called "a tremendous battle."[96] A few countries had lined up behind the US opposition to the reform: Brazil, Chile, Ecuador, and Uruguay (who, Trejo reported, "conducted themselves hypocritically after having promised a vote in our favor"[97]). But Trejo praised those countries who had voted in favor of the proposal, which, notably, included not only the smaller countries of Central America, the Andes, and the Caribbean, but also Argentina, "for defending Latin American ideals in a formidable fight sustained against threatening machinations and every class of efforts employed by the Yankees and their allies."[98] In the end, the reform affirmed the right of representation at the Inter-American conferences, allowed for a special representative to the Governing Board to be appointed in the case of nonrecognition, and mandated that the president and vice president of the board would now be elected positions.[99] The *bando latinoamericano* had prevailed.

At a ball given at the Casino Español after the close of the conference, Chilean president Alessandri greeted Trejo and said loudly to the assembled

Chilean and Argentine delegates, including Edwards, Álvarez, and Montes de Oca, "This is the Mexico that has driven the conference and has had such force in it." In response, Trejo demurred; it was simply the "natural development of the sovereignty and political consciousness of the people."[100] It was a consciousness, however, that had been raised by Mexico's insistence on equality of states and equal representation, made possible through concerted campaigning to change the very structure of international affairs and the institutions that governed them. As Inman recalled, despite not being an official delegate, the Mexican representative had indeed been "the most important person at the conference."[101]

CONCLUSION

After the close of the conference, Trejo wrote a lengthy and frank report for the ministry of foreign relations in which he related not only the minutiae of various sessions and plenaries but also his impression of his colleagues, who were judged on the basis of their political persuasions and independence from US influence. In many delegations, he had observed a split between forward-thinking and "modern" delegates and revanchist, conservative ones, which he summed up thus: "In the opposition of the new and old standards, there can be observed as well the economic aspect that works in the formidable struggle worldwide: the old men, that is to say, the representatives of the oligarchic systems of the different countries, were marked by adhesion, servility, and complicity with the dominion of capitalism, that is the principle enemy of all our nationalist efforts."[102] His judgments were often scathing (Leo S. Rowe was a "blockhead"; Brazil's Afranio Mello Franco was a "decrepit fool hostile to modern ideas"; Chile's Agustín Edwards was a "dummy for English capitalism"), but they reflected Trejo's understanding of the historical role of his country's revolution, and its principles, in shaping the future for the world.[103] Revolutionary Mexico, he argued, would have a crucial influence on Latin America's international interventions in the future.

The United States had come to the conference, in Trejo's estimation, thinking that the Latin American countries held the same worldviews and international policies as they had at the previous conference, in Buenos Aires in 1910. But the United States had not been aware, Trejo contended, that a collective awakening had been experienced in the intervening years, one that could not be overcome with the usual intimidation and subornation. At the center of that awakening, of course, was the Mexican revolution. "The reorganization of the Governing Board of the Pan-American Union," Trejo wrote to Pani, "constitutes without a doubt the most important point of the conference with respect to Latin American solidarity."[104] Having lost the battle over its control of the governance structures of the Pan-American Union, the United States came to recognize the limitations and dangers that multilateralism presented to its projection of power, but also the parameters within which multilateralism could work. It was, as Trejo put it, a "true revelation" for the US delegation: while it had been easy to dismiss criticism of US policy as ignorant anti-Americanism based on racial inferiority, the Santiago conference demonstrated that the Latin American countries could work together in concert to challenge US power using the language of that country's own ideals. This was a first step toward making the demands that would result in the Good Neighbor Policy—the beginning of a long, iterative process of learning that US national interests could be better served by cooperation than by intimidation.

In asserting the formal equality of sovereign nations within international institutions, Mexico's early interventions under Carranza and Obregón laid the ideological groundwork on which later Mexican campaigns would be built. Equality between states, Mexican officials argued, required recognizing the economic sovereignty of "weak" states as well as "strong" ones. In rejecting the Monroe Doctrine reservation in the League of Nations Charter, Carranza had insisted not only that sovereign states had a right to manage their own economic affairs at home, but also that this right would not be superseded by international organizations structured by hierarchy. All states, he insisted, had the same "rights and obligations" in the global order. Mexican officials then worked to put these ideas into practice in the campaign to turn the Pan-American Union from the "colonial division of the Department of State" into a more equitably representative institution. In so doing, they mobilized Carranza's political interventions into a technical reform of the governing statutes of the Pan-American Union. At a moment when officials in the United States were debating their new role in the world, this challenge was formative. Senator Miles Poindexter of Washington put it most bluntly. "America is now a world power and must play its part in the affairs of the world," he had argued in front of a crowd of hundreds of observers in early 1919; "its part is the leadership and hegemony of the New World."[105] But as Mexico's actions to bring together the *bando latinoamericano* made clear, such hegemony would not be achieved without struggle.

TWO

A New Legal and Philosophic Conception of Credit

REDEFINING DEBT IN THE 1930S

IN LATE 1933, MEXICAN FOREIGN MINISTER José Manuel Puig Casauranc arrived in Montevideo for the Seventh Inter-American Conference, the first meeting of representatives of the Western Hemisphere since the Great Depression had begun. In his briefcase, he carried what in ordinary circumstances would have been a dry, procedural document, proposing a revision of the conference's economic agenda. But the situation Puig faced was anything but ordinary; not only were countries around the region seeing their export economies evaporate and declaring default on their foreign debts, but they had also seen the promise of international economic cooperation disappear at the World Monetary and Economic Conference in London a few months earlier. In response to these circumstances, Puig arrived at Montevideo ready to advocate not only a set of specific policy prescriptions—a temporary moratorium on sovereign debt payments, mechanisms for increasing monetary use of silver, and the creation of a new financial institution for the hemisphere—but also an entirely new way of understanding international finance and the roles of debtor and creditor states within it. At Montevideo, Mexican advocacy for the rights of what had previously been conceived of as the smaller or weaker countries, as described in the previous chapter, became advocacy for the *debtor* countries, as well. That is, Mexico's advocacy, which had previously focused mainly on issues of representation, began to focus explicitly on issues of redistribution. While US representatives at Montevideo would maneuver to delay decisions on Mexico's specific proposals, Puig's ideas opened a breach in the inter-American system. Mexico's revolution in development was beginning to take shape.

If foreign debt had been a chronic issue for the Mexican government through-out the nineteenth century, it was an acute one for the postrevolutionary state. While the Mexican government managed to obtain a series of foreign loans in the early years of the revolution—which mainly served to allow the country to continue to meet its existing foreign debt service—in January 1914 the Victoriano Huerta government declared default, ushering in a quarter century of Mexican exclusion from foreign capital markets.[1] After Carranza took power he promised the Wilson administration that, in exchange for diplomatic recognition, he would review claims made by those whose property had been damaged or expropriated during the revolution. But he also declared that Mexico would only recognize and endeavor to pay "legitimate" foreign debt contracted before and during the revolution, thereby implicitly repudiating at least some of the country's financial obligations. In response to Carranza's perceived intransigence, capital began to organize into two powerful pressure groups: an association of holders of Mexican bonds, estab-lished in London in 1915 within the Corporation of Foreign Bondholders; and the International Committee of Bankers (ICB), created in 1918 and headed by Thomas Lamont of J. P. Morgan, which brought together US, British, and French banks to pressure Mexico to pay its debts.[2]

Together with the National Association for the Protection of American Rights in Mexico, an organization that advocated for the owners of property lost during the revolution, the ICB began a sustained campaign to force the Mexican government to the negotiating table. The US State Department, by then withholding diplomatic recognition from the Obregón administration, worked closely with the ICB. This effectively created a state-backed creditor's cartel, which worked to ensure that no institution would lend to Mexico until two conditions were met: first, the question of the outstanding claims had to be settled, and second, Mexico had to agree to a treaty stating that the application of Article 27 of the new constitution would not be retroactive. A halting series of agreements followed. Through an agreement negotiated between Lamont and finance minister Adolfo de la Huerta in 1922, Mexico recognized all outstanding federal debt contracted before 1910, the debt of a number of Mexican states, and the outstanding railroad bonds that had been issued under Díaz, and agreed to begin payments using taxes on oil revenues. This was followed by the Bucareli accords, negotiated by Alberto J. Pani in 1923, which finally specified nonretroactive application of Article 27 and paved the way for recognition of Obregón.[3] After de la Huerta rebelled against that agreement and launched an insurgency against Obregón that had to be put down by force, however, Obregón found himself without sufficient revenue and suspended debt payments again.

The subsequent administration of Plutarco Elías Calles, which took power in late 1924, then abrogated the Bucareli accords, and Calles used the oil taxes and a newly instated income tax to create the Banco de México, the country's central bank, in 1925.[4] Pani, appointed to head the ministry of finance under Calles, reopened negotiations with Lamont and the ICB, and as a result Mexico attempted to begin reservicing the debt in 1925. A downturn in the US economy, however, meant that Mexico faced declining export sales and therefore declining foreign exchange; Calles managed to make payments as promised in 1926 and 1927, but by early 1928 Mexico fell back into default.[5] In 1930 a new agreement was signed, but given the rapidly worsening economic conditions, it was quickly abandoned. Thus, for more than a decade and a half, Mexico had not only been excluded from foreign credit markets; it had faced the relentless pressure of organized capitalist interests and their advocates in the US government.

If Mexico's economic outlook had been difficult before the crash of 1929, its problems accelerated with the Great Depression.[6] Trade ground to a halt, with exports declining by nearly 65 percent from 1929 to 1932, and the terms of trade declining by 20 percent.[7] Lower agricultural productivity, declining demand for manufactured products, and the forced return of hundreds of thousands of laborers and their families deported from the United States had a destabilizing effect, stoking discontent among both peasant farmers and urban workers.[8] The governments of the period known as the Maximato—the period between 1928 and 1934, in which former president Calles exerted considerable influence over the administrations of a series of short-lived Mexican presidencies and remained "the arbiter of political life" in the country—sought to combat these economic problems through domestic reforms.[9] In August 1931, in response to rising urban labor unrest, the Ley Federal de Trabajo was passed, finally putting into effect the labor provisions of the 1917 constitution (and, it should be noted, beginning the process of institutionalizing the relationship between labor and the state that would be solidified after the founding of the PRI).[10] In 1932 the Abelardo Rodríguez government passed the new Agrarian Code, reviving land redistribution stalled over the previous few years, as well as a law mandating a minimum wage linked to the cost of living in each state.[11] Also in 1932, the government passed a banking reform law and instituted a series of countercyclical monetary measures.[12] Then, in 1933, the state founded its first national development bank, Nacional Financiera. But while these efforts helped reverse some of the downturn and cushion the blow of the Great Depression in Mexico, growing economic interdependence, particularly with the United States, meant that domestic policy solutions were necessarily insufficient. Solving Mexico's problems would require more than renegotiating its debt payments and increasing government spending; it would require international economic cooperation. Mexican representatives therefore looked forward eagerly to the World Monetary and Economic Conference in London, convened in the summer of 1933 by the League of Nations to devise cooperative solutions to the world's economic problems. Their faith in cooperation, however, would soon be tested.

MEXICO CALLS AT LONDON

Planners at the League of Nations hoped that the London conference might bring about closer central bank cooperation to stabilize currencies and therefore restore world trade. Many contemporary observers, however, understood that the United States, Great Britain, France, and Germany came to London with conflicting economic interests, particularly with regard to the gulf between their domestic economic priorities and the perceived sacrifices required for international cooperation.[13] While Great Britain had left the gold standard in 1931, the United States abandoned it only shortly before the conference convened, just after Franklin D. Roosevelt took office in early 1933; both countries hoped by doing so to expand their domestic money supply, increasing the availability of credit. In addition, Roosevelt's decision to take the United States off gold was an attempt to raise the prices of primary commodities for the benefit of domestic producers. For their part, many of the European representatives were anxious about questions of debt, particularly given the suspension of Germany's war reparations payments at Lausanne the year before, but the US representatives argued forcefully that discussion of intergovernmental debts fell outside the purview of the conference and should be negotiated separately.[14] These fundamental disagreements over what should be subject to international negotiation were a sign that the conference was not off to a propitious start.

In preparation for London, Mexico's Calles had declared that the global economy required "a fairer system of organization, so that it may not be possible for a few privileged individuals to have in their power the destinies of mankind by hoarding its wealth."[15] At the conference, it fell to Pani, as head of the Mexican delegation, to advance Calles's vision. When Pani had taken over as minister of finance in 1932, he had initiated an active countercyclical monetary policy that allowed the coinage of silver and devalued the peso, thereby increasing access to credit. This expansion of silver use was intended to reinvigorate the mining sector, putting more miners back to work and quelling some of the unrest that had developed in Mexico over the preceding years; further expanding silver use around the world would also provide an important source of foreign exchange for Mexico. In his remarks before the plenary session of the London Conference on June 15, Pani enumerated the domestic reforms he had undertaken, noting that the Mexican situation was "at present not only less critical than in recent years but is better than several other countries" in attendance at the conference, making the case for Mexico being in a proto-Keynesian vanguard. Despite this, however, he acknowledged that there were economic and financial questions that Mexico could not solve on its own: the prices of export products were still subject to international market fluctuations, and the stabilization of Mexico's currency in the international market required the currencies of Britain and the United States to be stabilized first. Nevertheless, Mexico was prepared, he assured the delegates, to make sacrifices in the name of "re-establishing the economic equilibrium of the world," and he called upon the other countries assembled to do the same.[16]

Of course the London Conference was an infamous failure precisely because its participants, most importantly the United States, refused to sacrifice their domestic considerations to reach an international agreement. Infuriated by the unrelenting attention to negotiations around a temporary currency stabilization agreement between the United States and Great Britain, Roosevelt released his famous "bombshell message" on July 3, declaring that such an agreement represented only the "old fetishes of so-called international bankers."[17] In the view of the president, the domestic well-being of the countries involved in the negotiations rested on balanced budgets, increases in commodity prices, and restoring and maintaining the purchasing power of the national currency. Though he still professed that currency stabilization was a worthy goal, it would have to come only after countries agreed to "live within their means," and after the restoration of world trade. While many saw Roosevelt's message as the effective end of the conference, work went on for the next few weeks, and

Mexico logged one of the few victories of the conference, negotiating a multilateral agreement on silver between India, China, and Spain (countries that had traditionally used silver for currency and were holding large stocks of silver that could potentially flood the market and depress prices) on the one hand, and Australia, Canada, the United States, Mexico, and Peru (countries that were producers of silver) on the other. With the strong support of Western senators like Key Pittman of Nevada, Mexico scored a clear win with the agreement, which resulted in the Silver Purchase Act of 1934 and an ongoing agreement between Mexico and the United States for the acquisition of Mexican silver, thereby shoring up Mexico's access to foreign exchange.[18]

Despite their victory on the silver question, the Mexican representatives took away from London the understanding that international economic cooperation was more necessary than ever—not least because it seemed possible that the United States might respond to the growing division of the global economy into regional blocs by trying to incorporate Latin America into a closed hemispheric system. Mexico's ambassador to the United States, Fernando González Roa, reported from London on the problem he saw developing: if the United States pulled back from cooperation with the European countries, he worried in a confidential memo sent during the conference, "there is no doubt that they will seek to form an American bloc and they will fight at the Montevideo conference to incorporate the majority of countries into their commercial system."[19] González Roa's worry was not just that the United States would continue to informally exercise its dominance over economically weak Latin American countries, but that it would attempt to codify such dominance in a formal agreement, what he called "a kind of economic Monroe Doctrine."[20] The League of Nations, for example, had created a system for the outside administration of bankrupt countries in Eastern Europe; González Roa worried that US secretary of state Cordell Hull might be looking to the League policy as a precedent for the Western Hemisphere.[21] Further, González Roa feared that Argentina, one of the few countries that hadn't defaulted on its federal loans, might also advocate such a system for the Americas; he reported that Isidoro Ruiz Moreno, a famous Argentine jurist and adviser to Argentina's foreign minister, had recently published a treatise arguing for "intervention of foreign nations in the state that was bankrupt." It was against the possibility of such intervention that Mexico began to prepare for the Montevideo conference.

Planning for Montevideo had been underway before Pani and his team traveled to London, but the stakes for Mexico's interventions were now clearer. In the preparations for the previous conference, which had taken place in Cuba in 1928, Mexican officials had considered economic issues, particularly relating to the need for foreign capital to be subject to national law, but in the midst of ongoing negotiations with the ICB over the debt, the Mexican delegation was wary of further antagonizing the United States.[22] By 1933, however, the Great Depression had revealed not only the extent to which servicing Mexico's foreign debt meant sacrificing domestic spending but also the extent to which the debt problem was not one faced by Mexico alone. Looking forward to Montevideo, Mexico's minister of foreign relations convened two commissions of technical experts to study the issues that would be discussed at the conference and assigned to them officials from not only the SRE but also the finance and economy ministries. In addition to these technical bodies, however, Calles used his power as *jefe máximo* to create a special commission consisting of just three people: the minister of finance, Pani, who had been Mexico's representative at London; the minister of foreign relations, Puig, who had previously been the ambassador in Washington; and most importantly, Calles himself, who was, among other posts, serving as a director at the Banco de México.[23]

While Pani had stressed the need to deal with the issues of monetary and commercial cooperation that had been sidelined in London, Calles insisted that the issue of debt was central, and a detailed study undertaken by SRE staffer Luis Sánchez Pontón had convinced Puig of the importance of the debt question as well.[24] Debt defaults were widespread by the time the conference preparations got underway: in 1931 and 1932 Bolivia, Peru, Chile, Brazil, Colombia, Uruguay, Costa Rica, Panama, the Dominican Republic, and Cuba had all announced at least partial moratoria on foreign debt service, and Mexico had already long been in default.[25] In an early meeting of the special commission, Calles asserted that two themes would be crucial to the upcoming meeting: the first was the creation of a bimetallist monetary system (continuing the silver negotiations undertaken at London), and the second was with regard to debts. He proposed a moratorium on foreign debt payments for five years at least, and ten if possible, which in his view would facilitate the "rapid economic recuperation of the continent." He demanded that the conference reject intervention to force debt payments, arguing that only with such an agreement would "the rich and strong countries . . . cease being exploiters of the weak countries." He continued: "That is how a moral and prudent credit will be established, that will not produce the effects of ruin and disaster that humanity suffers today."[26]

For many Mexican experts, the United States was the particular source of Latin America's problems. As early as May 1931, González Roa, who had been serving on the US-Mexico Claims Commission convened to settle outstanding property disputes from the revolution, drafted a memo for SRE staff on what he considered the most important points for Mexico at the next conference. The memo was harshly critical of the role of US finance capital in creating the economic situation in which the Latin Americans found themselves after the Great Depression, arguing that the United States had never been concerned with lending genuine help to the countries of Latin America; rather, González Roa wrote, "its tendency has always been to consider them as countries of economic action for its own benefit."[27] He followed this assertion with a laundry list of economic predations in the region and criticized the protectionism of US president Herbert Hoover, noting that many countries throughout the region had offered the United States their friendship, and in return the United States had "in fact declared a relentless economic war." In the context of the Great Depression, the economic sovereignty of countries all over Latin America was especially threatened by the attempts of private bankers to secure governmental intervention for the collection of their debts. Should the US government take further action on behalf of private creditors, the Mexican expert worried, this would mean "quickly achieving the conversion of American businessmen into territorial conquistadors and turning private investment into the buying of national sovereignty."[28]

Despite being deeply critical of the abuses of US capital and government support of it, however, Mexican officials faced two other considerations: the conference presented an opportunity to take advantage of the emerging "Good Neighbor" attitude of the Roosevelt administration, but it also revealed the skepticism of the other large countries in South America, particularly Argentina, Brazil, and Chile, with regard to the motives of both the United States and Mexico. Mexico's preparations required balancing these competing pressures, and Puig decided that the issue of economic recovery, particularly a focus on debt, put Mexico in the position to take a leadership role within Latin America. He wrote to Calles in May 1933 detailing the "role of real importance and decisive moral influence that Mexico could have at the Montevideo Conference," arguing for a self-appointed leadership role in the hemisphere.[29] Mexico's pretensions to leadership did not go unnoticed; in London, Paul Mason of the British Foreign Office had seen Pani's performance at the World Monetary and Economic Conference and reported to his superiors that it was likely the Montevideo conference was to bring a contest "between Argentina and Mexico for the theoretical leadership of Latin America." In that struggle for leadership, Mason continued, "Argentina has the resources, Mexico the theories."[30]

STRIKING A HEMISPHERIC BALANCE

If the debt question motivated Mexico's "theories," however, the issue of how to force them onto the agenda at Montevideo was complicated. In a meeting in Washington on the way back from London, Pani had advocated to State Department officials various changes to economic aspects of the conference agenda, and once he was back in Mexico City, he argued that this was particularly necessary given the failure at the London conference.[31] Puig had also already decided that a wholesale revision of the parts of the conference agenda related to economic and financial affairs would be necessary, and he designated a team of experts to begin to draft a new version. The Governing Board of the Pan-American Union in Washington, however, had been making preparations for many months regarding the conference program, and an agenda had already been approved by that body in May 1933.[32] By the end of the London conference, it was simply too late, according to the rules governing the Union, to submit a wholesale change to the agenda, which would require unanimous approval by the members of the board. Much easier, Puig decided, would be to attempt to reform the agenda once he was in Montevideo, where he only needed approval of two-thirds of the representatives.[33] As had been the strategy a decade before at Santiago, Puig therefore began a concerted campaign to bring the rest of Latin America on board with his plans.

Given the economic circumstances in which the meeting would take place, the agenda that had been approved by the Governing Board of the Pan-American Union was strikingly mundane; most of the items could have been lifted from any previous Inter-American conference. The proposal drafted by Puig's team, on the other hand, called for a complete revision of

Chapter IV of the program, which was to deal with economic issues. First and foremost on his agenda was debt; his proposal called for recognition of the Drago Doctrine—which forbade military intervention for the collection of foreign debts—and for an agreement on a debt moratorium, interest free, of no less than six but no more than ten years. On the subject of money and credit, the proposal called for a common bimetallist system, as against gold-standard exclusivism, and for the creation of what he called "an institution that would function as a Continental Central Bank" that would undertake currency stabilization efforts and facilitate capital flows and international payments.[34] Together, these proposals represented a radical departure from the agenda as it had been approved, and Puig began to circulate his plans to the governments in the rest of Latin America to solicit responses.[35]

In circulating his new agenda, Puig sought to strike a hemispheric balance. Some in the region feared that Mexico's intentions were too much in line with the United States and intended to bind the continent to a US-led economic system, while some in the United States feared a conspiracy of Latin Americans against their economic and political interests in the region. Puig understood this from the inception of planning for the conference; in a handwritten note to himself prepared for a meeting with Calles, Puig stressed the "necessity, also, that—so that it cannot be supposed that Mexico works as an agent of the United States in the preparations for the Pan-American Conference—Mexico introduces high themes of general convenience and policy for the Latin Americans."[36] Given how many countries were in various states of default, Puig knew that his ideas were not exclusive to Mexico, and he decided that he would therefore use the issue of debt to lead the rest of Latin America toward Mexico's goals.[37] Puig insisted at every turn that his proposals had been formulated considering the "sentiment, the thinking, and the general interest of Latin America," not of Mexico alone. Further, to demonstrate Mexico's anti-interventionist credentials and make clear that its proposals were not in the service of the United States, Puig included with his agenda revision a memorandum that urged an "update" of the Monroe Doctrine. By arguing for the "inviolability of the principle of national autonomy," the memo signaled to the rest of Latin America that Mexico was not simply pushing a US agenda.[38]

Just a few months before the conference, Puig met with US ambassador Josephus Daniels in Mexico City and subsequently followed up with a detailed memo reiterating Mexico's stance, which he not only circulated to the other Latin American countries but also published in both English and Spanish. The memo emphasized the centrality of the debt question and noted that the poorer countries in the hemisphere were not able to unilaterally declare a moratorium on their payments, "even if they are drowning, because of the influence that Wall Street has over them."[39] It would not be fair, he argued, for the strongest and most independent countries of Latin America to make unilateral policies regarding debt service and to leave the "weak countries, for fear of the 'bankers committees,' [to] have to continue squeezing their meager budgets and practically drowning their people," an action that would have the result, he argued of "thereby sowing, also, dangerous seeds of discontent and social dissolution."[40] In his reference to bankers' committees, Puig drew from Mexico's long and arduous negotiations with the ICB, but he also implied that if the banks were free to form such a creditors' cartel, the most effective way to counter it was with the organized, collective power of the Latin American states.

While Mexico's preconference advocacy pleased some smaller states, reports from the powerful countries in South America were less than enthusiastic. The British Foreign Office was keeping tabs on Mexico's campaign, and reported that the Mexican diplomat Alfonso Reyes was traveling throughout the region trying to drum up support for the Mexican proposal.[41] Reyes sent a number of reports back to the SRE on his discussions, and his report from Argentina expressed succinctly the Southern Cone skepticism prior to the conference: the Argentines feared that the agendas of Mexico and the United States would be too closely related at the conference, as a result of "the conversations that Mr. Pani had with Roosevelt in his visit to the United States returning from London."[42] In fact, Pani *had* repeatedly stressed the congruence between Mexico's economic program and that being pursued by Roosevelt, telling the *New York Times* that there was "a close agreement of views" between himself and the president, which only fueled suspicions.[43]

Further reports from South America indicated another reason for skepticism: because of ongoing trade negotiations in Argentina and Uruguay with Great Britain, leaders in those countries feared that attempts to solidify any hemisphere-wide economic agreement would compromise their negotiations in Europe.[44] Reyes continued his reconnaissance, however, and reported back to Puig that he thought that Brazil's finance minister, Oswaldo Aranha, as well as Chile's president Alejandro Alessandri and foreign minister Miguel Cruchaga, were sympathetic to the Mexican proposal. Representatives of Colombia, El Salvador, Panama, Peru, and a number of other countries also indicated that they would support Mexico.[45] But Reyes reported that the Uruguayan minister of finance, Pedro Cosío, who had been at the London conference, was reluctant to discuss economic issues at the conference, "for consideration that the colossus of the North will take all the advantage."[46] Reyes was apparently persuasive, however, and by late September he reported to Puig that he had obtained a promise from the Uruguayan foreign minister that he would cable Washington in support of the Mexican proposal, adding that the Uruguayan had told him, "with Mexico we will go wherever."[47] While Reyes won over some countries, however, Argentina remained staunchly opposed to the Mexican plans.

There was opposition in the United States as well, and many in Washington and New York were displeased with Puig's focus on debt, given Mexico's long history of intransigence with regard to its foreign creditors. As the newsletter *Affairs: Washington's Weekly Review* reported, Puig's circulation of his memo in both English and Spanish meant that the Mexican foreign minister had "won the reputation also of being one of its 'bad boys' as far as the United States is concerned."[48] While there was broad congruence between the Puig vision and some emerging New Deal economic ideas, particularly with regard to speculative finance, Secretary of State Hull was steadfast in his opposition to the Mexican plan. Upon receiving Puig's proposal in September, Hull called on Puig and attempted to prevent him from forcing the debt moratorium onto the agenda at Montevideo, implying that the United States would have to vote against any government action on debts, on the grounds that the US government simply didn't have any ability to intervene in the settlement of private debts.[49] He attempted to convince Puig that the newly mandated Foreign Bondholders Council, a nongovernmental body created under the Securities Act passed just a few months earlier, would provide the best venue for debt negotiations. Hull and Roosevelt hoped that the creation of the Bondholders Council would take debt negotiations off the intergovernmental table and thereby prevent controversy at the conference.

Controversy was inevitable, however, once Hull learned that Puig had shared his proposal not just with Washington but also with the other Latin American governments. Upon discovering Puig had included the additional memo on "updating" the Monroe Doctrine, Hull frantically cabled Daniels in Mexico City.[50] He implored the ambassador to get further information from Puig, concluding, "I wish to add for your information that this *démarche* is causing me some anxiety." But it wasn't just the Monroe Doctrine language that worried Hull; it was also the proposals on debt. Hull admitted to a representative from the British Foreign Office in October that he feared the Latin Americans would "put up a joint demand for a long moratorium on their commercial debts, public and private."[51] Puig, for his part, told Ambassador Daniels that while they were indeed circulating the proposed agenda changes, they simply sought the chance to discuss the proposals at the conference in an open manner.[52] As it became clear that Puig would not agree to forego discussion of the debt question at the conference, Hull drew up instructions for the US delegates that the United States wouldn't oppose the discussion but would "endeavor to see that no action at all be taken by the conference."[53]

In October, Puig traveled to Washington to meet with Hull and Roosevelt himself.[54] Puig described Roosevelt in glowing terms: "He gives one the impression of being a social revolutionary in the highest and noblest sense of the term."[55] For its part, the Roosevelt administration was publicly promoting the idea that it would arrive in Montevideo the most popular US administration in the history of the Pan-American gatherings.[56] Roosevelt and Hull hoped that they would maintain this popularity by restricting the conference to the least controversial, and thereby least pressing, of topics, a tactic they had used at the previous conference in 1928. On November 9, Roosevelt announced that because "unsettled conditions" in Latin American economic matters persisted, it made sense for the "United States to forego immediate discussions of such matters as currency stabilization, uniform import prohibitions, permanent customs duties and the like."[57] The US delegation would discuss, on the other hand, enhancing transportation and communications infrastructure, the political and civil rights of women, and how to further intellectual cooperation. But, Roosevelt signaled, the most urgent economic issues were off the table. Even the US press could see this was an untenable position. The *Washington Evening Star* noted that a similar ban on "controversial" topics in London was the reason the conference there had resulted in "futility and failure for that attempt at international recovery and reconstruction."[58] The *New York Times* observed, "In this case the good neighbor warmly shakes hands but tells his guests and hosts that they must not talk about what most concerns them."[59] If the Roosevelt administration thought its was the last word, however, the Latin American delegates certainly did not. Despite Roosevelt's attempts to keep them off the table, dueling economic proposals from Puig and Hull would dominate the conference.

Upon arrival in Montevideo, Hull met cordially with Puig but reported back to Washington that the US delegation should be able to defeat the proposals easily by putting them off, noting "our fight will be to postpone by referring to committee."[60] He was likely not prepared for the length or passion of Puig's address to the innocuously named Committee on Initiatives that met on December 4 to discuss the changes that Mexico proposed making to the conference agenda. In a rousing address, Puig delivered a sweeping indictment of the international financial system and a vision for its renovation. He told the assembled delegates that since at least 1920 there had been a "general economic tempest rising in America" with regard to the issue of credit.[61] Puig charged that the truth about the international economy and its inner workings was being kept hidden, in the interests of a set of what he called "superbankers who themselves know no fatherland and often know no law." This obvious reference to the International Bankers' Committee on Mexico was not, he assured the delegates, an attack on all bankers: "[T]he guilty parties are not the regular bankers, our denunciation is not of bankers as a professional class, it is not of capitalism," he argued. Rather, it was an attack on the "distorted conception of responsibility" that prevailed in what he called "orthodox economic science," which, he noted, "the great vested interests have known how to embody into principles and into treaties and into law." In Puig's view, this had been the folly of the capitalist state, leading to the massive financial crisis that emerged in 1929: the economic predations of speculative capital had been perfectly legal, and the state had not intervened to prevent these distorted conceptions of responsibility from becoming the very norms of international finance. These norms, he argued, had emerged to protect powerful private interests, to the detriment of the debtor nations.[62]

He then detailed the most radical aspect of his proposals: the recognition that international finance was, at its core, a social relation. Rather than a neutral, technical, economic practice with already constituted and inviolable rules, Puig argued, international finance was instead deeply rooted in the underlying social and political structures. With a crisis mounting in Europe over war debts, and with the wave of defaults in Latin America resulting from the Great Depression, these roots had suddenly been rendered visible. Part of the task of the financial sector, however, had been to obscure the social relations altogether, to render as natural and sacrosanct the rules of international finance. Referring to the interests of international capital, which "precisely because they are invisible are almost impossible to defeat," he argued that they would continue to obscure the real truth of what credit was: "a 'social function' . . . the same as property."[63] Here, Puig directly drew from the 1917 constitution's redefinition of property rights as vested not in the individual but in the nation. Property, in the Mexican conception, was a social function insofar as its delineation and use was intended to further collective well-being; in the Mexican conception, the property owner had obligations to provide benefits to community and nation, obligations that rested on interdependence and solidarity.[64] Extrapolating from this notion of property, Puig argued, it was necessary to formulate "a new legal and philosophic conception of credit" based on the recognition of international finance as an international social relation, one that should be based in that same interdependence and solidarity.[65]

The reciprocity inherent in understanding international finance as a social relation drew from Puig's insistence on a recognition that, in capitalism, the creditor needed the borrower as much as the reverse. He argued that international lending should not be based in asymmetrical power relations, because, as he said, "exactly the same service is rendered by the party who grants the loan as by the party that takes it."[66] To explain this point, Puig stressed that extending credit was a necessity for holders of capital, as only through investing and lending that capital could it bring any return. This was, of course, a core function of capitalism: to make more money out of money. Borrowers were crucial to this process, Puig insisted, as credit was "'an equation' of at least two terms." Given this fact, he insisted, there was no reason that, in addition to paying "often usurious charges of interest," that countries making use of borrowed surplus capital should have to "kowtow" to creditors, and to grant massive concessions. If international capitalism was to recover, Puig implied, the creditor needed to heed the situation of the borrower—and the United States would need to heed the situation of Latin America.

Puig's "new legal and philosophic conception of credit" was in many ways an international version of what Keynes would come to call, in the *General Theory*, a "somewhat comprehensive socialization of investment."[67] Puig's vision had three important implications: first, that repayment should be premised on a state's capacity to pay (and therefore that the practice of taking on further debt simply to meet existing repayment obligations should be abandoned); second, that there should be some mechanism for disciplining not just debtors but also creditors for their role in generating financial imbalance;

and finally, that the ultimate responsibility for the smooth operation of the credit system must fall to the state and be regulated through cooperation between states.[68] "It is the Governments," he wrote, "in the last analysis, who are the rock bottom support of credit," a fact that Hull's insistence on the US government's nonintervention in private debts was willfully ignoring.[69] The ideological debate about state intervention in the capitalist economy, however, was preventing those assembled from recognizing the crucial role of the state. Too often, Puig argued, economics was understood as a "science" when it benefited what he called "superfinanciers" but derided as self-interested political posturing when mobilized by governments.

The disjuncture in how economic rules were understood based on who promoted them was particularly egregious, he argued, because it was clear that the rules could be flouted by the more powerful countries when they deemed it necessary. He pointed out that France, Germany, and Great Britain had no need to consult their international bondholders in order to devalue their currency or make adjustments in their gold balances. The less-powerful countries, however, did not have the same freedom; their sovereignty over economic decision-making was less than absolute, and the credit form itself therefore had become an ordering principle for international politics. (Meant as a scathing criticism, this idea would be taken up as an explicit program by some neoliberals in the 1960s, who advanced what Quinn Slobodian has called an "interest rate theory of civilization.")[70] In arguing for an intergovernmental accord on debt and credit, Puig noted that there were gathered at Montevideo twenty debtor countries and only one creditor, a situation that had many parallels around the world. He hoped that his vision might help in establishing "a procedure that we wish to be continental, that may perhaps come to have some effect of a universal order."[71] The Mexican proposal, Puig argued, would present "something logically, decidedly, systematically and firmly on behalf of 'the many' as against the unjust privileges and interests of the few."[72]

After Puig's rousing speech, heated discussion of his proposals commenced. Argentina's Carlos Saavedra Lamas—whose disagreement with Puig's debt proposals resulted from the fact that his country was one of the few that had not defaulted on its federal loans—argued that the Pan-American Union was not the place for discussion of financial matters and called Puig's plan "a sort of continental bankruptcy of all the American countries," despite the fact that it was meant to alleviate the economic problems of only some of them.[73] Puig's response was incredulous; that the conference would refuse to discuss debts in a forum where there were twenty debtor countries and a single creditor was absurd.[74] Venezuela's César Zumeta, who had been a representative of his country before the League of Nations, got to the heart of the question: the fundamental error of hemispheric politics to that point was the apparent belief that "political independence should not have been complemented by economic independence."[75] Such economic independence, Zumeta insisted, would be achieved not by rivalry, but by the kind of cooperation being proposed by the Mexican delegation. The contentious discussion went on for days, until Argentina's Saavedra Lamas moved that Puig's proposal in its entirety be referred to the Inter-American High Commission in Washington—a suggestion that was equivalent to moving to kill the proposal, as the High Commission had been defunded by the US Congress some months earlier and had ceased to function. The committee reached a compromise with a proposal to convene a third Pan-American Financial Conference, to be held in Santiago, Chile, shortly after the closure of the Montevideo conference. Argentina, the United States, and Mexico could claim plausible victories in this compromise: Hull and Saavedra Lamas were satisfied that they had postponed any resolution of the question of debt at the conference, and Puig was satisfied that Mexico's agenda would soon be studied in detail in a planned multilateral forum.

Puig's interventions, however, did not end with the referral of his proposals to a future conference. After finally securing support from a reluctant White House to do so, Hull gave a speech to the conference on December 12 railing against economic nationalism and laying forth his free-trade vision for the hemisphere. Though some US historians recall the proposal as a diplomatic triumph for Hull, contemporary observers noted that his proposal "met with a mixed reception."[76] Puig led the criticism of the Hull proposal. In his response to Hull's speech, Puig noted that every nation desired increases in inter-American trade, but that "economic recovery, both national and international, demands a revision of tenets and systems."[77] Prefiguring in some ways the terms-of-trade thesis that would come to define the theories of Raúl Prebisch and his UN Economic Commission for Latin America in the decades to come, Puig argued that Latin America consisted of "countries whose economy is of the colonial type, countries exporting raw products and necessarily importing manufactured products."[78] Payments for such imports had deleterious effects on reserves and currency values and quite frequently led countries to contract further debt to cover balance-of-payment problems—all of which had adverse impacts on the workers in the primary exporting countries. In such a situation, he argued, it was natural that countries should resort to tariffs, exchange controls, and import restrictions, and it was unfair of the United States to ask countries to lift such measures without committing to buy more goods from them. For the debtor countries at Montevideo, the trend was obvious, and the need for a solution was urgent.

In the end, by agreeing at the Montevideo Convention to renounce military intervention—something that Latin American representatives had been advocating forcefully since the 1928 meeting—Hull secured in return a resolution calling for the American republics to undertake tariff reductions. Language was added to the tariff resolution, however, that carved out exceptions to such reductions for a number of reasons, including for "domestic programs, primarily for national economic recovery."[79] The criticisms leveled by Puig would persist as Hull moved forward with his reciprocal trade agenda, and while the Roosevelt administration tried to assuage its critics with the creation of the Export-Import Bank in 1934, Mexico and other Latin American countries would continue to push for deeper cooperation.[80]

CONCLUSION

Traditional diplomatic histories of the 1933 Montevideo meeting have understood it as the forum at which the United States was forced to abandon its military interventionism in Latin America, to finally recognize the territorial sovereignty of the Latin American nations.[81] Uncovering the campaign detailed here reveals the contours of a project to defend the *economic* sovereignty of those nations, as well, and to create international agreements and institutions that would help to govern the "wise circulation" of international capital, as Calles had put it. While some scholars have seen Mexico's intervention at Montevideo as one episode in a history of "anti-Americanism," the substance of the Mexican proposals examined here was both more complicated and more fundamentally important than simple anti-Americanism.[82] Puig's proposals, and the subsequent projects that would develop from them, were part of an emerging Mexican project that sought to foster Latin American solidarity in order to harness the productive potential of capitalism to an international regime of economic redistribution—and therefore to constrain the rising economic power of the United States with new international rules and agreements. In seeking to internationalize a "new legal and philosophic conception of credit," Puig and his contemporaries sought not only to legitimate Mexico's domestic programs at home in the eyes of a foreign audience, but also to use the principles of the Mexican revolutionary constitution as the basis for a new global understanding of how the world economy should be governed.

It was at Montevideo that Mexico's fight for representation within multilateral institutions became an explicit fight for redistribution through them, as Puig put forth a concerted program for restructuring the system of international credit. The Mexican analysis advanced at Montevideo was deeply shaped by Mexico's exclusion from world financial markets during and after the revolution, reflecting the frustrations of the long and torturous negotiations with organized bankers and bondholders that had defined Mexico's international standing over the previous two decades. Having faced the power of organized Northern capital, Mexican representatives sought to rewrite the rules of the international financial order to put states like theirs on a more even footing. What's more, the Mexican analysis also represented a sophisticated and prescient understanding of the structural problems of the Latin American economies with regard to production, trade, and investment. Puig's emphasis on overcoming the unequal terms of trade through the redistribution of capital from North to South, and his insistence on the recognition of the centrality of borrowers to the success of financial markets, prefigured some of the most important theoretical insights that would emerge within the structuralist and dependency schools in the postwar period. Though left out of the canon of Latin American developmentalist thought, Puig's intervention at Montevideo set the agenda not only for how Mexico and its Latin American allies would approach institutional negotiations over the next decade and a half—but also for how the United States would respond to their demands.

THREE

A Solidarity of Interests

MEXICO AND THE INTER-AMERICAN BANK

GIVEN THEIR EXCLUSION FROM INTERNATIONAL financial markets in the 1920s, Mexican officials would come to understand that a radical reorientation of the system of international finance would require not just interstate goodwill, but a permanent international institution. Mexican experts in the 1930s therefore began to make explicit their demands not only for a new international system of credit, as detailed in the previous chapter, but also for a specific institution to manage it: the world's first international development bank.[1] Such an institution, Mexican advocates and their allies hoped, would prevent the financial predations of private bankers, stabilize foreign exchange systems, and steer capital toward productive investment to develop the national economies of the Latin American countries. Mexican and other Latin American economists and diplomats undertook years of continued advocacy for what came to be the Inter-American Bank (IAB). By 1939 they had convinced US officials of the utility of such an institution, and that year the Treasury Department deputized a committee to draft a charter and bylaws for the IAB. While there has been renewed scholarly attention to the complicated negotiations within the United States about the IAB, we know relatively little about what the Latin American representatives who advocated this institution wanted from it and precisely how their proposals influenced the US vision for it.[2] This chapter demonstrates that Mexican economists and diplomats were at the forefront of the fight for the IAB, and their plans for the bank would be an important codification of their fight for representation and redistribution in international economic governance. Uncovering this history, then, not only reveals a vision for international economic development as it emerged from the Global South before the Second World War; it also traces how Latin American conceptions of development influenced how officials from the United States came to understand the global project of development and the place of their country within it.

SAVING CAPITALISM FROM SPECULATION

Though the financial problems resulting from the Great Depression represented an acute crisis throughout Latin America, regional leaders had already shown interest in the idea of creating a new multilateral financial institution for some time. In fact, Latin American representatives had discussed creating some kind of international bank at Pan-American conferences as far back as the 1890s. They had also studied the idea within the Inter-American High Commission, an economic and financial body that had been created by the Pan-American Union to foster increased trade between member countries. While some Mexican economic experts, such as longtime diplomat Fernando González Roa, thought that the High Commission was little more than an economic reconnaissance body for US business interests—not least because it was located in Washington and physically housed at the US Department of Commerce—it nevertheless served for a time as a central forum for the discussion of the hemisphere's economic and financial problems.[3] As early as 1922, Mexican High Commission representatives joined their counterparts from Venezuela to push a proposal for the creation of an international currency clearinghouse to stabilize exchange rates and provide credits for countries facing balance-of-payments problems.[4] The Mexican section attempted to rally the rest of the Latin Americans to Venezuela's proposal, calling for a conference to study the feasibility of creating the international institution.[5] In the context of the lending boom of the 1920s, however—an outpouring of private credit from which Mexico was excluded, due to its ongoing default— that conference never took place. Mexican officials spent the next few years engaged both in bilateral debt negotiations with the United States, as described in the previous chapter, and in the creation of their own central bank, the Banco de México, which was founded in 1925. After the stock market crash of 1929 and the resulting flight of capital from the region, however, Mexican representatives turned back to the idea of an international bank and intensified their efforts to bring such an institution into being.

In 1931 the Mexican experts on the High Commission undertook a detailed study of the various existing proposals for an international financial institution and produced a memo advocating such a project. The memo outlined the numerous ideas for international financial cooperation that had been put forward in Europe and the Americas over the preceding decades, noting that it had become increasingly clear that such cooperation would provide "the only solution to problems which would have been otherwise unresolvable."[6] Among those ideas surveyed by the Mexican representatives on the High Commission were Luigi Luzatti's proposal for central bank coordination in 1907; an international clearinghouse for trade between the United States and Latin America, proposed by J. J. Arnold of the First National Bank of Chicago in 1914; the 1920 Ter Muelen plan of the League of Nations; the Gold Reserve Bank, proposed in 1922 by National City's Frank A. Vanderlip; and the 1922 proposal by Germany's Hans Heymann for a Bank of Nations.[7] The Mexican national section was most interested, however, in the Bank for International Settlements (BIS), founded just a year earlier, in 1930. The BIS had been created to coordinate German reparations payments, but also to provide "an increasingly close and valuable link in the cooperation of central banking institutions" of Europe, which the founders deemed "essential to the continuing stability of the world's credit structure."[8] The Mexican representatives on the High Commission had Germany and the BIS at the forefront of their minds when they began to outline the project for what they were now calling the International American Bank.

Mexican experts were particularly interested in the changes made to the level of German reparations under the Young Plan of 1929, which, the Mexican report suggested, took into consideration Germany's means to pay what it owed—a principle that had only recently been introduced into the negotiations between Mexico and the International Committee of Bankers.[9] The Young Plan, the Mexican section wrote, "has inspired the principle that, before accepting that a people should restrict consumption to pay a debt, the base should be *the development of production.*"[10] Countries had already taken on international loans aimed at stimulating their national economic progress, they wrote, so there should be established an institution that would not only make fulfilling loan commitments less contentious but actually aim to increase the productive capacity of the borrowing country—thereby easing the conditions for loan fulfillment. In Germany, they argued, experts had decided to subordinate the financial question to the issue of reconstruction, thereby increasing Germany's chances of actually paying its reparations; this was a model that Mexican planners intended to follow.

Mexican experts also took from the BIS proposal the importance of coordination between the central banks of its member countries, many of which (like Mexico's) were quite new institutions. At the Fourth Pan-American Commercial Conference just a few months later, the international financial expert Edwin Kemmerer enthusiastically recommended such central bank cooperation.[11] For their part, the Mexican planners continued to insist that such cooperation would be beneficial not only for the "elimination of the costs of the movement of funds," which was crucial for interstate trade, but even more important, "for the distribution of credit and the cushioning of shocks resulting from business cycles."[12] In Mexico's vision, then, the bank could do more than facilitate international payments; it could actually provide productive credit to governments seeking to finance industrial and agricultural development. Surveying the region, the Mexican experts argued that the existing forms of international finance had left Latin American countries vulnerable to "prospectors," speculative financiers who had fueled the boom and bust of the 1920s "dance of the millions."[13] With a multilateral bank, the Mexican experts argued, such speculation and its resulting instability could be avoided, and the bank would thereby create what they called an "international solidarity of interests."[14] Over the next decade and a half, Mexican experts would work tirelessly to try to bring that solidarity of interests into being.

THE MONTEVIDEO MOMENT

The 1933 Montevideo conference presented an opportunity for Mexican planners to debut their plans for an international bank to a wider audience. As detailed in the previous chapter, Mexico's revisions of the economic and financial program had a particular focus on problems of debt and credit. An important solution to those problems was to be found, the Mexican delegation argued, in the creation of new, permanent international economic institutions: a Pan-American economic and financial organization to replace the Inter-American High Commission (the US section of which had been defunded by Congress just a few months earlier, causing it to cease to function), and, under its auspices, the Inter-American Bank.[15] In the proposal presented by José Manuel Puig Casauranc, the IAB was conceived of as "an institution that would function as a Continental Central Bank," that would not only allow for currency stabilization between the central banks of member countries but would also serve "as their means of contact with the general market of money and capital"—a market from which Mexico had been excluded for nearly two decades.[16]

Mexico's Daniel Cosío Villegas, then a young staffer at the ministry of the economy, provided important background for Puig's proposal in a long and detailed study on inter-American economic cooperation submitted to the conference.[17] He reviewed an existing Cuban proposal from 1931, which had advocated replacing the High Commission with a new body charged with comprehensively studying "the economic development of the American Republics and the promotion of economic relations among them."[18] Cosío Villegas, however, argued that while an institution like that proposed by Cuba was necessary, the plan had a number of flaws; among them was the proposal that the organization would be staffed by members of the diplomatic corps of member nations, who Cosío Villegas thought insufficiently prepared to handle technical economic matters. Beyond the Cuban proposal, Cosío Villegas also surveyed the changes that the various economic and financial organizations of the League of Nations had undergone in recent years and suggested that League economic mechanisms had been more efficient than the existing Pan-American ones because they had had "the disinterested collaboration of real experts."[19] While the formal study of economics was only beginning in Mexico—Cosío Villegas himself had founded an economics program within the Law School at the Universidad Nacional Autónoma de México (UNAM) only a few years earlier—there was an emerging cohort of Latin Americans with economics training from US and European institutions.[20] Cosío Villegas, having studied at Harvard, the London School of Economics, and Sciences Po, was among the most prominent of this new crop of experts, and he had worked to fill the ranks of the Mexican bureaucracy with trained economists. His report recommended creating two economic bodies within the Pan-American Union: a division of economic relations, appointed by the Governing Board of the Union, and an economic advisory committee, made up of three representatives from each country "chosen primarily for their knowledge of international economic matters."[21]

At the conference, the Mexican delegation drew from Cosío Villegas's study in introducing a proposal to create what it called an International Bank of the American Continent, stressing that such an institution needed to be of a truly "financial" nature: it should be, they argued, "authorized to intervene effectively in the exchange, liquidation, and discount operations among the American countries and contribute, thus, to the development of agriculture, industry, and commerce."[22] Separately, Peru's Felipe Barreda Laos also outlined a proposal for the creation and capitalization of an international bank, which, he argued, would need to help protect Latin American interests during "the reorganization of the international regime of credit and currency."[23] Peru was in the middle of a wave of social and political unrest, and like many countries in the region had defaulted on its foreign loans in 1931. Edwin Kemmerer himself had been dispatched to try to prevent Peru from repudiating its obligations, but to no avail, and the government declared a five-year moratorium on its debt.[24] It was in this context that Barreda Laos argued that his proposed bank would not only improve the methods for financing foreign loans, it would also "defend Latin America against abuses in those loans . . . which have up to date brought the American countries of small means to exhaustion, ruin, and economic slavery."[25] The Peruvian proposal, he went on, would provide "the definite economic liberation of Latin America" through multilateral financial oversight. He also called for the bank to be headquartered in Buenos Aires, rather than Washington at the Pan-American Union, because, he argued, increasing the existing "unbalanced conditions" of the Pan-American Union's structure "would be fatal for the very subsistence of the organization."[26]

Uruguay's Octavio Morató agreed with his Peruvian counterpart. But Morató also expressed an opinion shared by a number of other Latin American countries, arguing that while the United States could, on its own, solve many of their problems by simply agreeing to buy more Latin American goods, this would do little for those countries, like Argentina and Uruguay, that relied heavily on trade with Europe—unless the United States agreed to "an extraordinary increase" in imports.[27] Given the US policy of protection of its agricultural production, Morató saw little hope of US action in this regard. A multilateral economic institution would therefore be necessary, particularly because after the Great Depression, he argued, "international commercial, bank, and governmental credit which is favorable to the Latin American countries does not exist."[28] He called for the creation of what he called the Inter-American Institution of Economic and Financial Reconstruction, which would oversee the reestablishment of international finance for Latin America not only by regenerating commercial ties, but also by granting both loans *and* credits to Latin American countries for the "rehabilitation and consolidation of their domestic economies." This was a radical proposal of what he called "financial aid" for those countries that had been severely affected by the crisis in the United States, an international redistribution of resources. As to the location of the institution, he too argued that its seat should be in South America, so that US representatives would be "obliged to enter the atmosphere of these problems where they actually exist."[29]

Though these proposals were largely in agreement with the ideas presented by Mexico, some delegations raised concerns. A delegate from Brazil expressed reservations about both the feasibly and the desirability of creating international institutions without first settling domestic economic problems; a delegate from Ecuador pointed out that the bank was likely to be an extremely costly undertaking. After days of deliberation, however, the subcommittees considering the various proposals regarding economic and financial institutions produced a joint report, which recommended the creation of what it called the Inter-American Economic and Financial Institute to replace the High Commission, under which would be created the Inter-American Bank. The IAB, the proposal specified, would be a "cooperative and associated instrument" of the central banks and "a regulator of credit and currency."[30] Further, the institute and the bank would be necessary to rectify what the Latin American delegates saw as massive imbalances in an "unhinged" international financial system and would thereby "improve the onerous conditions in which many of the Latin American countries negotiate their foreign loans."[31] To achieve this, the conference recommendations put the consideration of the Inter-American Economic and Financial Institute and the IAB on the agenda of a to-be-scheduled Third Pan-American Financial Conference, to be held in Santiago, Chile.[32] The Mexican delegation claimed victory; Mexican delegate Constantino Pérez Duarte cabled Plutarco Elías Calles at his home in Puebla to gloat that the Mexican proposal had gone from having an "ornate burial" as a "body as dead as the High Commission was" to being the subject of a planned special conference.[33]

A CHANGING CONTEXT

For various reasons, the proposed Santiago financial conference never took place, though the creation of the broader financial institution and the bank was again recommended at the 1936 and 1938 Inter-American meetings.[34] In response to the continued Latin American demand, the United States attempted to provide more financing to Latin America through the creation of two new institutions: the Export-Import Bank (Ex-Im Bank) and the Exchange Stabilization Fund (ESF).[35] Roosevelt had created the Ex-Im Bank by executive order, giving it an initial capitalization of $100 million and a mission to finance US exports abroad. Notably, it was conceived explicitly to avoid competition with private banks and was later tasked with furthering US foreign policy goals in cooperation with the State Department.[36] While the Ex-Im Bank was of only limited importance in its early years, by the late 1930s the perception of a growing threat to US economic expansion from both radical economic nationalism (most vividly represented in the minds of those in Washington by the oil expropriations in Mexico and Bolivia) and from Nazi Germany's interest in Latin America caused the United States to reorient Ex-Im Bank attention toward Latin America.[37] Even with a significant increase in its capitalization, however, the Ex-Im Bank alone could not provide the economic resources that the Latin Americans sought from a new financial institution.

In Mexico, the postrevolutionary political economy was shifting. Lázaro Cárdenas, elected in 1934, redoubled efforts at land reform and began a concerted program of industrialization. As the early Cárdenas years saw increasing militancy by urban workers, the populist president also brought Mexican labor into a more centralized relationship with the state via the newly established Confederación de Trabajadores Mexicanos (CTM), thereby containing some of its power to pressure the federal government from below. As industrialization became more and more central to the Mexican development strategy, Cárdenas and his advisers conceded more political space to business leaders, including the ideologically laissez-faire Monterrey Group, composed of Mexico's most important industrialists.[38] By 1937, an ongoing strike by oil workers threatened the federal government with a serious crisis. When the oil companies decided to move their capital reserves to foreign banks and other investors followed, public and private financing in Mexico ground to a halt. Mexican officials found themselves without the means to continue to fund public works projects and unable to secure further investment from abroad. The Banco de México refused to continue to lend funds to the government, and the outflow of dollar reserves put serious pressure on the peso.

The head of the Banco de México, Eduardo Villaseñor, wanted to avoid a politically and economically costly devaluation, as did Cárdenas. So in late

1937 the president sent Eduardo Suárez, the minister of finance, to Washington to meet with Secretary of the Treasury Henry Morgenthau. Morgenthau agreed to further purchases of Mexican silver, thereby providing desperately needed foreign reserves to stabilize the peso, but he lectured Suárez on the need for balanced budgets. Suárez countered that the trade imbalances, as well as Mexico's blocked access to credit, were the main culprits of the country's financial problems.[39] As the crisis worsened, Cárdenas government seized an important strategy to retain domestic legitimacy: the nationalization of the petroleum sector.[40] The 1938 nationalization demonstrated to the United States that Mexico would make good on the ideas about economic sovereignty and state-led developmentalism that were written into the 1917 constitution. But as Mexican planners were well aware, Mexico was operating in the context of a larger economic system, its insertion into which determined important aspects of Mexican economic performance. Particularly after the onset of the Second World War in Europe, it was clear that domestic policy alone would not solve Mexico's problems; the international financial climate remained crucial.[41]

AN INSTITUTION OF A PERMANENT CHARACTER

In was in this changed domestic and international context that Mexican economic experts again began to advocate strongly for the creation of the IAB. In September 1939, after the German invasion of Poland, the United States convened an emergency meeting of the Western Hemisphere's foreign ministers in Panama to discuss continental security. In addition to declarations of solidarity and assurances of neutrality in the European war, the participants were deeply concerned with what the war might mean for economic and financial relations in the Americas, and the Latin American delegations repeatedly raised economic issues as key to their wartime cooperation. The head of the US delegation, Assistant Secretary of State Sumner Welles, outlined his country's willingness to support short-term, emergency solutions to economic problems resulting from the war. Despite the Latin American anxieties, however, the US delegation had worked out a policy before the conference in a meeting between representatives of the State Department, the Treasury Department, the Ex-Im Bank, and the Reconstruction Finance Corporation: no definite loan amounts would be mentioned at the conference; no promises would be made.[42]

It was clear to everyone at the Panama conference that the US position, while considering the creation of an economic advisory committee, was far from fulfilling the vision that had been laid out by Latin American delegates at earlier conferences. Even a memo prepared by Treasury Department staff about the resolutions drafted before the conference by the State Department noted, "It is well known that the resolution represents a watered-down version of a proposal to create a common fund to be used for stabilization of American currencies and for advances to Latin American republics."[43] Mexico once again took the lead among Latin American delegates who expressed their dissatisfaction with what they saw as vague promises of Ex-Im loans and private finance. The head of the Mexican delegation, Foreign Minister Eduardo Hay, countered Welles's resolution with a proposal to urge the finance ministers of all the American countries to create "an inter-American financial institution of a permanent character."[44] This institution would carry out the tasks that had been outlined by the Mexican delegation at Montevideo: facilitate international payments, enhance central bank cooperation, and solve monetary and exchange problems. By the end of the Panama conference, the delegates agreed to approve a mandate for the creation of the Inter-American Financial and Economic Advisory Committee (IFEAC) under the purview of the Pan-American Union in Washington, instructing that it convene not later than November 15, 1939—just a few months away.[45] The IFEAC began work in Washington quite quickly, finally replacing the long-defunct Inter-American High Commission.

Shortly after the Panama meeting of the region's foreign ministers, their finance ministers met in Guatemala. Latin American delegates quickly surmised that the meeting was of secondary importance to the United States, as the Treasury Department sent only Herbert Gaston, an assistant secretary; Mexico's Villaseñor would later remember that the United States had sent a "second-rate" treasury official.[46] The perceptions were probably true: writing on his way back from Panama, Welles had assured Hull that "there is no expectation that any agreements will be reached at Guatemala or any negotiations undertaken."[47] Despite the fact that the United States seemed to have written off the meeting, however, Villaseñor came prepared with a specific proposal for the "immediate establishment of Pan-American Central Bank."[48] Villaseñor laid out in detail a six-point proposal for the purview of the bank: it would (1) serve as a currency clearinghouse, (2) act as financial agent for the central banks in international capital markets, (3) help stabilize currency levels of member countries, (4) study trade and exchange problems,

(5) aid in settling international balances accepting both gold and silver, and (6) "act as a channel for the investment of capital which will promote sound economic development in the American Republics."[49] This function, the management of finance for development, was a centrally important aspect of the bank for Villaseñor, who was another of the new generation of Mexican economists with formal training abroad. The Latin American countries must accelerate their industrialization in order to solve the problems of international trade, he argued, and financing from the bank would be necessary for that acceleration. What's more, Villaseñor asserted echoing the Peruvian proposal from 1933, the new institution would be crucial to overcome the problems that speculative foreign investment had brought to the Latin American countries. He argued that the bank would have to "avoid in all cases the aspect of hegemony or privilege that [foreign] investment could represent in the internal economy" of the debtor countries.[50] For Villaseñor, then, concerns over both representation and distribution could be addressed with the creation of a new kind of international economic infrastructure: a multilateral development bank.

The final resolution of the conference echoed Villaseñor's language, with a declaration in favor of "promoting the sound economic development of the American Republics," which argued that capital should be directed toward agricultural and industrial development.[51] It was clear in the final language, however, that there was not yet unanimity on the idea of the bank, and the delegates noted that the creation of such an organization presented both political and technical problems in harmonizing the interests of the disparate countries of the Americas.[52] The conference therefore recommended that the newly created IFEAC take up the study of such an institution—something that it was, in fact, already doing.[53] Suddenly there was significant momentum for the creation of the kind of institution that Mexican experts had been advocating for many years. Despite feeling that the United States hadn't taken the meeting sufficiently seriously, Villaseñor would later call his work at the Guatemala meeting "the most important public manifestation" of his career.[54]

THE BANK COMES UNDER US DIRECTION

By the close of the Guatemala conference, it was becoming clear to the United States that the Latin Americans were not going to simply drop their proposal for the IAB, and that the United States would need to play an active role in its development to ensure US interests were protected.[55] Harry Dexter White, the Treasury Department official who would go on to be the most important US representative at the Bretton Woods Conference, had already been encouraging Roosevelt to consider large-scale economic aid for China, Russia, and Latin America to ensure future access to markets and to counter the German threat. He warned Roosevelt that unless the United States created an assistance program "on a scale appropriate to the problem with which we are faced, . . . Latin America will gradually succumb to the organized economic and ideological campaign now being waged by aggressor nations."[56] Assistant Secretary of State Adolf Berle had also come to see the useful role that such an institution could play, arguing that the bank might serve as a "laboratory study" in which the United States could develop techniques that could later be used in Europe and elsewhere.[57] Other officials were also beginning to recognize the specific advantages of the multilateral nature of the institution. The Treasury Department's Simon Hanson thought that technical assistance provided through a multilateral institution—even if the experts were still sent mainly from the United States—was less likely to repeat the "poor record of American advisors in Latin America," particularly given how the presence of US "money doctors" had often provoked political discord in the region.[58] Berle saw another advantage that a multilateral institution might provide, testifying to the Senate Foreign Relations Committee that the IAB would be an effective vehicle for both encouraging countries to borrow *and* ensuring that they would repay, because more than one country would have a stake in preventing default.[59] This was a view that White shared; he attempted to convince Treasury Secretary Morgenthau of the desirability of the bank proposal by arguing that "there would be less of a danger of defaulting on these obligations if the creditor were an Inter-American Bank than if it were a wealthy country."[60] Perhaps more important, however, and more to the point of US interest, "the charge of dollar diplomacy would be absent."

Now that US officials were outlining their interest in the institution, plans for a bank began to move very quickly within the IFEAC. Only a week into the IFEAC's existence (and while Villaseñor was still in Guatemala, making similar proposals), the Mexican delegate, Antonio Espinosa de los Monteros, outlined a proposal for the bank in a memo. Espinosa's proposal echoed the one Villaseñor was presenting in Guatemala, including that one of the key functions of the bank should be "directing the movement of capital toward countries of the American continent in which it may be invested to advantage and with requisite security."[61] There remained, however, some Latin American skepticism about the bank. Pedro Larrañaga, the Peruvian representative on the subcommittee and an economist affiliated with the Alianza Popular Revolucionaria Americana (APRA), argued that the bank as conceived was dangerously similar to an ordinary commercial bank, in which the United States would be the only depositor and the other twenty countries the likely debtors. If this was to be the case, he asked, "Why obscure the meaning of this solution, which instead of giving the Americas a new independent and neutral credit structure is merely going to increase our indebtedness to the United States?"[62] Even if US representatives had come around, nationalist resistance in Latin America remained strong.

This skepticism shaped the early debate among US officials; Treasury's Hanson argued to White that "the feasibility of the functions [of the Bank] is inverse to their desirability in the eyes of Latin America," adding that it would do little to facilitate trade.[63] There was also opposition emerging from Congress, focused especially on Mexico's role in the advocacy of the bank. Representative Fred L. Crawford, a Republican businessman from Michigan, argued strenuously against the "grandiose Mexican plan" for the bank, given what he called the "Moscowian doctrines engulfing Mexico."[64] New Deal economic experts, however, paid little attention to this Republican hyperbole. White, for his part, harbored little fear of Moscowian doctrines and was strongly in favor of state-interventionist economic policy and interested in the mechanics of Soviet planning.[65] White disagreed with Hanson's assessment of the bank and argued to Morgenthau that it *could* facilitate trade by guaranteeing short-term credits that commercial banks were unwilling to take on. Further, he indicated that it might be possible for the institution to grant long-term loans and offer some settlement of outstanding debts—both issues that Mexican officials had repeatedly stressed to White.[66]

After these initial volleys, it was clear to the Treasury officials that they needed to better understand precisely what the economic and financial needs of the Latin American countries were. White drafted a survey for the member countries that asked each to detail its needs for long- and short-term credit, as well as its need for assistance with currency stabilization and exchange.[67] Before sending Mexico's formal response to the survey, Finance Minister Suárez sent a note to the State Department's Sumner Welles, who had been the key figure in the negotiations over Mexico's oil nationalization.[68] In the note, Suárez outlined what he saw as the major problems facing Mexico's economy: closed European markets meant a need to increase sales to the United States, but competition from lower-wage countries, particularly from colonial economies, meant that increasing Mexico's reliance on agricultural exports could introduce additional precarity. The solution, Suárez argued, was to increase trade in select agricultural items where Mexico could compete, but also to encourage increased investment in Mexican industrialization, which was then beginning to increase the standard of living of Mexican workers (and thereby allowing them to buy imported finished goods from the United States). Therefore, Suárez argued to Welles, the United States should welcome Mexican industrialization and take steps to foster it.

In countries that had not yet begun extensive industrialization efforts, however, responses to White's survey indicated that the further extension of credit was of secondary importance to the expansion of markets for Latin American goods; as the foreign minister of the Dominican Republic put it, his country's main concern was "the intensification of foreign trade."[69] Where additional credit was requested, it was in most cases for infrastructure that would aid in transporting primary goods to market, as the Venezuelan response indicated.[70] Other responses were mixed. For instance, the Colombian response noted that the closing of European markets had been detrimental to that country's trade but also requested financing for short- and long-term agricultural loans and for infrastructural development. Bolivia's response, too, argued that "to offset the effects of the war, the United States should give more opportunities for Latin America trade," but also indicated that it sought long-term credits that would help develop its sources of production, including transportation infrastructure.[71] For some respondents, the whole idea was inadequate. Chile's IFEAC representative, Carlos Dávila, a well-known lawyer, journalist, and diplomat who would go on to become the secretary general of the Organization of American States in the 1950s, drew up his own plan, in which he argued that the extension of short- or long-term credits would be insufficient, but so would—contradicting responses from other countries—an increase in US purchases of Chilean goods. Instead, Dávila called for the creation of a mechanism to develop "enterprises having mixed American and Latin American capital" in agriculture, mining, and industry. The Dávila plan, a more market-based solution than the parallel Inter-American Bank idea, was circulated in other Latin American countries and was met with a favorable reception; the foreign minister of the Dominican

Republic professed to preferring it to the plans that had been circulating for the IAB.[72] As interest in the Dávila plan grew, one result was the creation of the Inter-American Development Commission, a body that brought industrialist and government officials together to promote commercial investment in the region.[73]

By February 1940, Mexico's Villaseñor had drafted a long reply to the White survey, in which he reiterated some of what had been argued in the earlier memo from Suárez, but he added a new and repeated emphasis: the importance of long-term financing for development. He reiterated Suárez's language about the need to increase certain classes of agricultural exports to the United States and added that they now had to compete not only with the low-wage colonies, but also with China. He also noted that "this situation will not have a definitive remedy if the standard of living in said colonies is not raised."[74] He emphasized that in the face of massive variations in prices of commodities in the United States, countries like Mexico were necessarily going to suffer exchange rate disequilibria, and therefore maintaining exchange rate stability might mean "obliging its residents to suffer with all rigor the consequences of a crisis originating in another country." But for Villaseñor, the way to solve this wasn't through "phantom credits" from the central bank or through short-term commercial credit to prop up the exchange rate; it was to fundamentally alter the nature of the economy. He summed up his view: "If the economic development of a country does not proceed on sound bases, any measure taken will do as much good as an aspirin does in cases of typhoid fever. You may relieve the headache, but you do not kill the disease."[75] The most important issue at stake in the creation of the bank for the poorer countries, he wrote, was to foster long-term investments that would serve economic development. Up to that point, obtaining such credit had proved difficult, he argued, because the investments offered low returns compared to the kind of speculative, short-term activities that bankers had undertaken in "states with a semi-colonial structure" during the 1920s.[76] The takeaway, as he told a news magazine later that year, was clear: if the intention was to expand international trade, "there is no other means . . . [than] the promotion of a steady stream of investments to enable these countries to increase production and export."[77]

White and the other planners at the IFEAC took these responses into consideration, and when the draft convention for the creation of the Inter-American Bank was completed, the Mexican vision for an institution that would provide long-term development financing was fully integrated into the design of the bank.[78] In fact, the proposed bylaws took up nearly all of the proposals of the Mexican planners (including inserting a provision about the "use and distribution" of silver), establishing a bank whose first purpose was listed as to "facilitate the prudent investment of funds and stimulate the full productive use of capital and credit," as well as to stabilize currencies; increase trade in the Western Hemisphere; facilitate research, data collection, and technical advising; and promote "the development of industry, public utilities, mining, agriculture, commerce and finance" in the Americas.[79] As White noted, the Latin American responses to his survey had given the unavoidable impression "that the bank is needed to provide long-term developmental capital to Latin America."[80] It might not have been the revolutionary "new legal and philosophic conception of credit" that Puig had argued for at Montevideo, but it was a profoundly new kind of institution. As Adolf Berle wrote in 1941, the new bank represented a departure from the nineteenth-century conception of international finance. Rather, he said, the IAB "should be the beginning of a system in which finance is the servant of exchange and development . . . in direct contrast to the older system, which insisted that the development and the commerce must serve finance, or it could not go forward."[81]

The draft convention for the establishment of the bank, as well as a charter and bylaws for the institution, were submitted by the IFEAC to the member states of the Pan-American Union on February 7, 1940. By the time of the official convention signing on May 10, seven of the Latin American countries had agreed to sign on: Bolivia, Brazil, Colombia, the Dominican Republic, Mexico, Nicaragua, and Paraguay. Chile and Peru, whose delegates had expressed such dissatisfaction with the project during the negotiations, were not among the initial signers. The next step in the bank's establishment was its ratification by the legislatures of its member countries, and Mexico was the first to ratify. Cárdenas himself made a statement in 1940 that the IAB would be essential in increasing continental solidarity, again reiterating Mexico's concern for the debtor countries of the world.[82] But the approval was far from unanimous. Peru's Felipe Barreda Laos, whose nationalism had shaped his skepticism of Mexico's interventions at Montevideo and who was now arguing against further involving Latin America in the US war effort, wrote remorsefully, "They have created in the United States an American Bank whose aims are very different and even opposed to the aims for the economic liberation and organization of Hispanic America which we, who were the authors of the beneficial initiative, proposed to be fulfilled."[83] Even as Mexico portrayed its interests as universal, important divisions in the region remained.

The rest of Latin America awaited US ratification of the convention. In the United States, business interests began to weigh in. The real estate firm Cushman & Wakefield printed up a brochure advertising the best site for the proposed bank and had it sent, in both English and Spanish, to the members of the Governing Board of the Pan-American Union. The firm proposed that the bank be housed at 39–41 Broad Street in New York's financial district and paired a quote from Bolívar with one from FDR to sell what they called "The Doorway to a New World."[84] Locating the bank in New York, the brochure boasted, would "greatly facilitate trade, credit, and security." But perhaps the proposed placement of the bank so near to Wall Street was seen as a threat, as almost immediately after the convention was signed, New York banking houses began to make clear their disapproval of the plan.[85] A letter to Treasury Secretary Morgenthau from the vice president of National City Bank, Randolf Burgess, plainly worried that despite the stated intentions of the bank not to compete with commercial banks, "it is not safe to rely on any statement of intentions."[86] He argued that the "privileged position" of a government-backed bank would mean unfair competition with the branches of commercial banks, such as his, and ended his letter with a veiled threat of withholding the cooperation of the banking sector if his concerns weren't addressed.

In response, State Department officials and Nelson Rockefeller, who was by then the chairman of the Inter-American Development Commission, held a series of meetings with bankers in New York, which seemed to secure some approval from the bankers—but at the cost of inserting further provisions in the IAB's bylaws to limit its short-term lending operations to only those loans with a government guarantee. Even these assurances, however, did not satisfy the bankers or their advocates in Congress, who needed to ratify the convention to bring the bank into being.[87] While a subcommittee of the Senate Foreign Relations Committee had approved of the ratification by May 1941, the chair of the Senate Banking and Currency Committee, Carter Glass, insisted that his committee review the bill as well. Glass polled the New York bankers for their opinions, and National City Bank's Burgess reiterated, and indeed strengthened, his opposition to the bank. Glass decided to take no further action on the bill, and despite multiple attempts to push the bill forward, including by Roosevelt himself in 1942, the bill languished in committee.

The few existing histories of the IAB project end here, and with good reason: the failure of ratification in the United States prevented the bank from coming into being, and the US representatives involved, particularly White, turned their attention to the creation of the new, global financial institutions that would be necessary when the war came to an end. But for the Mexican representatives, and Villaseñor especially, the battle was far from over, and they would continue to fight for the IAB even after the creation of the World Bank and the IMF, all the way up through 1948.

As debate about the bank got underway in the United States, Villaseñor published and spoke widely advocating its creation. He extolled the virtues of the bank to the Mexican press, arguing to those who were skeptical of foreign intervention in Mexico that the bank presented nothing to fear in regard to foreign control over national economic decision-making.[88] In February 1941, just before a meeting of the Mexican Bankers' Association, he reiterated the importance of the bank to the local newspapers, and when, days afterward, White traveled to Mexico to work on Mexico's stabilization agreement xswith the United States, many of those newspapers drew a connection. While the Treasury Department tried to downplay the reason for White's travel in Mexico, the newspaper *La Prensa* noted that "it has come to be known in financial circles that although [White's] presence in the capital is apparently owed only to a pleasure trip, it is intimately linked to the function of the Inter-American Bank."[89] After White's visit, Mexican papers closely followed the bank negotiations as they played out in Washington, reporting each bureaucratic step as the convention moved toward ratification.[90] Then in July, shortly after the Senate Foreign Relations Committee hearings on the bank in Washington, Villaseñor traveled to a conference at the University of Chicago, where he gave a long lecture on the world economic and financial conjuncture. He reiterated the theory that Puig had expounded at Montevideo, arguing that the United States found itself in a position of needing outlets for its surplus capital in order to continue to grow. With the war in Europe and the Pacific, and geopolitical considerations in Africa, he argued, Latin America would be the sole region where US capital would find productive investment outlets.[91] While he didn't speak specifically to the bank, he laid out a detailed case for the work it could do.

Shortly thereafter he published a piece in English in the US journal *Foreign Affairs* in which he tried to address the potential "dangers" that detractors had raised about the bank. In particular, he addressed concerns about short-term lending for balancing budgets and maintaining exchange rates, neither of which he thought was a particularly advisable practice. Ultimately, he argued, these short-term fluctuations would be best addressed only by long-term economic transformation, and that should be the goal of the bank. He also addressed the concerns expressed by financiers about the bank's ability to lend directly to central banks and to make loans for public works and infrastructure. In his estimation, these mechanisms should not be considered risky "if the country's ability to pay is considered as a function of its future economic development."[92] Villaseñor concluded that a bank that "extends credits only for the type of investment which leads to the economic development and improvement of the peoples of Americas . . . will assure its own life for a long term and it also will create a continental community of interests which is not yet entirely evident." Mexico's revolution in development had found its institutional form.

In both of these very public interventions in the United States, Villaseñor sought to broaden the conversation going on about the bank beyond Washington and to influence US public opinion on the issue. He redoubled these efforts when congressional action on the bank began to stall. In March 1942 Villaseñor gave a fifteen-minute interview on CBS radio that was not only broadcast in New York but simultaneously heard all over Latin America.[93] In the interview, he stressed that the creation of the bank was a matter of real urgency, particularly given the loss of markets in Europe. Before the war, he said, Mexico had used its trade surplus with the rest of the world to pay for its trade deficit with the United States; now, that was no longer possible. He made clear what the stakes were for a US audience: the United States, he said again, would "inexorably" have to export its surplus capital to maintain its own equilibrium, and in order for Latin Americans to continue buying North American products, this capital would have to be invested in "enterprises that lead to the economic development of Latin America."[94] The bank, of course, was the best vehicle to channel that capital.

By this time, the US and British plans for the new postwar global financial institutions were being circulated publicly in Mexico and around the world, and the question became how the new institutions might complement or supersede the IAB. An undated memo in Villaseñor's papers indicates that at least one member of his research team at the Banco de México thought it likely that the new institutions would make the bank irrelevant, but

Villaseñor continued to argue for it.[95] In May 1944, Villaseñor argued before Rockefeller's Inter-American Development Commission that the creation of the bank would complement and make successful the work of the new global institutions.[96] Together, he argued, these new institutions would overcome the seemingly intractable swing between war and massive unemployment—but only if, he asserted, concerted attention was paid to the less-developed countries. While he recognized the importance of the health of the US economy as a determining factor in the world economy, he stressed the linkages and interdependencies to the less-developed countries that made that health possible. In moving forward with its international proposals, he argued, the US planners would have to recognize this interdependence.

Villaseñor's attempt to sway public opinion, however, did little to counter the weight of the Wall Street bankers. Villaseñor made a final attempt to bring the bank into being in 1948, at the Inter-American Conference at Bogotá. There, Mexican foreign minister Jaime Torres Bodet joined others in Latin America in demanding that Latin American economic recovery be given equal consideration with reconstruction in Europe, arguing that Latin America deserved not only lending from the World Bank but also the type of resources that had been allocated under the Marshall Plan. Secretary of State George Marshall responded to Torres Bodet in no uncertain terms: there would be no Marshall Plan for Latin America.[97] But even in the face of this US resistance, which was coupled with a growing anti-communism that had begun to fuel suspicion of any state intervention in the economy, the Mexican delegation at Bogotá reintroduced the IAB proposal.

Taking up the language of security that Marshall himself had deployed, and that would come to dominate international economic discourse in the context of the emergent Cold War, Villaseñor argued at Bogotá that "economic security is the best basis of political security," warning that "the strength of a chain is only equal to that of its weakest link."[98] In light of this, he argued, the bank would be indispensable not only for Latin America but for the entire world. The US representatives countered that the most important condition for the promotion of economic development in Latin America was the creation of "suitable safeguards to private capital," and further discussion was put off.[99] Stymied at the Bogotá conference, Villaseñor then made his case before a domestic audience, in a speech at Mexico City's Palacio de Bellas Artes in June 1948.[100] He was still arguing for the creation of the bank, but he now made clear Mexico's path forward: if foreign capital was not forthcoming, he said, "the action of the State can and should supplement the lack of private investment in those fields that are most desirable."[101] The path was now clear: by the late 1940s, the "action of the state" in the form of import substitution industrialization would come to define the Mexican economy.

CONCLUSION

Even as the institution itself was languishing behind the locked doors of the US Senate Banking Committee, the ideas behind the IAB would soon find an even larger forum, as plans began to be formulated for the multilateral economic institutions that would help the world transition from wartime to peace. The IAB, as what one scholar has called a kind of "first draft of the subsequent plans," was of central importance to White as he was tasked with sketching out the institutions that would become the World Bank and the IMF.[102] If, as Berle had hoped, the United States had created a "laboratory study" in the Western Hemisphere for working out plans for a postwar global economy, officials like White had done so on the basis of Latin American, and particularly Mexican, demands. Crucially, the Mexican demand for an organization that would restructure how international credit markets operated, and how surplus capital was distributed, was accepted by central figures in the Treasury and State Departments—but it was rejected by Wall Street financiers, who exercised their leverage over the US state as a de facto veto, blocking the IAB from coming into existence. These negotiations therefore reveal an important mechanism through which capital has historically been able to fight efforts to reform international economic governance, even when those efforts are promoted by Northern state actors. The close working relationship between US and Mexican officials and the recognition of the benefits of multilateralism for the projection of US state power were simply not enough to overcome the opposition of private financial interests, who feared both competition from and constraint by a state-backed institution. Despite the defeat, however, US officials brought along much of what they learned from the hemispheric IAB negotiations as they set about making plans for new, global institutions at Bretton Woods. There, too, Mexico would continue its fight for both representation and redistribution.

FOUR

Voice and Vote

MEXICO'S POSTWAR VISION AT BRETTON WOODS

IN THE SUMMER OF 1944, representatives of the world's most powerful countries convened in Bretton Woods, New Hampshire, to create the institutions that would govern the world economy after the war. The creation of the IMF and the World Bank has long been understood as the culmination of a bilateral reconciliation of the competing visions of the declining hegemon, Great Britain, and the rising hegemon, the United States.[1] In such a reading, Bretton Woods has two protagonists of note: US Treasury Department official Harry Dexter White, who chaired the conference's first commission, on what would become the IMF, and Great Britain's John Maynard Keynes, who chaired the second commission, on what would become the World Bank. Almost always overlooked, however, was the existence of a third commission, tasked with considering "Other Means of International Financial Cooperation," chaired by Mexico's finance minister, Eduardo Suárez. The very existence of this commission raises the question: Why was Mexico—a country that had been in default on international loans for more than a quarter century and had just a few years earlier implemented wide-ranging land reform and nationalized its petroleum industry—offered such a prominent seat at the table upon which the postwar multilateral economic institutions would be framed?

Scholars have only recently begun to ask this question, however, as the prevailing wisdom has long been that development was not a concern at the conference and that, as a key study put it, "the delegates at Bretton Woods gave little thought to the Fund's potential impact on the less-developed countries."[2] Echoing the derisive judgments found in the archival records of the great powers, scholars have long dismissed the possibility that a country like Mexico made any difference to the Bretton Woods negotiations. Though

Latin American countries comprised nineteen of the forty-four countries in attendance, the State Department's Dean Acheson, for example, could be found arguing that the "Latin Americans will just sit there until they vote."[3] If some US officials thought they might be ignored, British officials worried that representatives of the poorer countries would be a disruptive presence. Keynes, for his part, famously lamented that the presence of so many Latin American delegates at the conference would turn the gathering into what he called derisively "the most monstrous monkey-house assembled for years."[4] Another British Treasury official, Wilfred Eady, was even more explicit in a memo lambasting White's ongoing and in-depth consultation of the countries of the Western Hemisphere. "It is also silly," Eady wrote to a superior, "to make the pretense that the Mexicans (even though their representative in July was, I understand, a graduate of the London School of Economics) and the Brazilians would discuss 'at the expert level' a document which the American Treasury was endorsing." Rather, he argued, the Latin American role was clear: "Their function," he wrote, "is to sign in the place for the signature." He concluded, "To compare that consultation with the consultation with the Belgians and the Dutch which [White] seems to suggest we might do is part of the gap in Dr. White's understanding of the practical way in which international exchange works."[5] This statement is perhaps only surprising in the bluntness of the racialized assumptions it makes vis-à-vis who is qualified to participate in "international exchange." This is particularly the case given that Eady had himself been born in the late nineteenth century in a small municipality in Córdoba, Argentina, the son of a railway engineer working on a British concession, whereas Víctor Urquidi, the LSE-trained representative referenced in his comments, had actually been born in France. But the sentiment behind Eady's protest—that even the cosmopolitan, educated, and elite Latin Americans appointed by their governments to undertake these negotiations were unfit for "expert level" discussions on the international economy—is one that is consistent with the way most history of Bretton Woods has been written.

Despite contemporary and retroactive judgments about its place, however, Mexico's leadership role at Bretton Woods was the result of not only the history of interventions traced in the previous chapters, but also an active partnership over the years preceding the conference between Mexican and US financial experts. At a time when the core and the periphery of the global economy were in the process of being defined by scholars and policy makers alike,

Mexican economists and diplomats repeatedly intervened in the international postwar planning processes to argue for the crucial role played by countries like theirs and to advocate for both representation within the new institutions and distribution through them. While histories written from US and British documents characterize the Latin Americans at Bretton Woods as "client supporters" of the United States, the Mexican archival record not only reveals far more contention than is usually assumed, but also demonstrates the extent to which the Mexican delegation foresaw—and attempted to forestall—many of the later criticisms regarding US power in the IMF and World Bank.[6]

STABILIZING MEXICO, STABILIZING THE WORLD

The Mexican representatives at Bretton Woods were sent by a state in the throws of a profound political and economic shift. The election of Manuel Ávila Camacho in 1940 had signaled a definitive turn in Mexican state policy away from a concern with agrarian development and issues of land distribution toward urban industrialization, inaugurating what one scholar described as an "orthodox development program."[7] During the 1940s, Mexican officials made industrialization into a nationalist political project, intended to spur the economic growth that would bring "wealth, sovereignty, and international influence."[8] Officials also recognized, however, that the prospects for Mexico's national development hinged on the international economy into which it was inserted. The exigencies of wartime trade had a profound effect on the Mexican economy, and even before the United States entered the war, Mexico agreed to prohibit the export of strategic materials to non-American countries, thereby tying Mexico's export economy to that of its Northern neighbor.[9] Therefore, for Ávila Camacho's industrial development strategy to bear fruit, he would not only have to bring disparate domestic constituencies on board with his industrial vision; he would have to ensure that both wartime economic policies and global postwar plans didn't undermine Mexico's place in the rapidly changing global economy. To do so, Ávila Camacho leveraged a narrative of reconciliation with the United States and played up Mexico's war efforts, which allowed his administration to negotiate the restructuring of outstanding debts and expropriation indemnities for mere pennies on the dollar, thus freeing up state funds for Mexico's national development program.[10] Even as officials finally reconciled Mexico's long-standing debts and entered the war on the side of the United States, however, Mexican experts were steadily building a case that postwar planning needed to take into account the needs of countries like theirs.

While the Inter-American Bank (IAB) project described in the preceding chapter was one important venue for Mexican experts to promote their vision of international economic governance, they were also pressing their case elsewhere. For much of his tenure at the US Treasury Department, White had in his portfolio of duties the oversight of the Exchange Stabilization Fund (ESF), a $200 million pool of funds used to buy and sell foreign currencies to stabilize exchange rates.[11] Congress authorized the creation of the ESF in 1934, giving the president and the Treasury Department full discretion in its use, without congressional oversight of its operations—thereby lending it an air of considerable secrecy. In its first few years, the ESF was famously used to stabilize the dollar in the face of competitive devaluations of the British pound and the French franc, resulting in the Tripartite Agreement of 1936. But the Tripartite Agreement was not the first stabilization loan; in fact, the first transfer of dollars to stabilize a foreign currency was made earlier that year, to none other than Mexico, and it was followed soon afterward by another agreement negotiated in 1941. According to two economists who have studied the history of the ESF, these Mexican agreements "became the model for subsequent stabilization loans."[12] In fact, a former general counsel for the IMF argued that the 1941 agreement with Mexico "contained the germ of the idea of combining regulatory and financial provisions that is so prominent a feature of the IMF."[13] The 1941 agreement was concluded just as White was beginning to elaborate his global plans for currency stabilization after the war—and it was much more than a simple currency swap.[14]

In February 1941, White traveled to Acapulco for the meeting of the Mexican Bankers' Association, accompanied by his good friend and former Harvard contemporary, Antonio Espinosa de los Monteros, the head of Mexico's national development bank, Nacional Financiera. (The two were so close, in fact, that Víctor Urquidi would later remember that White referred to Espinosa de los Monteros as "Tony" throughout the Bretton Woods conference.)[15] As he constantly flew between Washington and Mexico City to participate in the negotiations over Mexico's debt, Espinosa de los Monteros repeatedly advocated for new mechanisms to channel surplus capital from the United States toward Mexican development projects. As early as August 1940, one Treasury Department official had explicitly noted in a memo the "idea that Monteros [sic] has on Mexico's need of funds that won't have to be returned for a long, long time."[16] This was a case that Mexican officials had been making for years, as previous chapters have demonstrated, but Espinosa de los Monteros used his access to White and the Treasury to keep the pressure up. While little was disclosed in the United States about White's trip to Mexico—treasury secretary Henry Morgenthau told US reporters only that White had gone for "a general study"—White and his team indicated to the Mexican press that they would meet with high-level officials in Mexico, raising expectations about an eventual agreement.[17]

Back in Washington, officials at the State Department were struggling with the intransigence of both the international oil companies and the Mexican government, who were engaged in negotiations about the indemnification for the 1938 expropriation of petroleum. Secretary of State Cordell Hull sought Treasury's help in determining how the United States might meet Mexico's demands. The time had come, wrote Frank Coe, an assistant to White, "to discuss with Mexico what we may give to her so that the discussions concerning what we want from Mexico can be expedited."[18] What the United States wanted was the ability to transit planes protecting the Panama Canal through Mexican airfields and to ensure access to strategic materials that would aid US support of the Allies in Europe. State suggested that a Mexican negotiator would be called to Washington to work out a deal, and so in July 1941, just a few months after White returned from their trip together, Espinosa de los Monteros arrived in the US capital for a series of meetings.

During July and August 1941, Espinosa de los Monteros met repeatedly with White and other officials from Treasury and State to work out the details for the stabilization agreement. The Mexican economist extracted a number of concessions from the US negotiators, including increasing the stabilization loan amount from $30 million to $40 million and extending the window during which the funds could be recalled from thirty days to effectively one year (he did so by using the explicit threat that Mexico might put in place more stringent exchange controls, something the United States wanted to avoid). Both of these requests were intended not just to help smooth temporary balance-of-payments problems, Espinosa argued, but also to allow Mexico "to permit the use of a further portion of the existing reserves to import machinery and equipment, which would enable Mexico ultimately to reduce imports and increase exports."[19] As such, Espinosa saw the stabilization package as part of a larger vision for Mexican development, allowing Mexico to devote less of its foreign exchange to the service of overseas obligations and more to investment in the industrialization effort. The negotiations resulted in a broad plan, including the resumption of the US silver purchase program, which had been suspended following the oil expropriation; support for the stabilization of the peso; a reciprocal trade agreement between the two countries; and an Ex-Im Bank loan to be managed through Nacional Financiera, as a precursor to "other requests for credit for development in Mexico."[20] This was much more than a simple stabilization loan; it was the outline of a comprehensive development package. Bilateral negotiations over the "coordinated and over-all development of the economy of Mexico" would continue in the years to follow, with the creation in 1943 of the Mexican-American Commission on Economic Cooperation, on which White was a key delegate.[21] In these bilateral fora, then, representatives like Espinosa de los Monteros made Mexico's development demands quite clear.

MEXICO CONSIDERS THE US PLANS

Even as bilateral negotiations with Mexico were proceeding, White was working on his plans for a new global arrangement. White's first drafts for a new kind of international stabilization fund were written in 1941, and he further refined them in early 1942 into plans for both a fund and a "Bank for Reconstruction and Development of the United and Associated Nations."[22] As Eric Helleiner has argued, important aspects of White's plans for the postwar institutions reflected the concerns of the Latin Americans. In his first draft, for example, the bank was to provide loans that would "raise the productivity and hence the standard of living of the peoples of the member countries" and to "promote stability in prices of important commodities"— both concerns that had been raised by the Latin American representatives in the earlier negotiations over the IAB.[23] The importance of the "Latin American audience" for White's plans was made clear when, in January 1942, just a month after Pearl Harbor, the United States convened the Inter-American Meeting of Foreign Ministers in Rio de Janeiro.[24] The US officials wanted to use the meeting to pressure the Latin American countries to break relations with the Axis, but the Latin American representatives forced onto the agenda resolutions concerning capital flows, commodity production, and even postwar economic planning.[25] White, for his part, sought to use the conference to gauge Latin American support for the idea of an international stabilization fund, and he began holding informal discussions in Rio with various financial representatives about preliminary plans for the fund.[26]

When asked by Latin American delegates in Rio if they could review the text of his proposed plan, White argued that the conference could "hardly examine any plan, since a plan does not yet exist"—which was, of course, not strictly true.[27] Once the Latin American countries had signaled their collective interest in such a plan through a conference resolution, however, White prepared to share his drafts with Brazil and Mexico, in addition to Great Britain, China, Canada, and Australia.[28]

Mexican planners received White's preliminary proposal text in early July 1942, when the Inter-American Financial and Economic Advisory Committee (IFEAC) convened a meeting in Washington. Mexico sent a delegation of finance experts to the meeting headed by Antonio Carrillo Flores, an official with the Ministry of Finance, and including Eduardo Villaseñor, director of the Banco de México, and the young economist Víctor Urquidi. Urquidi was among the first generation of Mexicans to receive formal economics training, having studied at the London School of Economics; he spoke fluent English and was well versed in monetary policy. At a dinner banquet during the conference at Washington's Hotel Mayflower, Urquidi found himself sitting next to White, who invited the young Mexican economist to meet with him in his office the following day.[29] There are no records of what was said during that meeting, but Urquidi departed from White's office with a copy of the latter's April 1942 draft and with instructions to read it carefully and to convey it to central bank and finance ministry officials in Mexico.

Urquidi returned to Mexico and shared the proposal with staff at the Banco de México, who thought that it might be useful to publicize some of the US ideas in Mexican media. When Urquidi wrote to White to ask for permission to do so, however, he was told that it remained strictly confidential. Initial impressions in Mexico, therefore, were that the proposal seemed somewhat premature and undeveloped, and there was some skepticism regarding US intentions to actually carry out White's plans. Despite this doubt about the US intentions, however, officials at the Banco de México decided that they needed to begin to study postwar planning more generally, and they created a group within the Office of Economic Studies charged with investigating postwar issues.[30] When the next draft of White's plan was officially circulated for comment in April 1943, this group delegated a team, led by Urquidi and Daniel Cosío Villegas, to draft a formal study of the plan, which they did over the course of a month's retreat at a resort hotel in Acapulco.

If US officials expected their Mexican counterparts to simply go along with their plans, they probably would not have anticipated the scathing nature of Urquidi and Cosío Villegas's report. Concluding that the White plan "was in no way satisfactory," they lamented that it was not as thoroughly thought out as the British plan, also released in 1943.[31] (The Mexican finance minister, Suárez, remembered many years later that he would have preferred the Keynes plan to that which emerged from Bretton Woods, as it "would have, since then, resolved all of the problems that later presented themselves.")[32] Urquidi and Cosío Villegas were especially concerned about what the plans would mean for what they called the "weaker countries," fearing not only that the United States was quickly becoming an indomitable economic power, but that its officials seemed unprepared to effectively manage that role. The study lamented that "the United States, to whom the division of labor and good fortune now reserves the role of director of the world, has been able to present a project so immature for the first great international adventure of the postwar."[33] The Mexican analysts argued that many of the world's current problems actually *derived from* the rising power of the United States in the world economy, diagnosing the two main problems that Latin American economies had suffered over recent decades. Broadly, they wrote, the "United States is a country that wants to sell, but not buy; and what's more that it's a creditor that does not invest but hoards." Echoing the Mexican proposals for the need for the IAB, Urquidi and Cosío Villegas advocated a mechanism for the international coordination of investment, to ensure that this "hoarding" would not jeopardize the development of the smaller countries. Further, they linked the question of finance to the question of trade, arguing that "fundamentally, the case of Yankee protectionism is the rare case of a country that the whole world owes, that wants and demands to be paid, but in declining to buy that which its debtors produce, it in reality impedes payment." Proposals to stabilize currency and facilitate credit would do little, they argued, if the United States continued to refuse competition from Latin American exports.

In addition, Urquidi and Cosío Villegas highlighted dangers of the lopsided nature of US power in the planned organization, lamenting its deficiencies with regard to representation. The plan was not the heroically international effort that they had been sold in media and US government reports; rather, they wrote, "there have presided at a rather close distance North American interests, prejudices, fears and ideas."[34] If the United States truly wanted to create the propitious international economic circumstances that would underpin monetary and financial stabilization, they argued, it would require "taking very seriously the situation, needs and wishes of the debtor countries, in the process of economic development, anxious to accelerate their progress." After all, they wrote, the debtor countries were the vast majority of those who would join any new organization; any plan would be unsuccessful, they argued, if it didn't adequately address the needs of the weaker countries. This meant that Mexico and the rest of Latin America should "expect that the moment will come in which conversations can be initiated about other plans for international economic cooperation, above all in matters of international trade, customs and investment."[35]

On the basis of the study by Urquidi and Cosío Villegas, Rodrigo Gómez of the Banco de México convened a larger group of Mexican officials to consider their position in future negotiations about the new institutions. According to Urquidi, officials from the US Treasury, the Federal Reserve Board, and the New York Federal Reserve paid visits to Mexico for meetings on the topic, as did as the famous Argentine economist Raúl Prebisch.[36] While much attention was being devoted to the new Stabilization Fund, a memo prepared by the Banco de México argued that the fund would only be useful as part of a larger set of institutions that would address the particular problems of the less industrialized world, especially primary commodity producers. In outlining Mexico's negotiating stance, Banco de México officials wrote that their delegation should consider not just the advantages and drawbacks of the fund, "but of the other institutions whose organization and functioning are already aimed: the Bank of Reconstruction and Development, and, at least, an organization whose field of work will be the production, distribution and prices of primary products."[37] The need for long-term financing for development projects was paramount, and the memo stressed that Mexico's interests in a stable monetary regime were much less than the creation of an "institution that could facilitate, in liberal conditions and without political compromises, long term credit to better take advantage of its natural resources." In addition, an institution that would coordinate production, distribution, and prices of primary products would be especially important, as Mexico's exports were still largely in this sector. As to the fund itself, the Mexican experts worried, it seemed that White's successive proposals were "turning away each time more from the possibility of resolving, or helping to resolve, the fundamental economic problem of the next few years: the profound disturbance that the excessive wealth of the United States represents in the world." Therefore, they concluded that for the rest of the world, the Fund might have little utility. This didn't mean that Mexico shouldn't cooperate in the planning, however, and Cosío Villegas and Urquidi raised the possibility of Mexico's conditional approval of US plans: if Mexico would get relatively little benefit from the fund and a slightly greater benefit from other agreements, then perhaps "it would be advisable to plant the question of whether Mexico should give its approval to the Fund on the condition that the other organizations are created and that the organization of them is satisfactory."

In May 1943, Espinosa de los Monteros and Rodrigo Gómez traveled to Washington for the preliminary discussions on the International Stabilization Fund at the Treasury Department. During the last week of May, the Mexican officials met four times with White and his team. During those meetings, Espinosa again emphasized the need not just for currency stabilization, but also for long-term lending, something he had been stressing to White repeatedly over the previous years. In response, White indicated that his plans included the "other agencies for long term capital" that Espinosa thought so vital.[38] By this point in the planning, it was clear that Mexican officials had become key interlocutors for White; in June, White argued to Morgenthau, "If we get agreement by the U.S., U.K., Russia and China on the main points in the draft, we shall probably want to get an indication from Minister Suarez [sic] as to his reaction."[39]

VOICE AND VOTE: MEXICO'S INTERVENTIONS AT THE CONFERENCE

By the time the Mexican delegation arrived for preliminary meetings in Atlantic City in June 1944, its members—including Suárez, Gómez, Cosío Villegas, Espinosa de los Monteros, and Urquidi—had devoted considerable study to the plans for and implications of the new bank and fund and had developed an agenda for the conference that centered on raising the concerns of the "smaller nations" in the new international economic system. Mexico's objectives were summed up in a headline in Mexico City: "Mexico Will Seek Voice and Vote for the Weaker Nations at the Monetary Meeting."[40]

Despite their long experience negotiating directly with US representatives, the Mexican representatives now confronted some new multilateral stumbling blocks. In particular, British representatives found the Mexican and broader Latin American presence in the negotiations exasperating, and

Mexican attempts to reinforce the equality and sovereignty of countries like theirs set the Mexican delegation on a collision course with Keynes himself. In Atlantic City, during a discussion regarding the mechanisms by which countries might be suspended from the proposed fund, Espinosa de los Monteros argued vigorously "that suspension or compulsory withdrawal of a member, as a matter of national honor, must be voted by the entire Directorate representing the nations," rather than by just the most powerful nations.[41] Espinosa de los Monteros was drawing from the long tradition of Mexican defense of the formal equality of sovereign states, a theme that the delegates would continuously emphasize at Bretton Woods. Keynes replied scornfully that "the fund as a business organization is not concerned with questions of national honor."[42] These negotiations were technical and rational, Keynes implied; the Mexican concern was irrational and therefore inappropriate. The British contention that countries like Mexico were not fit for such negotiations was already palpable.

Despite Keynes's annoyance, however, Mexico's role at Bretton Woods had been assured years before the meeting convened, as US Treasury officials hoped that representatives of both Mexico and Brazil would make early and public demonstrations at the conference of their support for new institutions. As the largest participating economies in Latin America (Argentina was not a member of the United and Associated Nations and was therefore not invited to the conference), their leadership of the other seventeen Latin American republics in attendance—a group that Treasury documents at the time referred to as "friendly Latin America"—was vital for White and his staff.[43] In a preliminary conference plan drawn up in April 1942, Treasury staffer George H. Willis went so far as to draft the full text of speeches that the representatives of Brazil and Mexico might give, including one by the Mexican finance minister in support of the fund and one by the Brazilian finance minister in support of the bank, using ideas that Mexican and other Latin American representatives had stressed at the Rio conference.[44] The existence of this curious US ventriloquism of Mexico and Brazil might lend credence to the interpretation offered by the British Treasury official quoted previously—that the Latin Americans were there to "sign in the place for the signature"—if not for the fact that, alongside these speeches, Willis also drafted a speech for the British chancellor of the exchequer.[45]

Thus, when the conference opened in northern New Hampshire in July 1944, Mexican officials were appointed to important leadership roles at the conference. One of the first tasks was the nomination of the chairs of the commissions that would organize the conference deliberations. White and Keynes were joined as chairs by Mexico's finance minister, Eduardo Suárez, appointed to chair the third commission of the conference on "Other Means of International Financial Cooperation." Suárez's nomination to this leadership position was a reflection of the US estimation of the importance of Mexico vis-à-vis the rest of Latin America and also of the long and deep relationship he and his advisers had with Morgenthau and White. Suárez was also tasked with formally nominating Treasury Secretary Morgenthau as the president of the conference. His nominating speech praised New Deal planning, implying a congruence with Mexican policies, but also argued that one of the lessons of the New Deal experience was that external balance should not be sought at the expense of internal stability. Rather, he argued, the two should be pursued in tandem, to ensure the "harmonious development of the national economies of all countries."[46] With echoes of the earlier Mexican ideas about debt, credit, and the development of production, Suárez was implying that the powerful countries might have responsibilities no less than the weak ones when it came to international financial stability. Such harmonious development required coordination that would scale up the equitable distribution of resources to the international economy. Mexican representatives would then approach the remainder of the conference seeking to make such distribution possible, through a series of interventions.

"Questions of Sovereignty"

Mexican officials had long been concerned with protecting the sovereignty of the weaker nations, and they brought this advocacy to the planning meetings prior to Bretton Woods. As White explained to Morgenthau after the Atlantic City meetings, "The Mexicans feel that many matters to be considered by the Fund involve questions of sovereignty, and that small countries have interests and responsibilities no less than the large countries."[47] This was a perceptive summary of the Mexican view; if the institution was indeed to be a multilateral one, it must not benefit only a few countries at the expense of the majority, echoing the doctrine put forward by Carranza during the League of Nations debate. In preparing for the conference, Mexican officials had floated the "possibility of a differential regime" for the new institutions, one that would distinguish between countries with different economic bases, "so that the small primary producing countries should give a quota proportionately less than the great industrial countries, could receive proportionately more credits, and have greater margins to autonomously modify their exchange rates, etc."[48] Such a proposal was based in Mexico's recognition of the reciprocal nature of international financial transactions, as had been passionately outlined by Puig at the Montevideo conference a decade earlier. International finance, Puig had argued, did not just benefit the country on the receiving end of a loan, but accrued a profit—often a larger one than could be sought at home—to the lender. Similarly, international trade was based in mutual needs; certainly during the war, primary products from Latin America had been crucial to the US war effort. But, just as Puig had noted, the unbalanced nature of international trade, in which the poorer countries exported primary products but had to import their capital goods, inherently led to balance of payments problems, and the exigencies of wartime had created additional difficulties.

At Bretton Woods, the Mexican experts were once again keen to demonstrate the reciprocal nature of international financial transactions, arguing for shared responsibility in the creation of economic disequilibria. In their study of White's early plans, Urquidi and Cosío Villegas had noted, for example, that the fault for balance of payments problems lay as much with the surplus countries as with those that had deficits. They recommended therefore that corrective measures be taken in both—particularly in situations where the economy of the deficit country was highly dependent on that of the surplus country, as was clearly the case between Mexico and the United States.[49] The solution, the Mexican experts argued, depended on both countries, but fundamentally rested with the country with *more* economic power. At Atlantic City, the Mexican delegation made common cause on the issue with Australia, Canada, and even Great Britain, as White noted in a memo to Morgenthau. Even if the US planners admitted such a contention, however, the difficulty would be in "finding appropriate means of exerting pressure on the creditor countries" as White put it.[50] Because of the nature of the fund, he admitted, it was far easier for the body to sanction debtor countries for their role in creating disequilibria than creditors. Keynes, as representative of a debtor country himself, argued for the need for a mechanism for the fund to put pressure on the creditor countries in such circumstances. This led to the insertion of the "scarce currency" provisions in the fund's agreement, which would, Keynes explained, "commit the U.S. to finding a way out in the event of the balance of trade turning obstinately in its favour."[51] After some debate, the clause was deemed sufficient to address Mexico's concern about the responsibility of creditors, as well as debtors, for resolving financial disequilibria.[52]

The principle of sovereign equality also underwrote Mexico's attempts to ensure that the member countries of the new institutions were relinquishing sovereign prerogative in equitable ways. The original language of the fund proposal gave the power to determine the gold parity value of currencies only to the most powerful nations, thereby, in the Mexican view, effectively removing sovereignty over currency valuation from all but a few countries. In response, the Mexican delegation submitted a strenuous objection on behalf of the less powerful countries. The intervention was planned before the conference; the preparatory documents drafted by Cosío Villegas and Urquidi argued that while there had been no attempt to conceal that the rich countries would be given more power to govern the fund, the rule that allowed only the United States, Great Britain, and the USSR to determine gold parities "has reached a point of cynicism that should lead to some declaration of the small countries."[53]

At Bretton Woods, Espinosa de los Monteros made just such a declaration; when it came to the necessary cession of some degree of economic sovereignty, Espinosa de los Monteros argued at the conference, "how can we help cooperation by blind submission of small countries?"[54] It was unreasonable to expect the smaller countries to adhere to rules that the larger ones did not need to follow. Certainly, he argued, no major country would give up to a foreign power the right to fix the value of its currency. This was, he argued, "one of the attributes of sovereignty which they are prone to guard most jealously." Instead, Espinosa de los Monteros argued, a multilateral forum should serve to ensure that *all* countries were relinquishing certain aspects of their economic sovereignty together, and not some more than others. The Mexican delegation would vote against the proposal as written, he argued, not only because it disrespected the sovereignty of the weaker nations, but also "because it presupposes that small countries will change their laws and perhaps even their constitutions at a minutes notice, regardless of political, social or economic difficulties." In response, a US delegate pointed out that a special committee had already agreed to language that would allow countries to opt out of uniform currency valuation changes, if they gave the fund seventy-two hours' notice. White, serving as the chair of the commission, clarified for the benefit of the Mexican delegation: "Does it apply to small nations as well as large?" "Large and small," came the reply from Treasury's Ansel Luxford.[55] With that affirmation of the principle raised by the Mexican delegation on the question of sovereignty, the language was approved, and Espinosa de los Monteros was mollified.

Ensuring Representation

The fight for equity in treatment was complemented by a fight for fair representation in the new institutions, which played out in a vigorous debate over the quotas that each country would subscribe to the fund—that is, the share of the capital they would supply—and how that share would reflect their voting power. The means of calculating the proposed quota numbers was already quite controversial at the conference itself, and the US delegation took pains to keep the method for determining them quiet, since they were, as Marriner Eccles of the Federal Reserve admitted in a US delegation meeting, based "on a formula, with some exceptions for political reasons."[56] Early US drafts of conference plans indicate that Treasury officials paid close attention to regional and colonial blocs and divided quota totals among regions such as "British Empire" and "Friendly Latin America" (which excluded Argentina and Chile).[57] While the representatives of countries like Mexico certainly understood the preponderance of US power in the new institutions, the debate emerged around the distinction between US *influence in* and US *control of* them.[58] White had reassured Morgenthau that the Mexican view was not intended strictly to limit the voting power of any single country like the United States but was instead a "desire to see the smaller countries participate more fully in the decisions of the fund."[59] If White intended to convince his superiors of the fidelity of their southern neighbor, however, he may have been optimistic. Urquidi and Cosío Villegas had, after all, written that the main international problem was the "profound disturbance that the excessive wealth of the United States represents in the world."[60]

Indeed, Mexican experts had been concerned since obtaining White's early drafts with what proportion of representation Mexico might have, particularly in relation to that of the United States. Other Mexican experts weighed the representation they would be afforded in the proposed IAB with the new global institutions and lamented what seemed like a diminished ratio. The fundamental difference between the new fund and the IAB plans, wrote Antonio Carrillo Flores, director of the Credit Management Department at the Ministry of Finance, "resides primarily in the voting power of the participating countries."[61] In the IAB, each country would have a director with a single vote; in the new institutions, representation would be based largely on the quota system. To address this, Carrillo wrote to Eduardo Villaseñor at the Banco de México advocating that Mexico push for a "a more democratic mechanism" for fund leadership: "The democratic climate that seems to inspire the United Nations should be taken advantage of," he urged, "to suggest an administrative mechanism that will dispel any suspicion of intent for political control by one country or group of countries to the detriment of the countries that are weakest economically." For their part, Urquidi and Cosío Villegas went so far as to try to use the various formulas that appeared in White's early drafts to calculate Mexico's vote, computing the possibilities by hand using complicated spreadsheets; they concluded that "the points assigned to Mexico will not represent more than one or two percent in comparison with our neighbor to the North."[62] Urquidi and Cosío Villegas therefore urged that it was "advisable that Mexico fight" against the effective control of governance by the largest countries and for equitable representation.

Despite the will to fight, the Mexican delegation at Bretton Woods conceded that they were not seeking complete equality of representation within the new institutions. Espinosa recognized that it was a fundamental aspect of the plans that "creditor nations should have proportionately more power than the debtor nations."[63] He continued, however, in something of an aside, "Not that it should [necessarily] be so. We question from a higher point of view this principle established in international finance," again, echoing the interventions made at Montevideo by Puig. In a pragmatic attempt to limit the ability of the largest countries to impose decisions on the smaller ones, however, Espinosa intervened in the debate over what would constitute a quorum for decision-making within the fund. The original proposal defined a quorum as two-thirds of the total votes—a figure that in early formulations could nearly be mustered by the United Kingdom and the United States alone.[64] Espinosa argued that a two-thirds quorum "is really dangerous to the small countries" and proposed a successful amendment that for any decision to be made, there must be present not only two-thirds of the total voting power, but also one-half of the total member countries.[65] The intention, then, was to prevent the largest countries from making decisions without the input of any other member states—and given that nearly half of the original member countries were from Latin America, the new requirement ensured that Latin American representatives would have to be present for decisions to be made.

An additional venue in which the fight over representation played out was the election of the executive directors of the IMF, the governing body that would run the fund on a day-to-day basis (a much larger body, the Board of Governors, was composed of a representative from each member country, but it was to meet only annually, and its decision-making powers were delegated to the executive directors). The original draft proposal called for eleven executive directors, one appointed from each of the five countries with the largest quotas, and the remaining seven elected from among the thirty-nine other member countries.[66] Here, Mexico put regional solidarity at the forefront. Suárez later remembered, "The Latin American delegates came to form a powerful bloc that discussed issues in private so that were could then defend them in common in the Conference," and this group had decided that Latin America had a right to expect to be represented among the permanent members of the board.[67]

Mexican officials joined with the Cuban delegation to push a proposal to reserve two executive director seats for Latin America, to ensure that the region was always represented. The Mexican delegation then set out to survey their Latin American counterparts about the idea, and in response the Brazilian finance minister warned that they could expect other regions and groups of countries to demand the same.[68] During a subsequent conference session, the delegate from Egypt did just that; though supportive of the proposal pushed by Cuba and Mexico, he argued that "the proper application of the principle" of regional blocs of representation meant that it would be applied to all economic regions, not just Latin America.[69] But Mexican negotiators skillfully used their behind-the-scenes relationships with the US delegation to press their case, and they prevailed. Suárez remembered, "Our arguments convinced both Mr. Morgenthau and Mr. White, in good part for the sympathy that both felt toward us, and they agreed that we would have two permanent delegates on the board of the Monetary Fund."[70] As a result, the original IMF Articles of Agreement included a provision that of a total of twelve executive directors, "two shall be elected by the American Republics not entitled to appoint directors."[71] Mexico and its Latin American allies thereby ensured their representation on the fund's governing body.

Fighting for Development

Perhaps the most consequential fight Mexican officials waged at Bretton Woods was to ensure that the institutions to be created would focus not just on the needs of reconstructing a war-torn Europe, but also on the economic development of the less industrialized world. As Víctor Urquidi would later remember, "the Mexican delegation thus arrived at Bretton Woods ready to inject some interest in economic development issues into the debate."[72] Once the conference began, the Mexican delegation quickly submitted revisions to the proposals that had been negotiated for the new institutions, including an early amendment meant to ensure that the purview of the proposed International Bank would cover both reconstruction *and* development. While Keynes had delegated to committees nearly all other technical aspects of the bank's agreement, he asked for the full second commission's consideration of the Mexican proposal as "a matter which strikes so deep, that I think it is not appropriate for any single committee."[73] The young Víctor Urquidi rose to explain his country's position, echoing many of the sentiments Mexican experts had previously expressed in negotiations over the IAB: if the idea was to make an institution of permanent, and not temporary, character, then development considerations would prove crucial once reconstruction of Europe had been accomplished. "In the very short run," Urquidi addressed Keynes, "perhaps reconstruction will be more urgent for the world as a whole, but in the long run, Mr. Chairman—before we are all *too* dead, if I may say so—development must prevail if we are to sustain and increase real income everywhere."[74] Without denying the importance of devoting funds to reconstruction, Urquidi urged that development not be postponed or relegated within the bank. Resources allotted for development, he argued, would benefit not just those countries receiving them, but the entire world, as the development of the nonindustrialized nations would "provide better markets and better goods." What's more, he argued, countries like Mexico were being asked to contribute resources to the bank (which they would do "ungrudgingly," he added) using foreign exchange that might otherwise be used for the import of capital goods—and so, he argued, such countries must be assured that their requests for capital would not be overlooked in favor of reconstruction projects.

The representative from Cuba rose immediately to support the Mexican statement, but the Dutch representative pointed out that the wording seemed to imply too rigid a constraint on the distribution of lending, such that if the amount allotted to reconstruction declined, the amount for development would have to decline similarly. Urquidi later remembered that after his intervention, "there followed a silence. Keynes at one point shoved his eyeglasses to the tip of his nose, shuffled some papers . . . and said something like this: 'With regard to the amendment submitted by Mexico, I think it can be made shorter and can be adopted by substituting *equitable* consideration for *equal* consideration.'"[75] The transcript reveals little of the condescension implied in Urquidi's memory of the meeting, but does show that Urquidi again raised the issue before the adjournment of the session, to ensure that the new wording would be incorporated into the draft being written. Keynes replied, "No doubt they will seek to harmonize, give equal emphasis, to reconstruction and development. No doubt they will attend to that."[76] He assured Urquidi that if the final language didn't sufficiently account for development, he could raise it again. At the close of negotiations, the language suggested by Keynes was approved, and the articles of agreement stressed, "The resources and the facilities of the Bank shall be used exclusively for the benefit of members with equitable consideration to projects for development and projects for reconstruction alike."[77] Mexico had ensured that "development" was enshrined in the essential purposes of the new institution.

CONCLUSION

If the Mexican economic team had arrived at Bretton Woods with a concerted plan to put the needs of the poorer countries on the agenda of the new global financial institutions, they had succeeded in important ways, such as putting development issues front and center and ensuring that the US preponderance of power within the institutions wouldn't mean unilateral control over them. Bretton Woods signaled to the Mexican experts that it was possible to reform the rules of global economic governance in favor of the countries of the Global South, using multilateral rules to not only ensure voice and vote for the poorer countries, but to create institutions that might begin to redistribute resources, as well. But despite the success of Mexican interventions regarding sovereignty, representation, and development, there was no guarantee that the new organizations would function to the benefit of the debtor countries. Shortcomings became clear quite quickly, and in 1945, Urquidi published an analysis of the new institutions in which he noted that, as constituted, they "didn't attack the root of the problem of investments of world economic development."[78] Urquidi worried that Mexico's concerted focus on development finance might not materialize in the face of the reconstruction needs in Europe. If this were to happen, he wrote, "there are two roads: that each country initiates a process of accelerating internal capitalization with their own funds, or that they obtain help of the countries willing to export capital." Both would require, he wrote, the "intelligent intervention of the state."[79] That state intervention would be the hallmark of the Mexican economy for the next four decades.

The conventional narrative of Bretton Woods has understood each of the interventions made by the Mexican delegation during the conference as mere footnotes to the real historical story, unfolding in the negotiations between White and Keynes, between an ascendant United States and a war-torn and beleaguered Great Britain. But uncovering the context in which Mexico's interventions were made—the changes in US–Mexican diplomatic relations, the emphasis on domestic postwar planning within Mexico, and the history of the US program of international stabilization—as well as paying close attention to the points at which Mexico intervened in the planning process, reveals a Mexico much less peripheral than earlier scholarship has imagined. And indeed, many of the interventions made by Mexico weren't confined to the conference itself, but were part of ongoing struggles to define the place of what would become the "developing world" in the new, postwar world order. Having achieved some of their procedural goals within the new Bretton Woods institutions, Mexican experts would now work to bring their fights over both representation and redistribution to the broader United Nations organization—and to push the United States to follow through on its new-found interest in development.

FIVE

Within Limits of Justice

THE ECONOMIC CHARTER FOR THE AMERICAS
AND ITS CRITICS

AS HAD BEEN THE CASE during the financial negotiations at Bretton Woods, the larger postwar planning effort revealed how important Latin America was in defining the new role of the United States in the world. When it came to designing the new United Nations (UN) organization, it was clear to many US planners that the institution's legitimacy rested on approval not just by the other great powers but also by the rest of the countries who would become members—a sizable plurality of whom were the republics of the Western Hemisphere. From Dumbarton Oaks, where the structure of the new global organization was formulated; to Chapultepec, where the United States made clear the place of Latin America in its postwar economic vision; to San Francisco, where the UN was brought into being, Mexican officials used the flurry of international negotiations to once again fight the global imbalance of economic power. Having strongly advocated for the infrastructure of international development over the preceding decade, by the early 1940s Mexican officials recognized that their dual struggles for representation and redistribution had become inextricable. As the United States planned the new institutions through which it would now project its vision of world order, Mexican officials once again harnessed the professed liberal multilateral values of the rising hegemon not only to advocate for the *rights* of the poorer and weaker states, but also to assert the *duties* of the richer, stronger ones. The war had revealed how important Latin American labor, markets, and commodities were to the United States, and Mexican officials intended to use that importance to their benefit. In a speech in Philadelphia in 1942, the longtime Mexican ambassador to the United States, Francisco Castillo Nájera, asserted that "the World Organism will be in charge of an economy assuring production and distribution in such a way as to banish present absurdities, such as nations perishing of hunger while in others surplus crops are destroyed." Looking toward the postwar future, he declared "a system of laissez faire cannot last."[1] Mexican officials would use the opportunity presented by the creation of new postwar organizations and agreements to attempt to define the parameters of a new system.

THE STATE AND THE MARKET
IN A POSTWAR WORLD

Like the leaders of other Latin American nations, Mexican officials expected that their contributions to the Second World War would be rewarded after the completion of the fighting. Mexico had not only sent Bracero laborers to work in US fields and deployed the airmen of the famous Squadron 201 to the Pacific theater; like many of their neighbors, they had also made agreements to sell strategic materials exclusively to the Allies. Mexican president Manuel Ávila Camacho had negotiated a wartime trade agreement in 1942 that guaranteed US markets for Mexican agricultural and extractive products in return for supplying the United States with strategic materials for the war at reduced prices, thereby linking Mexico's economy even more deeply to that of its Northern neighbor. This "economic solidarity," as it was called at the 1942 Rio conference, carried with it a Latin American expectation of reciprocal benefit. Mexican officials had good reason to think that they would receive such benefits; by 1944, the Mexican-American Commission for Economic Cooperation, composed of government and business officials on both sides of the border, had worked out what it considered a "minimum program for Mexico's economic development," which included a targeted industrial development strategy that built on the agreements negotiated under the ESF in the preceding years.[2]

Domestically, as Mexican industrialization accelerated, the question of how the country's economy would be organized after the war was the subject of deliberation among economists, political figures, and Mexican industrialists. What role should the state play with regard to private industry? Once wartime controls were relaxed, what plans would guide continued Mexican industrialization, and who would have a say in formulating such plans? There was a fierce debate among a rapidly expanding set of interests. Experts in government agencies like the Banco de México continued to advocate for public intervention in investment, production, and trade, managed directly by the state. The relatively new National Chamber of Manufacturing Industry (CANACINTRA), founded in 1941 to bring together industrialists mostly in and around Mexico City, similarly wanted state protection and intervention, though under the direction of the industrialists themselves. Other regional industrialist associations, however, particularly those that comprised the northern Monterrey Group, were more ideologically committed to liberalizing reforms, and therefore skeptical of any state intervention.[3] Representatives of the Confederation of National Chambers of Commerce (CONCANACO), for example, produced a plan calling for the "reestablishment in the entire national territory of the regime of private property," bringing about an end to the "half-socialist and half capitalist" economy that they argued had prevailed in Mexico to that point.[4] In July 1944, still another industrial group, the nationwide Confederation of Industrial Chambers (CONCAMIN) got into a public spat with President Ávila Camacho over his formation of the Federal Commission for Industrial Development. The president intended to establish a centralized planning agency for industrial development to make up for what he saw as "deficiencies" in the private sector, which CONCAMIN resented.[5] But despite the fact that CONCAMIN and the Mexican Employers' Association (COPARMEX) denounced state intervention in the economy on ideological grounds—and even went so far as to label CANACINTRA industrialists and their collaborators in the Confederation of Mexican Workers (CTM) "pseudo-communists"—there was broad agreement about at least one issue: the need for protection for Mexican industry.[6]

The debate in Mexico reflected not only a broader global debate over the role of the state in the economy generally, but also a more specific argument about the role the US government, in particular, should play as the manager of an increasingly international economy. As New Deal postwar planners looked to Latin America, a debate emerged. Would private enterprise and unfettered trade would be sufficient for the region's economic development? Or would state intervention and government investment—and therefore some redistribution of capital from North to South—be necessary? After the sustained advocacy of Latin American officials throughout the 1930s and early 1940s, most US planners recognized that some modicum of industrialization would be necessary for Latin America's economic future; the final act of the 1942 Rio conference, for example, recognized industrialization as key to raising the living standards of the hemisphere.[7] Confronted with growing demands emanating from Latin America, then, US officials had to decide what rules might govern the new international organizations that might oversee industrialization efforts.

In mid-1943, at Roosevelt's request, the State Department set up an inter-departmental committee made up of officials from the State Department, the Commerce Department, the Board of Economic Warfare, and the Office of the Coordinator of Inter-American Affairs, among other agencies, to study the question of raising living standards in Latin America after the war.[8] The report submitted by the group, which included Dean Acheson, Emilio Collado, Nelson Rockefeller, and Will Clayton, recommended that the United States should be prepared to invest substantial sums of capital in the region—up to $3.5 billion over ten years, some three-quarters of which would need to be "under government auspices."[9] Then, in May 1944, the Inter-American Development Commission (IADC)—overseen by Rockefeller and composed of the national commissions of twenty-one Latin American countries—passed a resolution recognizing that long-term, low-interest credit would be necessary for the region's industrial development. At the same meeting, however, the question of private versus public investment was a key point of debate. The IADC passed other resolutions, urging that state capital not crowd out private enterprise and investment and pressing govern-ments to abandon the state-run activities that had emerged during the war as quickly as possible upon its conclusion.[10] Back in Mexico, president Ávila Camacho responded to the IADC's resolutions in a speech to the country's industrialists, reminding them that crucial Mexican industries—chemicals, cement, electrical equipment, and steel—would not exist without state inter-vention.[11] The debate over the role of the state in the economy, and therefore about Mexico's economic sovereignty, would continue to structure Mexico's interventions in the international negotiations to follow.

DUMBARTON OAKS

As plans for the UN began to take shape, questions of world security pre-dominated. Mexican and other Latin American diplomats and political fig-ures, however, continued to stress the centrality of economic issues to the postwar order. In early 1944, the United States announced plans to gather representatives of Great Britain, China, and the Soviet Union at Dumbarton Oaks, in Washington, DC, to begin the negotiations about the new postwar world institution. As more and more countries beyond the great powers began to protest their exclusion from the meetings, Secretary of State Cordell Hull gave a press conference assuring the "small nations" that their rights would be protected in the new organization.[12] To make good on his word, a month later, in July 1944, the State Department circulated a summary of its plans for the new organization to Latin American nations, including Brazil and Mexico.[13] The Mexican SRE received the outline with a memo indicating that Washington desired to know its opinion of the new organization and emphasizing the importance of "broad and free exchange of viewpoints of all Nations, both large and small."[14]

As a result, Mexico began its work on its own proposal for the postwar organization at nearly the same time that the British, Chinese, and Soviet negotiators gathered at Dumbarton Oaks received the initial draft of the US plans.[15] Foreign Minister Ezequiel Padilla appointed a team of Mexican experts who, just six weeks later in early September, transmitted to the State Department their own forty-point "Project for the Constitution of a Permanent Union of Nations," a competing vision for what the world body should look like.[16] While Mexico was formulating its draft, other important Latin American countries, such as Brazil, complained that they were being kept in the dark about US plans; the Brazilian ambassador in the United States protested to the State Department in 1944 about the "complete ignorance in which they had been kept" regarding what had been decided at Dumbarton Oaks.[17] (Even some small European countries, including Belgium, Holland, Yugoslavia, Czechoslovakia, and Greece, would complain as late as October to the Mexican ambassador in Washington that *they* had not even seen plans that the Mexicans had apparently seen.[18]) In response to the protests from the Brazilian ambassador and others, Secretary of State Hull convened two meetings in Washington with the ambassadors of the Latin American countries to hear their concerns. Though a newspaper reported that some Latin American representatives felt they had "merely been talked to" by Hull, Latin American figures had already spent months making their concerns, particularly regarding economic issues, abundantly clear.[19] The *New York Times* reported shortly after the meetings that "economic problems appear to be most pressing," and that, in the United States, the economic woes of the Latin Americans would soon become "our problem too."[20] Hull therefore stressed in his summary for the Latin Americans that economic issues would be of key importance in the new organization.[21]

The proposals were then transmitted to the allied and associated nations for comment, and over the months between Dumbarton Oaks and San

Francisco, no fewer than forty countries suggested amendments to the UN plans. These included not only the four negotiators themselves, but also seven other European countries; a not-yet-independent India; a host of nations from Africa, the Middle East, and Australasia; and fully eighteen countries from Latin America and the Caribbean, nearly half of the total. Equality of representation within the new organization emerged as a key early critique. Latin American responses repeatedly stressed that the organization required what the Uruguayan delegation called "the ideal of a fully democratic organization of the international league, in which there are no differences of prerogatives and treatment among its members."[22] A Mexican newspaper reported that the majority of Latin American countries were seeking "Equal Representation as the Four Great Powers."[23] The criticism that the proposals had been formulated without the input of the developing world was pervasive; the Venezuelan commentary stressed that the proposals had been prepared "without sufficient estimation of the rights and aspirations of the so-called medium and small nations," language reflected in other proposals, such as that of Egypt.[24] Representatives of Haiti righteously took this ideal to its logical extension; their comments insisted that together with the economic causes of the war, there be specific mention of "religious and racial discriminations" in the understanding of sovereign equality of states, and this was echoed by the Philippine proposal, which added language about racial equality.[25] Many country reports noted opposition to the imbalance of power accorded the Security Council and the General Assembly—even while recognizing the special duties of keeping the peace accorded to the Great Powers—and the proposals of countries such as Guatemala, Costa Rica, and Brazil, among others, sought not only to strengthen the power of the General Assembly but also to rectify the exclusion of Latin Americans from the Security Council through the reservation of one or more guaranteed seats for the region, as they had secured for the new IMF just months earlier.

Mexico presented the most comprehensive response to the Dumbarton Oaks framework. By November, after the conclusion of the fractious negotiations between the great powers, Mexico's comments and proposals ran to more than two hundred pages; China's suggestions, by contrast, as included in official UN documentation, comprised three paragraphs.[26] The Mexican dossier included not only a paragraph-by-paragraph comparison of the Mexican vision with the Dumbarton Oaks proposal, but also a series of commentaries on what it considered the other most relevant and credible proposals for the postwar organization, which had been published and circulated by groups of international jurists and other experts in foreign affairs from Great Britain, the United States, and Canada. The Mexican proposals, like those of many of the country's counterparts among what were repeatedly called the "medium and small powers," also stressed the imbalance of power between the Security Council and the General Assembly. To make their case, the Mexican experts pointed to those world institutions that had already been chartered—the United Nations Relief and Rehabilitation Administration (UNRRA), the Food and Agriculture Organization (FAO), and the IMF and World Bank—and argued that in those cases, "the supreme organ is the one in which all the Member States are represented," rather than a more limited body.[27] The tentative proposal for the new international organization, they argued, had offered precisely the opposite structure. Mexico's suggestions found many allies on this point, and nearly all of the criticism of the proposals from the less powerful countries argued for accountability of the Security Council to the larger General Assembly as a core democratic principle.

Beyond the question of representational power within the organization, Mexico's proposals offered other dramatic revisions to the plans introduced at Dumbarton Oaks. Mexico's draft began with a recognition of international law as the "fundamental basis for the conduct of governments" and argued that there should be a mechanism for the harmonization of international law and national legislation. As had been the case during the Montevideo negotiations over a decade earlier, this recourse to international law was meant to create a structure of accountability that would bind both rich and poor countries to an acknowledged set of rights and duties—both individual and national. Mexico's proposal argued that the relevant tenets of international law for the organization should be codified in two related documents, which were to be drawn up and appended to the Charter: a "Declaration on the Rights and Duties of Nations" and "Declaration of the International Rights and Duties of Man."[28] These were both proposals with important antecedents. The Mexican proposal appended a draft declaration on rights and duties of states that had been submitted by the delegation of Panama to the American Institute for International Law in 1916 but had languished since.[29] Further, the Inter-American Bar Association had emphasized just that summer the "necessity" of a declaration of the rights of man and instructed jurists to begin work on a draft at the conclusion of a tumultuous meeting in Mexico City in August.[30] For the Mexican experts, both legal frameworks would be necessary to ensure equality of treatment in the post-war organization.

The Mexican proposal also enumerated a number of principles central to the country's vision of a new world organization. In addition to codifying "respect for territorial integrity and for political independence," which was, the Mexican proposal argued, an obvious component of collective security, it argued that the General Assembly should collectively have the ability to oversee decolonization and the creation of new states and borders.[31] Another key principle was that of nonintervention of one state in another's domestic affairs, which the Mexican proposal highlighted as the "cornerstone of the Inter-American System," having been codified in the Convention on Rights and Duties of States at Montevideo in 1933. The Mexican proposal also called for the "equality of jurisdiction over nationals and aliens," which would preclude the abuse of diplomatic protection of foreign nationals, corporate or individual. Unlike the US proposal, which accorded membership only to "peace-loving states," the Mexican proposal argued that the new organization would mandate the obligatory membership of "all States, Dominions and Colonies having a free government." Universal representation was key to ensure that governments could not simply opt out of the international organization, along with its associated rights and duties. As a whole, then, the Mexican proposals were meant not only to address the shortcomings of the tentative US proposal but to establish a system that would serve to address the concerns of the smaller and less powerful nations. As a Mexican official later summarized, in Mexico's proposals, "the veto practically disappeared, the General Assembly had broader powers, the international protection of human rights was guaranteed in the Charter, the rights and duties of states were to be defined in an annex to the Charter and international law was to be automatically incorporated in to the national laws of the members."[32]

Despite Mexico's assessment of the shortcomings of many aspects of the Dumbarton Oaks proposals, however, there was one section for which the Mexican delegation offered broad support: the establishment of the Economic and Social Council (ECOSOC). The creation of an economic council was celebrated by many of the less powerful delegations, especially by the Mexican team, who heralded the democratic nature of its membership compared to the proposed Security Council and argued that it merited "the most enthusiastic applause."[33] They offered only minimal revisions to the language establishing the council and argued that ECOSOC should be considered an "essential organ" of the new organization (differentiating it from the International Court of Justice, which it argued should be autonomous from the body), a stance seconded by countries such as Venezuela.[34] Other delegations, however, demanded more specifics. A Bolivian proposal recommended that organized labor be given representation within ECOSOC, arguing that its purpose should be "to achieve concerted action destined to promote the economic development, the industrialization, and the raising of the standard of living of the less favored nations."[35] The Dominican Republic, which had been under the thumb of a US customs receivership for more than three decades—an arrangement that had ended only in 1941—stressed the "necessity for the existence of equality of treatment and the adoption of just and equitable procedures in international trade."[36] Cuba echoed this, with language about "the right to access, on equal terms" to trade, markets, and raw materials.[37] That the otherwise very comprehensive Mexican proposal simply celebrated the creation of ECOSOC and affirmed its "essential" nature suggests that the Mexican delegation understood the new economic body as a step toward fulfilling the mandate that Mexican officials thought would be necessary for postwar development. Ensuring that postwar planners actually worked to address the economic problems that Mexico and the rest of Latin America faced, however, would be an ongoing challenge. Mexican representatives would ensure that it received further discussion by inviting the rest of the region to Mexico City.

CHAPULTEPEC AND THE PLACE OF LATIN AMERICA
IN A US WORLD ORDER

In the immediate aftermath of Dumbarton Oaks in October 1944, Mexican foreign minister Ezequiel Padilla had suggested in a speech in Cuba that the foreign ministers of the Americas should soon convene to discuss the problems of the postwar settlement and the future of inter-American cooperation.[38] It was a proposal that had been floated already a number of times, including within the Pan-American Union's working group on postwar problems.[39] The question of whether and how to include the Farrell government in Argentina—which the United States had refused to recognize over suspicions of ties to the Axis—complicated negotiations over holding the meeting, and US officials hoped that the unresolved Argentina question would simply delay its convening. Though Padilla was resolutely anti-fascist, Mexico's Estrada Doctrine—a foreign policy mandate of not withholding recognition over political issues put in place under foreign minister Génaro Estrada in in 1930—meant that Mexico had not broken relations with Argentina, much to the frustration of the United States.[40] In early November, Padilla surprised US officials by announcing publicly that he had already consulted with the ambassadors of Brazil, Uruguay, and Cuba and had decided to call an inter-American meeting to discuss "matters of permanent general interest related to the postwar."[41] The traditional US strategy of simply running out the clock to avoid contentious inter-American negotiations hadn't worked.

Padilla—who was himself on the conservative, anti-Cardenista spectrum of the ruling Partido de la Revolución Mexicana (PRM) and was regarded by important representatives of the Mexican left as suspiciously close to the United States—would quickly link his principled anti-fascism in the Argentina debate to Mexico's real priority for the conference: the postwar economy. The State Department sent an envoy, Carl Spaeth, to Mexico City in December 1944 to discuss the meeting. In reviewing their talks, US ambassador George Messersmith noted Padilla's contention that the fight against fascism in the Western Hemisphere should be implemented through a "declaration of our determination to intensify programs in the other republics for the general improvement of basic economic conditions in the Americas."[42] By the end of December, with the obdurate but ailing Hull having been replaced as secretary of state by the former industrialist Edward Stettinius, the United States gave in to Latin American insistence about a hemisphere-wide meeting. Representatives of Mexico and the United States agreed on an agenda: the conference would now cover the proposals that had emerged from Dumbarton Oaks; the role of inter-American cooperation in the postwar world; the economic issues that the working group within the Pan-American Union had been studying; and "other matters of general and immediate concern to the participating Governments," which could include the Argentina question.[43] With this agenda established, the Mexican government then issued its formal invitation to the Inter-American Conference on Problems of War and Peace, to be held in February 1945 at Chapultepec castle in Mexico City.

Domestic material conditions and the bilateral US-Mexican relationship served as an important context for Mexico's interventions at Chapultepec. Wartime food shortages, compounded by the inability to buy grain abroad, had become acute by 1943, and inflation increased steadily throughout the war. The 1942 trade agreement that had tied Mexico into the US war effort had frozen and reduced tariffs on a host of goods; by 1946 more than 71 percent of Mexico's exports went to the United States, and 84 percent of its imports came from its Northern neighbor.[44] In some circles, this motivated an ideology of "reciprocal prosperity" in the initial surge of wartime cooperation, with figures such as Minister of Finance Eduardo Suárez arguing that the solution to Mexico's industrial issues lay in the United States. In other quarters, however, there was criticism of the subordination of the Mexican economy to the US war effort; despite the creation of the Mexican-American Commission for Economic Cooperation to coordinate industrial purchases, Mexico continued to have problems obtaining the capital goods it needed. The Banco de México's Eduardo Villaseñor repeatedly argued in speeches that US economic cooperation had amounted to little more than promises on paper, noting that what Mexico needed was not just open-book credit, but the provisioning of machinery, equipment, and technical assistance.[45] What's more, he argued, where capital goods exports had been sold in Mexico, US firms and Mexican industrialists with ties to US interests were frequently the recipients, limiting the benefits to the broader Mexican economy.[46]

With the prospect of increased competition from US manufactured goods overwhelming Mexico's domestic industries, Mexican workers and industrialists stepped up calls for a revision of the 1942 trade agreement. Further, the Mexican government began to threaten the introduction of new tariffs and import licenses on more than six hundred goods.[47] (Before Chapultepec, the Mexican government postponed the new tariffs, but afterward Ávila Camacho would impose import controls again.) In addition, in June 1944 Ávila Camacho issued an emergency decree that limited foreign ownership in a host of industries, requiring the approval of the SRE for majority ownership by foreign firms. Like other countries throughout the region, Mexico was attempting to protect its economy from the potential dislocations of the transition to peace.

With the clamor from Latin American workers, industrialists, and governments rising, US officials preparing for Chapultepec were forced to consider what one official called the "responsibility of the United States with respect to the economic well-being of the other American republics."[48] Because the new IMF and World Bank were unlikely to be up and running in time to provide adequate financing for Latin America's immediate postwar industrial and commercial needs—indeed, the US Congress hadn't yet ratified the Bretton Woods agreements, and wouldn't do so until December 1945, nine months after Chapultepec—there were immediate questions about postwar planning and financing for trade and investment to be resolved. The State Department designated a committee to prepare for the economic aspects of the conference and put Assistant Secretary of State for Economic Affairs William Lockhart Clayton in charge. Clayton, like Stettinius, was a businessman, having founded Anderson, Clayton, & Company, which was at one time the world's largest cotton trading firm. He had been brought into the Roosevelt administration as a disciple of Cordell Hull's reciprocal trade agenda, and he was known as a free-trade crusader. Clayton would therefore put free trade at the center of his approach to Chapultepec—and put the United States on a collision course with Mexican officials.

There was some dissent within the US team on the question of free trade. Merwin Bohan, a former commercial attaché and technical adviser to the US delegation who had a background in Mexican affairs, argued in a letter to Rockefeller that the United States "should stop making a religion of trade policy" and counseled flexibility toward Latin American demands.[49] But his advice fell on deaf ears; the reply thanked Bohan for his views but argued that the State Department's policy was for the Latin American nations to join the US agenda for the free flow of trade. Further, the letter announced that these ideas would be embodied in a new hemispheric agreement: what they called an economic charter for the Americas. Such a charter, the State Department emphasized, was intended to foster an "economy of abundance" in the Western Hemisphere, through the elimination of discriminatory trade practices and the reduction of trade barriers, as well as the "elimination of excessive economic nationalism in all its forms," the guarantee of equal treatment for domestic and foreign investment capital, and a guarantee of "adherence to a system of private enterprise."[50] Bohan was incredulous. Having met repeatedly with the Mexican committee that had been formed to address the economic aspects of the conference—which included Ramón Beteta, then serving as subsecretary of finance, and Antonio Espinosa de los Monteros, the head of Nacional Financiera, among others—he warned in a subsequent memo, "[T]he Mexicans are going to be very much disappointed if the United States comes to the Conference prepared only to discuss the reaffirmation of liberal trade principles."[51] As the conference drew nearer and Mexico revealed further details of its plan, Bohan reported, the Mexican delegation was in fact envisioning "an even more rigid control of international commerce," a highly regulated and protected order that ran directly counter to a liberal, free-trade vision, as well as the creation of new institutions to coordinate that control.[52]

In fact, Foreign Minister Padilla had already proposed to Bohan that postwar economic problems in Mexico would need to be approached in "TVA fashion," referring to the New Deal's Tennessee Valley Authority program—that is, with massive public investment and concerted planning.[53] Further, Beteta and Espinosa de los Monteros had emphasized that the US desire for equality of access to raw materials must be complemented by equality of access to capital goods for Latin American industrialization, as well as the means for financing their purchase.[54] What's more, the Mexican officials proposed, such financing should be a Western Hemisphere project, separate from the proposed World Bank; European votes within the Bank might stymie lending for Latin American initiatives in order to favor not only European reconstruction but also their imperial preferences in development lending. As such, the Mexican team raised the idea, once again, of the importance of something like an inter-American development corporation and lamented that the IAB had not been created.

While Mexican experts had been pushing their agenda behind the scenes in bilateral meetings with US officials, once the conference actually got underway, Mexico's fight for the twinned goals of representation and redistribution for the less powerful states reached the broader public.[55] In his speech opening the Chapultepec conference, Ávila Camacho underscored the emphasis on representation, telling the assembled delegates, "If the international order of tomorrow were to be established by taking into account the opinion of the powerful alone, in the final analysis this war would prove to be nothing more than a gigantic and grotesque farce."[56] But he also signaled the importance of distributional issues to the postwar plans, arguing that "without real support of a well-planned economic democracy, political democracy is precarious, both in a nation and in an assembly of nations, whether universal or continental." To achieve such plans, he asserted, the smaller countries did not want mere handouts, locking them into a kind of subservient dependency. Rather, the world needed an "economic cooperation that shall, by placing limits of justice on the spheres of activity of the most industrialized societies, will permit them to use their available resources to best advantage." The notion of "limits of justice" on the richest countries was key to the Mexican vision of a set of international rules and regulations that could level the playing field for the smaller powers—emphasizing again not just the rights of the developing nations, but the duties of the developed ones.

During the conference, questions of representation motivated the debates regarding both the shape of the new world organization as well as the future of the inter-American system. Mexican proposals on incorporation of international law into national law; preparing a declaration of the essential rights of man; and affirming principles such as nonintervention, juridical equality of states, and peaceful resolution of disputes, were all adopted.[57] These principles were written into the "Declaration of Mexico," which also demanded that economic and social principles be "harmonized with the rights of the individual," thereby internationalizing important tenets of the Mexican constitution.[58] With regard to the new UN, Mexican delegates worked together with other Latin American representatives to pass a resolution stating that the Latin American countries favored "amplifying and making more specific the powers of the General Assembly," as well as "harmonizing the powers of the Security Council with such amplification."[59] When, near the end of the conference, Secretary of State Stettinius announced the official invitations to San Francisco and circulated the State Department's "Yalta formula" on voting in the Security Council—which ensured that "no nation could be the judge on its own case"—Mexico's Padilla claimed credit for the Latin Americans.[60] His opening speech had aspired to a full realization of the democratic aims of the new world organization, and he heralded the new formula as one "of the most extraordinary democratic advances," noting that mechanisms had been established for the "small nations" to have their voices heard.[61] If Mexico and its allies felt they had won new mechanisms for representation, however, distribution would prove a thornier issue.

THE ECONOMIC CHARTER

Mexico's geopolitical position as a key interlocutor in the US quest for multilateral legitimacy was complicated by its economic position, as an industrializing country facing a dollar glut, inflation, and a lack of access to capital goods. This contradiction meant that Mexican officials had to walk a fine line in the new world order. In his opening speech at the conference, Padilla had sought to link Latin America's economic aspirations with the political and security goals that the United States was promoting. Reminding his audience of Mexico's participation in the fight against fascism, he railed against those who argued for what he called a "Phalangist Hispaniscism"—that is, a racialized vision of Latin American unity that excluded the United States.[62] Latin Americans could ill afford to turn their backs on the United States, he intimated, as the "expensive organization of social security and economic expansion" could only be accomplished by "pooling the energies, the resources, and the confidence of all the Americas."[63] Looking to the conversion of US industrial power from wartime to peacetime, Padilla argued that US production capacity would have to find an outlet somewhere, and therefore "a coordinating intelligence must organize the buying power of nations." Only through "fervent action and reciprocal confidence," he argued, would Latin America's economic problems be solved. Such action would also be beneficial to the United States, he noted, not only through expanding trade in US-made equipment and machinery, but also by expanding consumption as standards of living increased throughout the region.

Having established that there was a crucial role for the United States to play in Latin America's future, Padilla then outlined a program that looked very much like the "rigid control of international commerce" about which Bohan had earlier warned.[64] In order to increase trade, Padilla argued, it would be necessary to provide the kind of long-term credit that would expand production in Latin America; these would not be meager Ex-Im Bank loans, but rather "credits as large as are the resources of the whole continent."[65] He raised the issue of imbalance in the terms of trade created by dependence on agricultural commodities—which would become foundational to the Latin American structuralism of Raúl Prebisch just a few years later—arguing that his vision would allow Latin American countries to break "the shackles of our agricultural commodities which, incapable of creating large capital for industrialization, have continued producing only raw materials in the old colonial pattern, exploited by the highly industrialized countries." Padilla's speech was well received among the Latin Americans, and indeed, even among the US representatives, who reported back to Washington that "his address was helpful and its tone restrained."[66] Following the speech, Bolivia introduced a proposal lauding Padilla's speech and arguing that the ideas it enumerated represented "a body of doctrine, the statements of which should be considered as standards of continental policy"—urging that a "Padilla Doctrine" should be spread throughout the Americas.[67]

After Padilla had outlined the broad strokes of the Mexican vision for a new economic postwar order, representatives from the United States presented their own. The first address by Secretary of State Stettinius stressing the interdependence of the Americas and reaffirming the Good Neighbor policy was broadly welcomed in Mexico, where newspapers reported the speech under headlines like "Sovereign Equality Is the Basis for a Durable

Peace" and "The United States Declares, Through the Mouth of Stettinius, Equality and Sovereignty of All Nations."[68] The text of the speech was even admiringly reprinted in the leftist magazine *Futuro*, the organ of Vicente Lombardo Toledano's Workers' University of Mexico.[69] In affirming Mexico's long-standing commitment to sovereign equality, the secretary of state demonstrated just how much the United States had learned from the criticism leveled against it in the past.

The economic proposals soon introduced by the United States, however, ignored all of Mexico's teachings. The draft Economic Charter of the Americas, introduced by the US delegation just a few days into the conference, is striking for how little heed it gave to the protests Bohan had already lodged on behalf of the Latin Americans against the State Department's free-trade dogma. The document did take as a key objective "the constructive basis for the sound economic development of the Americas," reflecting a recognition of the demands for development that Latin American political figures had been making for more than a decade already, and it further included a provision on meeting the labor standards set out at the 1944 International Labour Organization (ILO) meeting in Philadelphia.[70] But it then outlined a rigid free-trade, private-enterprise program of precisely the type that Bohan had warned against: the draft called for equality of access to raw materials, demanded that American nations reduce tariff and nontariff barriers to trade, sought the "elimination of economic nationalism in all its forms," called for "just and equitable treatment for foreign enterprise and capital," and promoted private enterprise and discouraged state-owned enterprise. When these proposals were published in newspapers in Mexico, the United States, and throughout the hemisphere, they would quickly turn from the stuff of high diplomacy to the subject of street protests.[71] Daniel Cosío Villegas, who had been so central to the Mexican analysis of the Bretton Woods institutions, judged the US plans "a hackneyed economic philosophy which the United States exports to other countries but consumes less and less at home."[72]

When the Economic Charter was introduced, reaction on the ground in Mexico City was immediate and dramatic. Just a day after Will Clayton introduced the charter in a speech at Chapultepec, newspapers carried word that the industrialists in the Mexico City–based industrialist group CANACINTRA would strenuously oppose the plan, arguing that it would be ruinous for recently established and still-to-be-established Latin American industries.[73] In response, Padilla called a press conference to assure the manufacturers that there was no hostility toward Latin American industrialization at the conference and that the Economic Charter was simply a draft, yet to be modified, that didn't preclude a "prudent and vigorous defense" of Latin American industry.[74] Summarizing the controversy for a US audience, however, the *New York Times* ran a story under the headline "Clayton Trade Plan Praised by Padilla," which argued that the Mexican foreign minister, acting as the unofficial spokesperson for the entire region, had affirmed Latin America's satisfaction with Clayton's speech—a characterization that surely would have astonished most delegates.[75]

While Mexican labor groups and left-wing parties had largely supported Padilla's principled anti-fascism, their patience with his coziness with the US backers of a free-trade agenda that might damage Mexican industrialization was growing thin. A few days after CANACINTRA voiced its opposition, the Confederation of Mexican Workers (CTM) joined the factory owners in their criticism, placing a full-page newspaper ad that aligned Mexican workers with "'the progressive industrialist' in opposition to the 'archaic policy of the free trade.'"[76] (After the conference, the CTM would enter into a worker-employer pact with CANACINTRA to foster Mexican industrial development.)[77] The advertisement, a US memo reported, pointedly charged that the Economic Charter provided no guarantees for the less powerful countries to obtain the equipment they needed from the United States for their industrial development.

In trying to explain away the cross-class opposition to the charter, US officials cast it as mere nationalism and highlighted the simmering opposition to Foreign Minister Padilla himself. They pointed out that Vicente Lombardo Toledano, the Mexican labor leader who founded the Confederation of Latin American Workers (CTAL) and had recently been in London at the inaugural World Trade Union Congress, had just returned to Mexico. It was certainly true that Lombardo Toledano hated Padilla, regarding him as an *entreguista*, ready to sell out Mexico's national interests to the United States at any moment; just a few months later, as Padilla was gearing up for a presidential campaign, Lombardo Toledano's magazine *Futuro* would publish a number of articles lambasting Padilla with titles like "Who Does Ezequiel Padilla Serve?" and accusing him of backing the forces of "reaction and imperialism."[78] But if US officials blamed this animosity for the reaction to the Economic Charter on the ground in Mexico, they underestimated the congruence between Lombardo Toledano's ideas and the proposals that Padilla would put forward at the conference.

Lombardo Toledano circulated two forceful reactions to the Economic Charter, published in major periodicals throughout Mexico and later published as a pamphlet by CTAL.[79] The first, distributed even before the end of the conference, argued that Mexican labor and the other popular sectors, including the National Peasants Confederation (CNC) and the National Confederation of Popular Organizations (CNOP), were keen to raise the standard of living for the masses through a concerted focus on economic development in industry and agriculture. But while they recognized the dire need in the region for foreign capital, Lombardo Toledano stressed, they also required "fixing to foreign investment conditions that annul the danger that they could take control of fundamental sectors of national economies."[80] The proposal to abolish state intervention in the economy would, he argued, simply turn Latin American industrialization over to international monopolies and return agricultural production to the monocrop exports of the late nineteenth century. Instead, he argued for deeper public control over production, distribution, and consumption—which was, of course, precisely the kind of international coordination that Padilla and the Mexican delegation were arguing for at the conference.

Despite his antipathy to Padilla, therefore, Lombardo Toledano's responses to Chapultepec were in fact largely in line with Mexico's proposals—and gave the Mexican delegation the popular backing to fight. With important Mexican labor and industrial actors loudly opposing the economic agenda that the United States had introduced, the Mexican delegation joined with other Latin Americans to oppose the US plan. The Latin American proposals were wide ranging, but they reflected a broad-based desire for international economic planning, as Bohan had warned. Chile introduced resolutions on combating unemployment and furthering industrialization in the region.[81] Venezuela made proposals on coordinating postwar shipping and creating "multilateral agreements for the distribution of products."[82] Peru introduced similar resolutions on coordinating trade, urging that coordination be taken up at a planned technical economic conference.[83] The Dominican Republic advanced the "expansion and planning" of agricultural production and distribution and offered a proposal on worker protection.[84] Cuba submitted proposals encouraging foreign capital investment as long as it was coordinated with national economic needs and didn't displace national capital.[85] Honduras wanted a permanent inter-American economic organization, and Guatemala proposed financial and technical assistance and the creation of an international institution for the regulation of the production and sale of primary goods.[86] Brazil introduced a measure condemning export subsidies, directed squarely at the trade practices of the United States (Chile introduced a similar measure), as well as one aiming to correct for the "marked disparity" between agricultural and manufactured products and another arguing that rich countries should "recognize as a duty" the need for the investment of their capital, with favorable terms, in poorer ones.[87] An additional Brazilian proposal on the "Betterment of Mankind" argued that there was an unavoidable need for state action to complement private enterprise in order to ensure the most urgent needs of Latin American economies would be met.[88]

Complementing these, Mexico introduced more than a dozen resolutions for the conference and stressed the idea of international economic planning. Mexican proposals included resolutions that mandated coordinated action on the disposal of surpluses, regulated transportation of goods, advanced hemispheric industrialization, promoted the sale of primary goods, and advocated the creation of an inter-American finance company, among others.[89] A specific resolution on economic coordination used the "economy of abundance" language that the US delegation had been promoting, but also stressed "acceptance of the principle of mutual responsibility," arguing not just for rights, but for duties.[90] The proposal on primary goods called on the signatory countries to make agreements between the producing and consuming countries so that "there shall be guaranteed to the primary producers a non-discriminatory price."[91] Finally, the proposal on industrialization stressed concerted planning on the international level, "leaving nothing to chance" by creating new international agencies to oversee it. It also called for industrialized countries that produced capital goods to adopt "special measures" to meet the industrialization needs of the Latin Americans.[92]

Taken together, the Latin American economic proposals at Chapultepec reveal a broad vision of a planned international economy, with rules that would level the playing field for the less-industrialized and primary-exporting countries. In one area there was broad agreement between North and South: the United States had proposed reorganizing the Inter-American Financial and Economic Advisory Committee—the body formed to oversee the negotiations on the IAB—into the Inter-American Economic and Social Council; this was welcomed by the Latin American delegates.[93] In areas where there was disagreement, the US delegation worked hard to temper the stridency of the Latin American proposals. On March 7, the day the conference was scheduled to end, the committee working on economic issues approved fourteen resolutions that were, the US delegation reported, the result of long negotiations over the Latin American demands for various protections for their established and prospective industries.[94] In these resolutions, the United States was forced to take on some of the language that Mexico and other countries had put forward. In the final declaration on industrial development, for example, Mexico's proposal seeking "perfect collaboration with all possible energy" became an agreement in principle to "lend to one another the maximum amount of technical and financial cooperation and to agree upon certain basic principles which will guide their conduct."[95]

For their part, the Latin Americans also worked to blunt the edges of the most important US proposal, the Economic Charter for the Americas. A comparison of the original draft, submitted by the United States, with the final version adopted at the end of the conference is instructive.[96] In the clause regarding private enterprise, the suggested US language "to refrain from the establishment of state enterprises for the conduct of trade" was removed.[97] The final draft of the charter added to a paragraph on "equality of access" the principle that the participant countries would "likewise declare and accept the principle of equal access to the producers' goods which are needed for their industrial and economic development." A paragraph that was originally submitted under the title "Reduction of Trade Barriers" became "International Commercial Policy." It was originally intended simply to "find a basis for practice and effective cooperative measures to reduce barriers of all kinds to the flow of international trade," but the final version read "to find practical international formulae to reduce all barriers detrimental to trade between nations in accordance with the purpose of assuring all peoples of the world high levels of living and the sound development of their economies." Where the original draft contained a clause on the "elimination of economic nationalism in all its forms," the final version not only dampened this, calling only for "collaboration to eliminate the excesses which may result from economic nationalism," but also included in this category behavior ascribed to the rich countries, including "excessive restriction on imports and the dumping of surplus of national production in world markets." And on the equitable treatment of domestic and foreign capital, the original US proposal urged the signatories to work together to ensure "just and equitable treatment and encouragement for the enterprises, skills and capital brought from one country to another." In the final version, however, an exception was added: "except when the investment of the latter would be contrary to the fundamental principles of the public interest."

The extensive revisions of the charter's language were celebrated as a triumph in Mexico. In a radio address broadcast in Mexico City, Padilla argued that the revised charter would "reject the practice of aggressive economies" and would create economic policies allowing the countries of the Western Hemisphere to complement each other.[98] What's more, Padilla's left-wing critics from the labor movement seemed to agree. Lombardo Toledano greeted the new language with what he called "profound satisfaction," and the CTAL even had copies of both the original US proposal and the revised text published and circulated.[99] Achieving the addition of equal access to capital goods was, he argued, an "inappreciable conquest for the progress and emancipation of Latin America." What's more, Lombardo Toledano noted that the reforms introduced sought to protect against the danger that Latin American markets would be flooded with consumer goods from the industrialized countries and provided for the kind of technical collaboration that would make the further industrialization of agriculture possible. There were, however, still some shortcomings. Despite the advances, he lamented, the revisions didn't provide the kinds of limits on foreign capital that the CTAL had argued for in its previous publication, which were intended to end the era in which foreign investment represented what he called "the principal factor in the delay and the deformation of the economic development of Latin America." Nor did the agreement resolve the problem of the terms of trade, continuing to subordinate primary producing countries into a semicolonial status. Finally, he argued, the revised Economic Charter still contained the "anachronistic and harmful principle of non-intervention by the state in the national and international economy." Given these issues, Lombardo Toledano and the CTAL resolved to keep fighting the US economic agenda and what they were now calling "Plan Clayton." As broader global negotiations got underway with a US proposal to create an international trade organization, they would have ample opportunity, as the next chapter shows.

CONCLUSION

Upon the conclusion of the Chapultepec conference, Mexico and other Latin American nations were confident that they had secured assurances of US commitment to their economic development after the war. In stark contrast to the original free-trade proposals the United States submitted, the final resolutions adopted at the conference contained than a dozen agreements on economic issues, many of which not only enshrined the importance of Latin American industrialization, but also promised material resources for securing it. One key resolution committed the American governments to preparations for the Inter-American Technical Economic Conference just three months later in Washington, where they would work toward putting the declarations at Chapultepec into practice. After Roosevelt's death and the inauguration of Harry S. Truman just a month later, however, that conference never happened.[100] But even as Mexican officials had argued during and after Dumbarton Oaks for the kind of representation within the new international institutions that would allow the poorer countries to hold the rich ones to their professed principles, they already knew that the justice they sought would require continued struggle. Based on their experiences over the preceding decades in the inter-American system, Mexico and its Latin American counterparts had a long history of such struggle from which to draw lessons. They knew that, as had been the case with the Inter-American Bank, securing agreements from US state representatives during multilateral negotiations wasn't enough to ensure that such agreements would be fulfilled; the fight to guarantee not just the rights of the poor countries but to assert the duties of the rich ones would be ongoing. As had also been the case with the IAB, however, Mexican experts quickly realized after Chapultepec that US officials were now moving their attention from the hemispheric to the global level. Mexican leaders therefore prepared once again to organize their Latin American allies—as well as new counterparts in the burgeoning Third World—for the fight now on the horizon, for a new organization that would regulate global trade. The fight over the International Trade Organization would, perhaps more than any other institution, define the contours of the postwar world, and Mexican experts intended to ensure that the interests of the poorer countries, already outlined at Chapultepec, were now represented on the global stage.

SIX

Organizing the Terms of Trade

MEXICO AND THE INTERNATIONAL
TRADE ORGANIZATION

BY THE END OF 1945, new global infrastructure for security, financial stability, and investment had been outlined in the mandates for the UN, the
IMF, and the World Bank. But crucial economic issues remained unresolved
at the global level. Near the end of the Bretton Woods conference in the
summer of 1944, the third commission—chaired by Mexico's Eduardo
Suárez—raised two additional issues that were key for global economic cooperation: the creation of an "international agreement on maintaining high
employment" and consideration of "trade and its relation to other financial
policies."[1] Like many of their counterparts in the less industrialized world,
Mexican economic experts worried that both US reciprocal trade and British
imperial preferences would be detrimental to their economic future. Indeed,
even before the Bretton Woods conference began, the Banco de México's
Eduardo Villaseñor had argued in a speech to the Mexican Bankers
Association that the proposed IMF and World Bank would only solve the
world's economic problems if they were complemented by a body that regulated international trade to prevent massive price fluctuations and attendant
dislocations in employment levels. He insisted that "to ensure the success of
these plans, it is imperative that the three organizations function together;
any one of the three, working alone, might fail."[2] To keep employment high
and commodity prices stable, he argued, the international economic playing
field would have to be leveled in a way that acknowledged the interdependence of the richer and poorer countries and allowed the poorer countries to
take measures to protect and develop their economies—precisely the vision
that Mexico and its Latin American allies advanced at Chapultepec. As
the United States began to circulate its plans for organizing trade beyond the
Western Hemisphere, then, Mexican officials once again set out to shape

the parameters of a new multilateral institution: the International Trade Organization (ITO).

A CHANGING POLITICAL AND ECONOMIC CONTEXT

Having secured at Chapultepec what they understood as a basic commitment from the United States to ease the transition to a postwar economy and promote industrialization in Latin America, Mexican leaders moved quickly to put these promises into action. By early 1947, Mexican planners had submitted requests for $240 million worth of international loans for infrastructure projects that were intended to further Mexico's industrialization plans, including dams, irrigation projects, and oil and gas pipelines.[3] Mexican planners understood that both national capital and international private investment were insufficient for the scale and purpose of these projects. Interest rates in Mexico were relatively high, so domestic capital continued to prefer investment in real estate via mortgages and short-term loans rather than investing in industry or infrastructure.[4] Mexico therefore sought financing from both the new IBRD and the Ex-Im Bank, as well as stabilization loans from the IMF to combat pressure on the peso from the outflow of dollars. These loans became increasingly important as Mexico's foreign exchange reserves continued to decline: in early 1946, after the end of the war, Mexico held nearly $372 million in US dollars; by mid-1947, the dollar reserve had decreased precipitously to $200 million, and it would continue to fall.[5] The outflow of dollars would have a number of repercussions, including government decisions to increase import controls and, by 1948, to undertake a series of peso devaluations.[6] This economic uncertainty reinforced two key economic problems for Mexican planners: first, the continued dependence of Mexico's economy on US economic stability, and second, the semicolonial nature of an agricultural export economy whose terms of trade would prevent authentic development.[7]

In addition to the rapidly shifting economic terrain, there were important political changes underway as well, in both the United States and Mexico. Harry Truman took office in April 1945, just after the conclusion of the Chapultepec conference, and Miguel Alemán Valdés was sworn in in December 1946. Alemán oversaw a generational shift in the Mexican government, including the consolidation of the Cárdenas-era Partido de la Revolución Mexicana (PRM) into the Partido Revolucionario Institucional

(PRI), which would rule as a soft-authoritarian *dictablanda* for the next five and a half decades.[8] His administration intensified the conservative turn that had begun in the late Cárdenas period, passing dozens of probusiness laws and regulations and doling out contracts and support to cronies.[9] As the United States veered toward the imperatives of the Cold War, however, the Mexican state under Alemán took a more complicated path, committing Mexico to an anti-communist agenda while still promoting high levels of state intervention in the economy. For Alemán, industrialization became something of a "state religion," based on massive public and private investment and class collaboration between labor and capital.[10] Alemán cracked down on labor and peasant organizing, purged leftists from government positions, and formed the Dirección Federal de Seguridad (DFS), a countersubversive secret police force.[11] Demonstrating the business-friendly turn of his administration, he installed Antonio Ruiz Galindo, a prominent industrialist, as minister of the economy, and Carlos Novoa, a former powerful private sector banker and head of the Mexican Bankers Association, as head of the Banco de México.[12] Many of the officials who had overseen Mexico's previous international interventions—including Eduardo Suárez, Víctor Urquidi, and Daniel Cosío Villegas—left government for the academy. Under Alemán, questions of equity were secondary to questions of growth; as one scholar put it, "the president was fond of saying that there was no point in talking about distribution until there was something to distribute."[13]

Alemán had campaigned on deepening Mexico's industrialization as the key to strengthening not only its economic stability but its political independence, particularly from the United States. During his presidency, however, Alemán would increasingly accommodate the interests of both national capital and foreign investors, while still maintaining an emphasis on protecting Mexican industry.[14] The question of how that protection fit into the changing world trade regime, however, was complicated, as Truman administration officials made clear their preference for the kind of free-trade future that US officials had outlined at Chapultepec. Therefore, despite the political sea change underway in the country's domestic politics, Mexico remained committed to its policy of reforming global economic governance. At a speech before the UN General Assembly in May 1947—the first ever by a head of state—Alemán emphasized the role that the UN could play in promoting industrialization and in fostering "the development of international trade on a basis satisfactory for all nations—that is, both for those that export raw materials and those that manufacture capital goods."[15] In fact, a Mexican team of experts had already produced a detailed study of the US proposals for the new ITO—and had begun an advocacy campaign to ensure it would, indeed, serve "all nations," rather than deepening the postwar imbalance.

PLANNING FOR WORLD TRADE

In November 1945, the US State Department published its "Proposals for Expansion of World Trade and Employment," under the direction of William Lockhart Clayton—the very official who had introduced the Economic Charter of the Americas at Chapultepec. The proposals were the culmination of State Department efforts that had begun in the spring of 1943, including comprehensive negotiations with the British government. While scholars have rightly emphasized the negotiations with Great Britain as crucial to the US process for developing the proposals, some contemporary observers actually regarded the 1942 trade agreement with Mexico as a key antecedent—in much the same way that the 1941 stabilization agreement provided an important antecedent for the broader multilateral plans that became the IMF. The agreement with Mexico contained a set of general clauses, including the first escape clause ever inserted into a trade agreement, that were intended not just to set tariff levels but to secure the kind of open economic model that the United States favored. Reviewing the terms of the 1942 agreement after the ITO negotiations had finished, one expert noted that each of the seventeen general articles in the Mexican agreement had "a counterpart, more or less exact," in the proposals for the new organization.[16] Once again, bilateral agreements with Mexico had served as important precedent for the global negotiations to come.

The United States approached the negotiations over the new rules for world trade with a two-pronged strategy. First, US officials initiated multilateral tariff negotiations with a "nuclear group" of fifteen countries; this signaled the beginning of the negotiations on what would become the General Agreement on Tariffs and Trade (GATT).[17] In parallel, US representatives at the first meeting of the new UN Economic and Social Council (ECOSOC) in early 1946 urged the creation of a preparatory committee that would prepare a draft charter for the new ITO. A team of US officials completed an initial draft charter in July, then circulated it and conducted bilateral discussions with the nuclear group members to gauge their support before convening a preparatory committee meeting in London in October.[18]

While Mexico did not officially participate in that meeting, it sent an observer, Francisco Cuevas Cancino, a young attaché with the Mexican embassy.[19]

The London draft was universalist, in that it contained no special provisions for the less-industrialized countries, no recognition of differential positions within the global economy, and no mention of responsibility for economic development. Despite the fact that a prior ECOSOC resolution had argued for the inclusion of language about the "special conditions" of industrializing countries, US planners simply ignored the proposal.[20] Clair Wilcox, a chief US negotiator, argued that such issues fell outside the jurisdiction of the proposed ITO; they were better topics for agencies like ECOSOC and the World Bank.[21] This reflected, perhaps, the burgeoning influence of what Friedrich Hayek would come to call *isonomy,* or "same law," in which universal global rules for the protection of property needed to be constructed and defended.[22] But such a vision was patently unacceptable to the less industrialized countries, as revealed by comprehensive studies submitted in London by Brazil and India. Representatives of the Indian Department of Commerce came to London ready to "take the lead in presenting the case of all undeveloped economies and in suggesting changes in the scheme to safeguard their vital interests," as their study indicated.[23] The Indian report stressed that quantitative restrictions and state trading monopolies would be necessary parts of a planned industrialization strategy. Brazil's study made a similar case and included an alternative charter draft, which began with the primary goal "to promote the expansion of international commerce with due consideration of the levels of economic development of each member country" and called for the gradual reduction not of tariffs and trade restrictions but of the "existing economic inequalities" between countries.[24] The less industrialized countries, then, staked out a clear claim to their particular interests in the new organization. Upon receiving these proposals, Wilcox was incredulous, railing against what he called the "fetish of industrialization" and later writing, "some of the proposals advanced in the name of economic development must be seen to be believed."[25]

Despite Wilcox's annoyance, Australian officials rallied allies in London from India, China, Lebanon, Brazil, and Chile to argue for the necessity of protections for industrializing countries—particularly for the importance of quantitative restrictions such as import quotas, rather than just tariffs.[26] The negotiations over Australia's proposals were so contentious that they nearly derailed the London talks, but the United States eventually agreed to a set of concessions, including the inclusion in the London draft of an entirely new chapter on economic development, which included "an article under which a member of the trade organization might obtain permission, in a particular case, to employ an import quota in the promoting the development of a new industry."[27] While US negotiators had not originally considered development issues a necessary part of the new trade negotiations, their desire to achieve multilateral legitimacy for the new institution made this concession necessary.[28]

THE MEXICAN STUDY

Mexican government experts studied the proposals that emerged from London intently and made plans to send observers to the next two rounds of talks, which included a drafting meeting at Lake Success, New York (where the major aspects of the GATT were worked out) and a second preparatory committee meeting in Geneva in April 1947.[29] As soon as they received the London draft, in early January 1947, Mexican officials with the Consejo Superior Ejecutivo de Comercio Exterior (CSECE)—Mexico's foreign trade council—decided officially that their country should take part in the negotiations about the proposed charter and convened a team to review the proposals that had been published.[30] The president of the CSECE, Minister of Foreign Relations Jaime Torres Bodet, appointed a staff member, Pablo Campos Ortiz, to head the team, which also included representatives from the Finance, Economy, Labor and Social Provision, and Agriculture ministries, as well as a representative of the Mexican tariff commission and one from the Banco de México.[31] As a first step, the SRE cabled the Mexican ambassador in Washington, Francisco Padilla Nervo, requesting not only the final draft document from London but also the full texts of the proposals that both India and Brazil had submitted.[32] Reviewing this material, the Mexican experts sized up those they would approach to work with and decided that Chile, Australia, and India had had success in amending the draft, while Brazil, though presenting good ideas, was probably too economically tied to the United States to have forcefully advocated for change.[33] (The extent to which Mexico's own growing ties with the United States and its reliance on US capital might constrain their own future interventions was not noted.)

Torres Bodet instructed the group specifically that the Chapultepec resolutions, which they had successfully reformed, should act as a guide for their studies.[34] By March, the team in Mexico City had finished a detailed 177-page study, laying out Mexico's position toward the proposals and its goals for the upcoming Geneva meeting. The report was withering: the Mexican committee stressed that, based on the draft, "the intention of the industrial countries is revealed: to have free access to foreign markets for the placement of their products and the easy acquisition of primary materials. That is to say, it intends to impose a policy of open doors in international trade."[35] What's more, indications that the agreement might allow European countries to retain important aspects of their imperial preferences toward colonies led the Mexican team to argue that the proposed organization intended "to perpetuate the existing political structures." This would mean putting the independent countries of Latin America in unequal competition with those that retained colonial preferences, even if they had greater capital or technical resources. For Mexico in particular, because of the reliance on and integration with the economy of the United States, accepting the proposed charter as it stood would mean, they wrote, "converting ourselves into a semi-colonial country."[36]

Nevertheless, the analysts acknowledged that Mexico would not be strong enough to simply abstain from the proposed organization and would therefore have to seek modifications to its form as proposed. If Mexico didn't join with the other countries working to reform the draft charter, it might find itself in a situation in which the new organization made recommendations that would later become obligatory, which would mean subjecting Mexican trade to rules dictated by the larger countries. The report continued: "[I]n this case, nations like Mexico will not have the possibility of modifying their conditions of economic inferiority before the creditor countries of the world."[37] Given the massive inequalities in the global economy, the Mexican team argued, they would have to fight against the application of "equal rules" for all countries and rather work toward a charter that had what they called the "elasticity" to allow each country to protect its domestic economic needs while still supporting what they judged to be the "transcendent labor" of the new trade organization.

The Mexican experts also worried about what they understood as a "total threat" in Truman's recent speech at Baylor University. There, Truman had declared that the United States could "lead the nations to economic peace or we can plunge them into economic war."[38] If this *was* a threat of economic war, they wrote, Mexico had little choice; if the US president was going to use the agreement to try to protect the interests of his rich country, "Mexico can at least offer to fight so that the legitimate aspirations of its people and its government are respected."[39] The multilateral nature of the negotiations, they argued, presented an opening. "Because the U.S. has declared its intentions to negotiate with all friendly countries, this is an opportunity we must take advantage of," they wrote, concluding that Mexico would work to defend the common interest of nations that were economically similar. With this mandate, then, Mexican government officials launched yet another campaign to reform the infrastructure of the global economy.

PUBLIC OPINION IN THE UNITED STATES AND MEXICO

As the plans for the new organization progressed, the Truman administration began to undertake a concerted campaign to rally public opinion in the United States about the proposed ITO, and Mexican officials closely followed these efforts.[40] In February and March, the administration convened hearings on the charter in seven cities around the country, at which US government officials presented the case for the new organization, and business, labor, and citizen groups responded. Mexico sent observers to the meetings from their consulates, who reported back to the SRE on the opinions of both the promoters and the detractors of the ITO. Describing the public hearing in New Orleans in early March, the consulate reported back to Mexico City that Wilcox had described the objectives of the ITO as promoting the expansion of trade and consumption, the reduction of tariffs, and the elimination of commercial discrimination. In response to this description, staff at the SRE had written in the margin "Elevation of the standard of living? Industrialization?"[41] The Mexican observers also noted the growing opposition to the charter from the US business class on multiple fronts, including the desire for protection of US industry from low wage competition. The notes sent back from the Chicago meeting in March, for example, emphasized the skepticism and distrust regarding representation in the new organization expressed by business representatives, who argued that the charter "exposed the United States to the loss of its predominant economic position, by making it equal in rights to the rest of the members of the organization."[42] In San Francisco, the Mexican observer reported that the vice president of the American Trust Company had argued that the charter as drafted threatened the "possible abandonment of the principle of free private enterprise."[43] In New York, the representative of the National Foreign Trade

Council (NFTC) severely criticized the proposed charter for not including adequate protections from expropriation of US capital.[44] In addition to these public meetings, the House Ways and Means Committee also held hearings and solicited the testimony of Will Clayton, which Mexican observers immediately transcribed and sent back to Mexico City.[45] Together, these observations made Mexican officials keenly aware of the political nature of the trade debate in the United States. From New York, Octavio Barreda wrote to Torres Bodet that "in reality, all of this about the ITO and possible future trade conventions is not so much a subject of foreign policy as it is of domestic policy: the old fight between Republicans and Democrats over tariff rates."[46]

The partisan fight over trade was indeed heating up. The US midterm elections of November 1946 had been a stunning victory for protectionist Republicans, who were highly skeptical of the reciprocal trade agenda that had been pursued by the Roosevelt administration over the preceding years. The concerted opposition of US capital to a pure "free-trade" agenda, as evidenced in the various public hearings around the country, made clear to the promoters of the ITO that they would have to moderate their message. In his March 1947 speech at Baylor defending the ITO, Truman made the case himself, stressing that "there was no thought that the Geneva meeting would attempt to eliminate tariffs or establish free trade," only that tariffs would be lowered and *"freer* trade" would be promoted.[47] While Truman was able to use this moderation to gain the acquiescence of important Republican leaders to allow the Geneva negotiations to go forward, it was clear that there would be serious domestic opposition.[48]

At the same time, the Alemán administration was trying to bring Mexico and the United States closer together economically, with some success; in April 1947 Alemán appeared on the cover of *Time* magazine, which included an article that heralded what a "good friend" Mexico had become.[49] But the opposition to the "Plan Clayton"—a name first derisively floated for the Economic Charter of the Americas, as we saw in the previous chapter, but now referring to its global extension in the proposed charter for the ITO— was accelerating and beginning to have political consequences. When Truman made his state visit to Mexico in early 1947, *La Voz de México*, the organ of the Mexican Communist Party (PCM), published an editorial cartoon arguing that courtesy toward the US president shouldn't preclude the courage to stand up to him. The cartoon depicted President Alemán opening a door for Truman but requesting him to wipe the mud from his feet, which bore the label "Plan Truman, Plan Clayton, Imperialistas."[50] Cooperation with the United States was to be welcomed, but free-trade ideology had to be checked at the door. A few months later, a group of radical Mexican analysts from the Frente de Economistas Revolucionarios published an article arguing that the Clayton Plan was "nothing less than a plan for world domination and the abolition of competition and freedom, in which the United States is a metropolitan country and the rest of the world are satellites."[51] They continued, "only the United States is defending this neo-liberalism," arguing that the rest of the world was against it. The radicals were not alone in their opposition, and nationalists in the Mexican business class began to argue against the trade plan, as well. At an April meeting of the Mexico City–based industrialist organization CANACINTRA attended by Aléman and a group of foreign diplomats, manufacturers argued that complying with the Clayton Plan would mean a "death sentence" for Mexican industry.[52] This opposition in Mexico to what was perceived as an open-door, free-trade policy would only continue to grow as the global negotiations continued.

MEXICO AT GENEVA

In April 1947, the Mexican team of observers, which included Octavio Barreda, Gonzalo Robles, and Augustín Luna Olmedo, arrived in Geneva. Nuclear group tariff negotiations were already underway, and the new round of charter negotiations would begin in mid-May. While only the initial nuclear countries were to officially participate in the charter negotiations, observers were sent from organizations like the FAO, ILO, World Bank, and IMF, as well as from a host of other UN member countries from Eastern and southern Europe, the Middle East, and Latin America.[53] Once in Geneva, however, these observers—Mexico among them—found themselves shut out of the closed-door GATT negotiations and worried this would be the case for the ITO drafting meetings, as well. Barreda sent a report back to the SRE in Mexico City reporting his indignation at the exclusion: not only was Mexico not given access to the tariff negotiations, but observers were not being given official conference documents, meaning that Mexican state officials were no better informed than the general public. As he worked to remedy this exclusion, Barreda signaled his intention to build what he called a "bridge head" into the negotiations, as Mexico had done so often over the preceding decades in multilateral fora, by building close relationships with representatives of other Latin American countries as well as India and Canada, whose approaches seemed complementary to Mexican ideas.[54]

Barreda's first step was to seek the partnership of the other Latin American observers from Uruguay, Colombia, Ecuador, and Peru, then establish close relationships with the representatives of Cuba, Brazil, and Chile—who, he noted, as official participants in the negotiations, could transmit to the Mexican experts what was going on behind closed doors. Echoing the preparatory study that the Mexican experts had produced, Barreda had determined that Mexico's interests were most closely aligned with those of the Chilean delegation, and noted that the Chilean ambassador had told him confidentially that its delegation would not approve anything that did not "guarantee some way of not damaging the countries of incipient industrialization."[55] Mexico also sized up the other delegations to determine who might be allies. Colombia and Uruguay, also observers, indicated they were also in agreement with the agenda supported by Chile and Mexico, and Peru's representatives had indicated that they wanted to stand with Mexico, as well, while Ecuador was still studying the matter.[56] Initially, Barreda thought that Brazil was mainly in agreement with the proposals that Chile was putting forward, but he reasoned that they were unlikely to give vigorous support publicly given their growing economic ties to the United States—perhaps a reference to the recently opened Volta Redonda steel plant, which had been funded by US capital.[57] By May, Barreda had determined that Brazil would in fact support the US proposed reduction of tariffs but would fight for access to industrial equipment—one of the main problems plaguing the Latin American industrializers after the war—as compensation for these reductions. Cuban representatives, on the other hand, had indicated to the Mexican team that they would be willing to give up their infant industries to get more sugar and tobacco exports to the United States; Cuba was therefore unlikely, Barreda thought, to be an ally in the fight to secure the conditions for industrialization.[58]

As negotiations got underway, the Mexican team quickly found that many of the most contentious proposals were those regarding the promotion of economic development and industrialization. As expected, the Chilean delegation proposed a number of amendments intended to safeguard the interests of the less-developed countries, including a primary commodity price stabilization mechanism; a one-nation, one-vote principle within the proposed organization; and a set of proposals carving out exceptions to the universalization of the most-favored nation (MFN) principle. Obligatory

MFN, Chilean officials argued vigorously with the support of Syria and Lebanon, had been "conceived in the interests of highly industrialized countries" and didn't allow for preferences between neighboring countries, a question crucial to economies in both South America and the Middle East.[59] The Cuban, Brazilian, and Czechoslovak delegations, together with those from New Zealand and Australia, also similarly advocated language that would include various mechanisms excepting the less-industrialized countries from universal charter provisions in order to foster their development. The Mexican team also made special note of the interventions of the Indian delegate R. K. Nehru, who fought vigorously against the need for prior approval by the ITO of import limits, including quotas and other quantitative restrictions, which he argued were likely to be necessary in development planning—and which the United States vigorously opposed.[60]

Growing discord between the United States and Great Britain, combined with the cumulative effect of amendments in the interest of the industrializing countries, rapidly strained the conference to the point of breaking.[61] In a highly contentious session on June 9, Belgium introduced a proposal arguing that the negotiations to that point had carved out entirely too many exceptions, especially for what it called "under-developed countries," and that the draft as written to that point would represent a "death-sentence" for Belgium and Luxemburg unless it returned to the "original spirit of freedom" with which it had been initially conceived.[62] Barreda, writing back to Mexico City, saw the maneuvering of Wilcox and the interests of the imperial powers behind the outburst, against the work of New Zealand, Australia, Czechoslovakia, and Chile especially, countries that "had defended almost desperately positions and situations very similar to our own."[63] The Belgian proposal was meant, in Barreda's estimation, to shore up Wilcox's open door for US interests and to prevent the agreement from codifying a right to industrialization in countries like Mexico. Together, Barreda surmised, the imperial powers sought to "dampen the hopes that the rights of the economically weak countries would be respected and that there would be imparted decided assistance for their development." While the Belgian proposal to return to a draft unencumbered by development considerations was not advanced, it set an adversarial tone that would be difficult to overcome. In addition, Wilcox had managed, at the behest of US business interests, to insert language into the draft protecting international investment in the chapter on economic development.[64] As delegates looked toward the final negotiations at Havana, the disagreements appeared nearly insurmountable.

Surveying the growing discord within both the United States and Great Britain about the charter, Barreda reported back to Mexico City that the real problem might not even be the contentious international negotiations themselves. Rather, he argued, even if the charter made it through the negotiating process, it was likely to fail once it reached the legislatures of the member countries, where, he observed wryly, "in many cases all hope dies."[65] Domestic opposition in Mexico was certainly growing quickly. The organized Mexican Left, including the CTM and the PCM, had been consistently attacking what they were still calling "Plan Clayton" and arguing for a stronger stance toward the international agreements. Responding to pressure from labor and industry, Mexican officials had been petitioning the United States for months to enter into new trade negotiations that would revise the terms of the existing bilateral agreement, which had been negotiated in 1942.[66] As the balance of payments worsened—in July 1947 it was revealed that the Banco de México was losing more than a million dollars a day in foreign exchange—Alemán instituted a decree limiting the import of a series of manufactured goods, including automobiles, refrigerators, and electrical products.[67] Fearing that Mexico might be considering the use of even more drastic controls, in October the US State Department reluctantly agreed to preliminary trade negotiations.[68] Alemán then introduced a new tariff schedule on November 13, restoring many tariffs that had been cut during the war.[69] Just days from the start of the Havana negotiations, then, Mexico was ramping up its own trade protections.

Despite the declaration of increased tariffs, many in Mexico thought that the coming international negotiations still posed a threat to Mexican industry. Mexico's minister of finance, Ramón Beteta, had given a speech in late October at the National Convention of Foreign Trade in St. Louis that many Mexican industrialists had seen as too friendly to foreign capital.[70] To pressure the government, on Monday, November 17, 1947—with the Havana conference set to open that Friday—the Mexico City–based industrialist organization CANACINTRA and labor groups in the CTM called a mass demonstration in Mexico City.[71] The march organizers promoted what their announcement in *Novedades* called "the position of those authentic Mexicans who oppose with all their might our government's complicity in the approval of Plan Clayton in Havana."[72] According to Mexican surveillance sources, some five thousand people—including the famous Mexican muralists and communist militants Diego Rivera and David Alfaro Siqueiros—took to the streets to hear speeches vociferously condemning the trade plan.[73] Marchers carried massive posters that depicted Plan Clayton as the head of a wolf, devouring sheep labeled with the names of Latin American countries.[74] The PCM's *La Voz de México* used a front-page headline to urge the Mexican Left to form what it called a "National Democratic Front to Oppose Plan Clayton."[75]

Many radical factions of Mexico's Left, such as Acción Socialista Unificada (ASU), deeply opposed the proposed charter.[76] The ASU published a detailed critique of the plan, arguing that it would lead to irreparable damage to Mexico's infant industries, the closing of factories, mass unemployment, and the weakening of labor unions, thereby making Mexico a colony of the United States, locked into a subservient economic relationship.[77] If the radicals were united in their opposition, however, there was some disagreement within the broader CTM with regard to Plan Clayton; the more conservative and PRI-supporting sectors of the confederation saw the vigorous opposition to the charter as a distraction from the promotion of national development.[78] This was reflected during the demonstration itself, in which Alemán was largely shielded from criticism: one CTM militant argued that in fact the president was well positioned to carry out his plans to industrialize the country, but he could not do so if he was "betrayed" by Mexico's representatives at Havana—a pointed reference to Beteta.[79] As the *La Voz de México* put it, "[T]he interests of Mexico are under serious threat from the Havana Conference and must be defended."[80] As Beteta departed for Havana, then, he found himself squeezed between the US vision that promoted a free-trade, open-door world, on the one hand, and the combined agitation of Mexican business and labor, pushing for further trade protections and against US imperial pretensions, on the other.[81]

SETTING THE TONE AT THE HAVANA CONFERENCE

The United Nations Conference on Trade and Employment opened in Havana on November 21, 1947, with fifty-six countries represented, eighteen of which were from Latin America. Not only was the conference much larger and more inclusive than the preparatory sessions had been, the delegations themselves were large and quite heterogenous, with many including representatives from labor, industry, nongovernmental groups, and government. The

US delegation was headed by Will Clayton from the State Department, assisted by Clair Wilcox from State's Office of International Trade Policy, but also included congressional representatives, delegates from other cabinet departments, and representatives from a host of business groups like the National Foreign Trade Council, the National Association of Manufacturers, the Bankers' Association for Foreign Trade, and the Chamber of Commerce, as well as farm groups and representatives from both the American Federation of Labor (AFL) and the Congress of Industrial Organizations (CIO).[82] The British delegation sent by the Labour government of Clement Attlee was similarly diverse, though more poorly organized and operating under continually shifting instructions from London.[83] The Brazilian delegation, despite having participated in the preliminary meetings, was judged by its own leader to be ill equipped for the negotiations.[84] The Mexican delegation, by contrast, despite having participated only as an observer in preparatory negotiations, was quite prepared and ably managed, if still unwieldy. It included not only representatives from the important ministries—Foreign Relations, Finance, Economy, and Agriculture—but also industrialists and labor leaders. Once in Havana, the head of the delegation, Beteta, reported back to Alemán that his primary task was to keep the diverse and potentially unruly Mexican delegation unified: "Contrary to expectations," he reported, "neither the representatives of the private sector nor the workers have, up to now, given us any concern."[85] Signaling his dissatisfaction with other members of the delegation, however, he decried the "vagueness of the ideas" of the economy minister, Antonio Ruiz Galindo.[86] Ruiz Galindo was typical of the political appointees of the Alemán administration, a wealthy industrialist from Alemán's home state of Veracruz who had clashed with the leaders of smaller industrial concerns based in Mexico City.[87] Beteta, on the other hand, was not only one of the Mexican officials who had formal training in economics but was also one of the few who remained in the bureaucracy from the previous *sexenios*, setting him apart from many of Alemán's political appointees. It would be up to Beteta, therefore, to ensure that sectoral infighting among Mexican capitalist interests didn't subvert his strategy for the conference.

In his communication with Alemán, Beteta noted his intention to rally the rest of the Latin Americans to their cause, as the Mexicans had done so often before. The first fight on this front was procedural; Beteta campaigned to get the Cuban representative elected as the ceremonial president of the conference, rather than a Belgian, who was made vice president. The Latin

Americans further fought for representation on the various commissions so that they could continue to coordinate and "constitute a homogenous group that up to now is acting in common accord, and that will be with us to sustain the points of view expressed by Mexico."[88] Beteta's judgment of this Latin American unity was corroborated by a US observer, who wrote after the conference that "at times there appeared to be a sort of unorganized 'filibuster' on the part of the Latin American countries as a group."[89]

While the US delegation was frequently exasperated by the Latin American coordination, they also tried to use Mexico's leadership within Latin America to their advantage. Clair Wilcox had reasoned that Beteta might be able to bring the more recalcitrant Latin Americans into line, and he therefore recommended that Beteta be awarded the chairmanship of one of the important commissions at the conference, the Economic Development Commission.[90] With this leadership position secured, Beteta made early and very public interventions on behalf of the concerns of the developing world. At the first plenary session, Beteta gave a speech that "served notice," as the *New York Times* put it, that "the economically undeveloped and debtor nations were not fully satisfied" with the Geneva proposal.[91] Using striking Cold War language, Beteta argued that the new economic order being constructed had nothing to fear if it fulfilled its promises to the masses; if it failed to do so, however, "our peoples, by more or less violent means, will be obliged to seek other systems, other horizons, other procedures capable of inspiring in them the hope of a salvation which our regime could not or did not know how to give them."[92] The charter on offer, he argued, was inadequate to the task of providing such hope, as it offered negative prohibitions rather than a positive program for economic development. Beteta argued that the draft had "aroused misgivings among the working classes and also among the industrialists of the less developed countries"—clearly the marches in Mexico City were on his mind.

Though Beteta's criticisms of the industrialized countries were not extreme, they were unmistakable. He reiterated a theme he had touched on in a speech in St. Louis the month before, (and it should be noted, directly echoed Puig's interventions at the 1933 Montevideo conference), arguing that the imbalance of power in the global economy had created a situation in which creditor countries demanded payment from debtors but blocked their ability to pay by refusing to buy their exports. Therefore, the promises of equality of access to markets written into the charter draft, he argued, were insufficient. What was required was a "redistribution of acquisitive power"—

the ability of people to consume—from the creditor to the debtor countries. The stimulation of demand among the people of the less industrialized world was key to a real increase in world trade, and the charter as written was ill equipped to realize such a change. Although many exceptions had been carved out that would allow the less-industrialized countries some protection, he argued, "no long-term plan of the economies of these countries can be based on such expedients." It was his intention, therefore, to ensure that the conference built an infrastructure for such long-term development planning within the trade organization. Beteta reported back to Mexico City that his speech had a "magnificent effect among the Latin American delegations"—even Argentina, which had come to the conference, in Beteta's estimation, just to wreck its chances—as well as those in economically analogous situations, such as the Philippines, Egypt, and Iran.[93] Indeed, the *New York Times* reported that there was "sustained applause" after Beteta's speech.[94] The US delegation, of course, was less enthusiastic. Wilcox later remembered, "The conference opened with a chorus of denunciation in which the representatives of thirty undeveloped nations presented variations on a single theme: the Geneva draft was one-sided; it served the interests of the great industrial powers; it held out no hope for the development of backward states."[95] Beteta had been loud and clear.

THE REFORM AGENDA

Despite the publicly adversarial stance heralded by his opening speech, however, Beteta knew he had to work with the United States to achieve compromise; Mexico's intention was to modify the charter, not reject it. Beteta therefore met repeatedly with the object of the fervent protests in Mexico City, Will Clayton. The day after Beteta's speech, Clayton invited him as well as former minister of finance Eduardo Suárez and the Banco de México's Carlos Novoa to a private lunch, for what Beteta judged "the obvious proposition of personally answering some of the points in my speech," as well as to discuss the renegotiation of the US-Mexican trade agreement.[96] Beteta reported back to Alemán that Clayton indicated that the United States was willing to accept the tariff increases Mexico demanded in their bilateral trade negotiations. (Indeed, by December the United States would consent to Mexico's raising its tariff rates back to 1942 levels, reversing wartime reductions.)[97] Further, he reported that Clayton had promised that the United

States would not oppose Mexican efforts to include mechanisms for industrialization and development in the charter and would also promote "efficacious means of obtaining the international cooperation that will promote this development." Clayton also, however, laid out a theme that would continue over the next few months of negotiations: while the United States had grudgingly come to understand the logic of protective tariffs for industrial development, what it could not abide were the so-called administrative or quantitative prohibitions, such as import quotas, which the US delegate argued "are a cancer on international trade and . . . it is indispensable that they disappear."

Regulating the use of quantitative restrictions, however, was just one aspect of the proposals put forward by Mexico and the many other developing countries that introduced amendments. Over the course of the conference, some eight hundred amendments to the Geneva draft were proposed; Mexico put forward eighty-five of these.[98] In addition to fighting for the right to introduce quantitative restrictions, the Mexican delegation introduced proposals on rules for investment, on the obligation to undertake multilateral tariff reductions, on the requirement of prior approval by the organization for exceptions, and on the creation of an economic development committee within the ITO. (They also submitted proposals concerning the protections of migrant workers—in the context of the ongoing Bracero program—and other labor issues, taking up the mandate that had been set at the International Labour Organization meeting in Mexico City in 1946.)[99]

During the earliest working sessions of the conference, much of the Mexican energy was focused on the provisions concerned with economic development. The original draft of Article 11, for example, proscribed the use of "unreasonable or unjustifiable impediments" to obtaining the capital goods, technology, and skills required for industrialization. The Mexican revision, however, specified that "the Members shall make every effort necessary to ensure that the underdeveloped countries are able to obtain *on equitable terms* the facilities required for their economic development."[100] The Mexican delegation also proposed significant changes to the investment provisions that the United States had added in London, inserting language into Article 10 to discourage foreign investment from being directed to "speculative activities" and rewriting Article 12 to read "foreign investment should be made in a way which not only secures profits for the investors but takes into account the sound and balanced economic development of the countries receiving such investment."[101] The Geneva negotiations had already enshrined the principle that foreign investment could not be used to interfere in the domestic affairs or national policies of member countries; the Mexican draft specified further that foreign investors would not receive greater privileges than national ones, and that providing security for international investment would be "consistent with the limitations of their own legislation"; that is, expropriations would still be subject to national laws.[102] As Carlos Novoa argued in committee, this effectively codified the Calvo Doctrine, which prevented foreign capital from enjoying special privileges, in the ITO agreement—a proposal that Argentina, Uruguay, and China supported heartily and the United States roundly rejected.[103]

In addition to Mexico, many other delegations, including those from Chile, Argentina, Ceylon, Afghanistan, New Zealand, and Australia, also submitted amendments meant to ensure that foreign capital didn't enjoy special privileges, and that foreign investment couldn't be undertaken against the wishes of national governments.[104] Colombia also submitted a long proposal on the "special rules" relating to countries at an "early stage" of economic development, many provisions of which were incorporated into the charter.[105] And Mexico joined China, Burma, Argentina, and India in proposing substantive revisions to Article 13 on state intervention for development, which in the Geneva draft required prior ITO approval.[106] Mexico argued that Article 13 as written was "useless, complicated and dangerous."[107] Revisions instead suggested ex post facto judgment of such measures, to avoid what the delegation of El Salvador called the "time-wasting procedure" of prior approval, and suggested varying kinds of resolution procedures.[108] The discussions on development-related issues were highly contentious, and negotiations spilled over into the new year; it was quickly becoming clear that the conference was not going to meet its proposed January 15 conclusion. Once again, the smaller European countries lashed out against drawing a distinction between the industrial and underdeveloped countries, and the Latin Americans collectively submitted a response, insisting that their needs had not yet been met.[109]

Mexico and the other developing countries also worked to make sure that in addition to the investment provisions, the proposed trade regulations also took into account the needs of the industrializing world. In the third committee, on commercial policy, Mexican proposals argued that "the industrialized countries shall accord appropriate advantages to countries at an early stage of industrial development," and further, that in keeping with the principles Beteta announced in his opening speech, "creditor countries shall be required to grant to debtor countries advantages proportional to the degree of indebtedness of the latter, whether current or long-term."[110] Complementary proposals by Brazil and Colombia also pushed for special consideration for underdeveloped countries in trade negotiations.[111] Elsewhere, the Mexican delegation argued that with regard to the employment mandate of the organization, no measure that was intended to promote international trade should cause decline in the prevailing employment or wage levels; they also urged that in such a situation, countries could take the necessary steps to avoid unemployment.[112] Further, Mexico proposed revisions to Article 17, among the key articles of the charter, which covered most-favored nation treatment, reduction of tariffs, and the elimination of preferences. Among Mexico's proposals was that the organization should "take account of the economic position of the Members concerned before calling upon them to negotiate," and that countries should be free to choose which products they would negotiate over and should "retain the right to freely apply tariffs when necessary."[113] The Geneva draft, Mexico argued, had attempted to put all countries on a "plane of fictitious equality" for tariff reductions—a situation that was, as Beteta had said in his opening speech, the very negation of equity.

To consider the trade provisions, the conference designated a special working group of representatives from Australia, France, Mexico, Peru, and the United States. The Mexican committee member, Dr. Josué Sáenz, undertook what the Mexican delegation called an "intensive campaign" to reform the trade negotiation rules.[114] It took over a month of negotiations, but by the end of January, the working group had reached a compromise on language for Article 17, including substantial parts of the rules that Mexico had proposed.[115] The new rules granted that negotiations would be initiated by member countries, rather than by the organization, and be undertaken on a product-by-product basis, "taking into account the needs of individual countries and industries."[116] They also allowed members to refuse to grant concessions on any particular product, established that no member would be forced to grant unilateral concessions "without adequate concessions in return," and prevented the organization from punishing those that didn't fulfill their tariff reduction commitments.[117] While these may have seemed like small and technical revisions, they were in fact crucial rules for how the organization would oversee tariff negotiations going forward. A State Department guide to the charter published just after the conference listed Article 17 as one of the three key provisions of the new agreement, and a Mexican press release called the article "surely one of the most transcendent in the entire charter, and of vital importance for Mexico and its future development."[118] In a report to Alemán, the Mexican delegation wrote that their revisions to Article 17 had changed the fundamental nature of the charter: "The tariff negotiations are no longer the only goal of the organization," as the other aspects of the charter dealing with full employment and the development of less industrialized countries had been given equal footing.[119] It was a triumph, the Mexican delegation declared, that the conference had come to accept "the principles for which our delegation fought insistently, and frequently, alone."[120]

With these changes to the tariff negotiation provisions now settled, the US delegation decided in February that quantitative restrictions were the country's red line, and that they would go after the Latin Americans on this issue.[121] When Beteta and Clayton again met privately, Beteta noted the still ongoing mobilization of labor and industry in Mexico as a support for quantitative restrictions; the United States would have to compromise. Clayton responded by telling Beteta that his delegation had already reached the limit of what they could do for Mexico. He pointed out that Article 12 (on international investment) and Article 17 (rules for trade negotiation) had emerged almost exactly as Mexico proposed, and that he was disappointed that Mexico would not reach a further compromise. Beteta reported to Alemán that Clayton "expressed his sadness that Mexico has become a mortal enemy of the North American position."[122] Beteta was caught between the fervor for protection coming from Mexican industrialists and workers and the pressure from the United States; he suggested to Alemán that Mexico should back off of the issue and let another Latin American country take up the fight.

With the distributional struggles over investment and rules for negotiation apparently won, however, Mexico still had one more fight to wage, over representation in the organization for the underdeveloped countries. In various amendments, Mexico had not only recommended a one-country, one-vote principle for the organization's main negotiating body, the Tariff Committee; it had also recommended the creation of the Committee on Economic Development, which would operate parallel to the main committee.[123] The idea of a development committee as a core part of the ITO had been introduced at London and tabled; now, at Havana, the Mexican proposal was supported by the Latin Americans as well as by China and Pakistan.[124] The original Mexican draft reveals the extent to which the Mexican delegation, three years on from the completion of the Bretton Woods agreements, worried that the development mandate of the institutions created there might not suffice. The proposal suggested that the Committee on Economic Development could consider requests not taken up by the World Bank in a timely manner and that it would "take action" to "obtain for the Member the necessary facilities for its economic development."[125] Ultimately, the Mexican proposal for the Committee for Economic Development was rejected, but in such as a way as to incorporate some of the most important provisions of the idea within the structure of the ITO, by abandoning separate tariff and development committees altogether.[126] Rather, decision-making on tariff rates was instead vested in the ITO's Executive Board, on which the less industrialized nations had won sizable representation; therefore, it was reasoned, the developing countries wouldn't be shut out of tariff decisions, and with the Mexican rule changes, their interests could be adequately protected.[127]

At the end of March, after four contentious months of negotiations in Havana, the charter of the ITO was finalized and signed. It reflected the sustained advocacy of the developing countries for a trade organization that would take their needs into account, in uneasy tension with the desire to universalize the "freer trade" of the US vision. Looking over the conference, the British were astonished at the level of US concessions, arguing that "their attitude was dictated primarily by a wish to gain credit with the Latin American countries."[128] And given all the exceptions and escape clauses that had been built into the charter, one Australian official summarized, "the only really important trading country which will be subject to all the restraints which it imposes on the conduct of commercial policy for a long time to come is the United States."[129] For Mexico's part, Beteta's closing speech attempted to highlight some of the Mexican victories but was not sanguine about the chances for success; "within each country represented here," he observed, there exist "more or less powerful interests exist which feel injured by the Havana Charter."[130] Now, a document that satisfied nearly no one would be remitted to the legislatures of the member countries for ratification—and the campaign against it in the United States would intensify.

CONCLUSION

As had been the case with regard to the Inter-American Bank (IAB), the opposition of US capital to the ITO was overwhelming—and was once again was centered precisely on the concessions that Mexico and its allies had won. After the conference, representatives of the National Foreign Trade Council—like their counterparts in the National Association of Manufacturers and the International Chambers of Commerce—testified before Congress, arguing that the charter included "concepts alien and hostile to American principles of trade and investment," and therefore urged its rejection.[131] The NFTC especially opposed the perceived obligation to assist in the development of less industrialized countries; this would, it argued, be tantamount "to the signing of a blank check by the United States in favor of other members of the ITO."[132]

If the developing countries expected any such blank check, they were looking toward Europe for a model. On November 17, the very day that Mexican trade unions and industrialist groups had taken to the streets of Mexico City to protest the trade organization, Truman had appeared before a special session of Congress to obtain funding for a program for European recovery, the Marshall Plan. Though both the president and Will Clayton made the case that the ITO and the Marshall Plan would be complementary—the ITO would take over after the Marshall Plan had successfully reconstructed the European economies—the Latin Americans saw in the proposal precisely the kind of aid program they had argued for since at least Montevideo. Across the region, political figures took up the mantle of a Marshall Plan for Latin America, arguing that their wartime sacrifice and importance to the US economy merited such aid.[133] After being put off at the 1947 hemispheric defense conference in Rio, Latin Americans took up the cause at the eighth Inter-American Conference, which opened in Bogotá just a week after the Havana Charter was signed.[134] There, Mexico redoubled its fight for the IAB (as described in chapter 4), and the Latin Americans fought hard for further economic assistance. But the United States came to the Bogotá meeting to double down on the agenda it had been promoting over the preceding years; Secretary of State George Marshall himself arrived to tell the Latin Americans that the US government could finance only a "small portion of the vast development needed," and therefore they would be dependent on private capital.[135] There would be no Marshall Plan for Latin America.

Meanwhile, the process to ratify the charter of the new organization stalled, and in 1950 the Truman administration quietly dropped its attempts to advance the ITO in Congress; the General Agreement on Tariffs and Trade (GATT) would stand in its place. Many Latin American countries didn't join the GATT (only Brazil, Chile, and Cuba were original signatories). Mexico would debate doing so in 1979 after the Tokyo round of tariff negotiations, but only joined after the neoliberal restructuring of the 1980s.[136] Instead of joining the GATT, Mexico intensified its programs of import substitution industrialization, using the tariffs, subsidies, and quantitative restrictions it had argued for at Havana to bring about a period of growth known as the Mexican miracle. But an image of the system that underpinned that miracle as a closed, insular economy belies the massive influx of foreign capital that would soon begin to pour into the country. Despite the fact that Mexico didn't get the multilateral, planned trading system that the industrializing countries had advocated, Mexican officials would now take full advantage of the gains they had secured over the preceding years to make Mexico a major recipient of capital from the new development institutions. In the process, however, they would oversee a radical shift in the role Mexico played in the struggle to reform the global economy.

SEVEN

The Price of Success

NAVIGATING THE NEW DEVELOPMENT ORDER
DURING THE MEXICAN MIRACLE

SURVEYING THE INFRASTRUCTURE OF GLOBAL economic governance at the end of the 1940s, it would be easy to conclude that many of Mexico's goals over the preceding decades had not been met. Most obviously, the IAB had not come into being, and it looked as though the ITO would suffer a similar fate. While Mexican officials had managed to obtain US acquiescence to a number of their proposals for both institutions, the power of capital—organized into influential business associations with prominent defenders in Congress—had managed to prevent US ratification of either one. Nevertheless, Mexican officials during the 1950s and 1960s proceeded largely as though they had won the vision that their country's representatives had advocated over the previous decades. With the creation of the new UN system and the firm establishment of a mandate for development, the decades-long Mexican advocacy for representation and some modicum of redistribution of capital from North to South now had an established institutional framework. Having argued repeatedly for mechanisms for obtaining long-term capital that would support Mexican industrialization, Mexico would begin to reap the benefits of the concessions it had been able to squeeze out of multilateral institutions and the United States, contracting billions of dollars in foreign credit, both public and private. As economist Víctor Urquidi put it looking back on the period, "Bretton Woods fitted very nicely into Mexico's needs."[1] Once these new arrangements began to deliver benefits, however, Mexico's role as a champion of international reform began to shift.

As part of the negotiations over wartime cooperation, Eduardo Suárez had managed in 1942 to negotiate Mexico's outstanding foreign debt payments down to roughly 10 percent of the $500 million USD owed.[2] The resolution of the long-standing debt problem led to a "rapprochement with foreign capital" by the 1950s.[3] Between 1942 and 1959, Nacional Financiera, Mexico's state development bank, authorized nearly a billion dollars in foreign loans.[4] (Nominal GDP in the period grew from just over $2 billion in 1942 to over $11 billion in 1959, so this was a not insignificant amount.)[5] By the late 1960s, the total surpassed $4 billion in foreign loans authorized, a rapid acceleration of official foreign lending.[6] From the World Bank, Mexico received $205 million in loans from 1949 to 1959 to fund electrification, transportation, and industrial development projects, and then triple that from 1960 to 1969, with more than $646 million in project lending during that decade.[7] Loans to Mexico made up more than 20 percent of World Bank lending in Latin America and the Caribbean in the 1950s and 1960s, and despite some tension in Mexico's relationship with the institution, in 1970 World Bank disbursements to Mexico reached a staggering 14.2 percent of the *global* total.[8] There were also other important sources of official loans. The Mexican government continued to seek very large loans from the Ex-Im Bank to finance the purchase of capital goods from the United States, including a $100 million request in 1959. Mexican officials' appeal for such a large loan caused the Ex-Im Bank's head to remind them that as of the end of the 1950s, their country had the third highest level of Ex-Im Bank lending in the world.[9] During the 1960s, Mexico received an additional $660 million from the Ex-Im Bank.[10] And after the establishment of the Inter-American Development Bank (IADB) in 1959, Mexico received $530 million during the 1960s from that body for irrigation, agriculture, and transport projects.[11]

The administrations of Adolfo Ruiz Cortines (1952–1958), Adolfo López Mateos (1958–1964), and Gustavo Díaz Ordaz (1964–1970) pursued an import-substitution industrialization strategy that promoted significant investment of foreign capital and participation of foreign firms. Key figures included Rodrigo Gómez, head of the Banco de México through all three *sexenios*, and Antonio Ortiz Mena, who after working as the head of the Mexican Institute of Social Security (IMSS) under Ruiz Cortines became the minister of finance for both López Mateos and Díaz Ordaz, where he named and oversaw the project of "stabilizing development."[12] While there were certainly important flashpoints and differences among the three presidents, there was a basic continuity in the approach to Mexican developmentalism. Even when the López Mateos administration declared itself in 1960 to be "within the constitution, of the extreme left" and attempted to expand social programs and increase state involvement in the industrial sector, the organized pressure of Mexican business groups forced the state to reign in his progressive agenda.[13] While López Mateos pursued a more independent foreign policy abroad in the context of the global Cold War, the relative autonomy of the state from business interests at home had been seriously curtailed by the 1960s.[14]

In absolute terms, foreign direct investment increased by nearly a factor of five between 1950, when it was $556 million, and 1970, when it reached $2.8 billion.[15] Though the government continued to restrict foreign investment in what it classified as strategic areas, it welcomed foreign firms' participation in the national production of goods that had previously been imported.[16] While the absolute size of foreign investment in the period was low—approximately 10 percent of the total investment in the 1950s, declining to only 3 percent in the 1960s as private domestic investment increased—foreign firms played a disproportionate role in the growth of manufacturing in the period, representing nearly a third of production value by 1965, despite accounting for only 1 percent of all manufacturing firms.[17] By then, Díaz Ordaz oversaw the creation of a new wave of foreign investment under the 1965 Border Industrialization Program, which allowed US firms to set up assembly plants in Mexico in sectors like textiles, plastics, and electronics.[18] Even as domestic investment increased, therefore, the contribution of foreign capital to the rapid growth of the Mexican miracle period meant that maintaining access to such capital, even in the face of opposition from nationalist labor and business groups, was an important political goal during the 1950s and 1960s.

Further, Mexico's development and stabilization plans also made it a creditworthy borrower in international markets long before other developing countries received such inflows of capital.[19] Mexico was the destination of more than 44 percent of US portfolio investment in Latin America between 1954 and 1969.[20] In 1960, for example, the Prudential Insurance Company of America financed the $70 million purchase of American and Foreign Power Company as part of Mexico's nationalization of the electricity sector, representing the "first long-term credit granted to Mexico since the Porfiriato by a foreign private financial institution without prior conditions for its use."[21] Having been shut out after the revolution, Mexico also returned to the international bond market in 1963 with a successful $40 million float.[22] By 1965, Mexico had the highest credit rating of all developing countries.[23] The inflow of all this capital meant that by 1970, Mexico's foreign debt had reached more than $7 billion, with more than $3 billion coming from private sources.[24] During the heyday of the Mexican miracle, then, the kind of capital that Mexico had long argued for was beginning to flow into the country—and the political need to maintain access to this capital had serious consequences for the role that Mexico played in international debates over the rules and institutions of international development.

MEXICO, THE THIRD WORLD, AND THE COLD WAR

The international political context in which Mexico pursued its development strategy was shaped not only by bilateral relations between the United States and Mexico but by the larger struggle of the Cold War in the hemisphere and in the broader Third World.[25] During this period, Mexican officials sought political alliances that would further their developmentalist goals, meaning foreign policy was often made to maintain or expand their access to foreign capital and development assistance.[26] Early indications of Mexico's contradictory approach to foreign policy surfaced at the Organization of American States (OAS) conference in Caracas, Venezuela, in early 1954, where the United States pushed an anti-communist resolution in an attempt to obtain multilateral cover for the overthrow of the democratically elected government of Jacobo Árbenz in Guatemala. The Mexican delegation added language to the proposed resolution specifying that it was "designed to protect and not to impair the inalienable right of each American State freely to choose its own form of government and economic system"—meaning it carried the opposite implication than the original US intention.[27] Despite the amendment, however, in the end the Mexican delegation abstained from the vote rather than voting against the resolution—a stance for which the US representatives expressed gratitude.[28] While the United States managed to rally sixteen votes in favor of the resolution—fully half from dictatorships, through "an extravagant program of vote buying"—Mexican officials made sure not to appear among those countries that were bought off, while still not jeopardizing access to US-controlled credit.[29]

The coup in Guatemala convulsed the region, with protests in the streets of major cities as well as in the halls of the UN General Assembly. And it sent out other shockwaves, as well. Che Guevara, who had been living in Guatemala during the coup, decamped for Mexico, where he joined Fidel Castro and by 1955 was receiving logistical support from Mexican nationals and other exiles.[30] After the triumph of the Cuban revolution in 1959, and particularly after Fidel Castro signaled that Cuba would follow a socialist path, Mexico would attempt to use relations with Cuba—and with the Third World more broadly—to its advantage with the United States, outwardly supporting the Cuban government while facilitating surveillance and repression of Cubans and their supporters in Mexico. One consequence of Mexico's dogged insistence on maintaining relations with Cuba was that the Alliance for Progress—which looked in many ways like the culmination of the kind of economic assistance program Mexico had advocated for decades—actually played a minimal role in Mexico, and Mexico played a minimal role in the Alliance.[31] Once the conservative Gustavo Díaz Ordaz took office, the Mexican state became more dogmatically anticommunist, but the country's international stances remained ambiguous. Even after Mexican activists advocated armed struggle at the TriContinental Conference in Havana in 1966, Mexican diplomats still refused to vote for an OAS resolution condemning the conference. They did, however, begin a propaganda and counterintelligence campaign within Mexico that would paint student protestors as Cuban and Soviet sleeper agents, ultimately leading to the spectacular state violence at Tlatlelolco on October 2, 1968.

Similar ambiguities marked Mexican relations with the many Third World organizations and groups that proliferated through and around the UN, before which Mexican officials frequently equivocated, dissembled, and reversed themselves. Mexico's relations with the Non-Aligned Movement are particularly instructive. After coming to power in 1958, Mexican president Adolfo López Mateos assumed a Third-Worldist mantle, making official visits to nonaligned countries like India, Indonesia, and Yugoslavia and releasing joint statements with Nehru, Sukarno, and Tito affirming Mexico's commitment to a fairer international economic order.[32] Nonalignment seemed a natural fit, in some ways, for Mexico's long-standing international project, but Mexican officials decided that a flirtation with neutralism—without a full commitment to it—would provide them leverage with the United States without alienating their sources of credit. In 1961, at the same time as the planning for the Belgrade conference of nonaligned countries was underway, the Mexican government was in the midst of negotiating a new $400 million stabilization loan that was intended to shore up Mexico's reserves against ongoing capital flight.[33] Representatives from Yugoslavia and the United Arab Republic pressured Mexican diplomats to attend the conference, hoping to secure Latin American participation from a country other than Cuba.[34] Mexico followed rather than led, however, watching closely how countries like India and Brazil were approaching the conference. The US ambassador in Mexico perceptively summed up the Mexican strategy as "shrewd rather than weak, calculating, rather than uncertain."[35] Mexican officials declined in the end to participate in the conference or even send an observer, and subsequently the Ex-Im Bank and IADB agreed to some $500 million in loan commitments.

The next year, Mexico did send a delegation to the Non-Aligned Movement's 1962 Cairo Conference on the Problems of Economic Development, attended by thirty-six countries from Asia, Africa, the Middle East, and Latin America. But while the Mexican delegation continued its advocacy for easier access to capital and technical assistance, they went to the conference intent on defending, rather than criticizing, the existing development apparatus. Rodrigo Gómez, head of the Banco de México, sent instructions to Octaviano Campos Salas, a Chicago-trained manager at the Banco de México and head of the Mexican delegation, to "avoid any resolution critical of economic cooperation between the United States and Latin America."[36] Moreover, the SRE prepared instructions for the delegation that also called for Mexico to counter any criticism of existing international economic structures and to work against the creation of new economic institutions that might duplicate functions of UN bodies. The Mexican delegation was to favor increasing and stabilizing the prices of primary products and promote multilateral rather than bilateral technical assistance, both of which were mentioned in the speech given by Campos Salas at the conference.[37] But, the SRE's instructions argued, the delegation should abstain from discussions criticizing those institutions for "lending only to countries indicated or preferred by the largest Western powers." They would be permitted to argue for the establishment of a "non-discriminatory and equitable financing policy" from the international financial institutions, but not to criticize their existing practices.[38] Ultimately, the instructions argued, the delegation should avoid anything that went against the foreign policy of Mexico, which was, the foreign relations ministry argued, "not neutral, but independent."[39] Even in moments when Mexican officials sought broader Third World connections, then, the strategy of safeguarding their access to international capital frequently outweighed other considerations.

As previously chapters have shown, Mexican state officials had spent decades arguing for the creation and reform of international infrastructure for development—and after 1948, that infrastructure proliferated rapidly, both within the hemisphere and globally. Within the inter-American system, the newly reorganized OAS created the Inter-American Economic and Social Council (IA-ECOSOC). Other new regional institutions emerged as well, including the UN Economic Commission for Latin America (ECLA) and the long-anticipated IADB. Globally, UN bodies like the World Bank, the IMF, and the Food and Agriculture Organization (FAO) were supplemented by the work of the ECOSOC, which organized the Sub-Commission for Economic Development to work specifically on the problems of industrializing countries.[40] Early advocacy there for the United Nations Economic Development Agency would eventually result in the creation of a host of new bodies, including the Expanded Program of Technical Assistance (EPTA); the United Nations Special Fund for Economic Development (SUNFED) and its rival within the World Bank, the International Development Association (IDA); and finally, the United Nations Development Program (UNDP).[41] Further, in the 1960s the United Nations Conference on Trade and Development (UNCTAD) became a key forum for development thinking, creating the Group of 77 (G77) in 1964 to represent developing country interests within the UN. The creation of each of these institutions involved contentious North-South negotiations, particularly over questions involving trade relations and "soft financing"—that is, long-term concessional lending for projects that were not expected to turn a profit for investors—and therefore echoed the interventions that Mexican officials had made in earlier decades.[42] Officials from countries like India, Chile, Brazil, Yugoslavia, and elsewhere would push for the creation and reform of the development infrastructure in the 1950s and 1960s, forcing the United States and Western Europe to take up some of their demands. Mexico, however, largely took a back seat in these struggles.

Inter-American Development

Even as the development infrastructure expanded in the hemisphere, Mexican officials refrained from attempts to radically reshape new organizations and agreements; during the 1950s and 1960s, Mexico became a

follower rather than a leader. At the two inter-American economic conferences during the 1950s—in Rio in 1954 and Buenos Aires in 1957—delegates
considered a proposal to establish the General Economic Convention, a
treaty governing economic relations among the OAS countries. As they
had done so often in the past, Mexican leaders assembled a commission to
study the draft introduced by IA-ECOSOC, which produced a long document full of amendments, including language on avoiding disparities in
prices between manufactured goods and primary products, on using protection to promote development on "solid bases," and on the need for
greater technical cooperation.[43] The plan also argued that foreign capital
should be subject to national legal jurisdiction and called for more public
financing—especially multilateral lending—rather than private foreign
direct investment, arguing that it was easier to channel public capital in
line with Mexico's development plans. To operationalize these ideas,
Mexico introduced a resolution at the 1957 conference in Buenos Aires that
took what a US official called a "mild critical attitude" toward the World
Bank's lending programs, while approving of Ex-Im Bank practices.[44]
While these interventions initially looked quite similar to Mexico's earlier
efforts, in the end, US officials were able to convince both Mexican and
Brazilian officials to push the rest of the Latin Americans toward producing a mere declaration, rather than a binding treaty.[45] After the declaration
was passed, the US representative reported, "nothing specific was agreed of
any consequence at the conference."[46]

Given Mexico's desire to increase the level of public funding, especially, a
particularly illuminating aspect of the conference was the debate over the
creation of an inter-American financial institution—a new hemispheric
development bank. As detailed in chapter 4, Mexican officials had long been
the central advocates of such an institution. After a 1953 study by ECLA
calling for massive increases in investment was taken up at the 1954 Rio conference, Chilean representatives, including future president Eduardo Frei,
put forward a resolution on the creation of a new bank, supported by
Colombia, Costa Rica, Ecuador, and Haiti. It was approved by a vote of
20 to 1 and resulted in the creation of the "Santiago Draft" for the establishment of the Inter-American Development Bank, which was submitted to
IA-ECOSOC in 1955.[47] In 1957 at Buenos Aires, representatives of Chile,
Uruguay, and Cuba again strongly advocated the creation of such a bank,
though it remained an unresolved issue at the conclusion of the conference.
Throughout these negotiations, however, Mexico remained on the margins.

Though the United States had thus far managed to continue to fend off Latin American advocacy for an IADB, Brazilian president Juscelino Kubitschek's 1958 rollout of his Operação Panamericana made officials in the Dwight D. Eisenhower administration take the IADB proposal more seriously. Mexican representatives, however, acted as the "major holdout" on Operação Panamericana in the region, even going so far as to argue against the Brazilian proposal in private meetings with representatives of other states.[48] Together, Brazil's Kubitschek, Argentina's Arturo Frondizi, Venezuela's Rómulo Betancourt, and Costa Rica's José Figueres put serious pressure on the United States for more aid to Latin America, and the United States announced at the 1958 OAS meeting of foreign ministers that it would finally support the creation of the new bank. The IADB was finally chartered in 1959, with Brazil and Cuba pushing the United States for higher capitalization and better loan terms right up to the last minute.[49] Mexico, however, played no role in finally bringing the institution to fruition, sitting on the sidelines of the struggle. Even as development became the main framework through which the United States approached Latin America, Mexican officials had taken the position of working within the institutions they were receiving capital from, rather than creating new ones.

Mexico and ECLA: A Contentious Relationship

When it came to the UN Economic Commission for Latin America (ECLA), one of the region's most important organizations in promoting Latin American development thinking, Mexico's relations were also ambiguous. In 1951, for example, the existence of ECLA was on the line. The initial mandate of the organization, founded in 1948, was for a three-year term, and when that term was set to expire with the fourth ECLA meeting held in Mexico City in 1951, the United States floated a proposal to merge ECLA with IA-ECOSOC. By bringing it under the purview of the OAS rather than the UN, US officials thought the United States would have more leverage over the organization.[50] Merwin Bohan, who had insistently outlined the Latin American position in the face of free-trade orthodoxy during Chapultepec and Havana, had been appointed the US representative to the OAS, and he was charged with pushing the US merger agenda.[51] Mexico's intervention in the question demonstrated the fine line the country had to walk. Looking back at the negotiations, Mexican economist Víctor Urquidi remembered that Mexico gave a "strange, half-hearted support" to the US consolidation proposal; Prebisch's biographer asserted that the "U.S. convinced Mexico to play the role of stalking-horse," so that the proposal wouldn't seem like an imposition by Washington.[52]

The two key members of the Mexican delegation to the meeting were Antonio Carrillo Flores, the minister of finance, and Manuel J. Sierra, an old hand of the Mexican foreign ministry. Víctor Urquidi remembered that Sierra was keen on friendly relations with the United States and was not a fan of ECLA; considering the question of the organization and its leader Raúl Prebisch, Sierra had told a friend, "I will never accept him, that disgusting Argentinean."[53] But being seen supporting a US power grab within the international system was politically dangerous for Mexico, even if the Mexican delegates cared little about ECLA themselves. The question came to a head in dramatic fashion: Carrillo Flores had invited both Prebisch and Bohan for dinner before the fourth ECLA conference began. After they ate, Prebisch recalled, Carrillo Flores asked Bohan to read the merger proposal, then asked Prebisch what his opinion was. Prebisch replied that he had already made clear in Washington his strong opposition, and that he was resolutely against any merger. In response, Carrillo Flores grabbed the paper on which Bohan's proposal was written, tore it up, and threw it in the trash while Bohan looked on, helpless.[54] In dramatic fashion, the Mexican official had affirmed that his country was not a US stooge. With a renewed mandate, ECLA then expanded and opened a regional office in Mexico City, led by the Mexican economist Víctor Urquidi.

Despite the early show of support for the institution, however, the underlying Mexican ambivalence toward ECLA was deepened a few years later, when an ECLA study on Mexico was seen to be critical of the Mexican government's development strategy. In 1955, Prebisch asked the Brazilian economist Celso Furtado to conduct a study on the Mexican economy and appointed a team that included Osvaldo Sunkel, who had just returned from graduate study in London, as well as the Mexican economists Juan Noyola and Oscar Soberón. Noyola had worked at the IMF during its early years but was trained in the more Marxist-inflected economics program at the National Autonomous University of Mexico (UNAM). (After he was sent by ECLA to Cuba in 1959, he chose to remain there to study the Cuban economy and the new revolutionary model.)[55] This group, working under Furtado's direction, conducted research based in the regional office in Mexico City from 1955 to 1957. Soberón obtained access to Mexican national statistics that had not previously been made available to outside researchers, giving a clearer picture of the dynamics of the Mexican economy over the preceding decades. The report found that Mexico's economic model was generating both external disequilibria and internal inequality, and it flagged the mounting problem of the integration of Mexico's economy with that of the United States.[56]

The study, however, was never published. While there was controversy over whether the findings contradicted Prebisch's own theories on market integration, the underlying problem was perhaps less Prebisch's intellectual objections than the Mexican government's political ones.[57] While Furtado's group had worked in the ECLA Mexico City offices headed by Urquidi, ECLA had never obtained formal permission from the Mexican government for the study, believing it to be unnecessary. When the results of the study seemed to suggest Mexican government "ineptitude" in its handling of foreign exchange problems, the government pressured Prebisch to keep it from being published.[58] If supporting ECLA had earlier been a useful way of maintaining plausible distance from Washington, when the group's report indicated that Mexico's growing reliance on US capital might prove problematic, its findings were undermined and the work was censored. Having pushed for decades for organizations that would make Latin American economic ideas heard, the Mexican state in the 1950s was unwilling to countenance that such organizations might now question its development model.

A Special Fund for Development?

Ambiguity also marked the Mexican interventions in the debate over the creation of a Special United Nations Fund for Economic Development (SUNFED) under the auspices of the General Assembly. Debate over SUNFED lasted for nearly the entire decade of the 1950s, and the project came in for special criticism from the United States. While the experience of prior decades might suggest that the addition of new sources of multilateral development capital—particularly those that might provide better representation for the developing world in their governance structure—would have been welcomed by Mexican officials, Mexico approached SUNFED with caution. In 1952, when the project was first proposed, a study written by Mexico's Luis Weckmann argued that any new institution within the UN should be "practical" and therefore argued that it should not "obstruct the labor that is being done with such efficiency" at the World Bank and the Ex-Im Bank.[59] An important rationale for the fund, however, expressed within the ECOSOC Sub-Commission on Economic Development, was that the World Bank's lending capacity was proving inadequate to the massive capital needs of countries like India.[60] While Mexico defended the World Bank's "efficiency," then, other countries in the developing world still clamored for more capital.

ECOSOC formed a committee of nine prominent economic thinkers to study the proposal in early 1953. Mexico's Eduardo Suárez, who had been the head of the country's Bretton Woods delegation, chaired the committee, and members included Chile's Hernán Santa Cruz, a key proponent of the SUNFED idea, as well representatives from the United States, Western Europe, Yugoslavia, Pakistan, the Philippines, and India.[61] Their report, published and transmitted to ECOSOC in March 1953, recommended the creation of the fund, but with numerous caveats, including stressing the necessity of self-help—what one study at the time characterized as the "bootstrap operations" of "backward countries"—as well as avoiding the diversion of funds from other productive uses and ensuring the "efficient and prudent" use of funds in development projects.[62] US officials, for their part, wanted to ensure that development funds were channeled through institutions like the World Bank, over which they could exercise more control, rather than any new fund answerable to the General Assembly. US business associations in particular lobbied against the fund, as demonstrated by an article in the magazine *Nation's Business* with the headline "SUNFED: Your Name on a Blank Check," which argued that US taxpayer dollars would be used for an institution in which "the borrowers will run the bank."[63]

When the debate came up again during the General Assembly in 1956, Mexican finance minister Antonio Carrillo Flores advised that the Mexican UN delegation exercise extreme caution in expressing an opinion on SUNFED until the delegation knew that the proposal would get significant backing from other states—suggesting, again, that Mexico should follow rather than lead.[64] After refusing to express an opinion during the many months in which governments were polled for their ideas about the fund, in 1957 Mexican officials finally indicated that while they "sympathized" with the idea of the fund and supported any attempt to accelerate economic development, Mexico would take the position that the fund should complement, rather than duplicate, the work of existing institutions, only addressing areas that the World Bank and other such organizations didn't.[65] This allowed Mexico to support the idea of the fund and therefore not be seen as opposing the interests of other developing countries, but also to signal its continued support for the Bretton Woods institutions and therefore also not antagonize the United States and the existing mechanisms for development lending. While SUNFED was finally chartered in 1959, its purview had been strictly limited to supporting only technical assistance. Meanwhile, the United States responded to the clamor for more development funding with the creation of two new agencies *within* the World Bank: the International Finance Corporation, created to support private investment, and the International Development Association, created to undertake "non-self-liquidating investment"—that is, soft financing—for the poorest countries. As US representatives worked to keep such activities within the purview of the Bretton Woods institutions, rather than allowing authority to devolve to the General Assembly, Mexico remained a quiet ally.

The World Bank and the IMF

As the rapidly increasing loan figures make clear, the Bretton Woods institutions were of critical importance to Mexico's development strategy in the 1950s and 1960s, and Mexican officials worked diligently to ensure that capital would continue to flow from both the World Bank and the IMF. Beyond investment, monetary policy was also a crucial aspect of stabilizing development; maintaining both the rate of inflation and the balance of payments was critical for the sustainability of Mexico's industrialization. Central banker Rodrigo Gómez—described by a colleague as a "pragmatic monetarist" and therefore not an ideologue—represented what one scholar has called the "conservative developmentalist" tendency of the postwar Banco de México.[66] Gómez oversaw the devaluation of the peso twice in six years, first in 1948, when he was the subdirector, and then again in 1954. In this process, he and other Mexican state officials would come to learn how useful the multilateral imprimatur could be to undertake policies that might be politically unpopular. The 1948 devaluation had led to serious labor upheaval, with railroad workers launching an immediate strike and a coalition of worker and peasant organizations calling demonstrations that drew some forty thousand people in Mexico City and thousands more elsewhere in the country.[67] In carrying out the 1948 devaluation, Mexican officials had repeatedly ignored the advice of the IMF, allowing the peso to float for over a year in direct contravention of the fixed-rate Bretton Woods regime and finally fixing it at 8.45 pesos to the dollar, when the IMF and US treasury were pushing for 10.[68] By the time it became clear that another devaluation would be necessary in 1954, Gómez had come to understand not only the political consequences of devaluation but also the financial consequences of going along with IMF recommendations. The mechanics of the 1954 devaluation were worked out behind the scenes between Mexican financial experts and IMF officials. Only once completed were they presented as a fait accompli to President Ruiz Cortines.[69] Antonio Ortiz Mena, a close economic adviser of Ruiz Cortines who would go on to become the minister of finance in the next two administrations, made clear in an interview that the IMF's advice smoothed over the political problems created by devaluation: "We go to the IMF to make us do what we know we have to do," he said, and "this helps us control public opinion."[70] Four months after the IMF-directed devaluation, Mexico received a $61 million loan from the World Bank, then the largest project investment loan the Bank had ever made.[71]

While relations with the World Bank were not always smooth, Mexican officials worked to keep their country in the Bank's good graces. In 1950 the Bank argued that Mexican officials had failed to adequately consult them with regard to their plans for seeking foreign credit.[72] In response, in early 1951 Mexico's state development bank, Nacional Financiera, proposed to the World Bank that they form a joint commission to study Mexican economic development, "with particular reference to Mexico's capacity to absorb additional foreign investments."[73] The commission included two World Bank officials and two important Mexican economists, Raúl Ortiz Mena—brother of Antonio Ortiz Mena—and Víctor Urquidi, who had been on the Bretton Woods delegation and worked at the World Bank on Latin American issues in the late 1940s.[74] The study was completed mainly in Mexico over the course of a year and laid the groundwork for the foreign investment bonanza that was to come. It argued that Mexico was prepared to absorb much higher levels of foreign lending to both deepen its industrialization and continue to improve its agricultural output.[75] It also argued that the coming years would require more focus on "public facilities and social welfare projects," which would necessarily have a lower and slower return, meaning that continued growth would necessitate still higher investment levels. Therefore, Mexico would have to turn to more government borrowing, which would require increased coordination and planning on the part of the Mexican government.[76] "The time has come," the economists wrote, "when Mexico may want to abandon the project-to-project approach to economic development and look at the organic whole."[77] As a result, the Mexican government formed an investment committee to make a three-year plan, and the Bank now seemed satisfied that Mexican officials were willing to take its advice.[78]

As Urquidi would later remember, however, planning on paper and planning in practice frequently diverged; the investment committee was viewed with suspicion within some government circles, and the finance minister refused to consult the committee in making investment decisions.[79] As a result, Bank leaders grew increasingly frustrated with Mexican officials, and a few important loan requests were refused. Officials with the state-run oil company, Petroleos Mexicanos (PEMEX), sought lending from the Bank (as well as from the US government) for exploration activities and were rebuffed; the Bank's president, Eugene Black, was irked that PEMEX was a state-run monopoly and argued that the private sector was the more appropriate source of capital for the oil industry.[80] The Bank did participate in lending for the electricity sector, which was mixed between the state-run Federal Electricity Commission (CFE) and foreign-owned firms. Near the end of the Ruiz Cortines administration, however, the Bank began to argue that Mexican industries like electricity—together with railroads and petroleum—should be run on "sound business principles," and argued that electricity rates for users should be raised and that state intervention should be liberalized.[81] During a trip to review a power plant project in 1958, Black put Mexican officials on notice that the "Bank would not lend money to Mexico if they continued to follow a socialistic course."[82] The disagreement would only be resolved when in 1961 Antonio Ortiz Mena, now the minister of finance, convinced the new López Mateos administration to agree to an electricity rate increase.

The electric sector controversy, then, raised an early dispute over conditionality: the notion that loans from international financial institutions would have policy conditions attached.[83] In contravention of Black's recommendation, however, Mexico would soon nationalize the power companies at the heart of the dispute, using private loans. During the 1960s the Bank continued to recommend various means for increasing revenues to public sector industries, but as one internal Bank memo noted in late 1969, "there is little more that we can expect to achieve in the way of institution-building or influence over policy." Surveying Mexico's development progress, the Bank concluded that "the Mexicans naturally prefer the Bank's money to its advice ... [as] they can reasonably claim to have made a pretty good job of economic development."[84] Indeed, while the international economy was stable during the 1950s and 1960s, the so-called Mexican miracle was able to supplement public, multilateral funds with private lending, thereby affording Mexico some distance from Bank orthodoxy.

As long as the global economy continued to grow and Mexico continued to do its "pretty good job of economic development," then, Mexican officials largely defended the status quo from reforms that might threaten the country's continued access to capital. But the specter of economic crisis in the early 1970s put Mexico in an increasingly tenuous position on the international stage. Facing increasing pressure on the US dollar, in August 1971 the Richard Nixon administration effectively withdrew from the Bretton Woods monetary system by suspending the convertibility of dollars into gold and convening the richest countries, the G10, to work out a new temporary exchange rate regime.[85] The administration also imposed a 10 percent surcharge on imports to the United States, a move that was meant to force other countries such as Japan and West Germany to revalue their currencies against the dollar, but which countries like Mexico, whose major export market was the United States, took as a direct attack.[86] The response by Latin American nations tested the ambivalent stance toward far-reaching reforms in global economic governance that Mexico had developed over the preceding decades and set Mexico on a crash course with more radical leaders from throughout the Third World.

In direct response to the G10 action, the Group of 77 (G77) called a ministerial-level meeting for October 1971 in Lima, Peru, and in preparation, regional groups within the G77 gathered to work out their shared platforms.[87] The Latin American group, known as the Special Commission for Latin American Cooperation (CECLA), met in early September in Buenos Aires. Led by representatives of Argentina, Chile, and Mexico, CECLA issued a "manifesto" that urged reversal of the import surcharge and reduction in economic aid, pointing out the disproportionality of US action.[88] The manifesto stressed an issue that the Mexican delegation at the Bretton Woods conference had raised nearly three decades earlier: the inability of the IMF to force balance of payments corrections onto the rich countries. As such, the manifesto returned to a demand for further representation, urging "the need for full participation by the Latin American and other developing countries in current and future decision-making and in reform of the international monetary system."[89]

The apparent unanimity of the Latin American manifesto, however, concealed an ongoing disagreement over the nature of the reform of the international monetary order, in which Mexico's defense of the status quo became more difficult. The dispute came to a head when CECLA members gathered in Lima before the G77 meeting began. There, Peru's president, General Juan Velasco Alvarado, put forward a resolution to convene an economic conference that would, in his words, "create in the Third World the possibility of resisting the monetary rules dictated by the great powers."[90] Velasco's call to overturn established international monetary structures was linked to another even more politically explosive issue: the expropriation of foreign-owned property. Velasco, who had seized power in a military coup in 1968, had implemented wide-ranging leftist social reforms, including the nationalization of the transportation, communications, and electricity sectors and the expropriation of important US holdings in petroleum, and he had already been advocating an "inherent right to expropriation" within CECLA and the G77.[91] In response to a rising tide of nationalizations—not only in Peru, but also in Fidel Castro's Cuba and Salvador Allende's Chile—Texas representative Henry González introduced legislation in the US Congress that would require US delegates to the World Bank and IMF to vote against lending to any country that undertook expropriations without appropriate compensation. With the González amendment, questions of the right to expropriation were directly linked to the question of representation within the international financial institutions.

While the right to nationalization was written into Mexican law and had long been a key tenet of Mexican foreign policy, Mexico was actually a strong opponent of the Peruvian proposals in CECLA. Mexican delegates to the Lima CECLA meeting understood their Peruvian counterparts to be arguing that expropriations were legal *even without* compensation, a stance the United States was vehemently against. In response, Mexico issued formal reservations about the Peruvian language at the Lima meeting. The Mexican foreign minister advised that not only was such a resolution contrary to Mexico's long-standing foreign relations doctrine against interference in the domestic affairs of other countries—the right to nationalization wasn't subject to international agreements, Mexico had argued since the 1960s, as it was the stuff of domestic law—but that it also went against Mexico's clear position on expropriation *with* indemnification.[92] With Mexico's stellar credit rating facilitating huge capital flows into the country, the Mexican foreign ministry clearly did not want to be lumped into a group that might support uncompensated confiscation of foreign property.

Officials at the Mexican embassy in Lima worried, however, that Mexico's blocking of the Peruvian proposals was damaging what Ambassador Luis Zorilla called the country's "gallant image . . . as a bulwark for the values, the dignity and the defense of the interests of Hispanic America in particular and of peoples whom had been victims of abuses of any kind on the part of the big countries."[93] To underline his worries, Zorilla dispatched copies of the daily press coverage of Mexico's resistance, in which Peruvian reporters implied strongly that the Mexican refusal to adhere to Peru's proposal was due to US influence. One headline was blunt: "Some Countries Weaken Revolutionary Proposal for Fear of the Club of the Rich," it announced, and a subsequent article pointed the finger at "countries located to the north of our continent, principally Mexico."[94] To make matters worse, a Peruvian paper insinuated that Mexico's pushback against the Peruvian proposal was the result of a visit from the US envoy.[95] The implication that the government of Mexico was being bought off by the United States was a difficult one for the new administration of Luis Echeverría Álvarez, which, as the next chapter details, had begun a campaign as a champion of the Third World. The Peruvian press picked up on this tension and ran a story on demands for the reform of the international financial system coming from countries in Africa as well, under the rubric of the UN Economic Commission for Africa—demonstrating that Peru was not alone in its desire for radical change in global economic governance.[96]

If the González amendment was adopted by the US Congress, multilateral financial institutions like the World Bank and the IADB would be sanctioned as mechanisms through which the United States could punish expropriators. The Peruvian delegation therefore insisted on the need for the creation of *new* institutions and on the necessity of a conference outside the established channels to create them. While those countries that opposed Peru's proposal, such as Mexico, continued to argue that the IMF was an "adequate" organization for addressing the problems of the Third World, press coverage noted that most of the assembled countries had come around to Peru's proposal—including Chile's Hernán Santa Cruz, renowned jurist and representative of the Allende government at Lima.[97] Finally, after a week of debates that stretched until 4:30 in the morning, Argentine delegates proposed a compromise between the Peruvian and Mexican positions: the need to convene a global economic conference should be decided by a committee of developing countries created to act *within* the IMF itself.[98] Among the final resolutions adopted at the CECLA meeting, therefore, was one calling for the creation of an intergovernmental group of senior monetary and financial officials of the G77, together with the developing country executive directors of the IMF, which would consider whether to convene a conference "within the framework of the United Nations and its specialized agencies."[99]

If the Latin American countries had seemingly found a compromise in the final CECLA resolutions, however, it was not clear that the larger G77 could come to a similar agreement. As the Lima G77 meeting finally got underway, the group's acting president, Algerian foreign minister (and future president) Abdelaziz Bouteflika implored the developing countries to establish a "united front" before the G10, in order to achieve what he termed "participation in the reorganization of the international monetary system," language that was echoed by the overwhelming majority of those representatives who spoke during the plenary sessions of the meeting.[100] The most radical governments in Latin America, however, including Peru, Chile, and Cuba, continued to argue for the convening of a world monetary conference that would not reform but *replace* the current system. Speaking to the assembled delegates during the first plenary meeting, Peru's General Velasco took the less revolutionary governments to task. He argued that Peru's revolutionary path to development was a complete break with prior experiences, which "differed radically from the concept of modernizing development which aimed at altering, by a series of reforms, secondary aspects of a political and social situation."[101] Those countries that continued to work within existing systems, he argued, would simply be "reproducing foreign formulas and following paths which were not their own." The finger was pointed squarely at Mexico.

The next day, Allende's foreign minister, Clodomiro Almeyda, argued that "no machinery was more of an anachronism than the monetary system set up at Bretton Woods, and the International Monetary Fund (IMF) that was responsible for operating it."[102] As such, he stressed, the General Assembly should call a world monetary conference, "to revise or modify the entire Bretton Woods system, a conference in which all the countries of the world would participate on the basis of complete equality." A few days later, just after the Mexican delegate reiterated his country's support for the CECLA resolution calling for the intergovernmental group to work *within* the IMF, Cuba's foreign minister, Raúl Roa, went even further. His speech argued that the only way forward was to convene a new conference, "which would be preeminently political in character" and would "aim at abolishing the feudal overlordship which the United States had exercised over international money markets since the Second World War."[103] In the eyes of the radical socialist governments, then, a reform of the structures of the international financial system would be a failure; a revolution was necessary. They received some moral support from some of the new socialist governments in Africa. Victor Tamba Tamba of the People's Republic of the Congo, for example, said that his country would be willing to compromise, but he reiterated his country's Marxist-Leninist principles and argued that "the international monetary system could only be cured as part of the whole international situation."[104] Most representatives from African countries, however, did not wade into the intra–Latin American controversy; they instead focused on the need to use newly established special drawing rights at the IMF as a source of additional liquidity and financing for development.[105]

The insistence of Peru, Chile, and Cuba on the need to convene a conference *outside* the realm of the IMF therefore failed to gather more support, and the final resolutions of the conference took the route advocated by Mexico: the creation of a group within the IMF governance structure to advocate for Third World positions. The delegates drew up the Action Program of Lima, which declared it unacceptable that the rich countries had coordinated among themselves outside the framework of the IMF. The declaration argued for increased voting power within the IMF, as well as for the creation of an "intergovernmental group" of representatives of five countries from each of the developing regions—Asia, Africa, and Latin America—that would provide a mechanism for developing country participation in international monetary decision-making.[106] So it was within the IMF, as Mexico had been advocating, that new efforts at reforming the international financial system were undertaken. At this moment of international crisis, Mexico led the way in a collective attempt not to tear down or replace the IMF, but to *strengthen* the institution and make it more responsive to the needs of the developing world.[107] In returning to the question of representation within the institutions, Mexican officials hoped they wouldn't jeopardize their good standing in the international financial system.

CONCLUSION

Over the course of the 1950s and 1960s, Mexico had indeed done "a pretty good job of economic development," as the World Bank had recognized.[108] High levels of growth and industrialization had raised per capita GDP from $189 USD in 1950 to more than $725 in 1970.[109] Over this period, foreign direct investment and public and private lending had played an important role in Mexico's industrialization strategy, making the protection of foreign capital—and the institutions that supplied it—a key priority for the Mexican state. Even as some leaders during the period tried to strike a more Third-Worldist or radical tone in foreign policy, however, Mexican officials during the period overwhelmingly defended the status quo in international economic and financial policy. In contrast to earlier periods, Mexican officials repeatedly chose to follow, rather than lead, when reform efforts were proposed, and found quiet ways to avoid direct conflict with the United States, the source of so much of Mexico's necessary foreign capital. Mexican officials also repeatedly defended existing institutions, such as the World Bank and the IMF, and played little to no role in efforts to create new ones. In fact, Mexico often acted as a spoiler when other countries put such proposals forward, such as Brazil's efforts during Kubitschek's Operação Panamericana. After having spent the previous decades advocating for the creation of institutions that would support development and distribute capital to countries like theirs, Mexican leaders in the 1950s and 1960s took advantage of the mechanisms that had been created and positioned their country as a responsible developer and therefore a prudent market for credit and investment. The tensions raised by such a stance would soon make themselves felt, however, as Mexican leaders sought to retake a leadership role in the broader struggle that was emerging: the creation of the New International Economic Order.

EIGHT

A Mexican International Economic Order?

THE ECHEVERRÍA SYNTHESIS

As Mexico entered the 1970s, unease about rising inequality was growing, and especially after the spectacular violence at Tlateloco in 1968, cracks in the Mexican miracle were starting to show. In response, Luis Echeverría Álvarez campaigned for the presidency on a populist promise to turn the previous decades' stabilizing development into what he called "shared development." He rapidly expanded public sector spending, and after failing to pass a substantial tax reform, turned to foreign borrowing to cover government expenditures. Private banks were eager to find a return on their Eurodollar holdings in Latin American markets, and loans poured into Mexico. In the 1970s, the bonanza of foreign lending that had begun over the previous two decades accelerated rapidly; during the Echeverría *sexenio*, Mexico's foreign debt grew from $7.5 billion in 1971 to $24 billion in 1976.[1] Despite the fact that Mexico was able to access unprecedented levels of foreign credit, however, the broader international economic system had begun to falter, and particularly after the United States suspended gold convertibility and imposed a 10 percent import tax in August 1971, Echeverría would turn his attention to the system of global economic governance in which Mexico operated.

Echeverría's administration attempted to synthesize the two tendencies described in preceding chapters, combining the kind of leadership of a global effort to challenge international inequities in distribution and representation that Mexican officials had pursued from the 1920s through the 1940s with the insistence on the responsible, foreign-capital-friendly developmentalism that had been promoted in the 1950s and 1960s. The result was a campaign for a kind of global corporatist compromise, a framework that distilled the many decades of Mexican advocacy traced in the preceding chapters: the Charter of Economic Rights and Duties of States. In pursuing this charter at the UN, Echeverría repeatedly made the case that unless further distributional and representational concessions were made in how the global economy was managed, global insurgent politics would only spread—and therefore that his vision for reform stood between the status quo and revolutionary upheaval. In so doing, he positioned Mexico as a key interlocutor between the United States and a radical Third World, pursuing South-South cooperation in parallel to, and not in conflict with, Mexico's relationship with the Global North, especially the United States.[2] In the process, he also frequently reminded his US counterparts of the effectiveness of his own internal repression, bolstering his counterrevolutionary credentials in an attempt to paint Mexico's demands as moderate, reasonable, and above all, necessary.

INTERNATIONALISM AND REPRESSION

When Echeverría arrived in New York to address the UN General Assembly in early October 1971, Mexico's relationship with the United States was more uncertain than it had been in decades. Tensions had persisted for months after Nixon's Operation Intercept, a drug-interdiction program that shut down nearly all commerce across the US-Mexican border for three weeks in late 1969.[3] What's more, while the measures that Nixon had taken to address the economic crisis in the United States had had reverberations around the world, they seemed especially acute in Mexico, which sent nearly two-thirds of its exports to the United States, and which had seen big increases in US investment over the preceding years, as detailed in the previous chapter.[4] By the time Echeverría touched down in New York, Mexican officials had already registered their objections to the US economic policy changes. Immediately following Nixon's announcements, Echeverría sent a vigorous formal protest to Washington, in which he argued that Mexico's ability to keep "problems of a social character" under control was directly related to price stability and economic growth—which were threatened by the Nixon shock.[5] The threat was clear: economic instability could lead to political instability.[6]

In fact, Echeverría would repeatedly use his own history of repression within Mexico as a signal to the United States that he could be counted on as a Cold War ally. In his role as minister of the interior under president Gustavo Díaz Ordaz, Echeverría had infamously overseen the repression that culminated in the Tlatelolco massacre in 1968.[7] What's more, just a few months before Nixon's economic bombshell in 1971, a paramilitary group trained by the Directorate of Federal Security (DFS) known as the *halcones* attacked another student protest in Mexico City, beating protesters with poles and killing and disappearing dozens of people—an episode that became known in the United States as the Corpus Christi massacre.[8] Beyond the cities, in the countryside, state violence was more widespread, if less spectacular. In rural areas, guerrilla insurgents and those suspected of collaborating with them were regularly detained, disappeared, tortured, and killed, in what has come to be known as Mexico's Dirty War.[9] Echeverría would use this history over the next few years to continually remind the United States not only that revolution was lurking around every corner, and that economic crisis made insurgency more likely, but also that, given his long history of violently repressing dissent, he was best poised to contain it.

This repressive face loomed even at the UN General Assembly. At the UN, Echeverría began his remarks by reaffirming the centrality of the principle of sovereign equality of states and the importance of the UN as a universal organization in which all were represented. He emphasized the similarities between Mexico's history of colonialism and revolution and the struggles of the recently decolonized world, putting Mexico in the ranks of the "majority of the world" and therefore up against the powerful nations.[10] Arguing that the experiences of Latin America, and of Mexico in particular, had demonstrated that the achievement of formal independence and political sovereignty was insufficient for the achievement of justice, he expressed the hope that after "the era of political decolonization through which we have lived, there comes another, of economic decolonization." He argued that the structure of the current world economic system had created the conditions for the ongoing global crisis, which "originated in the deficiencies of the regulatory mechanisms created at the end of the Second World War," not least the inability to force the richest countries to adjust their own economies (as the Mexican representatives at Bretton Woods had argued at the time).

The Mexican president therefore reminded his audience of the crucial role played by the developing world in the functioning of the global economy— but also gave a stark warning. "There will be no peace in the world," Echeverría argued, "until there has been a basic reorganization of economic relations among nations." This threat of instability was picked up in the reporting on the visit: The Associated Press ran a piece noting that without changes in US policy, economic discontent might fuel extremists and even guerrilla fighters in Mexico. The Mexican leader's task in New York, as unnamed "presidential sources" told the reporter, was to convince the Nixon administration that a serious change in economic policy was the only thing standing between the United States and violent revolution in Latin America.[11] If Echeverría's warning was not heeded, the story noted, forces much more radical might find further justification for taking up arms.

Echeverría concluded his speech at the UN by looking forward to the upcoming meeting of the United Nations Conference on Trade and Development (UNCTAD) in Santiago, Chile, where, he argued, Mexico and its allies would "at last crystallize the main points upon which the hopes of the developing world rest."[12] What form that crystallization might take was not yet clear; Echeverría's two goals for the UNCTAD meeting were to demonstrate his firm support for the government of Salvador Allende, who was facing serious international pressure over recent nationalizations in the copper industry, and to deliver what his close aid Porfirio Muñoz Ledo referred to as a "discurso cardenista," thereby demonstrating Echeverría's own populist bona fides.[13] It fell to Muñoz Ledo to determine what Echeverría's intervention at Santiago would be.

Muñoz Ledo had worked with Echeverría since the presidential campaign, and his position in the office of the president made him an indispensable adviser; during the Santiago trip, one Mexico City newspaper would call him "a sort of Mexican Henry Kissinger."[14] His politics, however, were diametrically opposed to those of the US secretary of state; Muñoz Ledo would go on to be one of the founders, with Cuauhtémoc Cárdenas, of the Democratic Current, the left-wing group that split from the PRI and then became the Party of the Democratic Revolution after the fraudulent 1988 elections in Mexico. When he entered the Echeverría administration in late 1970, Muñoz Ledo was already an experienced public servant, having worked in the Ministry of Public Education under López Mateos and as head of the Mexican Institute of Social Security (IMSS) under Díaz Ordaz. He considered himself a man of the left: trained in law at the UNAM and the University of Paris, he had met Fidel Castro during his time as a student leader in Mexico City in the 1950s and had discovered Third-Worldism in a France beset by the Algerian war. He remembered being frequently mistaken for an Algerian in Paris and recalled that "it was there I assumed my nationality as a man of the Third World."[15] He met Echeverría not long after returning from France, and after Echeverría won the 1970 election, he moved Muñoz

Ledo from his position at IMSS to the Office of the Secretary of the Presidency, where he became a very close adviser.

In preparing for Echeverría's coming address at the UNCTAD meeting, Muñoz Ledo put together a small group that included Gustavo Petricioli from the ministry of finance and Eliseo Mendoza from the ministry of industry and commerce.[16] Together, they began to review what had happened at previous UNCTAD meetings, surveying the various international economic issues that were of importance to the developing world—especially transfers of technology, prices for primary products, and capital transfers and financing. The group shut themselves in an office for a weekend and plastered the walls with various studies and proposals on international finance, monetary policy, and trade.[17] As they finished up the speech that Echeverría would give in Santiago, they realized that they needed a strong conclusion, and they came to the idea that the various aspects of the proposals they had cobbled together could form the basis of a new international agreement, the Charter of Economic Rights and Duties of States.[18] Though it emerged as little more than a convenient rhetorical device, it was an idea that would come to define Echeverría's presidency abroad.

THE DEBUT OF THE CHARTER IN SANTIAGO

When Echeverría arrived in Chile, the political situation was tense: a massive march against Allende had brought an estimated 200,000 people into the streets of Santiago just before the UNCTAD conference opened on April 13, 1972.[19] The site of the conference, a modernist building constructed especially for the meeting by the Allende government, became a symbol of the struggle over economic justice—national and international—then taking place.[20] A few days after Echeverría arrived, protestors burned a US flag outside the conference, provoking a police response that resulted in foreign diplomats getting caught in the clouds of tear gas unleashed on the activists. Press reports indicated that among the protestors were militants from the Movimiento de Izquierda Revolucionaria (MIR), a then-illegal, underground group of Marxist guerrillas, who distributed leaflets decrying the UNCTAD meeting as a "sell-out" of the Third World countries.[21] In addition to the conflict on the streets, of course, tensions were also high in the meeting hall itself, particularly between the representatives of rich countries and those from the developing world.

Echeverría began his remarks to the assembled delegates by outlining the high hopes that had been established by previous UNCTAD resolutions, but noting that the world had not yet met those expectations: protectionism was on the rise, prices for primary products were falling, the adoption of various agreements had been put off, the transfer of financial resources was slowing, and the developing countries were taking on increasingly unsustainable debt loads. Underlying all of this, he lamented, was the fact that "the principle of joint responsibility had not been respected."[22] Just as it had been for Puig four decades earlier, joint responsibility, based in a notion of economic interdependence, was a crucial aspect of Echeverría's vision: "The progress of human society from here forward," he told the gathering, "is indivisible."[23] Addressing the looming crisis, therefore, required deep changes in how the world economy was governed, and he highlighted a number of the issues that were on the agenda for the meeting, including reforms to give developing countries more participation in decision-making at the IMF—as Mexican experts had been advocating within the G77—and orienting the World Bank further toward development.[24] Highlighting the success that the Marshall Plan had brought to Europe, Echeverría told the gathered delegates that there needed to now be a second massive transfer of resources, this time toward the periphery, which would correct the distortions plaguing the global economy and lead to shared prosperity. He forcefully added that international financing should not be made conditional on politics and therefore should not be denied to those countries using revolutionary means to achieve progress—no doubt an allusion to the economic blockade being levied against Allende, at the behest of the United States, through institutions like the World Bank.[25]

Achieving these goals, the Mexican president said, would require "strengthening the precarious legal basis of the international economy," moving it from the realm of goodwill to that of law. This meant, he declared, creating a Charter of Economic Rights and Duties of States, complementary, he said, to the Universal Declaration of Human Rights. He then outlined the basic tenets of such a charter in his speech:

> freedom to dispose of natural resources; the right of every nation to adopt the economic structure it considered most suitable and to treat private property as the public interest required; renunciation of the use of economic pressures; subjection of foreign capital to domestic laws; prohibition of interference by supranational corporations in the internal affairs of States; abolition of trade practices that discriminated against the exports of non-industrial nations; economic advantages proportionate to levels of development; treaties guaranteeing

stable and fair prices for basic products; transfer of technology; and greater economic resources for long-term untied aid.[26]

He concluded this list of principles with a warning: "The solidarity we demand," he said, "is a condition of survival."[27] There could never be stability if the majority of the peoples of the world found themselves impoverished and discontented: "Our people are aware that their misery produces wealth for others," he warned. Just as resentment toward the political structures of colonialism had produced the independence movements that had reshaped the world over the preceding decades, now Echeverría was convinced that resentment toward economic neocolonialism was producing a movement that had at its center the promotion of not just political sovereignty, but economic sovereignty as well.

Because the proposal for a charter—which would require a complicated international instrument designed to structure economic relations between states—was still little more than a set of talking points, it now fell to the assembled delegates to figure out what to do about Echeverría's idea. Over the next three weeks, Muñoz Ledo worked closely with other delegations and the Chilean hosts of the conference and met twice with Allende himself.[28] While there was some debate among the Mexican team about the form that a charter should take—an amendment to the UN Charter, a UN convention, or just a UN declaration—Muñoz Ledo stressed the necessity that a charter be legally binding and obligatory, to delineate both rights and responsibilities for all member countries.[29] The legal nature of the proposal was hotly contested, however, and US delegates told Mexican representatives that they were not sanguine about the possibility of adopting the charter for a host of reasons: the lack of consensus among UNCTAD countries, the broadness of the principles involved, and the extent to which such a charter would fortify the division between the rich and poor countries, "beyond any possibly of mutuality."[30] Despite US skepticism, however, the conference approved a final resolution to create the Working Group that would draft the charter, with ninety votes in favor and nineteen abstentions, including the United States and other industrialized countries.[31] Back in Mexico City, the Mexican press celebrated the approval as a major victory, not least that there hadn't been any votes against the proposal.[32] While the headline in El Día roared, "The Third World Will Participate in World Economic Decisions," others were more cautious: "There Will Be Obstacles to Economic Charter," warned La Prensa, the paper that billed itself as "the newspaper that says what others won't."[33]

While the proposal to draw up a charter had been approved, the Nixon administration had already made quite clear its skepticism about such an instrument. Therefore, when Echeverría arrived in Washington, DC, in June 1972, for a state visit in which he would meet personally with Nixon and Kissinger, as well as address that year's meeting of the OAS, he stressed the role his country could play in hemispheric, and indeed global, politics. In order to demonstrate why his vision for a new global economic system could be in the US interest, Echeverría made clear to Nixon that Mexico was prepared to serve as a bulwark between the United States and the growth of socialist revolution in the hemisphere and around the world. But Echeverría told Nixon that he planned to continue to make the case he had made in Chile for the principles of the Third World—a stance Nixon labeled the "Echeverría Doctrine," which the Mexican president accepted.[34] Echeverría put it bluntly: "If I don't take this flag in Latin America," he told Nixon, "Castro will. This is something I am very, very conscious of." Having seen in his travels throughout the Americas how workers, students, and intellectuals were increasingly receptive to revolutionary ideas and movements—and having monitored them for the Díaz Ordaz administration and intelligence officials in Washington—Echeverría played up the destabilizing threat represented by those to his left. He was also at pains to demonstrate his willingness to dialogue with important members of the US business class, explicitly mentioning that he would dine at the estate of Nelson Rockefeller with the leaders of corporations like Anaconda, General Motors, and Kimberly, where he would campaign for further joint US-Mexican investment. In doing so, he was positioning Mexico's plans—what he called "capitalist solutions of a mixed type"—as the responsible way to head off social conflict, and therefore attempting to make the economic vision represented by the charter indispensable to Nixon.[35] Nixon encouraged the Mexican president as an alternative to Castro and urged him to take a stronger role at the OAS. "In other words," he told the Mexican president, "let the voice of Echeverría rather than the voice of Castro be the voice of Latin America."[36]

Nixon seemed satisfied with the understandings to which the two had come. "The Mexicans are liberal as hell," Nixon told Chief of Staff H. R. Haldeman, "but they're anti-communist."[37] And so the Mexican president took his "Echeverría Doctrine" to the OAS headquarters in Washington, where he reiterated a commitment to the right to expropriation, the control

over natural resources, and limits on the activities of transnational corporations, and urged the OAS to support the Charter of Economic Rights and
Duties of States. His language was once again careful, never attacking the
United States by name but rather rejecting "any attempt to establish a hegemony," which could be read as much against the Soviet Union as the United
States. He argued that "the negligence of the great powers with respect to
the less-powerful countries has shaped, more than any other cause, a new
division of the world," which had created, he said, a "classist division of
international society."[38] But the metaphor of class struggle only went so far.
When he met Ronald Reagan and a group of California businessmen a
few days later, Echeverría stressed that the "Mexicanization" campaign
underway to ensure majority national ownership in industries operating in
the country was not threatening: "*Mexicanismo* is not communism, nor does
Mexicanization mean expropriation," he argued.[39] Reagan emerged, according to press reports, convinced of Echeverría's plans, saying he would encourage investment in Mexico, particularly along the border. Echeverría had
apparently succeeded in convincing crucial Republican leaders that his
mixed-economy approach was a sensible way forward, between the right-
wing authoritarian model of Brazil, for example, and the socialist projects of
Chile and Cuba.

Back in Mexico, just a few days after the end of the UNCTAD meeting,
Mexican foreign minister Emilio Rabasa formally designated a team to
draw up a draft for the charter, which consisted of the group that had originally written Echeverría's speech—Gustavo Petricioli, Eliseo Mendoza, and
Porfirio Muñoz Ledo—as well as Alfonso García Robles, Mexico's ambassador to the UN.[40] While the draft did mention issues of representation—
arguing that "the participation of developing countries in the decisions of the
international economic field has been only marginal despite the fact that
these decisions affect the entire world community"—issues of distribution
were paramount.[41] The draft drew heavily on language that had characterized
earlier Third-Worldist declarations; like the 1962 Cairo Declaration of
Developing Countries, it explicitly mentioned the growing distance between
the developed and developing worlds, and like the 1967 Algiers Charter, it
argued that the international community "had an obligation" to provide the
resources that would allow developing countries to ensure decent lives for
their citizens.[42] The initial Mexican proposal went even further than the
previous declarations, however, in stressing these international duties. In fact,
the Mexican proposal explicitly called for the structural adjustment of the

industrialized countries: "Developed countries have the duty to adopt and apply specific programs of conversion and structural readjustment in their economies," the Mexican planners wrote, "with the goal of bringing about a rapid transformation in the world economic order that does justice to the developing countries, through a more just and equitable international division of labor."[43] The original Mexican draft, then, while recognizing the importance of the coordinated efforts of the developing countries, laid a significant part of the burden for a new global economic system at the feet of the richest nations.

With the draft in hand, a Mexican delegation traveled to Geneva for the first Working Group meeting, in February 1973. Immediately, the question of the legal nature of the proposed charter surfaced, when Mexico's new UN ambassador Jorge Castañeda, who was elected as chairman of the Working Group, stressed the idea of "progressive development" of international law through the charter.[44] SRE staff member Sergio González Gálvez reiterated this idea in a speech that stressed the need for the Working Group to consider "not only norms of *lex lata* [current law], but of *lex ferenda* [future law]" as well.[45] He explained that the developed countries had argued that the charter should include only already accepted principles of international law and thereby avoid contentious issues.[46] But González Gálvez argued that international agreements should not simply reinforce existing conditions but actually serve as instruments for the creation of a more just world: "For the delegation of Mexico the charter that we are drafting should also be a stimulus, an aspiration, a guide of conduct, it should look to the future and not just consecrate the status quo."[47] In response, the stances taken by the industrialized countries in the Working Group—which included Canada, Denmark, West Germany, France, Italy, Japan, Holland, the United Kingdom, and the United States—consistently sought to confine the charter's draft within the existing principles of law as they saw it, particularly with regard to the rights of the developing countries to regulate foreign investment.[48] What's more, the US representative even went so far as to argue that any provisions requiring the rich countries to provide aid might be, in fact, be a violation of *their* state sovereignty, using the language of the Mexican proposal against its advocates.[49]

After two tense weeks of negotiations, at 2:30 in the morning on February 26 the delegates managed to produce a draft outline, which included a number of alternative suggestions for each section.[50] The text was then remitted to member states for comment, but not before the industrialized countries made sure to note that the circulation of the draft implied no commitment by the Working Group members. Some of the alternatives in the proposal demonstrated that the distance between the industrialized countries and the others was still significant; for example, a paragraph that proposed to enshrine "the right of each state to regulate and control the activities of transnational corporations and the duty of each state to cooperate in order to give effect to this right" carried an alternative supported by Canada, Denmark, Germany, Italy, the Netherlands, and the United Kingdom, as well as independently by Brazil, that simply read "The question of transnational enterprises; rights and duties." Going even further, France proposed deleting the paragraph altogether.[51] After the meeting concluded, Mexico's Castañeda judged the gathering to have been "extraordinarily difficult and turbulent."[52] While the reconciled proposal retained some of the character of the original Mexican draft, it demonstrated how much remained unresolved, not least the legal nature of the proposed instrument.

When the group reconvened in July 1973 in Geneva for the second Working Group meeting, Castañeda attempted to head off another lengthy discussion on the legal nature of the charter. He proposed not to reopen debate on that topic, arguing that this was to be decided finally by the General Assembly itself.[53] By tabling the legal question, Castañeda hoped to come to agreement on the principles of the charter, before deciding how it might be codified and enforced; the Mexican experts thought that the support of the overwhelming majority in the General Assembly would make the legal nature of the charter irrefutable. Despite this, however, the Mexican delegation repeatedly reintroduced language noting the "urgent need to strengthen the precarious legal bases of the international economy" into the new draft.[54] Those opposed to making the charter legally binding also continued to make their views clear; in response to a detailed Mexican proposal regarding permanent sovereignty over natural resources and the regulation of foreign investment, the industrialized countries as a group again proposed language arguing that such matters should be subject to the "relevant norms of international law" and proposed the outright deletion of language about transnational corporations.[55] Attempting to work through these disagreements over the course of the three-week session, the Working Group compiled the various competing proposals into a schematic draft that listed alternative suggestions for each article. But as time ran short, seeing that they would be unable to reconcile the different proposals themselves during the meeting, the members of the group resolved to ask the Trade and Development

Board at UNCTAD for an extension of its mandate, recommending two additional Working Group sessions before the General Assembly of 1974.

Outside the Working Group, Mexican representatives were using every possible international forum to promote the charter—but winning over the other countries of the Third World to Mexico's position was a complicated undertaking. In September 1973, before the General Assembly, Mexico had sent observers to the Non-Aligned Movement (NAM) meeting in Algiers to encourage that group to adopt a resolution in favor of the charter; they did so, calling for the coming General Assembly to give priority to the charter proposal.[56] (It was at Algiers Summit, as well, that the phrase "new international economic order" first appeared in a declaration.)[57] Getting the backing of the nonaligned countries was a crucial step in smoothing over a split that had emerged between the G77 and the NAM, as countries like Algeria and their allies had been consistently taking more radical positions than the ones Mexico and other Latin American countries were proposing.[58] A push toward self-reliance and a kind of radical rejection of foreign capital had emerged at the Georgetown Non-Aligned meeting, when Algeria's Abdelaziz Bouteflika had argued, pointedly, that "the road of Third World economic emancipation does not run through UNCTAD."[59] This stood in stark contrast to the ideas Mexico had been promoting over the preceding months and years, not only in the negotiations over the charter but also in its push for reform of the international monetary system (as discussed in the preceding chapter). The NAM was beginning to push a radical *rejection* of the existing international economic system, even as the Mexican experts were trying to rewrite its rules.

Late 1973 also marked the beginning of the oil embargo imposed by the Organization of the Petroleum Exporting Countries (OPEC) as a result of the Yom Kippur War; the price of oil would quadruple by mid-1974. The United States attempted to respond to the crisis by creating a kind of consumers' cartel, but partners in Western Europe, especially France, refused to join such an effort and instead suggested that the UN was the appropriate forum for coming to a solution.[60] With some space opening between Europe and the United States, Third World leaders like Algeria's Houari Boumediène sought to work with interlocutors in countries like France to build an alternative to US hegemony.[61] Boumediène therefore proposed a special session of the UN General Assembly to address not simply the energy crisis but "raw materials and development" more broadly.[62] That session met in April 1974, and Boumediène used the occasion to argue forcefully that the developed countries "must accept the conditions of the economic emancipation of the peoples of the third world," and agree to found the New International Economic Order (NIEO).[63] That the vision of the NIEO reflected so much of the work already being undertaken in the charter Working Group was not a coincidence; the background paper laying the groundwork for the special session had, in fact, been prepared in Geneva at the February Working Group meeting, meaning that the agenda was planned during the charter negotiations.[64] (Contrary to the idea that the charter was what one historian has called an "augmented sequel" to the NIEO, it was rather an important predecessor of and crucial context for the new declaration.)[65] The Mexican representatives made sure that the special session declarations would include language about the charter, working diligently to ensure other countries were on board. They were quite successful; the SRE noted that during the special session, at least twenty-three countries had publicly voiced support for the charter, including Henry Kissinger for the United States.[66] The final language of the NIEO declaration noted that it would provide "an additional source of inspiration" for the charter, and the NIEO Programme of Action included a chapter on the importance of the charter.[67]

In addition to these negotiations at and through the UN, Echeverría had been traveling around the world, promoting the charter and its underlying principles.[68] During 1973 he traveled to Ottawa, where he received important support from the Canadian prime minister, and then to London, Brussels, and Paris, where his reception was more lukewarm.[69] In Moscow, Leonid Brezhnev offered enthusiastic backing for the charter—particularly for the document's emphasis on nondiscrimination against countries with different socioeconomic systems—and in Beijing, the government of Zhou Enlai agreed with Mexico to undertake the "maximum efforts" for the formulation of the charter.[70] After a visit from UN secretary general Kurt Waldheim in Mexico City in January 1974, Echeverría then left in February for another world tour, attending the Club of Rome meeting in Salzburg and traveling to Munich, Bonn, Rome, Vienna, and Belgrade, where he met personally with Josip Tito, who offered his "full support" for the charter.[71] In July, Echeverría toured South America to meet with the presidents of Ecuador, Argentina,

Peru, Brazil, and Venezuela to promote the charter, and by September he had received expressions of support from Japan, Austria, Poland, Greece, and others.[72] Despite the growing support, however, Echeverría told an assembled group of reporters before he left for South America that while he was confident the charter would be adopted at the next General Assembly, "it will be a long fight . . . one of generations, before the document, destined to regulate international economic relations on equitable bases, will have full force."[73] Even as he had promoted the charter relentlessly for more than two years, Echeverría had come to believe that its passage would mark only the beginning of a longer struggle.

While securing support from around the world was crucial for the success of the Mexican plans, the most important interlocutor was still the United States. When Secretary of State William Rogers visited Mexico City as part of a larger tour of the region in May 1973, both Echeverría and the foreign minister, Rabasa, made sure to bring up the charter. The Mexican representatives positioned themselves as useful interlocutors between the United States and its more radical critics, and Rabasa noted that Mexico was anxious to find an agreement acceptable to both developed and developing countries; he explicitly pointed out that Mexico had "opposed Chile's extreme demands" for what he called an "unbalanced charter" and stressed the need for a "useful" draft.[74] Echeverría had even gone out of his way, once again, to signal his own anti-communism, and the US embassy made special note of his "comments concerning mischief making of the communists, foreign and domestic," which "gave strong indication he has not forgotten his experiences in controlling their activities as minister of interior before becoming president," a barely veiled reference to Tlatelolco.[75] "As he has often done in the past," the embassy concluded, "he left no doubt as to his belief in a firm hand when dealing with extremists." But if Echeverría hoped that he could trade on his willingness to use repression against left-wing critics to mollify the United States into cooperation on the charter, it had little effect. In response to Rabasa's plea for US help in clearing procedural hurdles for the charter, Rogers was frank: the United States, he said, questioned the "meaning and purpose" of the words "duties, rights, and responsibilities"; the United States could agree to a moral obligation to help other countries, but not a legal one.

After Kissinger took over as secretary of state a few months later, however, US representatives began to signal more cautious support for the effort. Behind the scenes, Kissinger had been pushing the Mexican team to put the charter in more "neutral" language, promising that if it was not critical of the developed nations, then, as he put it, "we will make a big effort to support it."[76] In his speech to the UN General Assembly in 1973, Kissinger reiterated this idea, noting that the charter would be historic if it reflected the "true aspirations of all nations," but that "it will accomplish nothing if it is turned into an indictment of one group of countries by another."[77] In his public response, Rabasa thanked the secretary for his indications of support, but he was forceful in his conception of what remained to be done: "Once and for all, let us put an end to economic discrimination. Let there no longer be *apartheid* in the distribution of benefits. Let not poverty be a constant stimulus for revolution and war."[78]

By this time, Kissinger had begun to fear that Mexico and other Latin American countries could be pulled in a more radical direction by the NAM, and he therefore proposed a "New Dialogue" for the region and called a meeting of foreign ministers of the Western Hemisphere in February 1974 in Mexico City.[79] Kissinger arrived with a single goal: to "prevent Latin America from sliding into the non-aligned bloc," by renewing the idea of a "special relationship" between the United States and the region.[80] National Security Council staff had decided that the charter could be an important means of accomplishing this goal, and they argued that Kissinger should therefore try to put the charter "on a more realistic and practical plane, while not depriving [Echeverría] of the pride of authorship."[81] At the conference, Kissinger surprised observers by arguing that the charter was not a unilateral set of demands but in fact a "farsighted concept of mutual obligations."[82] In order to make the charter a reality, however, he urged the Latin Americans to subscribe to the idea of an "American community," a concept that was met with skepticism even by those closest to the US agenda, like Brazil's military government.[83] Meeting with Echeverría afterward, Kissinger pressed the Mexican president on the relationship of Latin America to the Third World. When Echeverría expressed admiration for Algeria's Boumediène, Kissinger worried, "What happens when the non-aligned are more numerous than the aligned?," before concluding ruefully, "Then we are the non-aligned."[84] Echeverría allowed that, for instance, Castro's presence in the NAM stretched the definition of such a group, but reiterated: "For the first time the underdeveloped feel they are strong and have a weapon." Kissinger replied that this was a dangerous development; it was clear that Echeverría had succeeded in striking a nerve.

There were two final meetings of the Working Group, in Geneva in February 1974 and then in Mexico City in June.[85] For these meetings, Rabasa began to work more closely behind the scenes with US delegates Stephen Schwebel and Carlyle Maw, legal advisers at the State Department. The most controversial part of the charter—what would become Article II on permanent sovereignty over natural resources, nationalization, and the regulation of multinational corporations—was largely left for the final meeting. By the end of the third session, however, Rabasa noted that the US and Mexican teams had "agreed upon a formula" regarding language around nationalization and multinational corporations, which would be the basis on which they would enter into negotiations in the fourth and final session.[86]

Despite the burgeoning compromise reached behind the scenes between Mexico and the United States, when the delegates arrived in Mexico City for the final Working Group meeting, local newspapers ran headlines about the "grave divergences" between the parties.[87] Much of the Mexico City meeting was taken up by detailed negotiation around those differences, especially about the provisions for regulating transnational corporations and expropriations. By the end of negotiations, there were a few competing versions of the language for Article II. A US draft called for countries to "avoid arbitrary or capricious actions" on expropriation.[88] The version submitted by Mexico on behalf of the G77, on the other hand, reiterated established language from the 1962 UN Declaration on Permanent Sovereignty over Natural Resources, but added that "in the event of nationalization, payment of compensation, as appropriate, shall be in accordance with the domestic law of the nationalizing state." The 1962 Declaration, however, had referenced the rules in force in the state that was taking confiscatory action, *as well as* international law, which was the interpretation the US representatives preferred.[89]

Even as this dispute proceeded publicly, however, the US and Mexican teams continued to negotiate behind the scenes, and they developed a compromise proposal, which concluded that states seeking to nationalize resources or regulate transnational corporations should "fulfill in good faith their international obligations."[90] A group including representatives from the United States, United Kingdom, and Mexico then convinced the Philippines' Hortencio J. Brillantes to introduce the compromise proposal as his own, which he did at 2:00 a.m. on June 28—though he changed the language from "international obligations" to "international commitments and undertakings," which angered most of the developed countries, who thought it implied that only treaties were relevant and not "customary international law, as well." An all-night session the next day, ending at 7:00 a.m., produced a final proposal with a series of alternatives for all of the paragraphs not yet agreed upon, including the Brillantes compromise on Article II, which would be the basis for the final negotiations.[91]

While the legal negotiators quibbled over language—the United States agreed to remove the word *capricious* from its description of possible Third World actions, for example—Kissinger had come to believe that the charter's real value was as a political gesture of goodwill toward Mexico, in order to keep Echeverría from turning too far from the United States.[92] As Maw tried to convince him of the need to hold firm on particular language, he spat, "[N]obody gives a good God damn what's in this charter, no one will remember two minutes after it's signed, what it said."[93] When Maw suggested that the Council of the Americas, representing US businessmen in the region, was following the negotiations closely—that they, indeed, gave a good God damn—Kissinger replied that "American businessmen are certified morons." Kissinger urged Maw not to nitpick and to find an agreement acceptable to Mexico and the United States. For their part, Mexican officials also took a position of compromise, insisting to reporters in Mexico City that there were not "hard line" countries on either side, and that while Mexico would never compromise its sovereignty, there was still room to reach agreement.[94]

After weeks of debate that had kept the delegates up into the wee hours of the morning, the Working Group finalized a draft in June 1974. It was far from unanimous, and still contained a number of alternative suggestions that would have to be resolved for the final declaration.[95] When the document was circulated, Mexican media reported that the draft was 80 percent agreed upon, and UN ambassador Castañeda argued that, despite the fact that it was not yet final, the charter was now indisputably a reality.[96] This final draft was then sent from Mexico City to UNCTAD's Trade and Development Board, which then recommended an informal session of the Working Group in New York in October, during the General Assembly, to finalize the text.

A CHANGING CONTEXT

Even as it seemed that Kissinger and Rabasa had ensured that the United States and Mexico would reach a compromise, however, the political context in which they were working was rapidly changing. While the Working Group toiled in Mexico City, the House Judiciary Committee in Washington was in the thick of hearings on the impeachment of President Nixon. For Mexican officials, it was increasingly unclear whether even Kissinger might be forced out, and the uncertainty gave the Echeverría administration more breathing room in its relations with the United States.[97] Rabasa arrived in Washington in August 1974 to push the United States toward a reconciliation of the outstanding issues in the charter. At a meeting with Kissinger, Rabasa noted that even though Mexico and the United States had come to an agreement at the third Working Group meeting, it was clear during the final meeting in Mexico City that what he called the "unaligned" states continued to find their compromise unacceptable.[98] Further, he told Kissinger, the NIEO resolution that had passed in May was now causing problems, as the other Third World countries were now unwilling to accept anything less than the tenets of that declaration—particularly because it had been adopted without a vote, giving it the imprimatur of unanimity. While Rabasa hoped that he could use the demands of the more radical states as a wedge against US intransigence, Kissinger was blunt: the United States wouldn't be moved by the inflexibility of the Third World's "specialists in extortion," and he warned that threatening the United States was counterproductive. Rabasa tried to reassure Kissinger that the United States and Mexico weren't in disagreement; the problem was the nonaligned countries. Kissinger was unmoved; he said he would tell Schwebel and Maw to "hang tight" in the final, informal consultations on the charter, and that the United States had "gone to the limit" of its positions. If Rabasa had hoped that he could use the NIEO declaration to bring the United States closer to Mexico's position, he left the meeting disappointed.

In October, however, the Mexican team would get a new opportunity to push for further US cooperation, as new US president Gerald Ford traveled to the US-Mexican border for a state visit with Echeverría, his first trip out of the country as president. Not only had there been a change of administration in Washington; in Mexico, engineers had just discovered vast untapped reserves of oil, creating the possibility that Mexico would become an important oil producer. US officials had already expressed confidence that this would bring down world oil prices. The Mexican president, therefore, came to the meetings armed with this leverage, and the conversations held between the two presidents, attended also by Rabasa and Kissinger, reflected this new source of power. Rabasa attempted to push the language on Article II, governing expropriation, further than the established compromise. Kissinger argued back, "We want a charter consistent with the Maw-Rabasa agreement but we cannot go beyond that" and he concluded, "we do not want to elaborate principles of international law to be used against us."[99] But if Kissinger was trying to hold the line, Ford would soon give Mexico another opening. At a press conference on the border, Ford complimented Echeverría's authorship of the charter idea, asserting that the United States believed that the charter had "very great merit and very great support, and I compliment you for it."[100] Echeverría quickly seized on Ford's language, telling the assembled reporters, "actually this is a complete change from what it was before, and this is very valuable support" that the United States had not offered previously; he was now confident that the charter would be approved in the UN. The headline on the government-supported newspaper *El Nacional* in Mexico City blared, "The United States Rectifies Its Position and Offers Full Support to the Charter Proposed by Echeverría," and the *New York Times* ran an excerpt from the news conference that highlighted Echeverría's remarks.[101]

While the US delegation to the UN released a statement a few days later indicating that there had not, in fact, been a change in their position, Echeverría's comments were enough to stir up great controversy in the United States, not least among the business class. The NFTC, representing some six hundred US-based multinational firms, released a statement saying that the charter "would seriously deter if not fully shackle foreign private investment."[102] And even if Kissinger thought that US businessmen were "morons," as he had argued previously, and that their opposition to the charter was misguided, business interests were able to make their voices heard in Washington. Republican senator Charles Percy of Illinois, himself the former head of Bell and Howell Corporation, had argued to Kissinger that if the United States supported the charter, people in his position would face serious consequences from groups like the American Bar Association, the US Chamber of Commerce, and the International Chamber of Commerce, who were all reaching out to Percy to express their strident opposition.[103] Indeed, the American Bar Association had even convened a Subcommittee on Economic Rights and Duties and had already passed a resolution against US support for the charter unless it made explicit reference to established international law.[104] The interests of capital were mobilizing against the Mexican proposal, as they had done so often in the past, and their advocacy now threatened the delicate compromise.

In November, the final deliberations on the charter got underway at the UN General Assembly in New York. While the question of the legal nature of the charter was still unresolved, Castañeda signaled that he was willing to drop the question of the "progressive development of international law," justifying such a decision on the basis of Mexican experience: as the Mexican constitution had required enabling legislation to bring its provisions into operation, so the charter would require, over the coming years, just that sort of international codification; it was not necessary in the main text. With this agenda laid out, Castañeda requested that an accelerated series of meetings on the charter be held to try to reach consensus on a resolution draft.[105] For the next week, a drafting committee met regularly, and new amendments were introduced by various delegations.

If Castañeda hoped that postponement of the legally binding nature of the charter might mollify those who were still critical of the proposal, particularly the United States, this would prove unrealistic. Now that the General Assembly was underway, longtime US negotiators like Schwebel and Maw were joined by none other than Senator Percy—the senator who had been working tirelessly to amplify the voice of the US business community against the charter. This hardened the US stance. Deputy Secretary of State Robert Ingersoll, for example, insisted that it was important for the United States to have some "record of opposition to this for future international law"—thereby defending the status quo against the progressive development Mexico had envisioned.[106] This insistence on the codification of pro-capital international law reflected not only the influence of a long tradition of neoliberal thought, but also a concerted campaign against the emerging ideas of the NIEO by thinkers like Gottfried Haberler and Peter T. Bauer.[107] At a meeting with the Mexican team in Washington, Percy reiterated the emphasis on law, arguing that because the charter purported to replace a long-established body of international law, it would be necessary to explicitly reference it in the text. He fumed at the Mexican team, "Why won't you include a reference to international law?" Mexico's González Gálvez replied with some derision, "Many of the Group of 77 do not believe that there is any international law on the subject."[108]

For his part, Kissinger had come to hope they might find a way for the industrialized countries to simply abstain from the vote. When legal adviser Maw argued that the US business community opposed the charter entirely,

Kissinger was exasperated, reiterating that the vote was more important as a gesture of goodwill toward Mexico than as an actual international agreement. The charter would quickly be forgotten by everyone "except by the bar associations and a few businesses who will distinguish themselves by idiocy, no matter what we do," he argued.[109] Kissinger was growing increasingly angry, in particular, that Percy was jeopardizing the relationship with Mexico, noting that he had lectured Rabasa with "a speech about worldwide free enterprise" the previous day.[110] Kissinger fumed, "We cannot put a senator in charge of a negotiation like this; he doesn't know a damn thing." What's more, Kissinger thought that Schwebel's legalistic nit-picking, a phrase he used a number of times, was counterproductive: "I just don't accept the Legal Division's view. The price we're paying isn't worth it." While he hoped they might still find some compromise language, Kissinger was now fatalistic: "[T]here's no conceivable way we can fix the charter," he lamented.

On December 6, after additional compromise was introduced and after a failed attempt by the European delegations to delay the vote, the committee was set to vote on each individual article of the charter and to take a roll-call vote on the text as it existed.[111] Before the vote, however, US ambassador to the UN John Scali gave a speech to the General Assembly which, while never mentioning the Charter of Economic Rights and Duties of States, harangued the Third World for creating a "tyranny of the majority" and arguing that "paper triumphs are, in the end, expensive even for the victors."[112] This was a preview of the position that the United States would take in the roll-call vote that evening, when 115 countries voted to adopt the text, 10 voted to abstain, and 6 voted against: Denmark, the Federal Republic of Germany, Luxemburg, Belgium, the United Kingdom, and the United States.[113] In explaining the US vote against the charter, Percy acknowledged the tireless work put in by Rabasa and the Mexican delegation but argued that the charter remained "unbalanced" and insisted that it would discourage, rather than encourage, the capital flow needed for development.[114] The charter as written, he noted, was "meaningless without the agreement of countries whose numbers might be small but whose significance in international economic relations and development could hardly be ignored."[115]

Rabasa immediately called Kissinger to lament Scali's speech and the US vote, fuming in disbelief. Kissinger was apologetic and admitted, "assuming you're not going to quote me, I think our people behaved very badly."[116] Rabasa was incensed, saying the reaction in Mexico would be furious and sputtering, "we are all appalled at the outcome and the US comes up with no explanation." At a staff meeting that day, Kissinger laid out his disappointment with the outcome in New York. Rather than compromise, he argued, "Percy worked for a Mexican surrender."[117] He went on, "For three years now the Mexicans have not really carried out their preferences in the Latin America forums because of their relationship with us. We have thrown that, in my view, down the drain for nothing—for some lawyers' quibbles." He fumed that if the charter had been the project of any other Third World country, he wouldn't have expended any US effort to promote it. But he was worried, now, that without the need to keep the United States close for the sake of the charter, "Echeverría, who was always basically a third-worlder, is going to be unloosed." Rather than remaining an ally that sought to temper the most radical demands emanating from Latin America and the Third World, Mexico might instead lend its weight increasingly to efforts against US interests.

The next week, on December 12, the final resolution was brought for a vote. The text reflected a number of the compromises made over the preceding days: there was no mention in the preamble of the "progressive development" of international law, and reference was made there to cooperation based on "mutual advantage and equitable benefits."[118] One of the fundamentals of international economic relations that constituted the basic principles in Chapter I was the "fulfillment in good faith of international obligations," reflecting the language that the Mexican-US compromise had written for the Philippine proposal. But while Article 11—the most controversial, on the regulation of transnational corporations and the right to nationalization—was written to require "appropriate compensation" in the case of nationalization, it also stressed that such compensation would be made by a state "taking into account its relevant laws and regulations and all circumstances that the State considers pertinent." What's more, compensation was to be determined by national laws unless the states involved mutually agreed to seek other means; there was no automatic recourse to "the applicable rules of international law," as had been suggested by the developed countries in the Working Group.

Even with these compromises, however, the charter was a remarkable document. In the midst of a supposedly Cold War that had seen so much bloodshed on the soil of the Third World over economic ideologies, the charter declared the right of countries to choose their economic systems without interference or coercion. The charter recognized the rights of states to regulate foreign investment and transnational corporations according to their domestic needs, to expropriate foreign property, and to associate in primary producers' organizations. It argued that states had a duty to liberalize trade in a nonreciprocal and nondiscriminatory fashion, opening up US markets long protected in order to achieve "a balance more favorable to the developing countries."[119] It argued that it was a duty of states "to eliminate colonialism, *apartheid,* racial discrimination, neo-colonialism and all forms of foreign aggression, occupation and domination, and the economic and social consequences thereof, as a prerequisite for development," and that states that had practiced such policies were economically responsible for restitution. The charter was, then, a distillation of ideas about how to protect economic sovereignty in the context of an increasingly globalized economy—a document that argued not for the retreat from global economic forces, but for a reconfiguration of the rules about representation and redistribution.

Despite the lengths to which the negotiators had gone to come up with language acceptable to all sides and to find the "balance" that the United States and its allies had pushed for, however, the vote in the plenary session went the way it had gone in committee. Japan and a number of the European countries abstained, while the same group—Belgium, Denmark, Luxemburg, West Germany, the United Kingdom, and the United States, who together represented something like 45 percent of global GDP—voted against it. But from Afghanistan to Zambia, 120 countries voted in favor of the charter, and it therefore passed overwhelmingly. Rabasa noted in his remarks after the vote that those voting yes "represented 3.2 billion people, on five continents."[120] The Mexican representatives could now claim that the majority of the world had spoken, and it had done so with Mexico's voice.

CONCLUSION

The struggle to come to a compromise with the United States about the Charter of Economic Rights and Duties of States pointed up the complicated position Mexico now occupied. The long Mexican revolution in development had strengthened the mechanisms for the redistribution of capital from North to South, reinserting Mexico into financial markets and setting the stage to reap the benefits of the 1970s lending boom. As long as the capital flowed, Mexican officials could claim that their struggles for representation within international institutions had afforded them a measure of the economic sovereignty they had long sought. Other Third World countries, however, had not enjoyed the same access, and in pushing to overturn rules that Mexico and its allies had carefully negotiated, they threatened the very structures that buttressed Mexico's success. Mexican officials therefore found themselves in the contradictory position of trying to codify the underlying principles of Mexican developmentalism on the international stage without threatening their own access to foreign credit. In the negotiations spearheaded by Rabasa and Kissinger, it seemed for a time that they had succeeded. The contradiction between Mexico's geopolitical importance in the context of the Cold War and its position as a profitable outlet for US surplus capital, however, provoked serious tension within the ranks of US power—and ultimately the concerns of US investors served to override the countervailing geopolitical considerations. Capital's victory was illustrative of a larger reconfiguration happening within the US state, one that would become more apparent with the election of Ronald Reagan.

Mexican officials continued to believe that their vision for the charter was not only the best way forward for the Third World but was also the key to saving global capitalism from itself. After he left the presidency, Echeverría would insist that his vision for the Charter of Economic Rights and Duties of States was far from a declaration of war against the advanced countries, arguing that the US vote against it made sense in light of the power of their transnational corporations. "I am sure that someday, with a change in the real correlation of global forces," he told a reporter, "the United States will have to accept the charter."[121] For Muñoz Ledo, who had originally conceived of the idea, the charter was a collective expression analogous to class organization: "The developing countries are the workers; the industrialized countries are the capital. It's not about fighting but making good collective contracts, beneficial for both parties." He insisted, "it's not a Marxist thesis, it's another thesis"—a corporatist, developmental project meant not to overthrow global capitalism but to construct the rules within which it could be made to work for all.[122] If the Charter of Economic Rights and Duties of States represented the culmination of Mexico's long revolution in development, however, perhaps it also marked its last gasp. A new international economic order was, indeed, on the horizon, but not the one that Echeverría or Muñoz Ledo had envisioned.

Conclusion

HEGEMONY AND REACTION:
THE UNITED STATES IN OPPOSITION

THOUGH THE CHARTER OF ECONOMIC RIGHTS AND DUTIES OF STATES was approved overwhelmingly by the 1974 General Assembly, the negative votes of the world's industrial powers, including the United States, ensured that the struggle for the charter would continue. Soon after the vote, Mexican president Luis Echeverría began to publicly argue that the countries that had voted against the charter would realize their error and reverse their votes, "once they were convinced that the alternative to a new just international economic order is war."[1] The danger of Cold War rivalry became a theme for the Mexican president, and in nearly every public appearance, he stressed that there were two alternatives for the future of the world: *la carta o la guerra*—the charter or war.[2] In Mexico, the passage of the charter was narrated as a triumph for Echeverría, for Mexico, and for the Third World more broadly. It was hailed in the Mexican congress by deputies of all parties, and dozens of newspaper editorials celebrated its passage as a victory.[3] Echeverría and his subordinates undertook a vast publicity campaign to promote the charter, including the distribution of a forty-page broadsheet with the full text of the agreement and speeches about it, filled with photos of Echeverría speaking to crowds at the UN.[4] The government even printed a postage stamp that celebrated the charter, and distributed five million copies.[5] And officials gave dozens, if not hundreds, of speeches to labor and business groups, schools and universities, and even military battalions. In an address to the electrical workers union, Echeverría argued that the charter would be vital for what he called the "proletarian countries," drawing the parallel between the workers and the *patria*.[6] The organized Third World, he argued, could now collectively bargain for a fairer deal.

The US vote against the charter, however, meant that—as Kissinger had predicted—relations between Mexico and its northern neighbor were now seriously strained. They worsened after a controversial new trade law that bolstered government protections for US exporters took effect in January 1975, corroborating Third World accusations of unilateral, protectionist behavior on the part of the rich countries—a practice that Mexican officials had condemned since at least the 1930s, as the previous chapters have demonstrated.[7] While Mexico's Emilio Rabasa continued to try to get US representatives to reconsider their vote, serious divisions had emerged within the Ford administration concerning how to deal with the charter and with the Third World more broadly. Kissinger's strategy of "constructive appeasement" toward the G77 appeared to lose ground to the neoliberal wing of the administration when Ford appointed Daniel Patrick Moynihan as ambassador to the UN.[8] Moynihan had made his views on the Third World quite clear a few months before with the publication of a provocative essay titled "The United States in Opposition" in *Commentary* magazine.[9] In that piece he decried the "socialist" leanings of the Third World, which he argued operated on a "politics of resentment" and an "economics of envy."[10] Moynihan argued that instead of capitulating to the Third World, as prior administrations had done, it was time to launch a concerted campaign of opposition. Asserting that the multinational corporation was "arguably the most creative international institution of the 20th century," he turned his sights on Mexico and the charter: "It is time, that is, that the American spokesman came to be feared in international forums for the truths he might tell. Mexico, which has grown increasingly competitive in Third World affairs, which took the lead in the Declaration of the Economic Rights and Duties, preaches international equity. Yet it preaches domestic equity also. It could not without some cost expose itself to a repeated inquiry as to the extent of equity within its own borders."[11] The United States, Moynihan urged, should use the bully pulpit to denounce the hypocrisy of the Third World, "to turn their own standards against regimes for the moment too much preoccupied with causing difficulties for others, mainly the United States."[12] If countries like Mexico had long tried to hold the United States accountable to its own promises, Moynihan had now turned the tables.

Although Moynihan was ousted from his position as UN ambassador after little more than six months, he had outlined an enduring new doctrine within US foreign policy circles. Despite the US intransigence, however, Mexican officials continued to promote the charter internationally, and there were some signs they still had room for maneuver within ongoing North-South negotiations, particularly after Jimmy Carter was elected in the United States.[13] When José López Portillo announced his candidacy for the upcoming elections in 1976, he declared that fighting for the charter would be a crucial part of his platform.[14] Later that year, the G77 met in Mexico City for the Conference on Economic Co-operation among Developing Countries, and Echeverría continued to promote the charter. Then, in 1977, the World Bank appointed a group of economists from both the developed and developing worlds to form the Independent Commission on International Development Issues, led by West German chancellor Willy Brandt. After the Brandt Commission released its findings in the 1980 report *North–South: A Programme for Survival*, López Portillo invited the world to a renewed North-South dialogue, at a conference to be held in Cancún.[15]

Planning for the North-South meeting began in November 1980, the very month that Ronald Reagan was elected to the US presidency in a landslide. It was Reagan, therefore, who disembarked Air Force One in Cancún's sweltering autumn heat in late 1981 to share an embrace with Mexican president López Portillo. Reagan's professions of friendship with the leaders of what had come to be called the developing world, however, belied the message he would deliver in Cancún: not only would there be no consideration of any redistribution of global wealth, as the Brandt Commission report had urged the year before, there would be no further "global" negotiations on the matter either.[16] Instead, Reagan reiterated his insistence on the "magic of the marketplace," a refrain he had repeatedly used since taking office, arguing that "massive transfers of wealth" would not "somehow miraculously produce new well-being."[17] The prospect of reordering the global economy to take into consideration the needs of the developing world was all but dead; the "United States in opposition" had won the day. Rather than a new beginning, the North-South conference would mark an end. As López Portillo put it, "tragic paradoxes were raised in Cancún that could not be solved."[18]

THE MEXICAN PARADOX

By the early 1980s, Mexico did not lack for tragic paradoxes. In the early twentieth century, Mexicans had fought a revolution for democracy and against the predations of large landholders and capitalists, foreign and domestic. The revolutionary constitution of 1917 had enshrined a new understanding of property rights, endowing the state with a mandate for the collective well-being of its citizenry. But the postrevolutionary state had built a soft-authoritarian, single-party system whose mandate was to manage a corporatist development project that had become deeply dependent on foreign capital. Even the era of impressively high growth known as the Mexican miracle had produced destabilizing levels of inequality. Echeverría and López Portillo tried to address this inequality by rapidly expanding public spending; when Mexico's business class defeated substantive tax reform, both presidents relied on intensified foreign borrowing to finance government programs.[19] During the 1970s, Mexico took on tens of billions of dollars in new foreign loans, increasing its debt from $4 billion to over $50 billion in a decade. Then, in 1981 alone, as oil prices fell and Mexico's foreign exchange reserves were depleted, the country's foreign debt ballooned from $55 billion to $80 billion.[20]

Though the World Bank warned about Mexico's excessive foreign borrowing, those concerns were brushed aside by both Mexican officials and private lenders seeking profitable outlets for their surplus capital.[21] When Finance Minister Jesús Silva Herzog arrived in Washington in August 1982 to warn that Mexico would be unable to meet its intensifying foreign obligations, however, it was suddenly clear that the Mexican debt had become unsustainable. López Portillo was initially reluctant to seek help from the international financial institutions; reflecting on a painful 1976 currency devaluation at the beginning of his term, the Mexican president insisted, "I came in under the IMF yoke, and I'm not going out under it."[22] But the massive exposure of US banks to Mexican debt meant that a default would be costly not just for Mexico, but for the US-based financial system as a whole. The US government quickly worked with the private banks, the Bank for International Settlements, and the IMF to implement a rescue package, conditional on a painful austerity plan. A last-ditch effort by López Portillo to nationalize the Mexican banks was unsuccessful; Mexico's structural adjustment was underway.[23]

Thus, an unexpected consequence of Mexico's complicated history of interventions in systems of global economic governance was that IFIs like the World Bank and the IMF—the very institutions that Mexico had initially championed as necessary for the redistribution of capital and subsequently defended from the ire of more radical governments, arguing that better representation could solve the Third World's problems—would soon lead a total restructuring of the Mexican economy, bringing the developmental era to an end and marking the neoliberal transition. Of course, IMF prescriptions for the Mexican economy found willing backers among a class of Mexican business leaders that had been skeptical of state intervention for decades, as well as a new generation of government technocrats trained in US economics programs who filled the ranks of the new administration of Miguel de la Madrid.[24] When the World Bank granted Mexico a loan to encourage the liberalization of its trade policy—the first such loan in Bank history—it did so with eager partners in the Mexican state, whose zeal for reform even outstripped Bank recommendations.[25] Further World Bank loans in the 1980s would target the transformation of particular sectors of the Mexican economy for liberalization, and Mexico would finally join the GATT in 1986. While Mexican compliance with IFI conditionality was spotty given political and economic instability in the 1980s, important officials in the Mexican state worked hard to position Mexico as a "model debtor," and the administration of Carlos Salinas moved after 1988 to make permanent the structural transformations that had been supported by World Bank and IMF programs over the preceding years.[26] The institutions for which Mexico had fought as a means to secure its state-led developmental project were now those through which that very project was dismantled.

As the preceding chapters have detailed, this unexpected consequence resulted from Mexico's uneven and complicated path in its decades-long campaign for representation in international economic governance structures, meant to allow Mexico and countries like it to secure the redistribution of capital from North to South. What began as a fight for sovereign equality of states and equal representation in international institutions in the 1920s then heightened into a struggle over access to credit in the 1930s and 1940s, resulting in the creation of the infrastructure of international development as we know it today. While Mexican officials did not get the coordinated, planned international economy that they sought in the 1940s, they did get new institutions through which requests for long-term, productive, investment capital could be made—and fulfilled. Once those institutions began to supply Mexico with capital necessary for its industrialization strategy (thereby signaling Mexico's creditworthiness in global markets), Mexican officials largely abandoned efforts at radical reform during the 1950s and 1960s, arguing that working *within* the existing institutions was preferable to building entirely new ones. That experience then structured Mexico's project of compromise between the US and Third World positions in the 1970s. Such a compromise—between North and South, between producers and consumers, between debtors and creditors, between capital and labor—was meant to both prevent capitalism from succumbing to its contradictions and stave off the threat of revolution that lurked around every Third World corner. Putting their faith repeatedly in the reform of the rules and institutions that governed the global economy, Mexican officials thought a kind of global scaling-up of their own state-developmentalist project would lead the world forward to a fairer future. By the 1980s, however, that very project would be left behind.

LEARNING TO RULE

It is perhaps because of the spectacular collapse of Mexican state-led developmentalism, as the debt crisis gave way to the lost decade, that Mexican contributions to the history of global economic governance have been overlooked. While there were fleeting attempts in the late 1980s to form a debtors' cartel with other Latin American countries and push for a restructuring of the international debt system, neoliberal reformers within Mexico ultimately won the day, overseeing a program of punishing austerity and dizzying liberalization.[27] After the 1980s, Mexico assumed the role of dutiful pupil, as its officials absorbed the neoliberal teachings of the Washington Consensus. As Mexico liberalized its economy, the new, open, outward-facing Mexico was contrasted with the prior era's inward-looking, nationalist project of import substitution; as a result, the conventional wisdom became that, before Echeverría's work on the charter, "Mexico had generally taken a low profile on North-South issues," as one leading scholar put it.[28] As the preceding chapters have shown, however, the historical record flies in the face of this assertion: Mexican officials had repeatedly taken a strong leadership stance on North-South issues from the earliest days of the postrevolutionary state-building project. The assumption that Mexico had always been a dutiful pupil obscured the fact that Mexican experts had in fact had a great deal to teach US and European economic experts at key moments in the twentieth century.

Against an assumption that the United States suddenly emerged as the world's new hegemonic power in 1945 with a set of foolproof, fully formed, and coherent strategies of rule, this book has demonstrated that Mexico's demands, and those of the countries that Mexican officials allied with, structured how US hegemony would come to be exercised. Reading the construction of the twentieth century's most important international institutions "from the outside in" demonstrates that in fact the US officials who designed the postwar multilateral system had been engaging for decades with demands from the poorer, weaker, debtor countries of the world.[29] As Mexican officials and their allies levied repeated criticisms of the US failure to live up to its professed ideals, and as they demanded new institutions and agreements for the redistribution of capital from North to South, US officials would come to understand both the promise and the peril of the multilateral liberal project. The Wilson and Harding administrations were both forced by Mexican officials to face the disjuncture between multilateral legitimacy and unilateral prerogative. That immanent critique contributed directly to Good Neighbor policy making, and later New Deal officials would come to understand their experiments in responding to Latin American demands as a Western Hemisphere laboratory for their global ambitions.

Armed with a reciprocal understanding of the benefits of international financial exchange, Mexican officials forced US experts to take up the IAB project, for example, and thereby laid the foundations for the project of international development that was globalized in the postwar conjuncture. As the United States sought to delineate the rules that would govern new global institutions—from the World Bank and IMF to the UN General Assembly and the ITO—Mexican officials and the countries that rallied to their cause continued to press the case for taking the needs and wishes of the poorer countries seriously. They repeatedly found receptive audiences in the United States, as Northern officials conceded the importance of the development and industrialization of the emergent Third World. One of the central arguments of *Revolution in Development*, therefore, is that we should understand the construction of the international development apparatus at mid-century as the response to a set of sustained demands from below, rather than simply as some brilliant and nefarious imperialist imposition from above. It was through the dynamics of "interactive multiplicity"—variously rejecting, deflecting, and co-opting a series of demands made by Mexico and its allies in the nascent Third World—that the United States came to understand international development as a technology of power.[30] Rather than overseeing a hegemony constructed from the top down, it was through this contestation that the United States *learned* to rule.

The story told in these pages therefore reinforces an understanding of hegemony "not as a finished and monolithic ideological formation but as a problematic, contested, political process of domination and struggle."[31]

Highlighting that struggle requires reading the archives of US power both against the grain and in conjunction with the sources of the would-be dominated. Reading the Southern archival record against the Northern condescension of posterity reveals precisely the problematic and contested nature of the US rise to hegemony. Mexican consent to the US hegemonic project was not a given, even if some Northern officials hoped that countries like Mexico were there only to "sign in the place for the signature." The consent of countries like Mexico had to be won through a complicated process of struggle, in which the United States was forced to make substantive concessions to the Mexican vision for the world. Further, consent could easily be lost again. This book therefore challenges a conventional understanding of the history of global economic governance as one in which powerful states acted, and less powerful ones reacted. In fact, even the development of the ideology of the "United States in opposition" should be seen as a reaction by the declining hegemon to the conditions of that decline—the loss of consent of the Third World. As the United States turned away from the multilateral order it had itself designed, convinced that the UN was no longer a useful instrument of its hegemony, it did so in reaction to demands levied by Mexico and its Third World counterparts.[32] In *Revolution in Development*, then, we get a new angle of vision on the US rise to power: one in which Mexico's demands, and sustained campaigns to organize like-minded Third World actors to press their cause, structured the contours of legitimacy within which the United States sought to govern the global economy.

LESSONS

This new angle of vision allows us to see how a country like Mexico could have mattered to the governance of the global economy, providing a perspective that attempts to decenter an analytic focus on the Global North. While specific historical circumstances allowed Mexico to assume a particular role in the story told here, methodologically, such a perspective could be replicated for other Global South cases, and it is my hope that future scholars will take up the framework developed here to examine how this story might be different if told, for example, from Brazil or from India. The Mexican angle of vision is just one among many possible ways to approach the governance of the global economy "from the outside in." Particularly as scholars now seek to understand the potentialities for South-South cooperation, there are important lessons to be learned from overlooked earlier moments when the countries of the Global South organized to fight for their demands. But we should read those lessons as much for their possibilities as for their limits.

Ultimately, uncovering the history of Mexican interventions in crucial debates over global economic governance reveals the key constraints to some of the twentieth century's most important campaigns for international economic justice. It would be naive to take the position that Mexican officials themselves wanted to promote—the position illustrated on the cover of this book, for example—imagining a noble Mexican state seizing the revolutionary legacy to lead the world forward toward peace and prosperity, through the signing of international agreements. It might be tempting to imagine the Mexican actors in this book, having been written out of conventional histories based on Northern perspectives, as heroes of a Global South struggle for a fairer world order. But a careful reading of the historical record reveals a much more complicated history, one that troubles a simple normative understanding of heroic resistance from below. After all, the Mexican officials whose actions are traced here were representatives of an increasingly authoritarian, single-party, corporatist state, one that was born of violent struggle between agrarian leaders and liberal generals and that did not hesitate, at various points in its postrevolutionary history, to use force to suppress dissent. While the Mexican postrevolutionary state was deeply shaped by the ongoing struggles of workers and peasants—who among other achievements won a constitution that recognized a wide range of social and economic rights—the projects traced in this book were ultimately tied to the development of a Mexican vision for *capitalist* progress.

Mexico's revolution in development did not seek to overturn the global capitalist order, but rather to rewrite the rules within which global capitalism functioned, so that it might be made to work not just for the rich countries but also for poor ones. This ideology was distilled clearly in 1948 by Mexico's Jesús Reyes Heroles, then a young academic and adviser to the ministry of labor, who would go on to a long political career, including being an influential leader of the PRI. Reviewing the Soviet ideology of self-sufficiency, on the one hand, and the market-oriented theories of Friedrich Hayek and Ludwig Von Mises, on the other, he argued for a "third way" out of the domestic and international contradictions that capitalism had engendered thus far.[33] He summarized: "The technological potential of capitalism and the current methods of international economic planning make possible a global distribution of industrial production that creates complementary results among countries, and it is from this principle that we deduce that it is perfectly feasible, without disrupting substantially the global economic structure, to achieve the industrial development of backward countries."[34] Mexico's "third way" was of course a vision shared widely throughout the world, one that informed the ideology of welfare states in Europe as well as developmental states in Africa, in Asia, and throughout the Americas—underpinning what Giovanni Arrighi called the "developmentalist illusion."[35] That is, in important ways, this faith in a third way represents the undying dream of international development itself: that the productive power of global capitalism can be harnessed to a regime of equity, that the right rules and regulations can overcome capitalism's contradictions.

But even as they sought to avoid "disrupting substantially the global economic structure" and to harness the productive power of capitalism, Mexico's most important campaigns were in fact blocked by the organized power of capital in the Global North. The creation of the IAB, the substantial reforms to the ITO, and the Charter of Economic Rights and Duties of States were all actually accepted by US *government* officials who recognized the logic of Mexican and allied demands, only to be effectively vetoed by powerful organizations like the National Foreign Trade Council and the National Association of Manufacturers. That is, despite the Mexican faith that global capitalism could be constrained to create "complementary results" in North and South, organized capitalist interests and their allies in Congress and the executive branch in the United States repeatedly blocked Mexico's most substantial reforms, while allowing US planners to co-opt demands that did not interfere too much with the free functioning of US trade and finance. Mexico's revolution in development was based in an abiding faith that by organizing the debtor countries of the world into a kind of trade union of the poor nations, they could collectively rewrite the rules governing the global economy to benefit rich and poor, creditor and debtor, North and South alike. As today's projects of South-South cooperation and reform of international financial institutions resurrect this faith, Mexico's revolution in development should serve as a cautionary tale.

ACKNOWLEDGMENTS

Acknowledgments frequently reveal the dialectic between structure and contingency, and mine are no different. This book was certainly written in circumstances existing already, given and transmitted from the past, but was shaped in innumerable ways by the people whose paths I crossed along the way. Earliest thanks go to the late Patricia Bontempi, who was hired to teach Spanish for the first time ever at my tiny public high school in far northern New Hampshire. She not only taught me the Spanish language and my first lessons in Latin American history; she provided resources my own family didn't have to take me on my first trip to New York City to interview at colleges and took me abroad, to Spain, for the first time. My entire subsequent career can be traced to her classroom, and I am deeply grateful for her teachings. Thanks to Señora Bontempi and the Pell Grant program, I ended up at Barnard College, where Elisabeth Jay Friedman taught me about Latin American politics and social movements and put up with my teenage angst. I am profoundly lucky to still call her a mentor. With the financial support of a Truman Scholarship, I enrolled at Columbia School of International and Public Affairs and learned a great deal about how I didn't want to study the world. I was fortunate, however, to travel to Cuba and El Salvador to study, and to have the guidance of Eric Hershberg, who has been a mentor not only at Columbia but later at the Social Science Research Council and then at the North American Congress on Latin America (NACLA) and beyond. My five years as the executive director at NACLA were foundational to my intellectual development, not least because of the incredible community of scholars I was introduced to, including those people who would go on to be my mentors at New York University. Thank you to everyone who has sustained NACLA and kept it alive for all these years.

Research for this project was supported not only by the Graduate School of Arts and Sciences and Department of History at NYU, but also by the Barnard College Alumnae Association, the Social Science Research Council, the History Project of Harvard University and the Institute for New Economic Thinking, the Society for Historians of American Foreign Relations, the American Council of Learned Societies and the Mellon Foundation, the Conference on Latin American History, and a Frances R. Lax Award for Faculty Development at Rowan University. Crucial writing and research time was afforded by a fellowship from the Weatherhead Initiative on Global History at Harvard University. I am grateful for the generosity of these institutions. At Johns Hopkins University, Terri Thomas and Jessie Albee have provided invaluable support for both my research and teaching, for which I owe them deep thanks.

Tremendous thanks are also due to the archivists and librarians who aided in compiling the evidentiary base for this book. My sincere gratitude to the staff at the Archivo Histórico Genaro Estrada at the Secretaría de Relaciones Exteriores de México, especially Jorge Fuentes, Agustín Colín Huitron, and Mercedes de Vega, and to staff at the Colegio de México, especially Citlalitl Nares Ramos and Graciela Salazar in Víctor Urquidi's office. Additionally, many patient and knowledgeable archivists and librarians aided in my research at the Biblioteca Lerdo de Tejada, the Centro de Estudios de Historia de México, the Archivo General de la Nación, the National Archives and Records Administration in College Park, the National Archives of the United Kingdom, and the League of Nations Archives in Geneva, as well as at the FDR Library, the University of Texas Benson Latin American Collection, the Seeley G. Mudd Manuscript Library at Princeton, and the libraries of Columbia and Harvard Universities. In addition, many thanks to Raúl Gutiérrez Lombardo at the Centro de Estudios Filosóficos Políticos y Sociales Vicente Lombardo Toledano in Mexico City for his permission to use the image that graces the cover, to Daniela Spenser for the introduction, and to Joshua Everett at the Johns Hopkins libraries for his assistance in tracking down the physical copy of the magazine *Futuro* from which it is taken. I am also grateful for the careful research assistance of Diana Ávila Hernández in Mexico City.

My friends, colleagues, and comrades in graduate school were an incredible scholarly and activist community who shaped this work in so many ways. Extra thanks go to my cohort-mate and longtime collaborator Josh Frens-String, who has been an intellectual interlocutor from the first, as well as his partner Abby Weitzman. So grateful to count you as family. Deep thanks to my comrades from history, sociology, and American studies at NYU for the long nights in the library, at the bar, and at the bargaining table: Eman Abdelhadi, Jennifer Adair, Hillary Angelo and Ray Daniels, A.J. Bauer, Natalie Blum-Ross, Michelle Chase, Greg and Laura Childs, Daniel Aldana Cohen, Andy Cornell, Jeanette Estruth, Thomas Fleischman, Joan Flores, Eva Hageman, Anasa Hicks, Aaron Jakes, Ebony Jones, David Klassen and Boyda Johnstone, Sara Kozameh, Emma Kreyche and James Gatherer, Marisol LeBrón and Jenny Kelly, Tyesha Maddox, Alex Manevitz, Aldo Marchesi, Mike McCarthy, Liz Mesok, Max Mishler, Tej Nagaraja, Manijeh Nasrabadi and Ashley Dawson, Rachel Nolan, Michelle O'Brien, Amaka Okechukwu and Matt Birkhold, Claire Payton and Jonathan Katz, Nathalie Pierre, Natasha Raheja, Gabriel Rocha and Miranda Firestone, Daniel Rodríguez and Susan Rohwer, Shelly Ronen, Zach Schwartz-Weinstein, Samantha Seeley, Ernesto Semán, Martin Sivak, Marcio Siwi, Anna Skarpelis, Carmen Solíz, Jonathan Michael Square, Shauna Sweeny, Geoff Traugh, Nantina Vgontzas, Katy Walker and Jen Wilson, David Waschsmuth and Esme Webb, Beatrice Wayne, and Natan Zeichner. What a privilege to have found myself in graduate school alongside all of you. In addition, the Latin Americanist crew from Columbia University and Yale University played a huge role in my intellectual formation. Thanks especially to Yesenia Barragan and Mark Bray, Manuel Bautista, Mike Bustamante, Fredy González, Taylor Jardno, Christine Mathias, Rachel Newman, and Elizabeth Schwall. Among my farther-flung colleagues and conference pals, I'd like to especially thank Aaron Benanav, Danny Bessner, George Ciccariello-Maher, Vanessa Freije, Rebecca Herman Weber, Daniel Immerwahr, Jamie Martin, Nick Mitchell, Tore Olsson, Amy Offner, Thea Riofrancos, David Stein, Chris Taylor, and Simon Toner for their encouragement and friendship through the long process of research and writing.

A special word of thanks is due to my friends in the ciudad antes conocido como el D.F., especially Kimberly Nolan, who taught me everything I know about rifando y controlando. I was lucky too, to overlap there with Adam Goodman and Hilda Vázquez, who have become forever friends. Thanks also to my Narvarte crew, especially Gonzalo and Andrés, and to Tiana for the introduction, and to toda la banda chilanga: Yecatl, Fani, Violeta, Cheivi, Luis, Kuble, Blanca, Nadia, Tío, Dave, Abraham, Benjamin, and Roger, gracias a todos por los ensayos sin luz en Iztapalapa, las tocadas interminables en el Centro Histórico, y los mezcales inacapables en Coyoacán. In London, thanks to David Madden and Rachel Gurstein for making their home such a sanctuary at a crucial moment of writing, and endless thanks to the UK punks who put us up, took us in, and showed us around on many research trips: Ola, Dana, Emmanuel, Nani, Carlos, Clint (on his sojourns), Louis, Elissa, Ralph, Belma, Ralf, and most of all Paco. Que viva la vida comunale, friends.

My mentors among the faculty at NYU, Yale, and Columbia taught me a great deal about the responsibilities of the scholar, not only to each other and our students but to the broader world. I am grateful for the mentorship during graduate school of Karl Appuhn, Sinclair Thompson, Gil Joseph and the late Patricia Pessar, John Coatsworth, Manu Goswami, Ada Ferrer, the late and dearly missed Marilyn Young, Steven Hahn, Alejandro Velasco, Molly Nolan, Jennifer Morgan, Neil Brenner, Andrew Ross, and Nikhil Pal Singh. My greatest scholarly debts are to the two people to whom I always turn for advice, Barbara Weinstein and Greg Grandin. Barbara's deep wisdom is matched only by her endless fount of encouragement. When I returned from my dissertation research in Mexico and asked her for writing advice, she said something that has stuck in my head ever since: "You have to ask yourself, as you write every sentence and paragraph: Why does anyone have to know this?" Barbara's rare combination of practicality and positivity has been a sustaining force for so many of us, and I am endlessly grateful to her. Perhaps my deepest intellectual debt is to Greg Grandin, who introduced me to the study of history. While I will never match his level of productivity, I strive to emulate his approach to scholarship, rooted in asking questions that matter not just in the literature but in the world. His unflagging support has been invaluable in this process, and I am eternally grateful for his faith in my capacity as a scholar.

In various conferences, seminars, and less structured discussions, I've shared the ideas in this book with Alex Aviña, Sara Babb, Jennifer Bair, Johanna Bockman, Barry Carr, Linda Hall, Christina Heatherton, Luis Herrán Ávila, Fabián Herrera León, Amie Kiddle, Alan Knight, Susan Gauss, Julian Go, Paul Kramer, Carlos Marichal, Noel Maurer, Dawn Paley, Vanni Pettinà, Vijay Prashad, Louise Walker, Andrew Zimmerman, and Eric Zolov, all great sources of inspiration, healthy skepticism, and advice. In addition, William Booth kindly shared some of his research on the Mexican Left with me. Eric Helleiner has been an endlessly gracious interlocutor, always sharing his work, providing constructive feedback, and allowing me to ride his intellectual coattails. Jürgen Buchenau, Thomas Field, and two other anonymous reviewers provided invaluable feedback on the manuscript, as did Margaret Chowning, and I am deeply grateful for their careful engagement. I have also been lucky to count on the friendship and intellectual engagement of Micol Seigel and the entire community of the Tepoztlán Institute for the Transnational History of the Americas. It was at Tepoz that I met the incomparable Kate Marshall for the first time and pitched her the idea for this book, and she has been a source of endless guidance and incredible patience throughout this long process. I owe my deep thanks to her and her staff, especially Enrique Ochoa-Kaup, at University of California Press. Additional thanks go to my developmental editor, Megan Pugh, who helped me trim an unwieldy mess of a manuscript into the book I wanted to write.

At Rowan University, I was welcomed and mentored by Bill Carrigan and Emily Blanck, Corey Blake, Kelly Duke-Bryant, Chanel Rose, James Heinzen, and Ed Kazarian, and I'm lucky to count them as colleagues. At Harvard, I was grateful for the support of Sven Beckert, as well as for the clear-eyed vision of Walter Johnson and Kirsten Weld and the comradeship of Quinn Slobodian. Thank you also to Naghmeh Sohrabi and Greg Childs at Brandeis for allowing me to participate in the Mellon-Sawyer Seminar in Comparative Revolutions. In the Baltimore School, one of the most important sites for learning I've encountered, my deep gratitude goes to my teachers Lester Spence, Joshua Clark Davis, Jessica Douglas, Kate Drabinski, John Duda, Nicole Fabricant, Keegan Finberg, Sara Fouts, Rob Helfenbein, Andy Hines, Ailish Hopper, Nicole King, Brandon Soderberg, Steph Saxton, and Baynard Woods. I'm honored to learn with you.

At Johns Hopkins, special thanks goes to my Latin Americanist co-conspirators, especially Casey Lurtz and James Lynch, Alessandro Angelini and Nicole Labruto, Bécquer Seguín and Ilil Benjamin, as well as Elizabeth O'Brien, Debbie Poole,

Flavia de Azeredo-Cerqueira, Valeria Procupez, and Madga von der Heydt-Coca. Many thanks to the happy hour crew, without whom these first few years would have been unthinkable: Megan and Erem, Scot, Tom and Canay, Kyle, Carsten and Jess, Elanor and Patrick, Johannes and Zofia, Anicia and Steve, thanks for taking me in. The brilliant graduate students at Johns Hopkins have already taught me so much. Thanks to the participants of the Arrighi Seminar for reading the manuscript and offering your detailed feedback, and special thanks especially to Corey Payne, who read multiple drafts, and Luis Rodríguez, who helped me organize so much of my thinking about where this work fits across fields. A remarkable group of Hopkins faculty have held real interdisciplinary space for me: Bentley Allen, Jane Bennett, P.J. Brendese, Sam Chambers, Erin Chung, Nathan Connolly and Shani Mott, Jan Dutkewicz, François Furstenberg, Katie Hindmarch-Watson, Larry Jackson, Jessica Marie Johnson, Martha Jones and Jean Hebrard, Michael Kwass, Syd Morgan, Danny Scholzman, Todd Shepard, Robbie Shilliam, Lester Spence, and Vesla Weaver have all accepted me into their scholarly conversations as an equal. Thank you all. I am, of course, endlessly grateful to my colleagues in sociology, especially Rina Agarwala, Emily Agree, Joel Andreas, Katrina Bell McDonald, Ryan Calder, Stefanie Deluca, Ho-Fung Hung, Mike Levien, and Sasha White for their support and encouragement. I have no idea how to begin to repay the debt I owe Beverly Silver. She has deeply shaped my thinking in this book and beyond, and I'm so grateful for her mentorship and guidance.

Most important through these last few years, of course, has been my family, biological and intentional. My mother, Gail, was my first role model and made me in innumerable ways into the person I am. After she died during my second year of graduate school, I leaned hard on those who would bear my weight, and I thank so many for carrying me, in ways big and small. I am grateful to my brother Dan for his love, for his brilliance, and for bringing his giant brood into my life. I owe a great deal to mother's siblings, Rena, Beth, Meg, and John Gospodarek, and their families—without you all I would not have made it through those months and these years. I also want to thank Jane Marie Schrader for providing a home I can always turn to, and the late Mike Stoddard for sharing his wisdom and affection with me. He is greatly missed. My definition of family, though, encompasses a much broader set of people than those held close by blood or law, and centers especially on those who refuse to leave you behind even at your most broken. Matt Smith and Angela Gelso have provided endless sustenance. Margaret Wiatrowski and Anne Eller will always pick right back up with me, no matter how much time has elapsed. I'm so glad to call Holly Danzeisen, Erin Tomlinson, Renata Segura, Amy Withers, Kate Levitt, and Nick Wunder my council family. David and Libby McComb have been there, unquestioningly, whenever I needed them, to share a coffee or a meal or a stick-and-poke tattoo. Thera Webb stuck around when it might have been easier not to, and I hope she knows how much I appreciate it. Above all, Casey Hickey,

Shannon Kearns, and Jill Hubley have been the women who have long grounded me and shaped me into the person I am, over many years and through many bad haircuts. I am endlessly grateful to them and to Ian, John, Elliot, Stephen and Mary, and Ramona, for welcoming me into their families, as well.

The center of my chosen family is Stuart Schrader, whose quiet kindness and deep brilliance have taught me a way of being in the world that seemed impossible before him. His patience has been inexhaustible, and I know that I have tried it. Stuart is my sharpest editor, my most important intellectual interlocutor, and my partner in every sense. I have learned more from him than any other scholar, as we have turned over our ideas together, sharpening their dull edges before charging out into the world with them. In moments of unsteadiness, in Brooklyn and Baltimore, Buenos Aires and Barcelona, I have been so lucky to reach out my hand and find his there. As we face a deeply uncertain future in which our itinerant life has come to a sudden and disquieting stillness, I am so grateful to ground myself in the stability of his presence, and to fight alongside him as we struggle toward the horizon of justice. Pa'lante.

NOTES

INTRODUCTION

1. Though imperfect approximations for formations that have changed over time, this book uses Global North and Northern to refer to the United States and Europe, and Global South and Southern to refer to the regions of Africa, Asia, and Latin America, which were previously called the Third World or the developing countries. A North-South distinction is not simply a "matter of latitude," as some have argued, but a historically specific designation that emerged in a particular moment of contention; Chase-Dunn et al., "Democratic Global Governance," 45. For critical take on the term, see Palomino, "On the Disadvantages of 'Global South' for Latin American Studies." When possible, I try to avoid anachronisms, and in the empirical chapters that follow I use the terms employed by historical actors themselves, which included classifying countries that today make up the Global South as the smaller, weaker, poor, debtor, or formerly colonized countries.

2. On the pervasiveness of the developmentalist imaginary, see María Josefina Saldaña-Portillo, *The Revolutionary Imagination in the Americas.*

3. This requires recognizing "the contemporary social world [as] a specific configuration produced by historical struggle." Calhoun, "Explanation in Historical Sociology," 849–50.

4. See the review of this literature in Helleiner, *Forgotten Foundations of Bretton Woods*, 4–9. Exemplary is Gardner, *Sterling-Dollar Diplomacy.*

5. Eady to Padmore, January 12, 1944, The National Archives of the United Kingdom (TNA), Records of the Treasury, Papers of Lord Keynes, T247/27.

6. Arrighi et al., "Geopolitics and High Finance," 86.

7. Wallerstein, "New World Disorder," 175. Later, Chase Dunn et al., would argue that "semiperipheral development has historically played a large role in innovating economic and political systems and changing the world order," but they stress specifically the "communist states." Chase-Dunn et al., "Democratic Global Governance," 45–46.

8. For Arrighi and Silver, these interests represent distinct "angles of vision" for analyzing hegemonic transition. The approach followed in this book fleshes out another angle of vision on the construction of US postwar hegemony—that of relations with the weaker states. See Arrighi and Silver, *Chaos and Governance in the Modern World System*, 35.

9. Murphy, *International Organization and Industrial Change*, 166–68.

10. Cox, *Production, Power, and World Order*, 209–14.

11. Cox, *Production, Power, and World Order*, 260.

12. The dominance of such a perspective in the study of international political economy has only recently been challenged by calls to "globalize" its perspectives and objects of study. See, for example, Tussie and Riggirozzi, "A Global Conversation"; Cohen, *Advanced Introduction to International Political Economy*; Phillips, *Globalizing International Political Economy*; and Tickner, "Hearing Latin American Voices in International Relations Studies."

13. It should be noted that Bull considered a much longer historical trajectory for the struggle against "Western dominance," including the long Latin American histories of anti-interventionism. Bull, "Revolt Against the West," 217–28.

14. Krasner, *Structural Conflict*, 14–16. (Though he first introduced the concept in "Transforming International Regimes.") Of course, Third World attempts to change the rules came in response to the US decision to unilaterally rewrite those rules in the context of the crisis of the 1970s. See Arrighi, Silver, and Brewer, "Industrial Convergence, Globalization, and the Persistence of the North-South Divide," 21.

15. Cox, "Crisis of World Order and the Problem of International Organization in the 1980s," 373.

16. Commission on Global Governance, *Our Global Neighbourhood*; and Hewson and Sinclair, *Approaches to Global Governance Theory*.

17. Nye, "Globalization's Democratic Deficit," 2–6.

18. Glenn, "Global Governance and the Democratic Deficit."

19. Gray and Gills, "South–South Cooperation and the Rise of the Global South." See also Hopewell, *Breaking the WTO*.

20. See, for example, Acharya, "Studying the Bandung Conference from a Global IR Perspective"; Arrighi and Zhang, "Beyond the Washington Consensus"; Lee, *Making a World after Empire*; and Hardt, "Porto Alegre."

21. Toye and Toye, *UN and Global Political Economy*. On international organizations as bureaucracies, see Barnett and Finnemore, "Politics, Power, and Pathologies of International Organizations."

22. Helleiner, *Forgotten Foundations of Bretton Woods*; Helleiner, "Sun Yat-Sen as a Pioneer of International Development"; and Helleiner and Rosales, "Peripheral Thoughts for International Political Economy."

23. Manela, *Wilsonian Moment*, 6. For a similar perspective, see Garavini, *After Empires*. For histories written from a more traditional Northern frame, see Sluga and Clavin, *Internationalisms*; Pedersen, *Guardians*; Sluga, *Internationalism in the Age of Nationalism*; Clavin, *Securing the World Economy*; Mazower, *Governing the*

World; Mazower, *No Enchanted Palace*; and Iriye, *Global Community*, among others.

24. Acharya, "'Idea-Shift,'" 1160.

25. Getachew, *Worldmaking after Empire*.

26. Roseberry, "Hegemony and the Language of Contention," 360.

27. Gramsci, *Selections from the Prison Notebooks of Antonio Gramsci*, 52.

28. Go and Lawson, "For a Global Historical Sociology," 23–28.

29. Roseberry, "Hegemony and the Language of Contention," 360.

30. On revolutionary nationalism, see Smith, *United States and Revolutionary Nationalism in Mexico*; Brading, *Origins of Mexican Nationalism*; Gómez Villanueva, *Nacionalismo revolucionario*; and Meyer, *México para los mexicanos*, among many others. As Susan Gauss points out, of course, the ideological container of economic nationalism can actually be filled with quite divergent economic policies. See Gauss, "Politics of Economic Nationalism in Postrevolutionary Mexico."

31. Knight, "Ideology of the Mexican Revolution, 1910–40," 102.

32. Smith, *American Empire*, 114. Indeed, as Glenda Sluga points out, nationalism and internationalism have been "twinned ideologies" since the invention of "the international" in the late eighteenth century. Sluga, *Internationalism in the Age of Nationalism*, 3.

33. Smith, *United States and Revolutionary Nationalism in Mexico*, x. Of course, a similar argument might be made about the Haitian Revolution, in the context of a system of slavery intimately linked to the development of global capitalism. My thanks to Robbie Shilliam for this insight. See Beckles, "Capitalism, Slavery and Caribbean Modernity"; and Shilliam, "What the Haitian Revolution Might Tell Us about Development, Security, and the Politics of Race."

34. Smith, *United States and Revolutionary Nationalism in Mexico*, 83.

35. Grandin, "Liberal Traditions in the Americas," 75.

36. The field of Mexican foreign relations history is vast. This book draws especially from Zolov, *Last Good Neighbor*; Kiddle, *Mexico's Relations with Latin America during the Cárdenas Era*; Keller, *Mexico's Cold War*; Lajous, *Historia mínima de las relaciones exteriores de México*; Gómez Villanueva, *Nacionalismo revolucionario*; Herrera León, "México en la Sociedad de Naciones"; Pellicer de Brody, *México y el mundo*; Yankelevich, *La Revolución Mexicana en América Latina*; Spenser, *Impossible Triangle*; Schuler, *Mexico between Hitler and Roosevelt*; Hall, *Oil, Banks, and Politics*; Niblo, *War, Diplomacy, and Development*; Knight, *U.S.–Mexican Relations, 1910–1940*; Katz, *The Secret War in Mexico*; Gilderhus, *Diplomacy and Revolution*; Smith, *United States and Revolutionary Nationalism in Mexico*.

37. Thornton, "A Mexican International Economic Order?," 393.

38. The question of when the revolution "ended" and therefore how to date the emergence of a "postrevolutionary" state has been the subject of endless debate. For a summary, see Beezley, "Reflections on the Historiography of Twentieth-Century Mexico." Other scholars mark the transition in 1937–38, as mentioned in Knight,

"The End of the Mexican Revolution?" See, for example, Hamilton, *Limits of State Autonomy*.

39. On the development of an official nationalism, see Benjamin, *La Revolución*. On national-level processes of Mexican state formation (in addition to innumerable studies at the regional level of the *patria chica*), see Gillingham and Smith, *Dictablanda*; Jones, *War Has Brought Peace to Mexico*; Morton, *Revolution and State in Modern Mexico*; Meyer, *México para los mexicanos*; Gauss, *Made in Mexico*; Buchenau, *Last Caudillo*; Buchenau, *Plutarco Elías Calles and the Mexican Revolution*; Niblo, *Mexico in the 1940s*; López Villafañe, *La formación del sistema político mexicano*; Middlebrook, *Paradox of Revolution*; Aguilar Camín and Meyer, *In the Shadow of the Mexican Revolution*; Carr, *Marxism and Communism in Twentieth-Century Mexico*; Hamilton, *Limits of State Autonomy*; Lajous, *Los orígenes del partido único en México*; and Córdova, *La formación del poder político en México*, among others.

40. See Camp, "The Cabinet and the Ténico in Mexico and the United States"; and Babb, *Managing Mexico*.

41. John Dwyer has claimed that "a nation's elite can also be understood as subalterns when seeking to advance their interests against more-powerful international actors." Dwyer, *Agrarian Dispute*, 269. While I do not share this characterization, I do wish to highlight the power imbalance that Mexican officials faced in international fora.

42. On the study of elites, see Eley, "No Need to Choose," as well as Stern, "Between Tragedy and Promise."

43. On gender and global financial politics, see Marshall, "Gender Tropes and Colonial Discourses in the Turbulence of Global Finance."

44. My thinking follows Walter Johnson in a rejection of the epistemological individualism of the notion of agency in historical scholarship. Johnson, "On Agency."

45. Marx, "Eighteenth Brumaire of Louis Bonaparte."

46. See, for example, Monticelli, *Reforming Global Economic Governance*.

47. United States Department of State, *Proceedings and Documents, United Nations Monetary and Financial Conference*, 2:1179.

CHAPTER ONE. RECOGNITION AND REPRESENTATION

1. McCaa, "Missing Millions."

2. Dios Bojórquez, *Crónica del constituyente*, 160; and Niemeyer, *Revolution at Querétaro*, 139.

3. Grandin, "Liberal Traditions in the Americas," 75.

4. Constitution of Mexico, Article 27, in Joseph and Henderson, *Mexico Reader*, 398–401.

5. See, for example, "Protests to Mexico over Constitution," *New York Times*, January 26, 1917.

6. "Don Venustiano Carranza, al abrir el Congreso de sus sesiones ordinarias el 10. de septiembre de 1918," in México, XLVI Legislatura de la Cámara de Diputados, *Los presidentes de México ante la Nación*.

7. Buchenau, *In the Shadow of the Giant*, 27. On Porfirian foreign policy more broadly, see Lajous, *La política exterior del Porfiriato*.

8. The universal aspirations of the revolution had long been a theme for Carranza. See "Contestación del C. Primer Jefe," December 26, 1915, Centro de Estudios de Historia de México (CEHM), Fondo Venustiano Carranza (FVC), XXI 64/7058.

9. Manero, *México y la solidaridad americana* and Galindo, *La doctrina Carranza y el acercamiento indo-latino*. See also Yankelevich, "En la retaguardia de la revolución mexicana."

10. See Manela, *Wilsonian Moment*, 12.

11. Secretaría de Relaciones Exteriores (SRE) a Dejean, November 30, 1918, AHSREM, L-E-911; and Pani, *Mi contribución al nuevo régimen*, 250.

12. "To Oppose Alien Rights in Mexico," *New York Times*, January 23, 1919.

13. Pani's letters to Carranza are collected in Pani, *Cuestiones diversas, contenidas en 44 cartas al presidente Carranza*. Drafts and originals can be found in AHSREM, Fondo Embajada de México en Francia, Leg. XC, N 1–1458 and XC, N 2–1459.

14. Pani, *Mi contribución al nuevo régimen*, 251.

15. Kelley, *Bishop Jots It Down*; and Edward Mandell House Papers, Yale University Library, Series II, Diaries, vol. 7, May 3, 1919.

16. For León de la Barra's organizing, see, for example, León de la Barra a Eugenio Rascon, February 20, 1919, CEHM, Manuscritos de Francisco León de la Barra (FLdlB), carp. 9, leg.. 955. See also Henderson, *In the Absence of Don Porfirio*.

17. House Papers, Series II, Diaries, vol. 6, December 8, 1918, 56; León de la Barra a Tomas MacManus, December 18, 1918, CEHM, FLdlB, carp. 9, leg. 850; León de la Barra a Garcia Naranjo, January 19, 1919, CEHM, FLdlB, carp. 9, leg. 890; and Pani a Carranza, February 13, 1919, in Pani, *Cuestiones diversas*, 19.

18. Cover attachment to telegram, Mr. Cummins to Foreign Office, January 10, 1919, National Archives of the United Kingdom (TNA): Foreign Office Records (FO) 371/3826.

19. "Want Peace Parley to Aid in Mexico," *New York Times*, January 22, 1919; Hall, *Oil, Banks, and Politics*, 18.

20. For a survey of some of the legal discussions regarding the Monroe Doctrine in the period, see Scarfi, "In the Name of the Americas."

21. Hunter Miller, *Drafting of the Covenant*, 444, 459.

22. *El Pueblo* (México, D.F.), June 29, 1918; National Archives and Records Administration (NARA), RG 165, 10640/615. See also Gilderhus, "Wilson, Carranza, and the Monroe Doctrine."

23. SRE memorandum para la prensa, April 22, 1919, AHSREM, L-E-1845(1); and Bonillas a Polk, April 25, 1919, AHSREM, Fondo Embajada de México en las Estados Unidos (EMBEUA), 612/20.

24. Robert H. Murray, Telegram to the New York *World*, May 8, 1919, in *FRUS 1919*, 2:547.

25. Translation in Summerlin to Secretary of State, September 3, 1919, in *FRUS 1919*, 2:542.

26. Murray to the New York *World*, May 8, 1919, in *FRUS 1919*, 2:547.

27. Translation in Summerlin to Secretary of State, September 3, 1919, in *FRUS 1919*, 2:542. This is, of course, not dissimilar to the "Díaz Doctrine," described by Jürgen Buchenau as a belief that the Monroe Doctrine should be enforced multilaterally by all the countries of the Western Hemisphere. See Buchenau, *In the Shadow of the Giant*, 42–43.

28. Brown to Hughes, October 24, 1921, NARA, RG 56, State Department Decimal File (SDDF), Files Relating to the Monroe Doctrine, 710.11/539. See also Brown, "Fundamentals in the Foreign Policy of the United States."

29. Munro to Hughes, December 1, 1921, NARA, RG 56, SDDF 710.11/539.

30. See Gilderhus, *Diplomacy and Revolution*, 106–16.

31. Hall, *Oil, Banks, and Politics*, 54–59.

32. Hall, *Oil, Banks, and Politics*, 140–41.

33. Inman, *Inter-American Conferences*, 101; and Armendáriz del Castillo a Pani, June 2, 1923, AHSREM, L-E-191.

34. Inman, *Inter-American Conferences*, 104.

35. On the Santiago conference generally, see Salceda Olivares, "México y la V conferencia panamericana"; and Ramos, "Impact of the Mexican Revolution in InterAmerican Politics."

36. John Bassett Moore, "American Nations to Hold Conference," *New York Times*, December 20, 1921.

37. "Mexico Awaits Formal Invitation," *Christian Science Monitor*, October 7, 1922.

38. The text of the Rowe memorandum is attached to Tellez a Pani, October 25, 1922, AHSREM, L-E-191. It was published widely in various forms; see, for example, "Voice of the People," *Chicago Daily Tribune*, October 21, 1922.

39. Tellez a Pani, October 25, 1922, AHSREM, L-E-191.

40. Tellez a Pani, October 25, 1922, AHSREM, L-E-191.

41. The technique of withdrawing from an international gathering in protest was not without precedent for Mexico: in fact, at the Pan-American Commercial Conference in June 1919, Mexico withdrew its representatives over remarks made by Speaker of the House Frederick Gillett, who had argued before Congress that Mexico was the "greatest impediment to-day to full fellowship and international trade on this hemisphere." "Mexico Protests Charge It Is an 'Impediment,'" *New York Tribune*, June 10, 1919.

42. Pani a Trejo, January 24, 1923, AHSREM, L-E-191.

43. To the suggestion that a third country act as arbitrator between the United States and Mexico, Pani replied, "[A]s questions of sovereignty and national dignity are incontrovertible in not having a purely juridical character, they can not be sub-

jected, consequently, to any arbitration decision." Pani a Trejo, January 24, 1923, AHSREM, L-E-191.

44. This was reported by the US ambassador back to Washington. US Ambassador in Chile (Collier) to the Secretary of State, January 22, 1923, in *FRUS 1923* 1:291–92.

45. "Address Delivered by the President of the Republic, Mr. Arturo Alessandri, before the Delegates to the V Conference Assembled in the Reception Hall of Congress," March 25, 1923, in *Actas de Las Sesiones Plenarias de La Quinta Conferencia Internacional Americana.*

46. "Address Delivered by the President of the Republic, Mr. Arturo Alessandri."

47. The Ecuadorian delegate told him specifically that he had dispatched a cable home noting the reception that Mexico had been given, having been "cheered in a special and enthusiastic form." Trejo, "Informe sobre la Quinta Conferencia Panamericana: Tercera Parte—Carácter General de la Conferencia," May 1923, AHSREM, L-E-194.

48. Samuel Guy Inman, "Mexican Issue Shows in Pan-American Session," *Los Angeles Times*, March 27, 1923; and Trejo, "Informe sobre la Quinta Conferencia Panamericana: Tercera Parte," AHSREM, L-E-194.

49. Translation in Summerlin to Hughes, March 19, 1923, NARA, RG 43, entry 133, box 2.

50. Rowe to Fletcher, March 31, 1923, NARA, RG 43, entry 133, box 1.

51. "Memorandum 10: Preliminar sobre la actitud de la delegación mexicana en la conferencia," n.d., AHRESM L-E-195 (I).

52. Trejo, "Informe sobre la Quinta Conferencia Panamericana: Tercera Parte," AHSREM, L-E-194.

53. Trejo, "Informe sobre la Quinta Conferencia Panamericana: Primera Parte," May 1923, AHSREM, L-E-194.

54. See Roy T. Davis (San Jose) to Hughes, February 23, 1923 NARA, RG 43, entry 133, box 2.

55. "Alvarado Quirós y México," *Diario de Costa Rica*, May 31, 1923, AHSREM, L-E-191.

56. The proposal also suggested that regular ambassadors in Washington who were not representatives to the Pan-American Union were welcome to sit in on Governing Board meetings but not vote.

57. As summarized in Fletcher to Secretary of State, April 10, 1923, 8 p.m., NARA, RG 43, entry 133, box 2.

58. "Asks New Condition in Pan America Body," *New York Times*, April 10, 1923; "Proposes Ignoring U.S. Recognition," *Boston Daily Globe*, April 10, 1923.

59. Trejo a Pani, April 12, 1923, AHSREM, L-E-194.

60. Armendáriz del Castillo a Pani, June 2, 1923, AHSREM, L-E-191.

61. "La reorganización de la Unión Panamericana de Washington: Habla el ministro de Mexico, Señor Trejo Lerdo de Tejada," *La Nación* (Santiago, Chile), April 11, 1923, AHSREM, L-E-194.

62. Trejo a Pani, April 12, 1923, AHSREM, L-E-194.

63. "Delay Endangers Latin Arms Plan," *New York Times*, April 11, 1923.

64. Trejo, "Informe sobre la Quinta Conferencia Panamericana: Primera Parte," AHSREM, L-E-194.

65. Meeting of American Delegation, April 10, 1923, 9:30 a.m., NARA, RG 43, entry 133, box 1.

66. Fletcher to Hughes, April 9, 1923, NARA, RG 43, entry 133, box 2.

67. Meeting of American Delegation, April 10, 1923, 9:30 a.m., NARA, RG 43, entry 133, box 1.

68. Fletcher to Hughes, April 9, 1923, NARA, RG 43, entry 133, box 2.

69. Hughes to U.S. Delegation, April 19, 1923, NARA, RG 43, entry 133, box 2.

70. Meeting of American Delegation, April 10, 1923, 9:30 a.m., NARA, RG 43, entry 133, box 1.

71. Trejo a Pani, April 12, 1923, AHSREM, L-E-194.

72. US delegation to Hughes, April 10, 1923, noon, NARA, RG 43, entry 133, box 2.

73. Meeting of American Delegation, April 10, 1923.

74. Notes on the First Portion of Meeting of the Delegation, April 9, 1923, NARA, RG 43, entry 133, box 1.

75. Trejo a Pani, April 21, 1923, AHSREM L-E-194; and Armendáriz del Castillo to Pani, June 2, 1923, AHSREM, L-E-191.

76. Trejo, "Informe sobre la Quinta Conferencia Panamericana: Tercera Parte," AHSREM, L-E-194.

77. Trejo also reported that his adherence to US positions during the conference meant that some delegates came to refer to him as "Fletcher's pageboy" and "Mister Edwards." Trejo, "Informe sobre la Quinta Conferencia Panamericana: Tercera Parte," AHSREM, L-E-194.

78. Trejo, "Informe sobre la Quinta Conferencia Panamericana: Tercera Parte."

79. Trejo, "Informe sobre la Quinta Conferencia Panamericana: Tercera Parte."

80. Fletcher to Hughes, April 18, 1923, NARA, RG 43, entry 133, box 2. This was, however, a resolution already reached at the 1910 Buenos Aires Conference; as such, it didn't constitute an actual reform of the existing rules. "Official Documents: The Fourth International American Conference, General Records of Proceedings," *Bulletin of the International Bureau of American Republics* 31, no. 5 (November 1910): 798–801.

81. Trejo a Pani, April 18, 1923, AHSREM, L-E-194.

82. Samuel Guy Inman, "Two Santiago Plans Opposed," *Los Angeles Times*, April 21, 1923.

83. "Brazil Alone Stands with United States," *Boston Daily Globe*, April 19, 1923.

84. Trejo, "Informe sobre la Quinta Conferencia Panamericana: Primera Parte," May 1923, AHSREM, L-E-194.

85. Fletcher to Hughes, April 20, 1923, NARA, RG 43, entry 133, box 2.

86. Fletcher to Secretary of State, April 10, 1923, 9 p.m., NARA, RG 43, entry 133, box 2; and "Brazil Alone Stands with the United States," *Boston Daily Globe*, April 19, 1923.

87. Trejo, "Informe sobre la Quinta Conferencia Panamericana: Tercera Parte," AHSREM, L-E-194.

88. Trejo, "Informe sobre la Quinta Conferencia Panamericana: Primera Parte," AHSREM, L-E-194.

89. Trejo, "Informe sobre la Quinta Conferencia Panamericana: Tercera Parte," AHSREM, L-E-194.

90. Trejo, "Informe sobre la Quinta Conferencia Panamericana: Primera Parte," AHSREM, L-E-194.

91. Trejo a Pani, April 23, 1923, AHSREM, L-E-194.

92. Fletcher to Hughes, April 20, 1923, NARA, RG 43, entry 133, box 2.

93. Fletcher to Hughes, April 24, 1923, NARA, RG 43, entry 133, box 2.

94. Trejo a Pani, April 18, 1923, AHSREM, L-E-194.

95. "Discurso del Delegado de Argentina al Presentar a la Comisión Política la 'Formula de los Once Paises,'" April 25, 1923, AHSREM, L-E-194.

96. Trejo a Pani, April 25, 1923, AHSREM, L-E-194.

97. Trejo a Pani, April 25, 1923.

98. Trejo a Pani, April 25, 1923.

99. "Resolution Adopted by the Fifth International Conference of American States at Santiago, May 1, 1923," in *Report of the Delegates of the United States of America to the Fifth International Conference of American States*, 125.

100. Trejo, "Informe sobre la Quinta Conferencia Panamericana: Tercera Parte," AHSREM, L-E-194.

101. Inman, *Inter-American Conferences*, 101.

102. Trejo, "Informe sobre la Quinta Conferencia Panamericana: Primera Parte," AHSREM, L-E-194.

103. Thanks to Kirsten Weld for the translation of *cerebro cuadrado*. Trejo, "Informe sobre la Quinta Conferencia Panamericana: Primera Parte," AHSREM, L-E-194.

104. Trejo, "Informe sobre la Quinta Conferencia Panamericana: Primera Parte," AHSREM, L-E-194.

105. "Sees Peril to US in Nations' League," *New York Times*, February 1, 1919 (emphasis added).

CHAPTER TWO. A NEW LEGAL AND PHILOSOPHIC CONCEPTION OF CREDIT

1. Bazant, *Historia de la deuda exterior de México*, 183.

2. Wynne, *State Insolvency and Foreign Bondholders*, 66.

3. Bazant, *Historia de la deuda exterior de México*, 194.

4. Gómez-Galvarriato, "La política económica del nuevo régimen," 386.

5. Bazant, *Historia de la deuda exterior de México*, 205.

6. Cárdenas, *La industrialización mexicana durante la gran depresión*, 28–36.

7. Morton, *Revolution and State in Modern Mexico*, 70.

8. On the depression of 1926–32, see Haber, *Industry and Underdevelopment*, 150–70. On the forced repatriation of Mexican workers, see Balderrama and Rodríguez, *Decade of Betrayal*.

9. Buchenau, *Plutarco Elías Calles*, 144.

10. Hamilton, *Limits of State Autonomy*, 94–96.

11. Buchenau, *Plutarco Elías Calles*, 159–165.

12. Pani, *Mi contribución al nuevo régimen*, 326–345.

13. Clavin, *Securing the World Economy*, 84–122.

14. League of Nations Monetary and Economic Conference, *Draft Annotated Agenda*, reprinted in *FRUS 1933*, 1:464. For the British insistence on debts, see The British Ambassador (Lindsay) to the Secretary of State, Washington, April 12, 1933, in *FRUS 1933*, 1:487–89.

15. Calles, "Worldwide Economic Conditions" and "The Rehabilitation of Silver," English translation of interview in *El Nacional* (México, D.F.), February 19, 1933, AHSREM, L-E-245.

16. "Statement made by Mr. Alberto J. Pani, President of the Mexican Delegation at the Plenary Meeting of the Monetary and Economic Conference on June 15, 1933," AHSREM, III-1184-3 (IV). The expansionism pursued by Pani, and by his successors at the crucial economic conjunctures to come, including Eduardo Suárez and Ramón Beteta, was distinctly developmental in nature. This developmentalism is described in detail in Suárez Dávila, "Desarrollismo y ortodoxia monetaria (1927–1952)." Buchenau has argued that President Abelardo Rodríguez was more Keynesian than Pani, who, he argues, had more orthodox economic views on balanced budgets, causing Rodríguez to force Pani's resignation. This is the view expressed in Daniels to Roosevelt, October 9, 1933, FDRPL, President's Secretary's File, box 44.

17. Telegram, President Roosevelt to the Acting Secretary of State, USS Indianapolis, July 2, 1933, in *FRUS 1933*, 1:673.

18. Herrera León, "México en la Conferencia Económica Mundial de Londres."

19. González Roa, Informe Confidencial Num. 1, June 21, 1933, AHSREM, L-E-245.

20. González Roa a Puig, May 28, 1933, AHSREM, L-E-245.

21. González Roa a Puig, September 22, 1933, AHSREM, L-E-247.

22. See, for example, Secretaría de la Legación de México en Tegucigalpa, "Temas para la formación del programa oficial," in AHSREM, L-E-196(II), and "Preliminar sobre la actitud de la delegación mexicana en la conferencia," L-E-202. For more on the conference, see Sheinin, *Argentina and the United States at the Sixth Pan American Conference*.

23. The text of the presidential accord establishing the commission is in AHSREM, L-E-231. Mention of it as one of the preparatory commissions leading up to the conference is in AHSREM, L-E-230.

24. Luis Sanchez Pontón, "Las deudas de guerra y su influencia en la crisis económica presente," UNAM, 1933, AHSREM, L-E-254. For an analysis of this study, see King, "Mexican Proposal for a Continent-Wide Debt Moratorium."

25. Marichal, *Century of Debt Crises in Latin America*, 203. While Argentina had avoided default on federal loans, the Mexicans were quick to point out that payments had been suspended on provincial and municipal loans. See Puig, "Memorandum para ampliar—en un terreno personal y no oficial—la plática de Puig, de esta mañana, con el señor Embajador Daniels," September 14, 1933, AHSREM, L-E-210(I).

26. Memo IV, Circunstancias políticas internacionales características del momento actual, n.d., AHSREM, L-E-245.

27. Fernando González Roa, "Memorandum Num. 1, Relativo a los puntos mas importantes que tendrán que tratarse en la séptima conferencia de los estados americanos," May 26, 1931, AHSREM, L-E-230.

28. González Roa, "Memorandum Num. 1." This echoed colonial criticism of foreign financial power elsewhere, such as when the Indian nationalist economist and politician Dadabhai Naoroji argued, "English capitalists do not merely lend, but with their capital they themselves invade the country." Quoted in Goswami, *Producing India*, 224.

29. Puig a Calles, May 23, 1933 AHSREM, L-E-245.

30. Cover attachment to Thompson to Foreign Office, October 4, 1933, TNA, FO 371/16530.

31. Memorandum of Conversation with the Mexican Minister of Finance (Pani), July 29, 1933, in *FRUS 1933*, 4:8; and "Declaraciones del Señor Ingeniero Alberto J. Pani, Secetarío de Hacienda y Credito Público, sobre la actitud de México en la conferencia de economía," *El Nacional* (México D.F.), August 17, 1933, AHSREM, L-E-245.

32. "Program of the Seventh Conference of American States, Approved by the Governing Board of the Pan-American Union in the Session of May 31, 1933," in International American Conference (7th, Montevideo, Uruguay 1933), *Plenary Sessions*. Puig counseled Pani in August that insisting on changing the program at this late date was ill-advised. See Puig a Pani, August 4, 1933, AHSREM, L-E-231.

33. Puig a Todos los jefes de misión mexicanos en Latinoamerica, telegram, September 30, 1933, AHSREM, L-E-210(II).

34. The proposal and the accompanying studies were reprinted in Mexico, Secretaría de Relaciones Exteriores, *Temario economico financiero sometido por México*.

35. The circular memo and summaries of the responses from throughout the region are in AHSREM, L-E-247.

36. Puig, handwritten note, "Para junta con Sr. Gral Calles," n.d., AHSREM, L-E-245.

37. Puig, Memorandum, n.d., AHSREM, L-E-245.

38. Proyecto de Memorandum, October 6, 1933, AHSREM, L-E-211.

39. Puig, "Memorandum para ampliar," September 14, 1933, AHSREM, L-E-210(I).

40. Puig, "Memorandum para ampliar."

41. Thompson (Santiago) to Foreign Office, October 4, 1933, TNA, FO 371/16530.

42. Reyes a Puig, August 22, 1933, AHSREM, L-E-247.

43. "Daniels Hails Pledge of Amity by Calles," *New York Times*, August 1, 1933. Pani had been quick to point out, at and after the London conference, that the monetary and fiscal policies pursued by Mexico only differed from those being pursued by Roosevelt in that they "anticipated by more than a year" the US moves—that is, Mexico had put them in place first. "Declaraciones del Señor Ingeniero Alberto J. Pani," *El Nacional* (México, D.F.), August 17, 1933, AHSREM, L-E-245.

44. For instance, the Roca-Runciman pact on Argentine beef, an important export for Argentina, was negotiated in April and May 1933.

45. AHSREM, L-E-247. See also "Ibero-American Unity Cited as Mexican Aim," *New York Times*, November 20, 1933.

46. Reyes a Puig, August 20, 1933, AHSREM, L-E-247; Reyes a Puig, August 22, 1933, AHSREM, L-E-247; and Puig, Memorandum IV. Circunstancias Políticas internacionales características del momento actual, AHSREM, L-E-245.

47. Puig a González Roa, September 27, 1933, AHSREM, L-E-247.

48. *Affairs: Washington's Weekly Review* 6, no. 43 (October 27, 1933), AHSREM, L-E-232.

49. Puig a Cancillerías de Latinoamérica, September 25, 1933, AHSREM, L-E-210(I); and "Memorandum by the Secretary of State, Washington, September 22, 1933," in *FRUS 1933*, 4:16.

50. Telegram: Secretary of State to the Ambassador in Mexico (Daniels), Washington, September 28, 1933, in *FRUS 1933*, 4:17.

51. Leith-Ross to Overton, October 14, 1933, TNA FO 371/16530.

52. Puig, "Memorandum para ampliar," September 14, 1933, AHSREM, L-E-210(I).

53. "Instructions to Delegates," in *FRUS 1933*, 4:147.

54. AHSREM, L-E-259 contains details of the trip and meetings.

55. Quoted in Daniels to Roosevelt, October 24, 1933, FDRPL, President's Secretary's File, box 43.

56. "Dr. Puig Confers with Roosevelt," *New York Times*, October 19, 1933.

57. Franklin D. Roosevelt, "Statement on the Conference of American States," November 9, 1933, The American Presidency Project Online, www.presidency.ucsb.edu/documents/statement-the-conference-american-states.

58. "A Limited Conference," *Washington Evening Star*, November 9, 1933, AHSREM, L-E-232.

59. "Pan-American Limited," *New York Times*, November 10, 1933, AHSREM, L-E-232.

60. Chairman on the American Delegation (Hull) to the Acting Secretary of State, Montevideo, December 4, 1933, in *FRUS 1933*, 4:157.

61. Puig, *Remarks on the Position Taken by Mexico at Montevideo*, 23. The quotes that follow are all taken from this English translation, published and distributed by the Mexican government after the conclusion of the conference.

62. Puig's vision represents a powerful precursor to what Ogle describes as the "state rights against private capital" emphasis of the later efforts of the new

international economic order in the 1970s. Ogle, "State Rights against Private Capital."

63. Puig, *Remarks on the Position Taken by Mexico at Montevideo*, 24.

64. This is in contrast to the liberal conception of property, in which property is delimited to exclude the rights of others, and the property owner has obligations only to himself. For an analysis in international property law, see Foster and Bonilla, "Introduction: The Social Function of Property."

65. Puig, *Remarks on the Position Taken by Mexico at Montevideo*, 29.

66. Puig, *Remarks on the Position Taken by Mexico at Montevideo*, 28.

67. Keynes, *General Theory of Employment, Interest, and Money*, 377.

68. The Mexican insistence on the capacity to pay drew not from Keynes but from Pierre Jaudel, whom Luis Sánchez Pontón saw as the intellectual progenitor of the Dawes Plan. Luis Sánchez Pontón, "Las deudas de guerra y su influencia en la crisis económica presente," UNAM, 1933, AHSREM, L-E-254.

69. Puig, *Remarks on the Position Taken by Mexico at Montevideo*, 25.

70. Slobodian, *Globalists*, 168–74.

71. Puig, *Remarks on the Position Taken by Mexico at Montevideo*, 30.

72. Puig, *Remarks on the Position Taken by Mexico at Montevideo*, 29.

73. International American Conference (7th, 1933, Montevideo, Uruguay), *Plenary Sessions*, 166. Saavedra Lamas had held this opinion since before the conference, telling the US ambassador in November "that in his opinion the Montevideo Conference was badly planned *(mal preparada)* and that in all the circumstances the subjects discussed should be limited to those juridical rather than political in character; that Cuba, the Chaco, Leticia, and also debts (which, he added, Mexico would like to see discussed) should be tabu." The Ambassador in Argentina (Weddell) to the Secretary of State, November 7, 1933, *FRUS 1933*, 4:39.

74. International American Conference (7th, 1933, Montevideo, Uruguay), *Plenary Sessions*, 167.

75. International American Conference (7th, 1933, Montevideo, Uruguay), *Plenary Sessions*, 174.

76. "Reciprocity Pacts Proposed by Hull," *New York Times*, December 13, 1933. For the hagiographic view of Hull, see Butler, *Cautious Visionary*.

77. Puig, *Remarks on the Position Taken by Mexico at Montevideo*, 63.

78. Puig, *Remarks on the Position Taken by Mexico at Montevideo*, 69.

79. International American Conference (7th, 1933, Montevideo, Uruguay), *Final Act*, 22.

80. "Reciprocity Pacts Proposed by Hull," *New York Times*, December 13, 1933.

81. See, for example, Dallek, *Franklin D. Roosevelt and American Foreign Policy*.

82. The revolution's thinkers and makers of foreign policy redefined intervention in this period, marking economic control, not just military intervention, as a central issue. Britton, "Redefining Intervention," 48. For a striking reconsideration of anti-Americanism as immanent critique of US liberalism, see Grandin, "Your Americanism and Mine."

1. Helleiner, *Forgotten Foundations of Bretton Woods*, 53.

2. Most recently, Eric Helleiner has undertaken a detailed analysis of the negotiations around the IAB within the United States in *Forgotten Foundations of Bretton Woods*, 52–79. The bank was first discussed in some detail in Green, *Containment of Latin America*, and is mentioned in passing in the semiofficial history of the World Bank by Oliver, *International Economic Co-operation*. In addition, the Inter-American Development Bank has recently published a few works on the origins of that institution, also surveying the history of the IAB proposal. See Comas, *Los origenes del BID*, and Díaz-Bonilla and del Campo, *Long and Winding Road*.

3. Fernando González Roa, "Memorandum Num. 1, Relativo a los puntos mas importantes que tendrán que tratarse en la séptima Conferencia de los Estados Americanos," May 26, 1931, AHSREM, L-E-230; and Moore, "Pan-American Financial Conferences and the Inter-American High Commission," 344.

4. On the Venezuelan proposal, see Kains and Warburg, *Memoranda to Accompany Draft of Treaty*. The meetings at which the debate took place are summarized in Alta Comisión Interamericana, Consejo Central Executivo, *Informe presentado al Consejo Central Ejecutivo de la Alta Comisión Inter-Americana*. On Mexican representation at the High Commission, although a 1922 list of the members doesn't list a Mexican national section, the 1933 summary of the antecedents to the Bank written by Puig insists that the Mexican section had "never ceased to function since the creation" of the High Commission. Mexico, Secretaría de Relaciones Exteriores, *Temario económico financiero sometido*, 32. For the membership list, see Inter American High Commission, Central Executive Council, *List of Officers of Commission*.

5. Alta Comisión Americana, Sección Nacional Mexicana, Memorandum, "Asunto: Se propone que en el nuevo programa de actividades de la Alta Comisión Interamericana figuren los trabajos preliminares para la fundación de un Banco Internacional Americano," June 15, 1931, AHSREM, L-E-210(I).

6. Alta Comisión Americana, Sección Nacional Mexicana, Memorandum, June 15, 1931, AHSREM, L-E-210(1). Some of the same topics are discussed later in Luis Sánchez Pontón, "Las deudas de guerra y su influencia en la crisis económica presente," UNAM, 1933, AHSREM, L-E-254.

7. "Build Up Trade Relations with the Americas," *Commercial West* 26, no. 18 (October 31, 1914): 14; "Frank A. Vanderlip's Proposal for World Bank—Gold Reserve Bank," *Commercial and Financial Chronicle* 113, no. 2 (1922); "Bank of Nations Is Hitchcock's Plan," *New York Times*, January 19, 1922; and Heymann, *Plan for Permanent Peace*. The memo was quick to point out that the idea of an international bank was proposed first not in Europe, but in the Americas, with the founding of the Pan-American Union in 1889. Alta Comisión Ameri-

cana, Sección Nacional Mexicana, Memorandum, June 15, 1931, AHSREM, L-E-210(I).

8. Art. 3 of the BIS Statutes (1930), quoted in Toniolo, *Central Bank Cooperation at the Bank for International Settlements*, 1.

9. Of course, as Adam Tooze points out, the Young Plan was conceived at least in part to make sure that state-to-state reparations payments didn't "crowd out Germany's private debts to Wall Street." See Tooze, *The Deluge*, 488.

10. Alta Comisión Americana, Sección Nacional Mexicana, Memorandum, June 15, 1931, AHSREM, L-E-210(I) (emphasis added). This echoes Puig's thinking as published in Puig, *Una política social-económica de "preparación socialista."*

11. Kemmerer, "Currency Stabilization in Latin America," in Pan-American Union, *Fourth Pan-American Commercial Conference: Proceedings*. For the final resolutions, see Pan-American Union, *Fourth Pan-American Commercial Conference: Final Act*.

12. Alta Comisión Americana, Sección Nacional Mexicana, Memorandum, June 15, 1931, AHSREM, L-E-210(I).

13. On the dance of the millions, see Bulmer-Thomas, *Economic History of Latin America Since Independence*, 165–207.

14. Alta Comisión Americana, Sección Nacional Mexicana, Memorandum, June 15, 1931, AHSREM, L-E-210(I).

15. "Instructions to Delegates, Seventh International Conference of American States Held at Montevideo, December 3–26, 1933," *FRUS 1933*, 4:98.

16. "Modifications for Chapter IV of the Program: Mexican Proposition," in International American Conference (7th, 1933, Montevideo, Uruguay), *Plenary Sessions*, 176.

17. Cosío Villegas, "Study on the Establishment of an Inter-American Economic and Financial Organization," in International American Conference (7th, 1933, Montevideo, Uruguay), *Plenary Sessions*, 59. Meetings of the preparatory committee are summarized in AHSREM, L-E-230.

18. The resolution of the Fourth Commercial Conference is reprinted in Pan-American Union, *Special Handbook for the Use of Delegates*, 78–81.

19. Cosío Villegas, "Study on the Establishment of an Inter-American Economic and Financial Organization," 77. On the economic mandate of the League, see Clavin, *Securing the World Economy*.

20. Babb, *Managing Mexico*, 28–32.

21. Cosío Villegas, "Study on the Establishment of an Inter-American Economic and Financial Organization," 78.

22. "Proposition of the Mexican Delegation on the Creation of an International Bank of the American Continent," in International American Conference (7th, 1933, Montevideo, Uruguay), *Plenary Sessions*, 30.

23. "Report Presented by the Delegate from Peru, Mr. Felipe Barreda Laos," in International American Conference (7th, 1933, Montevideo, Uruguay), *Plenary Sessions*, 29.

24. Aggarwal, *Debt Games*, 293–98.

25. "Address Delivered by the Ambassador of Peru, Mr. Felipe Barreda Laos," in International American Conference(7th, 1933, Montevideo, Uruguay), *Plenary Sessions*, 51.

26. "Address Delivered by the Ambassador of Peru, Mr. Felipe Barreda Laos."

27. "Propositions on Economic Topics: Mr. Octavio Morató, Delegate of Uruguay," in International American Conference (7th, 1933, Montevideo, Uruguay), *Plenary Sessions*, 55–57.

28. "Propositions on Economic Topics," 56.

29. "Propositions on Economic Topics," 57.

30. "Statement of Motives Concerning the Establishment of an Inter-American Economic and Financial Organization," in International American Conference (7th, 1933, Montevideo, Uruguay), *Plenary Sessions*, 48–49.

31. "Statement of Motives Concerning the Establishment of an Inter-American Economic and Financial Organization," 49.

32. United States Department of State, "Seventh International Conference of American States Held at Montevideo, December 3–26, 1933," *FRUS 1933*, 4:159–71.

33. Pérez Duarte a Calles, December 15, 1933, AHSREM, L-E-231. Of course, as detailed in chapter 2, Hull and the US delegation claimed victory, as well, in postponing the Mexican projects to the forthcoming meeting.

34. Eduardo Villaseñor, "Memorandum sobre el Banco-Interamericano," n.d., Archivo Histórico del Colegio de México (COLMEX), Fondo Eduardo Villaseñor (FEV), caja 32.

35. White's role in the stabilization fund is discussed in chapter 4.

36. This provision was made explicit in hearings before the Senate Committee on Banking and Currency in February 1939. See Oliver, *International Economic Co-operation*, 91.

37. Oliver, *International Economic Co-operation*, 88–91n355. See also Gardener, *Economic Aspects of New Deal Diplomacy*, 57–60.

38. See Hamilton, *Limits of State Autonomy,* 184–215.

39. Schuler, *Mexico between Hitler and Roosevelt*, 63–89. Schuler details an important struggle between Morgenthau and others at Treasury and the Hull-led State Department in regard to how to confront the Mexican crisis. Hull wanted to use the crisis to extract concessions from the Mexicans, but Morgenthau thought that Hull had "too many angles to this situation that I do not understand and they do not smell good." FDRPL, Morgenthau Diaries, book 104, roll 27, December 29, 1937.

40. On the expropriation, see Hamilton, *Limits of State Autonomy*; and Meyer, *Mexico and the United States in the Oil Controversy.*

41. Urquidi, "La postguerra y las relaciones económicas internacionales de México."

42. Memorandum of Conference, September 13, 1939, NARA, RG 56, Division of Monetary Research (TDMR), box 30, folder: Records of Special Conferences (Misc).

43. Conference at State Department between Mr. Welles and Mr. Bailie and Mr. Burgess, September 7, 1939, NARA, RG 56, TDMR, box 30, folder: Records of Special Conferences (Misc).

44. Welles to State, September 25, 1939, NARA, RG 56, TDMR, box 30, folder: Records of Special Conferences (Misc).

45. And indeed, the first IFEAC meeting was held on November 16, 1939. See Pan-American Union, "Inauguration of the Inter-American Financial and Economic Advisory Committee."

46. Villaseñor, *Memorias-testimonio*, 257–81.

47. Welles to Secretary of State, October 94 1939, in *FRUS 1939*, 5:42.

48. "Initiativa de México que fue bien recibida," *Excélsior* (México, D.F.), November 16, 1939, COLMEX, FEV, caja 32, exp. 9.

49. Villaseñor, "The Inter-American Bank," 165–74.

50. Villaseñor, "Problemas financieros y de comercio interamericano," 394.

51. "First Meeting of the Finance Ministers of the American Republics at Guatemala: Final Act," Department of State *Bulletin*, December 2, 1939, 629.

52. Hanson to White, December 7, 1939, NARA, RG 56, TDMR, box 65, folder: Inter-American Bank Memoranda etc., vol 1.

53. Assistant Secretary of State Sumner Welles was named the chair of the IFEAC, and given its location in Washington (even after the ardent insistence of so many Latin American delegates at Montevideo that any economic organization be headquartered anywhere but in the US capital), there was constant communication between the new body and the State and Treasury Departments, as well as with the Board of Governors of the Federal Reserve and the National Loan Agency. United States Department of State, "Program Proposed by the United States for Inter-American Economic Cooperation," *FRUS 1940*, 5:359.

54. Villaseñor, *Memorias-testimonio*, 127–33.

55. Green, *Containment of Latin America*, 60–72.

56. White to Morgenthau, March 31, 1939, Princeton University, Harry Dexter White Papers (HDWP), box 5, folder 5.

57. Memorandum of Conversation re: Proposed Inter-American Bank, January 23, 1940, FDRPL, Morgenthau Diaries, vol. 237, pt. 2.

58. Hanson to White, December 7, 1939, NARA, RG 56, TDMR, box 65, folder: Inter-American Bank Memoranda etc., vol 1.

59. *Inter-American Bank: Hearings Before a Subcommittee of the Committee on Foreign Relations, United States Senate, Seventy-Seventh Congress, First Session on Executive K* (May 5-6, 1941).

60. White to Morgenthau, "Proposed Inter-American Bank," November 28, 1939, NARA, RG 56, Treasury Records of the Assistant Secretary for Monetary and International Affairs, Chronological File (CFHDW), box 3, file 14.

61. Memo No. 2, Mexico, November 20, 1939, NARA, RG 59, SDDF 710. FEAC/143.

62. Memo No. 10, Peru, November 29, 1939, NARA, RG 59, SDDF 710. FEAC/143.

63. Hanson to White, December 7, 1939, NARA, RG 56, TDMR, box 65, folder: Inter-American Bank Memoranda etc., vol. 1. These debates have been very ably summarized in Helleiner, *Forgotten Foundations of Bretton Woods*, 52–79.

64. US Congress, "Silver and the Inter-American Bank," *Congressional Record* 86, no. 67 (1940): 6080.

65. For a provocative discussion of White's interest in Soviet planning, see Steil, *Battle of Bretton Woods*.

66. White to Morgenthau, "Proposed Inter-American Bank," November 28, 1939, NARA, RG 56, CFHDW, box 3, file 14.

67. See NARA, RG 56, TDMR, box 65, folder: Monetary: Inter-American Bank Memoranda etc., vol. 1, and SDDF 710.FEAC/143 for the finalized survey as distributed.

68. The less-than-formal nature of the correspondence perhaps reflects the comprehensive nature of ongoing financial and economic negotiations elsewhere between the two countries, particularly vis-à-vis the oil sector. Suárez to Welles, December 13, 1939, NARA, RG 59, SDDF 710.FEAC/143.

69. U.S. Legation in Ciudad Trujillo to State, February 8, 1940, NARA, RG 59, SDDF 710.BANK/11.

70. "Venezuela: Contestacion al cuestionario transmitido de acuerdo con la Resolucion X," NARA, RG 59, SDDF 710.FEAC/143.

71. "Bolivia: Contestacion al cuestionario transmitido de acuerdo con la Resolucion X," NARA, RG 59, SDDF 710.FEAC/143.

72. U.S. Legation in Ciudad Trujillo to State, February 8, 1940, NARA, RG 59, SDDF 710.BANK/11.

73. Mecham, *United States and Inter-American Security*.

74. Villaseñor, Memorandum en respuesta, February 21, 1940, NARA, RG 59, SDDF 710.BANK/59.

75. Villaseñor, "Inter-American Bank: Prospects and Dangers," 171.

76. Villaseñor, Memorandum en respuesta, February 21, 1940, NARA, RG 59, SDDF 710.BANK/59.

77. "The Inter-American Bank: How It Will Work to Increase Trade in the Americas," *Revista Hoy* (México, D.F.), November 1940, COLMEX, FEV, caja 32.

78. Helleiner, *Forgotten Foundations of Bretton Woods*, 63–66.

79. Inter-American Financial and Economic Advisory Committee, *Convention for the Establishment of an Inter-American Bank*.

80. White to Morgenthau, March 12, 1940, NARA, RG 56, CFHDW, box 3, file 15.

81. Berle, "Peace Without Empire," 107.

82. Daniels to State, January 31, 1940, NARA, RG 59, SDDF 710.BANK/10.

83. Barreda Laos, *Hispano América en guerra?*, 226.

84. Cushman & Wakefield to Berle, May 23, 1940, FDRPL, Berle Papers, box 59.

85. This has been discussed in detail in Green, *Containment of Latin America*.

86. Burgess to Morgenthau, May 9, 1940, NARA, RG 59, SDDF 710.BANK/193.

87. See Collado to Duggan, Berle, and Welles, November 7, 1940, NARA, RG 59, SDDF 710.BANK/219.

88. See, for example, "The Inter-American Bank: How It Will Work to Increase Trade in the Americas," *Revista Hoy* (México, D.F.), November 1940, COLMEX, FEV, caja 32.

89. "Los Banqueros con el Secretario de Hacienda," *La Prensa* (México, D.F.), February 4, 1941, COLMEX, FEV, caja 32. See next chapter for more on White's trip to Mexico.

90. See, for example, "Proximo tramite para crear el Banco Interamericano," *Excélsior* (México, D.F.), March 22, 1941, and "Se aplazará un proyecto," *Excélsior* (México, D.F.), May 25, 1941, COLMEX, FEV, caja 32.

91. Eduardo Villaseñor, "Inter-American Trade and Financial Problems" speech presented at the University of Chicago, July 9, 1941, COLMEX, FEV, caja 22, exp. 3 (published in Laves, *Inter-American Solidarity*).

92. Villaseñor, "Inter-American Bank: Prospects and Dangers," 174. The quote that follows in this paragraph is also from this source.

93. "Se está tratando en N. York la creación de un gran Banco Interamericano," *La Prensa* (México, D.F.), March 12, 1942; "Es urgente la creación de un banco para las Americas," *Excélsior* (México, D.F.), March 12, 1942; "Estados Unidos deben exportaer capital," *Novedades* (México, D.F.), January 12, 1942; and "Inter-American Bank Is Urged by Banker," *New York Times*, March 12, 1942. He also apparently met with Winthrop Aldrich of Chase National Bank, according to the *Novedades* story.

94. "Se está tratando en N. York la creación de un gran Banco Interamericano," *La Prensa* (México, D.F.), March 12, 1942.

95. Memorandum sobre el Proyectado Banco Internamericano frente a la organizacion propuesta por el Departamento del Tesoro de los Estados Unidos con apoyo en el plan del Dr White, n.d., COLMEX, FEV, caja 32, exp. 5.

96. His remarks are published in Villaseñor, *América Latina en la economía mundial*.

97. "Latin-Americas Informed by Marshall They're out of Financial Aid Plan," *Los Angeles Times*, April 2, 1948.

98. Villaseñor, "El Banco Interamericano," 192.

99. "Marshall Urges Latins to Put Need of Our Help after ERP," *New York Times*, April 2, 1948.

100. "La II Guerra Mundial convirtió a EE. UU., en el único imperio económico," *Excélsior* (México, D.F.), June 24, 1948; and "La Posición de México ante el Banco Interamericano," *El Popular* (México, D.F.), June 24, 1948.

101. Villaseñor, "El Banco Interamericano," 192.

102. Oliver, *International Economic Co-operation*, 99. Mason and Ascher also mention that "White's exposure to the technical discussions concerning the Inter-American Bank obviously influenced his 1942 proposal for a Bank for Reconstruction and Development." Mason and Asher, *The World Bank Since Bretton Woods*, 16.

CHAPTER FOUR. VOICE AND VOTE

1. See, for example, Gardner, *Sterling-Dollar Diplomacy*; and James, *International Monetary Cooperation since Bretton Woods*.
2. Gardner, *Sterling-Dollar Diplomacy*, xxi. For the revision, see especially Helleiner, *Forgotten Foundations of Bretton Woods*; and Scott-Smith and Rofe, *Global Perspectives on the Bretton Woods Conference*.
3. Acheson cited in Dormael, *Bretton Woods*, 177.
4. Keynes to Sir David Walley, May 30, 1944, cited in Keynes, *Collected Writings of John Maynard Keynes*, vol. 26, 42.
5. Sir Wilfred Eady to Padmore, January 12, 1944, TNA, Treasury Files, Papers of Lord Keynes, T247/27.
6. Eckes, *Search for Solvency*, 154.
7. Niblo, *Mexico in the 1940s*, 75.
8. Gauss, *Made in Mexico*, 16. See also Contreras, *México 1940*. Nora Hamilton makes the case that the turn began earlier, in the late Cárdenas period. Hamilton, *Limits of State Autonomy*.
9. Niblo, *War, Diplomacy, and Development*, 75.
10. Niblo, *Mexico in the 1940s*, 90.
11. Schwartz, "From Obscurity to Notoriety."
12. Bordo and Schwartz, "From the Exchange Stabilization Fund to the International Monetary Fund," 7.
13. Gold, "Mexico and the Development of the Practice of the International Monetary Fund," 1127.
14. Oliver, *International Economic Co-operation*, 110; and Helleiner, *Forgotten Foundations of Bretton Woods*, 100.
15. Urquidi, "Reconstruction vs. Development," 50. Espinosa de los Monteros received his master's degree from Harvard in 1927; White was there beginning in 1925 and finished his PhD in 1930. Cosío Villegas was also at Harvard in 1925. See Wilkie and Monzón Wilkie, *Daniel Cosío Villegas*; and Babb, *Managing Mexico*, 30. Niblo speculates that the nomination was likely "an attempt to commit the world's major silver producer to a monetary settlement," and that Suárez was "feted to win over the silver bloc." Niblo, *War, Diplomacy, and Development*, 255.
16. Hanson to White, August 27, 1940, NARA, RG 56, TDMR, box 31, folder LA/6/15: Inter-American Economic Cooperation.

17. "Treasury Experts in Mexico," *New York Times*, February 11, 1941; "Eventual colaboración de los Edos. Unidos en el programa para la establización de nuestra moneda," *Excélsior* (México, D. F.), February 13, 1941; and "Personajes de las finanzas de E. Unidos," *El Universal* (México, D. F.), February 4, 1941. A translation was included in the files of the Treasury Department: Ortiz to White, February 13, 1941, NARA, RG 56, TDMR, box 51, folder MEX/0/70: Records of Special Missions.

18. Coe to Morgenthau, May 21, 1941, NARA, RG 56, CFHDW, box 4.

19. Southard and Spiegel to White, summary of conference on proposed Mexican Stabilization Operation, August 2, 1941, NARA, RG 56, CFHDW, box 5.

20. Department of State *Bulletin*, November 22, 1941; followed up in April 1942 with "additional agreements for collaboration with Mexico." *Bulletin*, April 11, 1942.

21. Messersmith to Secretary of State, September 24, 1943, *FRUS 1943*, 6:422; and Silva Herzog, *Imagen y obra escogida*, 156.

22. Helleiner, *Forgotten Foundations of Bretton Woods*, 101. Histories that insist that a "first draft" didn't mention development, only reconstruction, reference later circulated versions, not this provisional draft. See, for example, Kapur, Lewis, and Webb, *World Bank*, 57. The draft is Harry Dexter White, "Suggested Plan for the United and Associated Nations Stabilization Fund and a Bank for Reconstruction and Development of the United and Associated Nations," n.d., Princeton, HDWP, box 6, folder 6.

23. Helleiner, *Forgotten Foundations of Bretton Woods*, 101–8; White, "Suggested Plan for the United and Associated Nations Stabilization Fund."

24. Helleiner, *Forgotten Foundations of Bretton Woods*, 106.

25. "Final Act, Third Meeting of Ministers of Foreign Affairs of the American Republics Rio de Janeiro, January 15–28, 1942," Department of State *Bulletin* 6 (February 7, 1942): 117–41.

26. Southard Memo for the files, January 15, 1942, NARA, RG 56, CFHDW, box 6.

27. Observations made by Mr. Harry Dexter White, Sub-Committee of II Commission, Meeting, January 21, 1942, NARA, RG 56, entry UDUP/734A1, box 29, folder LA/0/75: Records of Special Conferences (Rio 1942).

28. "Suggested Procedure for an International Consultation on a Stabilization Fund and a Bank for the United and Associated Nations," July 2, 1942, NARA, RG 56, CFHDW, box 8. The idea that on the fundamental basics of the institutions, Mexico had been "informed rather than consulted" and that Mexico had experienced "minimal preliminary consultation," as one historian put it, is not borne out by a careful reading of the documentary record. Niblo, *War, Diplomacy and Development*, 255.

29. Urquidi, "Reconstruction vs. Development," 32.

30. This group included Cosío Villegas, Urquidi, Josué Sáenz, José Medina Echavarría, Javier Márquez, and Raúl Martínez Ostos. See Turrent y Díaz, *México en Bretton Woods*, 26.

31. Banco de México, Departamento de Estudios Económicos, "El proyecto norteamericano de éstabilización monetaria internacional," June 1943, AGN, Archivo Particular Gonzalo Robles, caja 43, exp. 21.

32. Suárez, *Comentarios y recuerdos*, 136. He acknowledged that political problems—including the fear that the legislatures of Great Britain and the United States would never approve the Keynes Plan—made the US-led plan that emerged from Bretton Woods more expedient.

33. Banco de México, "El proyecto norteamericano de estabilización monetaria internacional." The quotes that follow in this paragraph are also from this source.

34. Banco de México, "El proyecto norteamericano de estabilización monetaria internacional." The quotes that follow in this paragraph are also from this source.

35. The April 1943 "preliminary draft outline," which the Mexicans referred to as the "second project," was published in Mexico in the July 1943 issue of the journal *El Trimestre Económico*, the research organ of the prestigious Fondo de Cultural Económica at the Colegio de México.

36. Urquidi, "Reconstruction vs. Development," 34.

37. Banco de México, Conferencia Monetaria Internacional, Memorandum No. 3, "Orientación general para la delegación mexicana," n.d., folder marked July 10, 1943, COLMEX, FVU, caja 9, exp. 5. The quotes that follow in this paragraph are also from this source.

38. "Memorandum of a Meeting on the International Stabilization Fund," May 25, 1943, NARA, RG 56, Memoranda of Conferences held in Harry Dexter White's Office, 1940–1945, entry 360T, (HDWO), box 20.

39. White to Messersmith, June 26, 1943, NARA, RG 56, entry UDUP/734A1, box 51, MEX/o/oo General vol 1. White even told Morgenthau he should meet with Suárez in Washington just before the meeting: "His representatives here are very helpful and are likely to prove invaluable at Bretton Woods in winning support for our views young the Latin American States." White to Morgenthau, Memorandum for the Secretary, June 24, 1944, NARA, RG 56, Records of the Secretary of the International Monetary Group—Records of the Bretton Woods Agreements, 1938–46 (BWA), box 1.

40. "Mexico pedirá voz y voto para los países débiles, en la junta monetaria," *Excélsior* (México, D. F.), June 14, 1944.

41. Minutes of the Pre-Conference Agenda Committee at Atlantic City, June 28, 1944, NARA, RG 56, BWA, box 1.

42. Minutes of the Pre-Conference Agenda Committee at Atlantic City, June 28, 1944, NARA, RG 56, BWA, box 1.

43. Willis to White, May 21, 1942, NARA, RG 56, BWA, box 46.

44. "Statement of Finance Minister of the Republic of Mexico on the Need for an International Stabilization Fund" and "Statement of the representative of the United States of Brazil on the Need for a Bank for Post-War Reconstruction," April 29, 1942, NARA, RG 56, BWA, box 47.

45. Indeed, there was also a draft of a speech for Secretary Morgenthau, and an entire "British" proposal for the structure of the Bank. See "Statement of the Representative of the United Kingdom on the Need for a Bank for Post-War Reconstruction," April 23, 1942, NARA, RG 56, BWA, box 46.

46. United States Department of State, *Proceedings and Documents, United Nations Monetary and Financial Conference*, 1:76.

47. White to Morgenthau, Memorandum for the Secretary, June 23, 1944, NARA, RG 56, BWA, box 1.

48. Banco de México, Memorandum no. 3, COLMEX, FVU, caja 9, exp. 5.

49. Banco de México, "El proyecto norteamericano de establización monetaria internacional," 34–35, AGN, Archivo Particular Gonzalo Robles, caja 43, exp. 21.

50. White to Morgenthau, Memorandum for the Secretary, June 23, 1944, NARA, RG 56, BWA, box 1.

51. Keynes memo, February 15, 1945, in *Collected Writings of John Maynard Keynes*, 26:189.

52. In practice, however, the fund never invoked the scarce currency clause, and the United States was never sanctioned for its role in generating balance of payments problems for other members; periodic reform attempts to bring it into force continue to this day. See, for example, Skidelsky, "Resurrecting Creditor Adjustment."

53. Banco de México, Memorandum No. 3, COLMEX, FVU, caja 9, exp. 5.

54. United States Department of State, *Proceedings and Documents*, 2:1179.

55. "Commission I International Monetary Fund Fifth meeting: transcript July 14, 1944, 10:00 a.m," in Schuler and Rosenberg, *Bretton Woods Transcripts*.

56. Transcript of US delegation meeting, July 9, 1944, 11 a.m., NARA, RG 56, BWA, box 8.

57. Willis to White, "Participation and Voting Strength in the Bank for Reconstruction and Development of the United and Associated Nations," May 21, 1942, NARA, RG 56, BWA, box 46.

58. "Summary of Commission I, Committee 3, Organization and Managements of the Fund, Third Meeting: Transcript," July 5, 1944, in Schuler and Rosenberg, *Bretton Woods Transcripts*.

59. White to Morgenthau, Memorandum for the Secretary, June 23, 1944, NARA, RG 56, BWA, box 1.

60. Banco de México, Memorandum No. 3, COLMEX, FVU, caja 9, exp. 5.

61. Antonio Carrillo Flores a Villaseñor, July 2, 1943, COLMEX, FEV, caja 32, exp. 5. The quote that follows is also from this source.

62. Banco de México, "Memorandum No. 2, El segundo y tercer proyectos norteamericanos," n.d., folder marked July 10, 1943, COLMEX, FVU, caja 9, exp. 5. The quote that follows is also from this source.

63. "Commission I, Committee 3, Organization and Managements of the Fund, Third Meeting: Transcript," July 5, 1944, in Schuler and Rosenberg, *Bretton Woods Transcripts*.

64. The 1945 quota schedule put the UK subscription at $1.3 billion and the US one at $2.7 billion, out of a total of $6.6 billion (the USSR, which ultimately decided not to subscribe, was allotted $1.2 billion.) See United States Department of Treasury, *United Nations Monetary and Financial Conference Articles of Agreement*, 42.

65. "Commission I, Committee 3, Organization and Managements of the Fund, Third Meeting: Transcript," July 5, 1944, in Schuler and Rosenberg, *Bretton Woods Transcripts*.

66. In the quotas as assigned by 1945, the five largest would have been the United States, the United Kingdom, the USSR, China, and France.

67. Suárez, *Comentarios y recuerdos, 1926–1946*, 134.

68. Suárez, *Comentarios y recuerdos, 1926–1946*, 135.

69. "Commission I, International Monetary Fund, Fourth Meeting: Transcript," July 13, 1944, in Schuler and Rosenberg, *Bretton Woods Transcripts*.

70. Suárez, *Comentarios y recuerdos, 1926–1946*, 134.

71. United States Department of Treasury, *United Nations Monetary and Financial Conference, Articles of Agreement*, 24. The number of executive directors elected by the Latin Americans increased to three after Argentina joined the fund in 1956, but after a large number of African countries joined in the 1960s and the number of directors increased to twenty, many thought the original provisions unsustainable. In 1976, the provision to reserve seats for Latin American directors was dropped. See Garritsen de Vries, *The International Monetary Fund 1972–1978* 2:764–67.

72. Urquidi, "Reconstruction vs. Development," 40. Indeed, at the planning conference at Atlantic City, the Mexican delegation had argued that the purpose of the bank should be "to encourage permanently the economic development of member countries." Quoted in Helleiner, *Forgotten Foundations of Bretton Woods*, 163.

73. "Commission II, International Bank for Reconstruction and Development (World Bank), Second Meeting: Transcript," July 11, 1944, in Schuler and Rosenberg, *Bretton Woods Transcripts*.

74. "Commission II, International Bank for Reconstruction and Development (World Bank), Second Meeting: Transcript." See also United States Department of State, *Proceedings and Documents*, 2:1176.

75. Urquidi, "Reconstruction vs. Development," 42.

76. "Commission II, International Bank for Reconstruction and Development (World Bank), Second Meeting: Transcript," July 11, 1944, in Schuler and Rosenberg, *Bretton Woods Transcripts*.

77. United States Department of Treasury, *United Nations Monetary and Financial Conference, Articles of Agreement*, 56.

78. Urquidi, "Elasticidad y rigidez de Bretton Woods," 615. This is one reason Mexican experts such as Villaseñor continued to advocate for the creation of the IAB even after the Bretton Woods institutions came into being.

79. Urquidi, "Elasticidad y rigidez de Bretton Woods," 614.

1. Castillo Nájera, "Organization of Peace," 70.
2. See "Operation of the Mexican-American Commission for Economic Cooperation," *FRUS 1944*, 2:1198–1212.
3. On industrialization and debates over planning, see Gauss, *Made in Mexico*.
4. "Que vuelva el régimen de la propiedad privada," *Novedades* (México, D. F.), September 10, 1944.
5. Niblo, *War, Diplomacy, and Development*, 180.
6. Gauss, *Made in Mexico*, 189–91.
7. Pan-American Union, "Third Meeting of Ministers of Foreign Affairs of the American Republics, Final Act," 74.
8. Green, *Containment of Latin America*, 124–36.
9. "Industrial and Other Economic Development in the Western Hemisphere," November 22, 1943, FDRPL, President's Official File (OF) 5300—Living Standards Abroad.
10. Conference of Commissions of Inter-American Development, *Proceedings*.
11. Niblo, *War, Diplomacy, and Development*, 195.
12. "Hull Gives Pledge to Small Nations," *New York Times*, June 2, 1944.
13. "Peace Plan Reported," *New York Times*, July 4, 1944.
14. "Memorandum: Opinion of the Department of Foreign Relations," in *Documents of the United Nations Conference on International Organization, San Francisco*, Vol. 3, *Dumbarton Oaks Proposals* [hereafter *Dumbarton Oaks Proposals*], 55.
15. Reproduced as "United States Tentative Proposal for a General International Organization," July 18, 1944, in *FRUS 1944*, 1:653.
16. "Project for the Constitution of a 'Permanent Union of Nations' Submitted by the Department of Foreign Relations of Mexico to the Government of the United States of America on September 5, 1944," *Dumbarton Oaks Proposals*, 166.
17. "Brazilian Comment on Dumbarton Oaks Proposals," November 4, 1944, *Dumbarton Oaks Proposals*, 232; and "Memorandum of Conversation, by the Acting Director of the Office of American Republic Affairs, Washington, September 12, 1944, in *FRUS 1944*, 1:924.
18. "Conferencia con el Señor Embajador de los Paises Bajos en Washington," October 27, 1944, AHSREM, Fondo de Dirección General de Asuntos Diplomáticos (DGAD), III-1946-1(I).
19. Memorandum of Conversation by the Chief of the Division of Caribbean and Central American Affairs (Cabot), Washington, September 16, 1944, in *FRUS 1944*, 1:929.
20. Bertam Hulen, "South American Issues Sharpen as Peace Nears," *New York Times*, September 24, 1944.
21. Memorandum of Conversation by the Chief of the Division of Caribbean and Central American Affairs (Cabot), Washington, September 15, 1944, in *FRUS 1944*, 1:925.

22. *Dumbarton Oaks Proposals*, 27–28.

23. "Representación igual a la de los 4 grandes," *El Universal* (México D. F.), February 3, 1945.

24. "Observations of the Government of Venezuela on the Recommendations Adopted at the Dumbarton Oaks Conferences for the Creation of a Peace Organization," October 31, 1944, *Dumbarton Oaks Proposals*, 189.

25. *Dumbarton Oaks Proposals*, 52, 535. The question of racial equality in the new organization was also a topic followed closely by Black newspapers in the United States, such as the *New York Amsterdam News*. See A. M. Wendell Malliet, "Fate of Small Nations Weighed in Balance at Dumbarton Oaks," *New York Amsterdam News*, September 2, 1944.

26. Tello circular, November 22, 1944, AHSREM, DGAD, III-1946-1(I); and "Chinese Proposals on Dumbarton Oaks Proposals," *Dumbarton Oaks Proposals*, 25.

27. "Memorandum: Opinion of the Department of Foreign Relations," *Dumbarton Oaks Proposals*, 102.

28. "Memorandum: Opinion of the Department of Foreign Relations," *Dumbarton Oaks Proposals*, 60. See also Castañeda, *Mexico and the United Nations*, 26.

29. *Dumbarton Oaks Proposals*, 272–73.

30. Sikkink, "Latin American Countries as Norm Protagonists of the Idea of International Human Rights," 394.

31. "Memorandum: Opinion of the Department of Foreign Relations," *Dumbarton Oaks Proposals*, 66–69.

32. Castañeda, *Mexico and the United Nations*, 45. As Castañeda points out, these positions, particularly regarding the definition of "domestic affairs," would change as the new organization was negotiated at San Francisco.

33. "Memorandum: Opinion of the Department of Foreign Relations," *Dumbarton Oaks Proposals*, 145.

34. "Observations of the Government of Venezuela," *Dumbarton Oaks Proposals*, 217–19.

35. *Dumbarton Oaks Proposals*, 586.

36. *Dumbarton Oaks Proposals*, 571.

37. *Dumbarton Oaks Proposals*, 498.

38. Messersmith a SRE, November 3, 1944, AHSREM, L-E-452.

39. "Junta de ministros de relaciones, aquí," *Excélsior*, November 17, 1943; "Informe del comite ejecutivo sobre problemas de la post guerra: Conferencia técnico-económica interamericana," Presentado al Consejo Directivo de la Unión Panamericana en la session del 5 de abril, 1944, AGN, Fondo Manuel Ávila Camacho (MAC), 433/489; and De la Colina a SRE, December 30, 1944, AHSREM, L-E-452.

40. See Estrada, *La doctrina Estrada*.

41. Messersmith a SRE, November 3, 1944, AHSREM, L-E-442; Messersmith to the Secretary of State, Mexico City. November 8, 1944, in *FRUS 1944*, 7:39. See also Soledad Loaeza, "La política intervencionista de Manuel Ávila Camacho."

42. Messersmith a Padilla, December 12, 1944, AHSREM, L-E-442.

43. Memorandum, US Embassy, Mexico City, January 6, 1945, AHSREM, L-E-452.

44. Gauss, *Made in Mexico*, 180.

45. Villaseñor, "La economía de guerra en México"; Villaseñor, "Medios de cooperacion económica entre los Estados Unidos y México."

46. Niblo, *War, Diplomacy and Development*, 112.

47. Department of State to the Mexican Embassy, January 14, 1944, in *FRUS 1944*, 7:1213.

48. Bohan to McClintock, January 27, 1945, in *FRUS 1945*, 9:64.

49. Bohan to Rockefeller, January 29, 1945, in *FRUS 1945*, 9:71. For Bohan's role at Chapultepec and elsewhere, see Oral History Interview with Merwin L. Bohan, Dallas, Texas, June 15, 1974, Truman Library, www.trumanlibrary.org/oralhist /bohanm.htm.

50. Acting Secretary of State (Grew) to the Ambassador in Mexico (Messersmith), Washington, February 5, 1945, in *FRUS 1945*, 9:83.

51. Economic Memorandum No. 1 by Merwin Bohan, February 12, 1945, in *FRUS 1945*, 9:105.

52. Economic Memorandum No. 2 by Merwin L. Bohan, February 13, 1945, in *FRUS 1945*, 9:112.

53. Memorandum of Conversation by Merwin L. Bohan, January 29, 1945, in *FRUS 1945*, 9:73.

54. Economic Memorandum No. 1 by Merwin Bohan, 103.

55. "Mexico Talks Designed to Link Hemisphere to Dumbarton Oaks," *New York Times*, February 19, 1945; and Lisa Sergio, "Column of the Air," WQXR, February 21, 1945, AHSREM, L-E 442.

56. "Inaugural Address by His Excellency General Manuel Ávila Camacho, President of the Republic of Mexico, Chamber of Deputies," February 21, 1945, AHSREM, DGAD, III-1098-1. The quotes that follow in this paragraph are also from this source.

57. For Mexican proposals, see "Draft Presentation of the Mexican Delegation on Reorganization of the Union of the American Republics," Doc. No. 43, CI-PR-23, AHSREM, L-E-481.

58. Political Memorandum No. 3 by Mr. William Sanders, February 2, 1945, in *FRUS 1945*, 9:79.

59. Pan-American Union, *Final Act of the Inter-American Conference on Problems of War and Peace*, 74.

60. Francis O. Wilcox, "The Yalta Voting Formula," 945.

61. "Extemporaneous Address by the Secretary of Foreign Affairs of Mexico and Chairman of the Conference, Lic. Ezequiel Padilla," March 5, 1945, AHSREM, L-E-478.

62. For context on fascist mobilization in Mexico, see Schuler, *Mexico Between Hitler and Roosevelt*.

63. Discurso de Lic Padilla (en inglés), AHSREM, L-E-480. The quotes that follow in this paragraph are also from this source.

64. Economic Memorandum No. 2 by Merwin L. Bohan, February 13, 1945, in *FRUS 1945*, 9:112.

65. Discurso de Lic Padilla (en inglés), AHSREM, L-E-480. Unless otherwise indicated, the quotes that follow in this paragraph are also from this source.

66. The American Delegation to the Acting Secretary of State, Mexico City, February 23, 1945, *FRUS 1945*, 9:123.

67. Delegation of Bolivia, "Draft Declaration," Doc. No. 183, CI-PR-157, AHSREM, L-E-508.

68. "La igualdad soberana es la base para una paz duradera," *El Informador* (Guadalajara), February 25, 1945; and "Estados Unidos proclama, por boca de Stettinius, la igualdad y soberanía de todas la naciones," *La Prensa* (México, D.F.), February 23, 1945.

69. "La conferencia de cancilleres: Discurso de Mr. Edward R. Stettinius Secretario de Estado de los EE. UU.," *Futuro*, March 1945.

70. United States Delegation, "Draft Economic Charter of the Americas," February 24, 1945, Doc. No. 98, CI-PR-78, AHSREM, L-E-490.

71. "U.S. Proposals at Mexico City Parley for a Hemisphere Charter," *New York Times*, February 27, 1945.

72. Cosío Villegas, *American Extremes*, 181.

73. "La Industria nacional se opone a la Carta Económica de América," *Novedades* (México, D. F.), February 28, 1945.

74. "Tranquiliza el Sr. Padilla a los industriales," *Excélsior* (México, D.F.), February 28, 1945.

75. "Clayton Trade Plan Praised by Padilla," *New York Times*, March 1, 1945.

76. The American Delegation to the Acting Secretary of State, Mexico City, March 2, 1945, in *FRUS 1945*, 9:138.

77. Gauss, *Made in Mexico*, 187.

78. Manuel Méndez, "A quien sirve Ezequiel Padilla?," *Futuro* 98 (September 1945); and "Ezequiel Padilla, candidato de la reacción y el imperialismo," *Futuro* 106 (December 1945).

79. Confederación de Trabajadores de América Latina (CTAL), *Balance de la Conferencia Inter-Americana de Chapultepec*.

80. CTAL, *Balance de la Conferencia*, 11–12.

81. Delegación de Chile, "Medidas para aliviar la desocupación," Doc. No. 52, CI-PR-32; and "Plan Americano de industrialización," Doc. No. 53, CI-PR-33, AHSREM, L-E-465.

82. Delegation of Venezuela, "Draft Resolution, Organization for Post-War Transportation," Doc. No. 77, CI-PR-57, and "Draft Resolution, Multilateral Agreements for the Distribution of Products," Doc. No. 79, CI-PR-59, AHSREM, L-E-481.

83. Delegation of Peru, "Draft Resolution, Economic Demobilization of the Hemisphere during the Transitions Period," Doc. No. 122, CI-PR-102, and "Convention for the Development of Post-War Commercial Policy," Doc. No. 123, CI-PR-103, AHSREM, L-E-482.

84. Delegation of the Dominican Republic, "Draft Resolution, Agricultural Production and Distribution," Doc No. 66, CI-SP-46, and "Draft Resolution, Social Legislation to Protect Workers," Doc No. 67, CI-PR-47, AHSREM, L-E-481.

85. Delegation of Cuba, "Investment of Capital in the American Republics," Doc. No. 130, CI-PR-110, and "Coordination of Foreign Investment with National Economies," Doc. No. 135, CI-PR-115, AHSREM, L-E-482.

86. Delegación de Honduras, "Proyecto de resolucion sobre creación permanente del comite consultivo económico financiero interamericano," Doc. No. 125, CI-PR-105; Delegación de Guatemala, "Ayuda financiera y técnica a los países americanos para elevar su nivel de vida," Doc. No. 170, CI-PR-150; and "Establecimiento de un organismo internacional para regulación de la producción, distribución y precios de materials primas," Doc. No. 176, CI-PR-152, AHSREM, L-E-465.

87. Delegação do Brasil, "Projeto de resolução," Doc. No. 109, CI-PR-89, and "Capital Investments," Doc. No. 138, CI-PR-118, AHSREM, L-E-482.

88. Delegation of Brazil, "The Betterment of Mankind," Doc. No 136, CI-PR-116, AHSREM, L-E-490.

89. All contained in AHSREM, L-E-490.

90. Delegation of Mexico, "Draft Resolution, Economic Coordination of the Resources of the Continent," Doc. No. 59, CI-PR-39, AHSREM, L-E-490.

91. Delegation of Mexico, "Draft Resolution, Organized Sale of Primary Products," Doc. No. 62, CI-PR-42, AHSREM, L-E-490.

92. Delegation of Mexico, "Draft Resolution, Industrialization of America," Doc. No. 60, CI-PR-40, AHSREM, L-E-490.

93. Report by Dudley B. Bonsal, Washington, February 15, 1945, in *FRUS 1945*, 9:120.

94. The American Delegation to the Acting Secretary of State, Mexico City, March 7, 1945, in *FRUS 1945*, 9:148.

95. Pan-American Union, *Final Act of the Inter-American Conference on Problems of War and Peace*, 90.

96. Original proposals contained in AHSREM, L-E-490; final in Pan-American Union, *Final Act of the Inter-American Conference on Problems of War and Peace*, 92–96.

97. Most of these changes were hashed out early in the conference; a February 24 working draft by the fourth commission already included most of them, despite the fact that the unrevised versions were published in newspapers a few days later. "Informe del Comite 1—Venta y distribución de productos, de la Subcomisión A de la Cuarta Comisión," n.d., AHSREM, L-E-466.

98. Text of radio remarks by his Excellency Doctor Ezequiel Padilla, March 8, 1945, AHSREM, L-E-486.

99. CTAL, "Balance de la Conferencia." The quotes that follow in this paragraph are also from this source.

100. On the Washington conference, see Rabe, "Elusive Conference."

1. "Commission III: Other Means of International Financial Cooperation, Third (final) meeting: Transcript," July 20, 1944, in Schuler and Rosenberg, *Bretton Woods Transcripts*.

2. Eduardo Villaseñor, "Some Aspects of Mexico's Post-War Economy," English translation of speech to the Asociación de Banqueros de México, 1944, in COLMEX, FEV, caja 5, exp. 1.

3. Beteta a Torres Bodet, April 22, 1947, AHSREM, Fondo Jaime Torres Bodet (JTB), exp. 14.

4. Niblo, *War, Diplomacy, and Development*, 193.

5. Niblo, *War, Diplomacy, and Development*, 205.

6. Babb, "Embeddedness, Inflation, and International Regimes."

7. Villaseñor, "Some Aspects of Mexico's Post-War Economy."

8. See Alexander, *Sons of the Mexican Revolution*.

9. Niblo, *Mexico in the 1940s*, 207–15.

10. Carr, *Marxism and Communism in Twentieth-Century Mexico*, 143.

11. See Navarro, *Political Intelligence and the Creation of Modern Mexico*.

12. Maxfield, *Governing Capital*, 44.

13. Niblo, *Mexico in the 1940s*, 189.

14. Alexander, *Sons of the Mexican Revolution*, 146.

15. "Text of President Aleman's Address before U.N.," *New York Times*, May 4, 1947.

16. Brown, *United States and the Restoration of World Trade*, 20–22. See also Hudec, *Developing Countries in the GATT Legal System*, and Irwin, Mavroidis, and Sykes, *Genesis of the GATT*, 83n110 and 133–34.

17. Three more countries, Chile, Lebanon, and Norway, were subsequently added. See Oral History Interview with John M. Leddy, Washington, DC, June 15, 1973, Truman Library, www.trumanlibrary.gov/library/oral-histories/leddyj.

18. "Suggested Draft of a Charter for International Trade Organization of the United Nations" Executive Committee on Economic Foreign Policy (ECEFP) Document D-70/46, July 25, 1946; and Steffek, *Embedded Liberalism and Its Critics*, 44–46.

19. UN E/PC/T/33.

20. Hudec, *Developing Countries in the GATT Legal System*, 28.

21. Wilcox, *Charter for World Trade*, 141.

22. Slobodian, *Globalists*, 10, 261, 271-72.

23. UN E/PC/T/W.14.

24. Comite preparatorio de la Conferencia Internacional Sobre Comercio y Trabajo, "Carta de la Organización Internacional de Comercio de las Naciones Unidas, Sugestiones presentadas por el Gobierno de Brasil," UN E/PC/T/W.16, AHSREM, DGAD, III-2849-1(1a).

25. Wilcox, *Charter for World Trade*, 30, 142.

26. Zeiler, *Free Trade, Free World*, 72–73.

27. Wilcox, *Charter for World Trade*, 41.

28. Richard Toye has argued that the United States made concessions to the developing world in an attempt to "extend its concept of multilateralism so as to allow a wide range of countries to help to design the new organization, rather than hoping that they would accede, passively, to a U.S. blueprint." This is certainly true, but to conceive of this as a novelty in 1947 plainly ignores the history detailed here in the preceding chapters. Toye, "Developing Multilateralism," 284.

29. The London draft was published and circulated around the world. United States Department of State, *Preliminary Draft, Charter of the International Trade Organization of the United Nations*.

30. Torres Bodet a Andrés Serra Rojas, January 22, 1947, AHSREM, DGAD, III-2849-1(1a).

31. "Informe que la Comisión Intersecretarial encargada del estudio preliminar del proyecto de Carta Constitutiva de la Organización Internacional de Comercio de las Naciones Unidas rinde al Consejo Nacional de Comercio Exterior," March 25, 1947, AHSREM, DGAD, III-2849-1(1a).

32. SRE a Padilla Nervo, February 176, 1947, AHSREM, DGAD, III-2849-1(1a).

33. "Informe que la Comisión Intersecretarial," 85.

34. Niblo, *War, Diplomacy and Development*, 205.

35. "Informe que la Comisión Intersecretarial," 18.

36. "Informe que la Comisión Intersecretarial," 34.

37. "Informe que la Comisión Intersecretarial," 102.

38. Harry S. Truman, Address on Foreign Economic Policy Delivered at Baylor University, March 6, 1945, www.trumanlibrary.gov/library/public-papers/52/add ress-foreign-economic-policy-delivered-baylor-university.

39. "Informe que la Comisión Intersecretarial," 61. The quote that follows in this paragraph is also from this source, same page.

40. SRE al EMBAMEX DC, January 21, 1947, AHSREM, DGAD, III-2849-1(4a).

41. Aguilar a SRE, March 19, 1947. AHSREM, DGAD, III-2849-1(3a).

42. Aguilar a SRE, March 14, 1947, AHSREM, DGAD, III-2849-1(3a).

43. Memorandum, "Observaciones al margen de las audiencias informales sobre la propuesta Carta para la Organización Internacional del Comercio," San Francisco, March 17, 1947, AHSREM, DGAD, III-2849-1(4a).

44. Lelo de Larrea al EMBAMEX DC, March 14, 1947, in AHSREM, DGAD, III-2849-1(4a).

45. Enrique R. Ballesteros, "Memorandum: Sesión del comité denominado de 'Ways and Means' de la Cámara de Diputados," March 26, 1947, AHSREM, DGAD, III-2849-1(4a).

46. Barreda a SRE, March 15, 1947, AHSREM, DGAD, III-2849-1(3a).

47. "Economic War Due if Trade Bars Stay, Truman Warns U.S.," *New York Times*, March 7, 1947.

48. Irwin, Mavroidis, and Sykes, *Genesis of the GATT*, 82.

49. "Mexico: Good Friend," *Time*, April 28, 1947; see Niblo, *Mexico in the 1940s*, 208.

50. Juan Brochas, "Lo cortés no quita lo valiente," *La Voz de México*, February 23, 1947, cited in Booth, "Taming the Dead."

51. Fouque, Benítez, and Morros, "Protección a la industria," 58.

52. Quoted in Niblo, *War, Diplomacy, and Development*, 207.

53. UN E/PC/T/186.

54. Barreda a SRE, April 22, 1947, AHSREM, DGAD, III-2849-1(4a); for Chile's and India's speeches, see UN E/PC/T/PV.2/4.

55. Barreda a SRE, April 22, 1947, AHSREM, DGAD, III-2849-1(4a).

56. "Opiniones de los gobiernos de las repúblicas latinoamericanas sobre la proyectada carta para una Organización Internacional de Comercio," May 9, 1947, AHSREM, DGAD, III-2849-1(4a).

57. See Hilton, "United States, Brazil, and the Cold War, 1945–1960."

58. Despite this, however, the Cuban delegation would later reveal in a speech that the United States was—hypocritically, in their view—continuing to defend their use of quantitative restrictions, including quotas to protect their own agricultural production, even while working to convince the rest of the world to abandon such controls. Barreda judged the Cuban intervention a "magnificent speech" when he sent its text back to Mexico City. UN E/PC/T/A/PV/22; Barreda a SRE, July 3, 1947, AHSREM, DGAD, III-2849-1(5a).

59. UN E/PC/T/EC/SR.2/7.

60. Raúl Noriega (ONU) a SRE, July 30, 1947, AHSREM, DGAD, III-2849-1(4a); and UN E/PC/T/A/PV/22.

61. Irwin, Mavroidis, and Sykes, *Genesis of the GATT*, 88.

62. UN E/PC/T/90.

63. Barreda a SRE, June 20, 1947, AHSREM, DGAD, III-2849-1(5a).

64. Wilcox, *Charter for World Trade*, 146.

65. Barreda a SRE, April 22, 1947, AHSREM, DGAD, III-2849-1(4a).

66. Secretary of State to the Mexican Ambassador (Espinosa de los Monteros), Washington, June 12, 1947, in *FRUS 1947*, 8:775.

67. Niblo, *War, Diplomacy, and Development*, 208.

68. Secretary of State to the Embassy in Mexico, Washington, October 22, 1947, in *FRUS 1947*, 8:781.

69. Niblo, *War, Diplomacy, and Development*, 210; and Gauss, *Made in Mexico*, 130.

70. "Invitación de Beteta al capital extranjero," *El Informador* (Guadalajara), October 22, 1947; and Niblo, *War Diplomacy, and Development*, 209.

71. "Mexicans Protest Tariff Cut," *New York Times*, November 18, 1947.

72. "C.T.M.: A la opinión pública y a la clase obrera del país," *Novedades* (México, D.F.), November 17, 1947, cited in Booth, "Taming the Dead."

73. Cited in Booth, "Taming the Dead."

74. "Tuvo lugar la manifestación en contra del 'Plan Clayton,'" *El Informador* (Guadalajara), November 18, 1947.

75. "Debe formarse un frente democrático nacional para oponerse a la acotación del Plan Clayton," *La Voz de México*, November 19, 1947, cited in Booth, "Taming the Dead."

76. The ASU was founded in 1946 by Hernán Laborde after his ousting from the PCM over opposition to the assassination of Trotsky. See Carr, *Maxism and Communism in Twentieth-Century Mexico*, 149.

77. Acción Socialista Unificada, "A los trabajadores, al pueblo de México," AGN, Dirección General de Investigaciones Políticas y Sociales (DGIPS), caja 796, cited in Booth, "Taming the Dead."

78. Booth, "Taming the Dead."

79. "Tuvo lugar la manifestación en contra del 'Plan Clayton,'" *El Informador* (Guadalajara), November 18, 1947.

80. "La manifestación contra el Plan Clayton, será una demostración general," *Novedades* (México, D. F.), November 17, 1947, cited in Booth, "Taming the Dead."

81. "Absolute Free Trade Opposed by Mexico," *New York Times*, November 20, 1947.

82. "U.S. Delegation to Trade and Employment Conference," Department of State *Bulletin*, November 23, 1947, 981–82.

83. Toye, "Developing Multilateralism," 289.

84. Antônio de V. Ferreira-Braga to Raul Fernandes October 10, 1947, cited in Breda dos Santos, "Latin American Countries and the Establishment of the Multilateral Trading System," 325.

85. Beteta a Alemán, November 29, 1947, AGN, Fondo Miguel Alemán Valdés (MAV), exp. 433/216.

86. Babb, *Managing Mexico*, 41.

87. Gauss, *Made in Mexico*, 172–78; and Alexander, *Sons of the Mexican Revolution*, 88.

88. Beteta a Alemán, November 29, 1947, AGN, MAV, exp. 433/216.

89. Brown, *United States and the Restoration of World Trade*, 136.

90. Zeiler, *Free Trade, Free World*, 140.

91. "Old Issue Enters Cuba Trade Talks," *New York Times*, November 27, 1947.

92. Address by Lic. Ramón Beteta, President, the Mexican Delegation, United Nations Conference on Trade and Employment, Havana, November 26, 1947, UN Press Release ITO/32. The quotes that follow in this paragraph and the next are, unless otherwise noted, from this source.

93. Beteta a Alemán, November 29, 1947, AGN, MAV, exp. 433/216.

94. "Old Issue Enters Cuba Trade Talks," *New York Times*, November 27, 1947.

95. Wilcox, *Charter for World Trade*, 47.

96. Beteta a Alemán, November 29, 1947, AGN, MAV, exp. 433/216. The quotes that follow in this paragraph are also from this source.

97. "Duties on Imports Raised by Mexico," *New York Times*, December 14, 1947.

98. Zeiler, *Free Trade, Free World*, 139.

99. For example, UN E/CONF.2/C.l/C/W.l; E/CONF.2/11/Add.3; and E/CONF.2/11/Add.31. On the labor provisions, see see Jensen, "Negotiating a World Trade and Employment Charter," 83–109.

100. UN E/CONF.2/C.2/6/Add.14 (emphasis added).

101. UN E/CONF.2/C.2/6/Add.14; and Zeiler, *Free Trade, Free World*, 128.

102. UN E/CONF.2/C.2/6/Add.14.

103. UN E/CONF.2/C.2/SR.13.

104. UN E/CONF.2/C.2/9.

105. UN E/CONF.2/C.2/6/Add.3; and Wilcox, *Charter for World Trade*, 143.

106. UN E/CONF.2/C.2/9.

107. UN E/CONF.2/C.2/SR.14.

108. UN E/CONF.2/C.2/9.

109. UN E/CONF.2/C.2/D/W.2; and E/CONF.2/32.

110. UN E/CONF.2/C3/1/Add.43.

111. UN E/CONF.2/C.3/A/W.15.

112. UN E/CONF.2/11/Add.31.

113. Boletín para la prensa, January 28, 1948, AGN, MAV, exp. 433/216.

114. Boletín para la prensa, January 28, 1948, AGN, MAV, exp. 433/216.

115. UN E/CONF2./C.3/A/W.37.

116. United States Department of State, *Havana Charter for an International Trade Organization*, 46.

117. UN E/CONF2./C.3/A/W.37; and Zeiler, *Free Trade, Free World*, 140.

118. United States Department of State, *Havana Charter for an International Trade Organization*, 4; and Boletín para la prensa, January 28, 1948, AGN, MAV, exp. 433/216.

119. Boletín para la prensa, January 28, 1948, AGN, MAV, exp. 433/216.

120. Boletín para la prensa, January 28, 1948, AGN, MAV, exp. 433/216; and "Triumfo decisivo de México en la Habana," *El Informador* (Guadalajara), January 30, 1948.

121. Toye, "Developing Multilateralism," 295.

122. Beteta a Alemán, February 5, 1948, AGN, MAV, exp. 433/216.

123. UN E/CONF.2/C.6/2/ Add.10; and E/CONF.2/C2/6/Add.17.

124. Brown, *United States and the Restoration of World Trade*, 156.

125. UN E/CONF.2/C2/6/Add.17.

126. UN E/CONF.2/58; Wilcox, *Charter for World Trade*, 143; and Brown, *United States and the Restoration of World Trade*, 158.

127. Zeiler, *Free Trade, Free World*, 140; and Brown, *United States and the Restoration of World Trade*, 158.

128. Quoted in Toye, "Developing Multilateralism," 296.

129. Quoted in Zeiler, *Free Trade, Free World*, 135.

130. UN Press Release ITO/192.

131. National Foreign Trade Council, *Position of the National Foreign Trade Council*, 2.

132. National Foreign Trade Council, *Position of the National Foreign Trade Council*, 3.

133. See Long, *Latin America Confronts the United States*, 28; and López-Maya, "Change in the Discourse of U.S.-Latin American Relations," 143.

134. Mexico compiled press clippings on the topic from throughout the region; they are found in AHSREM, JTB, exp. 15.

135. George C. Marshall, "Interdependence of the Americas," Department of State *Bulletin*, April 11, 1948, 469–73.

136. See Story, "Trade Politics in the Third World."

CHAPTER SEVEN. THE PRICE OF SUCCESS

1. Transcript of interview of Víctor L. Urquidi by Thomas G. Weiss, Oslo, June 18–19, 2000, United Nations Intellectual History Project, 23.

2. Aggarwal, *Debt Games*, 281–86.

3. Maxfield, "Politics of Mexican Financial Policy," 242.

4. Cline, *Mexico*, 245.

5. Mexican GDP data from Aparicio Cabrera, "Series estadísticas de la economía mexicana en el siglo XX," 74.

6. Morton, *Revolution and State in Modern Mexico*, 82.

7. World Bank data, http://projects.worldbank.org.

8. Urzúa, "Five Decades of Relations between the World Bank and Mexico," 62.

9. "Memorandum of a Conversation, Mexico City," August 1, 1958, *FRUS 1958–60*, 5:832.

10. Marichal, "Deuda externa y política en México, 1946–2000," 458.

11. Marichal, "Deuda externa y política en México, 1946–2000," 461.

12. See Ortiz Mena, "Desarrollo estabilizador."

13. Quoted in Keller, *Mexico's Cold War*, 61; see also Cypher, *State and Capital in Mexico*, 72; and Whiting, *Political Economy of Foreign Investment in Mexico*, 73.

14. See Cypher, *State and Capital in Mexico* and FitzGerald, "Financial Constraint on Relative Autonomy."

15. Because of the rapid growth of the economy, this represented a slight decline as a share of GDP over this period. Stallings, *Banker to the Third World*, 125.

16. Whiting, *Political Economy of Foreign Investment in Mexico*, 70.

17. Whiting, *Political Economy of Foreign Investment in Mexico*, 31, 69.

18. Whiting, *Political Economy of Foreign Investment in Mexico*, 77.

19. Babb, *Managing Mexico*, 84.

20. Stallings, *Banker to the Third World*, 89.

21. Whiting, *Political Economy of Foreign Investment in Mexico*, 75.

22. Stallings, *Banker to the Third World*, 89.

23. Babb, *Managing Mexico*, 84; and Thompson, *Inflation, Financial Markets and Economic Development*, 181.

24. See Marichal, "Deuda externa y política en México, 1946–2000." Despite this increase, Mexico's debt to GDP ratio was fairly steady until the Echeverría administration. See Babb, *Managing Mexico*, 115.

25. See Zolov, *Last Good Neighbor*.

26. Pettinà, "'Adapting to the New World'."

27. Friedman, "Fracas in Caracas," 680.

28. "Memorandum of Discussion at the 189th Meeting of the National Security Council on Thursday, March 18, 1954," in *FRUS 1952–1954*, 4:304–5.

29. Friedman, "Fracas in Caracas," 674.

30. Keller, *Mexico's Cold War*, 43–48.

31. Rabe, "Alliance for Progress."

32. Pettinà, "Global Horizons," 747.

33. Pettinà, "Global Horizons," 750.

34. On the similar Brazilian ambiguity, see Hershberg, "'High-Spirited Confusion'," 373–88.

35. Quoted in Pettinà, "Global Horizons," 754.

36. SRE a EMBAMEX Cairo, July 5, 1962, AHSREM, Dirección General de Organismos Internacionales (DGOI), XII-758-10.

37. "Discurso pronunciado por el licenciado Octaviano Campos Salas, gerente del Banco de México y presidente de la delegación mexicana ante la Conferencia Sobre Problemas de Desarrollo Economico," July 13 1962, AHSREM, DGOI, XII-758-10. Published in Non-Aligned Movement, *Conference on the Problems of Economic Development*.

38. "Pliego de instrucciones confidenciales para la delegación mexicana que asistiera a la Conferencia Sobre los Problemas Económicos del Desarrollo que tendrá lugar en Cairo a partir de 9 de Julio 1962," AHSREM, DGOI, XII-758-10.

39. "Pliego de Instrucciones," AHSREM, DGOI, XII-758-10.

40. Lorenzini, *Global Development*, 97.

41. Browne, *United Nations Development Programme and System*, 13.

42. See Singer, "Terms of Trade Controversy and the Evolution of Soft Financing: Early Years in the UN."

43. "Observaciones del gobierno de México al anteproyecto de Convenio Económico General Interamericano," August 2, 1957, AHSREM, DGOI, XII-1047-1.

44. "Summary Notes of a Meeting of the Delegation's Steering Committee, Buenos Aires," August 26, 1957, in *FRUS 1955–1957*, 6:528.

45. "Memorandum from the Deputy Assistant Secretary of State for Inter-American Affairs (Snow) to the Secretary of State," Washington, August 22, 1957, in *FRUS 1955–1957*, 6:525.

46. "Minutes of a Staff Meeting, Bureau of Economic Affairs, Department of State, Washington," September 11, 1957, in *FRUS 1955–1957*, 6:559.

47. Dell, *Inter-American Development Bank*, 9.

48. Long, *Latin America Confronts the United States*, 44–45.

49. Long, *Latin America Confronts the United States*, 55.

50. "The Acting Secretary of State to Diplomatic Offices in the American Republics, Washington," November 27, 1951, in *FRUS 1951*, 2:1072.

51. Dosman, *Life and Times of Raúl Prebisch*, 270.

52. Transcript of Interview of Víctor L. Urquidi, United Nations Intellectual History Project, 76; and Dosman, *Life and Times of Raúl Prebisch*, 270.

53. Transcript of Interview of Víctor L. Urquidi, 76.

54. Pollock, Kerner, and Love, "Raúl Prebisch on ECLAC's Achievements and Deficiencies," 14.

55. See Carmona, "Homenaje a Juan F. Noyola Vazquez."

56. See Fonseca and Salomão, "Furtado vs. Prebisch."

57. Transcript of Interview of Víctor L. Urquidi, 93.

58. Transcript of Interview of Víctor L. Urquidi, 94.

59. "Proyecto de acuerdo sobre la consulta remitida por el Secretario de la ONU Sobre la creación de un Fondo para el Financiamiento de Países Insuficientemente Desarrollados," in AHSREM, DGOI, XII-325-11.

60. Jolly et al., *UN Contributions to Development Thinking and Practice*, 74.

61. United Nations, *Report on a Special United Nations Fund for Economic Development*, E/2381.

62. Elder and Murden, *Economic Co-operation*, 5.

63. Quoted in Elder and Murden, *Economic Co-operation*, 13–14.

64. Carrillo Flores a SRE, March 15, 1956; and SRE a Representante Permanente de México ante las Naciones Unidas, July 18, 1956, in AHSREM, DGOI, XII-820-3.

65. Carrillo Flores a SRE, June 20, 1957, in AHSREM, DGOI, XII-820-3.

66. Babb, *Managing Mexico*, 248 fn. 12; 91.

67. Middlebrook, *Paradox of Revolution*, 119.

68. Urzúa, "Five Decades of Relations between the World Bank and Mexico," 53.

69. Maxfield, *Gatekeepers of Growth*, 97.

70. Maxfield, *Gatekeepers of Growth*, 95.

71. Urzúa, "Five Decades of Relations between the World Bank and Mexico," 57.

72. World Bank, *OED Study of Bank/Mexico Relations*, 92.

73. Combined Mexican Working Party, *Major Long-Term Trends in the Mexican Economy*, i.

74. Babb, *Managing Mexico*, 85.

75. Combined Mexican Working Party, *Major Long-Term Trends in the Mexican Economy*, 13.

76. Combined Mexican Working Party, *Major Long-Term Trends in the Mexican Economy*, 208.

77. Combined Mexican Working Party, *Major Long-Term Trends in the Mexican Economy*, 151.

78. World Bank, *OED Study of Bank/Mexico Relations*, xvii.

79. Transcript of Interview of Víctor L. Urquidi, 91; and World Bank, *OED Study of Bank/Mexico Relations*, 93.

80. Urzúa, "Five Decades of Relations between the World Bank and Mexico," 58.

81. World Bank, *OED Study of Bank/Mexico Relations*, 93.

82. Despatch from the Embassy in Mexico to the Department of State, Mexico City, July 21, 1958, in *FRUS 1958–60*, 5:829.

83. World Bank, *OED Study of Bank/Mexico Relations*, 6.

84. World Bank, *OED Study of Bank/Mexico Relations*, 130.

85. Eichengreen, *Globalizing Capital*, 131.

86. See Irwin, "The Nixon Shock after Forty Years."

87. The Mexican representatives to the G77 lobbied to host in Mexico City owing to "the broad participation that the country has always had in international economic conferences," but they were unsuccessful. "Memorandum de conversación," Tlatelolco, February 4, 1971, AGN, Fondo Luis Echeverría Álvarez (LEA), caja 530.

88. "Manifesto of Latin America, XI Special Meeting of the Special Commission for Latin American Coordination (CECLA), Buenos Aires, September 1971," reprinted in US Congress, Senate Foreign Relations Committee, *Inter-American Relations*, 277–79.

89. "Manifesto of Latin America," 278.

90. "Algunos países debilitan propuesta revolucionaria por temor a club de ricos," *Expreso* (Lima), October 23, 1971.

91. SRE Memo: Confidencial—expropriaciones, February 3, 1972, AGN, Archivo Particular Porfirio Muñoz Ledo (PML), caja 27, exp. 8. On the Peruvian revolution and the United States, see Brands, "United States and the Peruvian Challenge, 1968–1975."

92. SRE Memo: Confidencial—expropriaciones, AGN, PML, caja 27, exp. 8.

93. Zorrilla (Lima) a SRE, 28 October 1971, AHSREM, Fondo SubSecretario, B1-415-1(3a).

94. "Algunos países debilitan propuesta revolucionaria por temor a club de ricos," *Expreso* (Lima), October 23, 1971; "Propuesta peruana siguen debatiendo," *Expreso* (Lima), October 24, 1971; and "Impase en la CECLA," *Expreso* (Lima), October 25, 1971, AHSREM, Fondo SubSecretario, B1-415-1(3a).

95. "Impase en la CECLA," *Expreso* (Lima), October 25, 1971.

96. United Nations Economic Commission for Africa, "Draft Resolution: Reform of the International Monetary System," 9th Session, Addis Ababa, Ethiopia, February 3–14, 1969.

97. "África: Por nuevo sistema monetario internacional," *Expreso* (Lima), October 26, 1971.

98. "Latinoamérica: Unida frente a problema monetario internacional," *Expreso* (Lima), October 27, 1971.

99. Resolution 27/XII, in CECLA, "The Consensus of Lima," Twelfth Meeting of the Special Committee on Latin American Coordination, Lima, October 20–27, 1971, in Group of 77, *Third World without Superpowers*, 1:553–92.

100. Statement by Mr. Boteflika, President of Algeria, in Summary Record of the First Plenary Meeting, October 28, 1971, in Group of 77, *Third World without*

Superpowers, 2:30. There were sixty-two plenary addresses, including twenty-five representatives of African countries; twenty-two Asian and Middle Eastern representatives, and eleven Latin Americans, plus a representative from Yugoslavia. In addition, Raúl Prebisch and representatives of both ECLA and UNCTAD spoke. But while a few representatives of socialist governments in Africa reaffirmed their commitment to revolutionary change in general, only the representatives of Chile, Cuba, and Peru called for circumventing the IMF entirely. See Group of 77, *Third World without Superpowers*, 2:26–198.

101. Summary Record of the First Plenary Meeting, October 28, 1971, in Group of 77, *Third World without Superpowers*, 2:33. The quote that follows in this paragraph is from the same page in the same source.

102. Summary Record of the Third Plenary Meeting, October 29, 1971, in Group of 77, *Third World without Superpowers*, 2:69. The quote that follows in this paragraph is from the same page in the same source.

103. Summary Record of the Sixth Plenary Meeting, November 1, 1971, in Group of 77, *Third World without Superpowers*, 2:117–18.

104. Summary Record of the Seventh Plenary Meeting, November 1, 1971, in Group of 77, *Third World without Superpowers*, 2:142.

105. Summary Record of the Seventh Plenary Meeting, November 1, 1971, in Group of 77, *Third World without Superpowers*, 2:139. This had been a part of the Addis Ababa declaration. See Report and Action Programme, Addis Ababa, October 8–14, 1971, in Group of 77, *Third World without Superpowers*, 1:497–531.

106. The Declaration and Principles of the Action Programme of Lima, 28 October–7 November 1971, in Group of 77, *Third World without Superpowers*, 2:203.

107. This point is emphasized by Henning, "The Group of Twenty-Four," 1:142.

108. World Bank, *OED Study of Bank/Mexico Relations*, 130.

109. Aparicio Cabrera, "Series estadísticas de la economía mexicana," 74.

CHAPTER EIGHT. A MEXICAN INTERNATIONAL
ECONOMIC ORDER?

1. Moreno-Brid and Ros, *Development and Growth in the Mexican Economy*, 129.

2. See González Marín, "México ante el Diálogo Norte-Sur," 332.

3. See Letter from President Nixon to President Díaz Ordaz of Mexico, Washington, November 18, 1969, and Telegram 1588 from the Embassy in Mexico to the Department of State, April 3, 1970, in *FRUS 1969–1976*, vol. E-10, docs. 445 and 451.

4. See FitzGerald, "Financial Constraint on Relative Autonomy," 220.

5. Telegram 4659 from the Embassy in Mexico to the Department of State, August 17, 1971, *FRUS 1969–1976*, vol. E-10, doc. 469. The administration proposed

a plan to end the 10 percent import tax just before Echeverría arrived. Edwin L. Dale, "U.S. Offers Plan for Termination of Import Surtax," *New York Times*, October 1, 1971.

6. Telegram 3330 from the Embassy in Mexico to the Department of State, June 17, 1971, *FRUS 1969–1976*, vol. E-10, doc. 463. See also Keller, *Mexico's Cold War*, 221–26.

7. Kate Doyle, "Tlatelolco Massacre: Declassified U.S. Documents on Mexico and the Events Of 1968," National Security Archive Electronic Briefing Book No. 10, October 2, 1998, https://nsarchive2.gwu.edu/NSAEBB/NSAEBB10.

8. Kate Doyle, "The Corpus Christi Massacre: Mexico's Attack on its Student Movement, June 10, 1971," National Security Archive Electronic Briefing Book No. 91, June 10, 2003, https://nsarchive2.gwu.edu/NSAEBB/NSAEBB91/.

9. See Herrera Calderón and Cedillo, *Challenging Authoritarianism in Mexico*.

10. UN A/PV.1952. Original Spanish version can be found as "Discurso del Presidente de México en la Sede del ONU," *Documentos de política internacional* (México, D.F.: Secretaría de la Presidencia, Departamento Editorial, 1975). The quotes that follow in this paragraph are also from this source.

11. "Mexico, Canada Complain of US Economics," *Boston Globe*, October 4, 1971.

12. UN A/PV.1952.

13. Muñoz Ledo, Wilkie, and Monzón Wilkie, *Porfirio Muñoz Ledo*, 201.

14. Leopoldo Mendív, "Oficio: Reportero," *El Heraldo* (México, D.F.), May 25, 1972; and Moises Martinez, "Política nacional," *La Prensa* (México, D.F.), May 30, 1972.

15. Muñoz Ledo, Wilkie, and Monzón Wilkie, *Porfirio Muñoz Ledo*, 100.

16. Later, as head of Nacional Financiera, Petricioli would argue against the structural adjustment agenda pushed by the World Bank after the debt crisis, but he would be overruled by Jesús Silva Herzog. See Woods, *Globalizers*, 92.

17. Documents from this session, such as "UNCTAD: Orígines y antecedentes," March 28, 1972, and "Tercera Conferencia de las Naciones Unidas Sobre Comercio y Desarrollo: Proyecto de discurso," n.d., can be found in AHSREM, Inventario Secretaría Particular (ISP), A-1117-1(IV).

18. Muñoz Ledo, Wilkie, and Monzón Wilkie, *Porfirio Muñoz Ledo*, 201–3.

19. "200,000 Anti-Marxists March in Chile," *New York Times*, April 13, 1972.

20. See Talesnick, "Monumentality and Resignification: The UNCTAD III Building in Chile."

21. "U.S. Rejects Attacks in Chile as Clichés," *New York Times*, April 22, 1972.

22. Echeverría, "Discurso pronunciado por el C. Presidente Constitucional de la República Mexicana, 119.

23. Echeverría, "Discurso pronunciado por el C. Presidente Constitucional de la República Mexicana," 120.

24. Bank president Robert McNamara also advocated this. See "Address to the United Nations Conference on Trade and Development," Santiago, Chile, April 14, 1972, in McNamara, *McNamara Years at the World Bank*, 169–90; and Hugh

O'Shaughnessy, "Mexico's Next Revolution," *The Observer* (London), October 1, 1972.

25. See Kedar, "World Bank–United States–Latin American Triangle."

26. As translated in "Summary of Address Given at the 92nd Plenary Meeting, April 19, 1972, by Mr. Luis Echeverría Alvarez, President of the United Mexican States," in United Nations, *Proceedings of the United Nations Conference on Trade and Development*, 186.

27. Echeverría, "Discurso pronunciado por el C. Presidente Constitucional de la República Mexicana," 126–27.

28. Muñoz Ledo, Wilkie, and Monzón Wilkie, *Porfirio Muñoz Ledo*, 202–12.

29. "La Carta Echeverría, fórmula para lograr un orden económico justo," *Novedades* (México, D.F.), May 25, 1972. For the Mexican debates on the form the charter could take, see Dirección General de Organismos Internacionales, "Informe resumido sobre los resultados de la Tercera Conferencia de las Naciones Unidas sobre Comercio y Desarrollo", June 22, 1972, AHSREM, Fondo Embajada de México en la Unión Soviética (EMBURSS), caja 71, exp. 5.

30. Telegram, May 4, 1972, AHSREM, ISP, A-1117-1(IV).

31. Revised draft UN TD/L.84, adopted as Resolution 45(III). See "Documento de trabajo que contiene un anteproyecto de Carta de Derechos y Deberes Económicos de Estados," July 5, 1972 in AHSREM, ISP, A-1117-1(IV); for abstentions see United Nations, *Proceedings of the United Nations Conference on Trade and Development*, 36.

32. "La Carta de Derechos y Deberes de México será sometida a la ONU," *Excélsior* (México, D.F.), May 25, 1972; and Leopoldo Mendív, "Oficio: Reportero," *El Heraldo* (México, D.F.), May 25, 1972, AGN, PML, caja 25-2, exp. 2.

33. "El Tercer Mundo participará en las decisiones economicas mundiales," *El Día* (México, D.F.), May 25, 1972; and "Habrá obstaculos a la carta sobre economía," *La Prensa* (México, D.F.), May 25, 1972, AGN PML, caja 25-2, exp. 2.

34. Transcript of Conversation No. 735-1, cassette nos. 2246–2248, June 15, 1972, 10:31 a.m.–12:10 p.m., Oval Office, Digital National Security Archive (DNSA).

35. The translator interpreted this as "close to capitalism" to Nixon and Kissinger.

36. Transcript of Conversation No. 735-1, cassette nos. 2246–2248, June 15, 1972, 10:31 a.m.–12:10 p.m., Oval Office, DNSA.

37. Transcript of Conversation No. 736-2, cassette no. 2253, June 15, 1972, 5:25–6:43 p.m., Oval Office, DNSA.

38. "Discurso del Presidente de México en la sede de la OEA," June 16, 1972, in Mexico, Secretaría de la Presidencia, *Documentos de política internacional*, 148, 154.

39. "Nueva etapa en las relaciones México–E. Unidos," *El Informador* (Guadalajara), June 20, 1972.

40. Rabasa a Echeverría, May 22, 1973, AHSREM, ISP, A-1117-1(IV).

41. Documento de trabajo que contiene un anteproyecto de Carta de Derechos y Deberes Económicos de Estados, July 5, 1972, AHSREM, ISP, A-1117-1(IV).

42. In fact, a few years later Echeverría would remember the charter as an "extension of the document that emerged in Algiers, with an enrichment of the thesis." Suárez, *Echeverría rompe el silencio*, 146.

43. Documento de trabajo que contiene un anteproyecto de Carta de Derechos y Deberes Económicos de Estados," July 5, 1972, AHSREM, ISP, A-1117-1(IV).

44. UN TD/B/AC.12/1.

45. Intervención del Lic. Sergio Gónzalez Gálvez, representante de México en el Grupo de Trabajo sobre la Carta de los Derechos y Deberes Económicos de los Estados, pronunciada en la Sexta Sesión Plenaria de Dicho Grupo efectuada el 15 de febrero de 1973, AHSREM, ISP, A-1117-1(IV). See also Partido Revolucionario Institucional, *México y el nuevo orden económico internacional*, 13.

46. The subgroup of industrialized countries was, in the original group of thirty-one, twice as big as any of the other groupings of countries from Africa, Asia, Latin America, or the Socialist bloc. See "Paises que integran el grupo de trajabo encargado de preparar un proyecto de Carta Sobre los Derechos y Deberes Económicos de los Estados," AHSREM, ISP, A-1117-1(IV). By agreement in November 1972, nine more countries were added to the working group, bringing its total to forty.

47. Intervención del Lic. Sergio Gónzalez Gálvez, AHSREM, ISP, A-1117-1(IV).

48. UN TD/B/AC.12/1, 7.

49. UN TD/B/AC.12/1, 8.

50. Memoradum para información del Señor Secretario, Tlatelolco, February 26, 1973, AHSREM, ISP, A-1117-1(IV); the draft is reproduced in UN TD/B/AC.12/1, 16–24.

51. UN TD/B/AC.12/1, 21.

52. Memoradum para información, AHSREM, ISP, A-1117-1(IV).

53. UN TD/B/W.12/2.

54. UN TD/B/AC.12/2, 15.

55. UN TD/B/AC.12/2, 32–33.

56. Memorandum para información del Señor Secretario, September 24, 1973, AHSREM, ISP, A-1117-a(II); and UN A/9330 and corr. 1, 73.

57. UN A/9330.

58. Cuba was the only Latin American country to formally join the NAM. Mortimer, *Third World Coalition*, 33–34.

59. Quoted in Mortimer, *Third World Coalition*, 37.

60. Henry Kissinger had complained, "The Europeans behaved like jackals. They gave us no support when we needed it." *FRUS 1969–1976*, vol. 25, doc. 250, quoted in Sargent, "North/South," 204.

61. See Garavini, "From Boumedienomics to Reaganomics."

62. Mortimer, *Third World Coalition*, 49.

63. UN A/PV.2208.

64. Hudes, "Towards a New International Economic Order," 102.

65. Burke, "Competing for the Last Utopia?," 49.

66. Memorandum para información del Señor Presidente de la Republica, n.d., AHSREM, ISP, A-1117-1(II); and Kissinger, "Address to the Sixth Special Session of the United Nations General Assembly."

67. UN A/RES/S-6/3201; and A/RES/S-6/3202.

68. As discussed in Asunto: Proceso de elaboración de la Carta de Derechos y Deberes Económicos de los Estados, Tlatlelolco, October 25, 1973, AHSREM, ISP, A-1117-1(II).

69. Echeverría, "Documentos y comentarios en torno al viaje del Presidente Echeverría." See also Echeverría, "Problems of Developing Countries," 420. On British skepticism, see Secretary of State to U.S. Embassy in Mexico City, May 24, 1973, Wikileaks document 1973STATE100257.

70. Echeverría, "Documentos y comentarios en torno al viaje del Presidente Echeverría," 24–54. It was after these trips, on which he professed great solidarity with the Soviet Union and China, that he would stress his anti-communist credentials to the US secretary of state. United States Embassy, Mexico to Secretary of State, May 19, 1973, Wikileaks document 1973MEXICO03586_b.

71. "Charlaron Tito y Echeverría," *El Informador* (Guadalajara), February 14, 1974. Mexican newspapers noted the president's intentions to reclaim relations with Europe so as to lessen dependence on the United States. "Recabará la presencia de Europa LEA," *El Informador* (Guadalajara), February 2, 1974.

72. "Necesaria unión de Latinoamérica," *El Informador* (Guadalajara), July 22, 1974; "Acuerdan México y Japon luchar en la ONU por la Carta de Derechos," *Excélsior* (México, D.F.), September 17, 1974; "La Carta de Derechos 'Podrá abrir el camino a la cooperación económica internacional': Austria," *Excélsior* (México, D.F.), September 27, 1974; "Polonia apoya la carta Echeverría," *Novedades* (México, D.F.), September 23, 1974; and "Optimismo en la ONU ante la carta de LE," *Novedades* (México, D.F.), September 26, 1974, in Biblioteca Lerdo, Archivos Económicos, E01318.

73. "No debe temer las ideologías," *El Informador* (Guadalajara), July 7, 1974.

74. United States Embassy, Brazil to Secretary of State, May 19, 1973, Wikileaks document 1973RIODE01735_b.

75. United States Embassy, Mexico to Secretary of State, May 19, 1973, Wikileaks document 1973MEXICO03586_b.

76. Telecon, Mexican Foreign Minister Rabasa/HAK, September 18, 1973, 1:47 p.m., DNSA.

77. UN A/PV.2124.

78. UN A/PV.2139.

79. Before the meeting, Kissinger told a group of senators, "[I]f we do not have a relationship with Latin America, in the UN we will be in ten years in a worse position than Russia was in the early days." Memorandum of Conversation, February 7, 1974, 9:30–10:30 a.m., DNSA. See also Address by Secretary of State Kissinger, Mexico City, February 21, 1974, in *FRUS 1969–1976*, vol. 38, pt. 1, doc. 28; and Secretary's Staff Meeting, November 26, 1973, DNSA. At a meeting with Kissinger at Los Pinos, the presidential residence, Echeverría again opened with the specter of youth extremism, impressing the threat of Cuban-style revolution once again on Kissinger.

See Memorandum of Conversation, President's Residence, "Los Pinos," February 21, 1974, 6:00 p.m., DNSA.

80. Transcript of Secretary of State Kissinger's Staff Meeting, Washington, February 14, 1974, 3:15 p.m, in *FRUS 1969-1976*, vol. E-11, pt. 1, doc. 10.

81. Memorandum from William Jorden of the National Security Council Staff to the President's Assistant for National Security Affairs (Kissinger), Washington, January 28, 1974, in *FRUS 1969–1976*, vol. E-11, pt. 1, doc. 9. For the conference declaration, see Organization of American States, "Conference of Tlatelolco."

82. Address by Secretary of State Kissinger, Mexico City, February 21, 1974, in *FRUS 1969–1976*, vol. 38, pt. 1, doc. 28.

83. Telegram 47899 from the Department of State to All American Republic Diplomatic Posts, Washington, March 9, 1974, in *FRUS 1969–1976*, vol. E-11, pt. 1, doc. 14; see also "Dialogue at Tlatelolco," *New York Times*, February 25, 1974.

84. Memorandum of Conversation, President's Residence, "Los Pinos," February 21, 1974, 6:00 p.m., DNSA. The quote that follows in this paragraph is also from this source.

85. The third meeting draft is found in UN TD/B/AC.12/3; the fourth is in TD/B/AC.12/4.

86. Memorandum of Conversation, Secretary's Office, August 29, 1974, 11:15 a.m., DNSA; and Maw to Secretary of State, July 1, 1974, Wikileaks document 1974STATE141990_b.

87. "Graves divergencias para redactar la carta de LEA," *El Informador* (Guadalajara), June 9, 1974.

88. See US Mission Geneva to Secretary of State, June 12, 1974, Wikileaks document 1974MEXICO04825_b.

89. General Assembly Resolution 1803 (XVII), December 14, 1962; and UN TD/B/AC.12/4.

90. Secretary of State to USUN Geneva, July 1, 1974, Wikileaks document 1974STATE142000_b. The quote that follows in this paragraph is also from this source.

91. UN TD/B/AC.12/4, Paragraph 2, Alternative 2. A footnote in the passive voice explains, "The view was expressed that this proposal could serve as a useful basis for further negotiations" (8). The fact that it had been drafted as a compromise behind the scenes remained confidential, and Castañeda took care to not associate Mexico with the proposal, instead noting that Alternative 1 had been introduced by Mexico on behalf of the G77.

92. "Más concesiones en la junta de los 40," *El Informador* (Guadalajara), June 27, 1974.

93. Telecon, Mr. Maw/Secretary Kissinger, June 21, 1974, 9:40 a.m., DNSA. The next quote in this paragraph is from the same source.

94. "Mexico no transigiría en asuntos de soberanía," *El Informador* (Guadalajara), June 22, 1974.

95. UN TD/B/AC.12/4, Paragraph 2, Alternative 2.

96. "No hubo acuerdo completo," *El Informador* (Guadalajara), June 29, 1974.

97. "Possible renuncia del Srio. de Estado Kissinger," *El Informador* (Guadalajara), July 14, 1974.

98. Memorandum of Conversation, Secretary's Office, August 29, 1974, 11:15 a.m., DNSA.

99. Memorandum of Conversation, Talks between President Ford and President Echeverria, October 21, 1974, DNSA.

100. News Conference of the President and President Echeverria of Mexico in Tubac, Arizona, October 21, 1974, American Presidency Project, www.presidency.ucsb.edu/ws/index.php?pid=4497. The next quote in this paragraph is also from this source.

101. "Estados Unidos rectifica su posición y ofrece pleno apoyo a la carta propuesta por Echeverría," *El Nacional* (México, D.F.), October 22, 1974; and "Excerpts from Ford-Echeverria News Conference," *New York Times*, October 22, 1974.

102. Quoted in Kathleen Teltsch, "New Declaration Voted in the U.N.," *New York Times*, December 13, 1974.

103. Telecon, Senator Percy/Secretary Kissinger, October 18, 1974, DNSA.

104. Charles N. Brower, letter to the editor, *New York Times*, December 8, 1974.

105. UN A/C.2/SR.1640.

106. Memo, The Secretary's 8:00 a.m. Regional Staff Meeting, December 3, 1974, DNSA.

107. Slobodian, *Globalists*, 220–21.

108. Memorandum of Conversation, Washington, December 4, 1974, in *FRUS 1969–1976*, vol. E-11, doc. 72.

109. Memo, The Secretary's 8:00 a.m. Regional Staff Meeting, December 3, 1974, DNSA.

110. Memo, The Secretary's 8:00 a.m. Regional Staff Meeting, December 5, 1974, DNSA. The quotes that follow in this paragraph are also from this source.

111. UN A/C.2/L.l419.

112. "The Text of the Address by Scali before the United Nation General Assembly," *New York Times*, December 7, 1974.

113. UN A/C.2/SR.1648.

114. "Statement by Senator Percy," December 6, 1974, Department of State *Bulletin* 72, no. 1858 (February 3, 1975).

115. UN A/C.2/SR.1649.

116. Telecon, FM Rabasa/Secretary Kissinger, December 6, 1974, DNSA.

117. Memo, Secretary's Staff Meeting, December 9, 1974, DNSA. The quotes that follow in this paragraph are also from this source.

118. UN A/RES/3281(XXIX).

119. UN A/RES/3281(XXIX). The quote that follows in this paragraph is also from this source.

120. Teltsch, "New Declaration Voted in the U.N.," *New York Times*, December 13, 1974.

121. Suárez, *Echeverría rompe el silencio*, 150.

122. Muñoz Ledo, Wilkie, and Monzón Wilkie, *Porfirio Muñoz Ledo*, 371.

1. "Pronto adoptarán la carta quienes votaron en contra: LE," *El Nacional* (México, D.F.), December 14, 1974.

2. This was the title of a hagiographic book published in Mexico in 1975. Casanova Álvarez, *La carta o la guerra*.

3. See, for example, "Triunfo mexicano, dicen los diputados" and "Para los 4 partidos políticos, la carta es un triunfo legítimo," *El Universal* (México, D.F.), December 13, 1974.

4. "Piden a la SEP que se divulgue en las escuelas la Carta de Deberes y Derechos," *Novedades* (México, D.F.), January 8, 1975; and Secretaría de la Presidencia, "Nuevo orden mundial," AHSREM, DGAD, III-6030-1.

5. "Fue emitido un timbre postal sobre la 'Carta económica,'" *El Nacional* (México, D.F.), February 8, 1975.

6. "Pronto adoptarán la carta quienes votaron en contra: LE."

7. Briefing Memorandum from the Assistant Secretary of State for Inter-American Affairs (Rogers) and the Director of the Policy Planning Staff (Lord) to Secretary of State Kissinger, Washington, January 14, 1975, *FRUS 1969–1976*, vol. E-11, doc. 27.

8. Sargent, "North/South," 202.

9. On neoconservative reaction to the NIEO, see Franczak, "Losing the Battle, Winning the War."

10. Daniel P. Moynihan, "The United States in Opposition," *Commentary*, March 1, 1975.

11. Moynihan, "United States in Opposition."

12. Moynihan, "United States in Opposition."

13. See, for example, "Inglaterra buscará apoyar la 'Carta 'Echeverría'," *Novedades* (México, D.F.), February 26, 1975; "La Carta Echeverría, insuficiente para controlar las transnacionales," *El Heraldo de México* (México, D.F.), March 23, 1975; and "Las decisiones unilaterales, devantajosas para países industrializados y pobres: Brandt," *Excélsior* (México, D.F.), March 29, 1975. On Carter's approach to the Third World, see Franczak, "Human Rights and Basic Needs."

14. "La Carta económica, 'Propósito de nuestra soberanía de reforzarse con otras,'" *Excélsior* (México, D.F.), February 27, 1976.

15. Independent Commission on International Development Issues, *North–South*; and González Marín, "México ante el Diálogo Norte-Sur."

16. Goldstein, "Redistributing the World's Wealth," 40.

17. Howell Raines, "Reagan Meets with Chinese and Mexican Leaders," *New York Times*, October 22, 1981; and Ronald Reagan, "Remarks to Reporters Upon Departure for the International Meeting on Cooperation and Development in Cancun, Mexico," October 21, 1981, The Public Papers of the President: Ronald Reagan, 1981–1989, Ronald Reagan Presidential Library.

18. López Portillo, "Las Naciones Unidas en la encrucijada," 1244.

19. Cárdenas, *La política económica en México*, 86–106.

20. Aggarwal, *Debt Games*, 335.

21. Kapur, Lewis, and Webb, *World Bank*, 603.

22. Quoted in Roos, *Why Not Default?*, 130.

23. See Lustig, *Mexico*.

24. Babb, *Managing Mexico*, 175–83.

25. Pastor and Wise, "Origins and Sustainability of Mexico's Free Trade Policy"; and Babb, *Managing Mexico*, 181.

26. Roos, *Why Not Default?*, 147–57; and Aggarwal, *Debt Games*, 333–75.

27. Aggarwal, *Debt Games*, 373.

28. Krasner, *Structural Conflict,* 54.

29. Manela, *The Wilsonian Moment*, 6.

30. Go and Lawson, "For a Global Historical Sociology," 23.

31. Roseberry, "Hegemony and the Language of Contention," 358.

32. Getachew, *Worldmaking after Empire*, 179.

33. Reyes Heroles, *La Carta de la Habana*, 9.

34. Reyes Heroles, *La Carta de la Habana*, 16.

35. Arrighi, "The Developmentalist Illusion."

BIBLIOGRAPHY

ARCHIVE AND MANUSCRIPT COLLECTIONS

United States

United States National Archives and Records Administration, College Park, MD (NARA)

> RG 43: Records of International Conferences
>
> RG 56: Records of the Department of the Treasury
>
> RG 59: Records of the Department of State
>
> RG 165: Records of the War Department
>
> RG 256: Records of the American Commission to Negotiate Peace, 1918–1931

United States Department of State, *Papers Relating to the Foreign Relations of the United States* (FRUS)

Princeton University, Seeley G. Mudd Manuscript Library

> Papers of Harry Dexter White (HDWP)

Franklin Delano Roosevelt Presidential Library (FDRPL)

> Papers of Adolf Berle
>
> Papers of Oliver Cox
>
> Papers of Henry Morgenthau
>
> Morgenthau Diaries
>
> President's Personal File
>
> President's Secretary's File

Yale University Library

> Edward Mandell House Diaries

University of Delaware Library

> George S. Messersmith Papers

The National Security Archive, Washington, DC

> Digital National Security Archive
>
> Electronic Briefing Books

United Nations Online Document Repositories (NY)

> World Trade Organization: GATT Documents
>
> United Nations Audiovisual Library of International Law
>
> United Nations Official Document System

United Kingdom

The National Archives of the United Kingdom, Kew

> Records of the Foreign Office
>
> Records of the Treasury

Mexico

Archivo Histórico Genaro Estrada, Secretaría de Relaciones Exteriores, México, D.F. (AHSREM)

> Archivo Particular de Luis Quintanilla
>
> Archivo Particular de Francisco Castillo Nájera
>
> Fondo Dirección General de Asuntos Diplomáticos (DGAD)
>
> Fondo Dirección General de Organismos Internacionales (DGOI)
>
> Fondo Jaime Torres Bodet (JTB)
>
> Fondo SubSecretario
>
> Fondo Embajada de México en Estados Unidos de América (EMBEUA)
>
> Fondo Embajada de México en Francia
>
> Fondo Embajada de México en la Unión Soviética (EMBURSS)
>
> Inventario Secretaría Particular (ISP)
>
> Legajos Encuadernados (L-E)

Archivo General de la Nación, México, D.F. (AGN)

> Archivo Particular Gonzalo Robles
>
> Archivo Particular Lázaro Cárdenas (microfilm)
>
> Archivo Particular Porfirio Muñoz Ledo (PML)
>
> Ramo Dirección General de Investigaciones Políticas y Sociales (DGIPS)
>
> Fondo Secretaría de Hacienda y Credito Público

Archivos Presidenciales:

    Fondo Obregón-Calles

    Fondo Lázaro Cárdenas del Río

    Fondo Manuel Ávila Camacho (MAC)

    Fondo Miguel Alemán Valdes (MAV)

    Fondo Luis Echeverría Álvarez (LEA)

Centro de Estudios de Historia de México, México, D.F. (CEHM)

    Fondo XXI Primer Jefe del Ejército Constitucionalista Venustiano Carranza (FVC)

    Fondo CDLXXX Miscelánea de Venustiano Carranza

    Fondo X-I Manuscritos de Francisco León de la Barra (FLdlB)

Archivo Histórico, Colegio de México, México, D.F. (COLMEX)

    Fondo Eduardo Villaseñor

    Fondo Víctor L. Urquidi

    Fondo Ramón Beteta

Biblioteca Lerdo de Tejada, México, D.F.

    Hemeroteca

    Archivos Económicos

PUBLISHED PRIMARY SOURCES

Periodicals

Atlanta Constitution

Boston Daily Globe

Chicago Daily Tribune

Christian Science Monitor

El Demócrata (México, D.F.)

El Heraldo (Santiago, Chile)

El Informador (Guadalajara)

El Nacional (México, D.F.)

El Pueblo (México, D.F.)

El Universal (México, D.F.)

Excélsior (México, D.F.)

Futuro (México, D.F.)

La Nación (Santiago, Chile)

La Prensa (México, D.F.)

Los Angeles Times

New York Sun

New York Times

New York Tribune

Novedades (México, D.F.)

San Francisco Chronicle

Books, Pamphlets, and Articles

Alta Comisión Interamericana, Consejo Central Executivo. *Informe presentado al Consejo Central Ejecutivo de la Alta Comisión Inter-americana sobre la visita que el consultor jurídico del mismo hizo a los Estados Unidos de Venezuela con el objeto de conferenciar sobre los trabajos de la misma Alta Comisión con el Ministro de Hacienda y la Sección Venezolana de este organismo.* Washington, DC: Imprenta del Gobierno, 1921.

American Society of International Law. "Consultative Meeting of Foreign Ministers of the American Republics." Supplement: Official Documents, *American Journal of International Law* 34, no. 1 (1940): 1–20.

Barreda Laos, Felipe. *Hispano América en guerra? A la juventud hispanoamericana.* Buenos Aires, Argentina: Linari y Companía, 1941.

Berle, Adolf Augustus. *Navigating the Rapids, 1918–1971: From the Papers of Adolf A. Berle.* New York: Harcourt Brace Jovanovich, 1973.

———. "Peace Without Empire." *Survey Graphic* 30, no. 3 (1941): 102–8.

Beteta, Ramón. "Mexico's Foreign Relations." *Annals of the American Academy of Political and Social Science* 208, no. 1 (1940): 170–80.

Bojórquez, Juan de Dios. *Crónica del constituyente.* México, D.F.: Ediciones Botas, 1938.

Brown, Philip Marshall. "Fundamentals in the Foreign Policy of the United States." *Annals of the American Academy of Political and Social Science* 114 (1924): 97–101.

———. "Mexico and the Monroe Doctrine." *American Journal of International Law* 26, no. 1 (1932): 117–21.

Brown, William Adams. *The United States and the Restoration of World Trade: An Analysis and Appraisal of the ITO Charter and the General Agreement on Tariffs and Trade.* Washington, DC: Brookings Institution, 1950.

Brum, Baltasar. *The Peace of America: American Solidarity.* Montevideo, Uruguay: Imprenta Nacional, 1923.

Carnegie Endowment for International Peace, Division of International Law. *The International Conferences of the American States, 1889–1928.* New York: Oxford University Press, 1931.

Casanova Álvarez, Francisco. *La carta o la guerra: Hacia un nuevo orden internacional.* México, D.F.: Organización Editorial Novaro, 1975.

Castañeda, Jorge. *Mexico and the United Nations.* New York: Manhattan Publishing, 1958.

Castillo Nájera, Francisco. "Organization of Peace." *Annals of the American Academy of Political and Social Science* 222 (1942): 60–73.

Ceniceros, José Ángel. *Mexico's Attitude in Its International Relations: Assertion and Development of Doctrines.* México, D.F.: Press of the Ministry of Foreign Affairs, 1935.

Combined Mexican Working Party. *The Major Long-Term Trends in the Mexican Economy, with Particular Reference to Mexico's Capacity to Absorb Additional Foreign Investments: Report of the Combined Mexican Working Party.* Washington, DC: International Bank for Reconstruction and Development, September 1952.

Confederación de Trabajadores de América Latina. *Balance de la Conferencia Inter-Americana de Chapultepec.* Mexico, D.F.: n.p., 1945.

Conference of Commissions of Inter-American Development. *Proceedings of the Conference of Commissions of Inter-American Development, New York, May 9 to 18, 1944.* Washington, DC: The Inter-American Development Commission, 1944.

Cosío Villegas, Daniel. *American Extremes.* Austin: University of Texas Press, 1964.

———. "La Conferencia de Chapultepec." *Cuadernos Americanos* 4, no. 3 (May 1945): 19–45.

Dios Bojórquez, Juan de. *Crónica del constituyente.* México, D.F.: Ediciones Botas, 1938.

Echeverría Álvarez, Luis. "Discurso pronunciado por el C. Presidente Constitucional de la República Mexicana, Lic. Luis Echeverría Álvarez, en la reunión plenaria del tercer período de sesiones de la Conferencia de las Naciones Unidas Sobre Comercio y Desarrollo." *Estudios Internacionales* 5, no. 18 (abril–junio 1972): 119–27.

———. "Documentos y comentarios en torno al viaje del Presidente Echeverría (marzo-abril de 1973)." *Foro Internacional,* 14, no. 1 (July–September 1973): 1–54.

———. "Problems of Developing Countries." *American Journal of Economics and Sociology* 32, no. 4 (October 1, 1973): 419–20.

Elder, Robert, and Forrest Murden. *Economic Co-operation: Special United Nations Fund for Economic Development (SUNFED).* New York: Woodrow Wilson Foundation, 1954.

Estrada, Genaro. *La Doctrina Estrada.* México, D.F.: Instituto Americano de Derecho y Legislación Comparada, 1930.

Fabela, Isidro. *Historia diplomática de la revolución mexicana.* México, D.F.: Comisión Nacional para las Celebraciones del 175 Aniversario de la Independencia Nacional y 75 Aniversario de la Revolución Mexicana, 1985.

Fabela, Isidro, and Josefina E. de Fabela, eds. *Documentos históricos de la revolución mexicana.* México, D.F.: Fondo de Cultura Económica, 1970.

Foreign Policy Association. "The Sixth Pan American Conference, Pt. I–II," *Information Service* 4, no. 4 (April 27, 1928): 50–222.

Fouque, Augustín, Carlos Benítez, and Abel Morros. "Protección a la industria." *Revista de Economía* 10 (May 31, 1947): 54–60.

Galindo, Hermila. *La Doctrina Carranza y el acercamiento indo-latino.* México, D.F.: n.p., 1919.

Group of 77. *The Third World without Superpowers: The Collected Documents of the Group of 77.* Vols. 1–4. Edited by Karl P. Sauvant and Joachim W. Müller. New York: Oceana Publications, 1981.

Heymann, Hans. *Plan for Permanent Peace.* New York: Harper & Brothers, 1941.

Hunter Miller, David. *The Drafting of the Covenant.* New York: G. P. Putnam, 1928.

Independent Commission on International Development Issues. *North–South: A Programme for Survival.* London: Pan Books, 1980.

Inman, Samuel Guy. *Inter-American Conferences, 1826–1954: History and Problems.* Washington, DC: University Press of Washington, DC, 1965.

Inter-American Financial and Economic Advisory Committee. *Convention for the Establishment of an Inter-American Bank.* Washington, DC: Government Printing Office, 1940.

Inter-American High Commission, Central Executive Council. *List of Officers of Commission.* Washington, DC: Government Printing Office, 1922.

International American Conference (1st, 1889–1890, Washington, DC). *Reports of Committees and Discussions Thereon.* Washington, DC: Government Printing Office, 1890.

International American Conference (2nd, 1901–1902, Mexico). *Actas y Documentos de la Segunda Conferencia Pan-Americana.* México, D.F.: Tipografía de la Oficina Impresora de Estampillas, 1902.

International American Conference (7th, 1933, Montevideo, Uruguay). *Final Act, Seventh International Conference of American States, Montevideo, Uruguay, December 3–26, 1933, Including the Conventions and Additional Protocol Adopted by the Conference.* Montevideo, Uruguay: J. Florensa, 1934.

———. *Plenary Sessions: Minutes and Antecedents, Fourth and Ninth Committees; Economic and Financial Problems.* Montevideo, Uruguay: n.p., 1933.

International Bureau of American Republics. *Bulletin of the International Bureau of American Republics* 31, no. 5 (November 1910).

Kains, Archibald, and Paul Moritz Warburg. *Memoranda to Accompany Draft of Treaty for the Establishment of an International Gold Clearance Fund.* Washington, DC: Government Printing Office, 1916.

Kelley, Francis Clement. *The Bishop Jots It Down: An Autobiographical Strain on Memories.* New York: Harper & Brothers, 1939.

Keynes, John Maynard. *The Collected Writings of John Maynard Keynes.* 30 vols. Edited by Elizabeth S. Johnson and D. E. Moggridge. Cambridge, UK: Cambridge University Press, 2012.

———. *The General Theory of Employment, Interest, and Money.* New York: Harcourt, Brace & World, [1936] 1964.

Kissinger, Henry A. "Address to the Sixth Special Session of the United Nations General Assembly." *International Organization* 28, no. 3 (1974): 573–83.

Laves, Walter H. C. *Inter-American Solidarity.* Chicago: University of Chicago Press, 1941.

League of Nations. *Official Journal,* Special Supplement 93 (1931).

List, Friedrich. *National System of Political Economy.* Philadelphia: J. B. Lippincott, 1856.

Luquín, Eduardo. *La política internacional de la revolución constitucionalista.* México, D.F.: Instituto Nacional de Estudios Históricos de la Revolución Mexicana, 1957.

Manero, Antonio. *México y la solidaridad americana: La Doctrina Carranza.* Madrid: Editorial América, 1918.

Marván Laborde, Ignacio, ed. *Nueva Edición del diario de debates del Congreso Constituyente Querétaro de 1916–1917.* Vol. 1. México, D.F.: Suprema Corte de Justicia de la Nación, 2006.

Marx, Karl. *The Eighteenth Brumaire of Louis Bonaparte.* New York: International Publishers, 1963.

McNamara, Robert S. *The McNamara Years at the World Bank.* Baltimore, MD: Johns Hopkins University Press, 1981.

México, Comisión Nacional de Planeación para la Paz. *Temario.* México, D.F.: Banco de México, 1945.

México, XLVI Legislatura de la Cámara de Diputados. *Los presidentes de México ante la nación: Informes, manifiestos y documentos de 1821 a 1966.* Vol. 3. México, D.F.: Cámara de Diputados, 1966.

Mexico, Secretaría de la Presidencia. *Documentos de política internacional.* México, D.F.: Secretaría de la Presidencia, Departamento Editorial, 1975.

Mexico, Secretaría de Relaciones Exteriores. *Labor internacional de la revolución constitucionalista de México.* México, D.F.: Secretaría de Gobernación, 1918.

———. *Temario económico financiero sometido por Mexico a la Septima Conferencia Internacional Americana.* México, D.F.: Imprenta de la Secretaría de Relaciones Exteriores, 1934.

Moore, John B. "The Pan American Financial Conferences and the Inter-American High Commission." *American Journal of International Law* 14, no. 3 (1920): 343–55.

Moynihan, Daniel P. "The United States in Opposition." *Commentary,* March 1, 1975.

Muñoz Ledo, Porfirio, James W. Wilkie, and Edna Monzón Wilkie. *Porfirio Muñoz Ledo: Historia oral, 1933–1988.* México, D.F.: Penguin Random House Grupo Editorial México, 2017.

Murkland, Harry B. "Latin America at Havana." *Current History,* June 1, 1948, 332–35.

National Foreign Trade Council. *Position of the National Foreign Trade Council with Respect to the Havana Charter for an International Trade Organization: Hearing before Committee on Foreign Affairs, House of Representatives,* 81st Cong., 2nd sess. (April 27, 1950).

Non-Aligned Movement. *The Conference on the Problems of Economic Development* [papers]. Cairo: General Organisation for Government Printing Offices, 1962.

Organization of American States. "Conference of Tlatelolco: Declaration on Inter-American Relations." *International Legal Materials* 13, no. 2 (1974): 465–70.

Ortiz Mena, Antonio. "Desarrollo estabilizador: Una década de estrategia económica en México." *Trimestre Económico* 37 (1970): 417–50.

———. "Stabilizing Development: A Decade of Economic Strategy in Mexico." Paper presented at the annual meeting of the World Bank and IMF, 1969.

———. *Final Act of the Inter-American Conference on Problems of War and Peace, Mexico City, February–March, 1945.* Washington, DC: Pan-American Union, 1945.

———. *Fourth Pan-American Commercial Conference: Final Act with Annexes and a Summary of the Work of the Conference.* Washington, DC: Pan-American Union, 1931.

———. *Fourth Pan-American Commercial Conference: Proceedings.* Vol. 1, *Addresses Delivered at Plenary Sessions.* Washington, DC: Pan American Union, 1931.

———. "Inauguration of the Inter-American Financial and Economic Advisory Committee." *Bulletin of the Pan-American Union* 74, no. 1 (January 1940): 1–7.

———. *Pan American Commerce, Past–Present–Future: Report of the Second Pan American Commercial Conference.* Washington, DC: Pan American Union, 1919.

———. *Proceedings of the First Pan-American Financial Conference, Washington, May 24–29, 1915.* Washington, DC: Government Printing Office, 1915.

———. *Proceedings of the Pan American Commercial Conference, February 13–17, 1911.* Washington, DC: Pan American Union, 1911.

———. *Special Handbook for the Use of Delegates, Seventh International Conference of American States.* Baltimore, MD: Sun Book and Job Printing Office, 1933.

———. "Third Meeting of Ministers of Foreign Affairs of the American Republics, Final Act." *American Journal of International Law* 36, no. 2 (1942): 61–95.

Pani, Alberto J. *Cuestiones diversas, contenidas en 44 cartas al presidente Carranza, 1 carta al presidente de la Huerta, 1 artículo de "El Universal" y 4 brindis.* México, D.F.: Imprenta Nacional, S.A., 1922.

———. *El problema supremo de México: Ensayo de crítica constructiva de la política financiera.* 2nd ed. México, D.F.: Inversiones A.R.P.A., 1955.

———. *La cuestión internacional mexicana-americana, durante el gobierno del General Don Álvaro Obregón.* México, D.F.: Editorial Cultura, 1949.

———. *La política hacendaria y la revolución.* México, D.F.: Editorial Cultura, 1926.

———. *Los orígenes de la política crediticia: Con la réplica y las contrarréplicas sucitadas.* México, D.F.: Editorial Atlante, 1951.

———. *Mi contribución al nuevo régimen (1910–1933).* México, D.F.: Editorial Cultura, 1936.

———. *Obsesiones y recuerdos.* México, D.F.: Talleres de A. Mijares Hno., 1953.

———. *Tres monografías.* [Vol.] I, *Revolucionarios y reaccionarios*; [Vol.] II, *La política hacendaria del nuevo régimen*; [Vol. 3], *La industria nacional del turismo.* México, D.F.: Editorial Cultura, 1941.

Partido Revolucionario Institucional. *México y el nuevo orden económico internacional: Documentos.* México, D.F.: Comisión Nacional Editorial, 1976.

Prebisch, Raúl. *The Economic Development of Latin America and Its Principal Problems.* New York: United Nations, 1949.

Puig Casauranc, José Manuel. *De nuestro México: Cosas sociales y aspectos políticos.* México, D.F.: n.p., 1926.

———. *Remarks on the Position Taken by Mexico at Montevideo.* México, D.F.: Ministry of Foreign Affairs, 1934.

———. *Una política social-económica de "preparación socialista".* Del México actual no. 5. México, D.F.: Imprenta de Secretaría de Relaciones Exteriores, 1933.

Quintanilla, Luis. "La política internacional de la revolución mexicana." *Foro Internacional* 5, no. 1 (1964): 1–26.

———. *A Latin American Speaks.* New York: Macmillan, 1943.

———. *Pan Americanism and Democracy.* Boston: Boston University Press, 1952.

Reagan, Ronald. "Remarks to Reporters upon Departure for the International Meeting on Cooperation and Development in Cancun, Mexico," October 21, 1981, The Public Papers of the President: Ronald Reagan, 1981–1989, Ronald Reagan Presidential Library.

Reyes Heroles, Jesús. *La Carta de la Habana: Comentarios y digresiones.* México, D.F.: EDIAPSA, 1948.

Rippy, James F. "The Question of Responsibility for the Exclusion of Mexico from the League of Nations in 1919." *World Affairs* 96, no. 1 (1933): 34–38.

Roosevelt, Theodore. *Roosevelt in the Kansas City Star: War-Time Editorials.* Boston: Houghton Mifflin, 1921.

Schuler, Kurt, and Andrew Rosenberg, eds. *The Bretton Woods Transcripts.* New York: Center for Financial Stability, 2013.

Silva Herzog, Jesús. *Meditaciones sobre México: Ensayos y notas.* México, D.F.: Cuadernos Americanos, 1948.

Spencer, John H. "The Monroe Doctrine and the League Covenant." *American Journal of International Law* 30, no. 3 (1936): 400–413.

Suárez, Eduardo, *Comentarios y recuerdos, 1926–1946.* México, D.F.: Senado de la República, 2003.

Suárez, Luis. *Echeverría rompe el silencio: Vendaval del sistema.* México D.F.: Editorial Grijalbo, 1979.

Truman, Harry S. "Address on Foreign Economic Policy." Delivered at Baylor University, March 6, 1945. www.trumanlibrary.gov/library/public-papers/52/address-foreign-economic-policy-delivered-baylor-university.

United Nations. *Documents of the United Nations Conference on International Organization, San Francisco.* Vol. 3, *Dumbarton Oaks Proposals, Comments and Proposed Amendments.* New York: United Nations Information Organization, 1945.

———. *Economic Development of Under-Developed Countries.* New York: United Nations, 1954.

———. *Proceedings of the United Nations Conference on Trade and Development, Third Session, Santiago de Chile, 13 April to 21 May 1972.* Vol. 1A, part 1. New York: United Nations, 1973.

———. *Report on a Special United Nations Fund for Economic Development.* New York: United Nations, 1953.

United Nations Economic Commission for Africa. "Draft Resolution: Reform of the International Monetary System." 9th Session, Addis Ababa, Ethiopia, February 3–14, 1969.

United States Congress. *Investigation of Mexican Affairs, Preliminary Report and Hearings of the Committee on Foreign Relations of the United States Senate*. Vol. 1. Washington, DC: Government Printing Office, 1920.

United States Congress, Senate Foreign Relations Committee. *Inter-American Bank: Hearings before a Subcommittee of the Committee on Foreign Relations, United States Senate, Seventy-Seventh Congress, First Session, on Executive K, May 10, 1940*. Washington, DC: Government Printing Office, 1941.

———. *Inter-American Relations: A Collection of Documents, Legislation, Descriptions of Inter-American Organizations, and Other Material Pertaining to Inter-American Affairs, 93rd Congress, 1st Session, 1973*. Washington, DC: Government Printing Office, 1973.

United States Department of State. *Bulletin*. Vols. 1–19. 1939–1948.

———. *Havana Charter for an International Trade Organization: March 24, 1948, Including a Guide to the Study of the Charter*. Washington, DC: Government Printing Office, 1948.

———. *Peace and War: United States Foreign Policy, 1931–1941*. Publication 1983. Washington, DC: Government Printing Office, 1943.

———. *Preliminary Draft, Charter of the International Trade Organization of the United Nations*. Washington, DC: Government Printing Office, 1946.

———. *Proceedings and Documents, United Nations Monetary and Financial Conference (1944: Bretton Woods, NH)*. Washington, DC: Government Printing Office, 1948.

———. *Proposals for Expansion of World Trade and Employment*. Publication 2411. Washington, DC: Government Printing Office, 1945.

———. *Report of the Delegates of the United States of America to the Fifth International Conference of American States, Held at Santiago, Chile, March 25 to May 3, 1923*. Washington, DC: Government Printing Office, 1924.

United States Department of Treasury. *Report of the Secretary of the Treasury to the President on the Second Pan American Financial Conference at Washington, January 19–24, 1920*. Washington, DC: Government Printing Office, 1921.

———. *United Nations Monetary and Financial Conference, Articles of Agreement, International Monetary Fund and International Bank for Reconstruction and Development*. Washington, DC: Government Printing Office, 1944.

Urquidi, Víctor L. "Elasticidad y rigidez de Bretton Woods." *El Trimestre Económico* 11, no. 44 (1945): 595–616.

———. "La postguerra y las relaciones económicas internacionales de México." *El Trimestre Económico* 10, no. 38 (September 1943): 320–44.

———. "Reconstruction vs. Development: The IMF and the World Bank." In *The Bretton Woods-GATT System: Retrospect and Prospect after Fifty Years*, edited by Orin Kirshner and Edward M. Bernstein, 30–51. Armonk, NY: M. E. Sharpe, 1996.

———. Transcript of interview by Thomas G. Weiss, Oslo, June 18–19, 2000. United Nations Intellectual History Project, Columbia Center for Oral History, Columbia University Libraries.

Villaseñor, Eduardo. *América Latina en la economía mundial*. México, D.F.: Cuadernos Americanos, 1944.

———. "El Banco Interamericano." *El Trimestre Económico* 15, no. 58 (1948): 177–93.

———. "The Inter-American Bank: Prospects and Dangers." *Foreign Affairs* 20, no. 1 (1941): 165–74.

———. "Inter-American Trade and Financial Problems," speech presented at the University of Chicago, July 9, 1941. In Walter H. C Laves and Norman Wait Harris Memorial Foundation, *Inter-American Solidarity*. Chicago: University of Chicago Press, 1941.

———. "La Economía de guerra en México." *Investigación Económica* 3, no. 1 (1943): 7–33.

———. "Medios de cooperacion económica entre los Estados Unidos y México." *El Trimestre Económico* 11, no. 44 (1945): 587–94.

———. *Memorias-testimonio*. México, D.F.: Fondo de Cultura Económica, 1974.

———. "Problemas financieros y de comercio interamericano." *El Trimestre Económico* 8, no. 31 (1941): 355–97.

Wilcox, Clair. *A Charter for World Trade*. New York: Macmillan, 1949.

Wilcox, Francis O. "The Yalta Voting Formula." *American Political Science Review* 39, no. 5 (1945): 943–56.

Wilson, Woodrow. *Americanism: Woodrow Wilson's Speeches on the War—Why He Made Them and What They Have Done*. Edited by Oliver Marble Gale. Chicago: Baldwin Syndicate, 1918.

World Bank. *OED Study of Bank/Mexico Relations, 1948–1992*. Report no. 12923. Washington, DC: World Bank, 1994.

SECONDARY SOURCES

Acharya, Amitav. "'Idea-Shift': How Ideas from the Rest Are Reshaping Global Order." *Third World Quarterly* 37, no. 7 (2016): 1156–70.

———. "Studying the Bandung Conference from a Global IR Perspective." *Australian Journal of International Affairs* 70, no. 4 (2016): 342–57.

———. "Who Are the Norm Makers? The Asian-African Conference in Bandung and the Evolution of Norms." *Global Governance* 20, no. 3 (2014): 405–17.

Aggarwal, Vinod K. *Debt Games: Strategic Interaction in International Debt Rescheduling*. New York: Cambridge University Press, 1996.

Aguilar Camín, Héctor, and Lorenzo Meyer. *In the Shadow of the Mexican Revolution: Contemporary Mexican History, 1910–1989*. Austin: University of Texas Press, 1993.

Alacevich, Michele. *The Political Economy of the World Bank: The Early Years*. Washington, DC: World Bank Publications, 2009.

Alexander, Ryan M. *Sons of the Mexican Revolution: Miguel Alemán and His Generation*. Albuquerque: University of New Mexico Press, 2016.

Álvarez, Edgar Llinás. *Vida y obra de Ramón Beteta*. México, D.F.: Libros del Umbral, 1996.

Aparicio Cabrera, Abraham. "Series estadísticas de la economía mexicana en el siglo XX." *Economía Informa* 369 (2011): 63–85.

Arndt, H. W. *Economic Development: The History of an Idea*. Chicago: University of Chicago Press, 1989.

Arrighi, Giovanni. "The Developmentalist Illusion: A Reconceptualization of the Semiperiphery." In *Semiperipheral States in the World-Economy*, edited by W. G. Martin, 11–42. Westport, CT: Greenwood Press, 1990.

———. *The Long Twentieth Century: Money, Power, and the Origins of Our Times*. New York: Verso, 1994.

Arrighi, Giovanni, Po-keung Hui, Krishnendu Ray, and Thomas Ehrlich Reifer. "Geopolitics and High Finance." In *Chaos and Governance in the Modern World System*, edited by Giovanni Arrighi and Beverly Silver, 37–96. Minneapolis: University of Minnesota Press, 1999.

Arrighi, Giovanni, and Beverly Silver, eds. *Chaos and Governance in the Modern World System*. Minneapolis: University of Minnesota Press, 1999.

Arrighi, Giovanni, Beverly J. Silver, and Benjamin D. Brewer. "Industrial Convergence, Globalization, and the Persistence of the North-South Divide." *Studies in Comparative International Development* 38, no. 1 (2003): 3–31.

Arrighi, Giovanni, and Lu Zhang. "Beyond the Washington Consensus: A New Bandung?" In *Globalization and Beyond: New Examinations of Global Power and Its Alternatives*, edited by Jon Shefner and María Patricia Fernández-Kelly, 25–57. University Park: Penn State University Press, 2011.

Aviña, Alexander. *Specters of Revolution: Peasant Guerrillas in the Cold War Mexican Countryside*. New York: Oxford University Press, 2014.

Babb, Sarah L. "Embeddedness, Inflation, and International Regimes: The IMF in the Early Postwar Period." *American Journal of Sociology* 113, no. 1 (2007): 128–64.

———. *Managing Mexico: Economists from Nationalism to Neoliberalism*. Princeton, NJ: Princeton University Press, 2001.

Baer, Werner. "Import Substitution and Industrialization in Latin America: Experiences and Interpretations." *Latin American Research Review* 7, no. 1 (1972): 95–122.

Balderrama, Francisco, and Raymond Rodríguez. *Decade of Betrayal: Mexican Repatriation in the 1930s*. Albuquerque: University of New Mexico Press, 1995.

Barnett, Michael N., and Martha Finnemore. "The Politics, Power, and Pathologies of International Organizations." *International Organization* 53, no. 4 (1999): 699–732.

Bazant, Jan. *Historia de la deuda exterior de México, 1823–1946*. México, D.F.: Colegio de México, 1995.

Beatty, Edward. *Institutions and Investment: The Political Basis of Industrialization in Mexico Before 1911*. Stanford, CA: Stanford University Press, 2001.

Beckles, Hilary. "Capitalism, Slavery and Caribbean Modernity." *Callaloo* 20, no. 4 (1997): 777–89.

Beezley, William H. "Reflections on the Historiography of Twentieth-Century Mexico." *History Compass* 5, no. 3 (2007): 963–74.

Benjamin, Brett. "Bookend to Bandung: The New International Economic Order and the Antinomies of the Bandung Era." *Humanity: An International Journal of Human Rights, Humanitarianism, and Development* 6, no. 1 (2015): 33–46.

Benjamin, Thomas. *La Revolución: Mexico's Great Revolution as Memory, Myth & History*. Austin: University of Texas Press, 2000.

———. "The Leviathan on the Zocalo: Recent Historiography of the Postrevolutionary Mexican State." *Latin American Research Review* 20, no. 3 (January 1, 1985): 195–217.

Bennett, Douglas, and Kenneth Sharpe. "The State as Banker and Entrepreneur: The Last-Resort Character of the Mexican State's Economic Intervention, 1917–76." *Comparative Politics* 12, no. 2 (1980): 165–89.

Bethell, Leslie, and Ian Roxborough. "Latin America between the Second World War and the Cold War: Some Reflections on the 1945–8 Conjuncture." *Journal of Latin American Studies* 20, no. 1 (1988): 167–89.

Block, Fred L. *The Origins of International Economic Disorder: A Study of United States International Monetary Policy from World War II to the Present*. Berkeley: University of California Press, 1977.

Boianovsky, Mauro. "Friedrich List and the Economic Fate of Tropical Countries." *History of Political Economy* 45, no. 4 (2013): 647–91.

Booth, William. "Taming the Dead: The Mexican Marxist Left, 1945–47." PhD diss., University of London, 2012.

Bordo, Michael, and Anna J. Schwartz. "From the Exchange Stabilization Fund to the International Monetary Fund." NBER Working Paper Series. National Bureau of Economic Research, January 2001. www.nber.org/papers/w8100.

Borgwart, Elizabeth. *A New Deal for the World: America's Vision for Human Rights*. Cambridge, MA: Belknap Press, 2005.

Bortz, Jeffrey, and Stephen Haber, eds. *The Mexican Economy, 1870–1930: Essays on the Economic History of Institutions, Revolution, and Growth*. Stanford, CA: Stanford University Press, 2002.

Brading, David. *The Origins of Mexican Nationalism*. Cambridge, UK: Centre of Latin American Studies, 1985.

Brands, Hal. "The United States and the Peruvian Challenge, 1968–1975." *Diplomacy & Statecraft* 21, no. 3 (2010): 471–90.

Breda dos Santos, Norma. "Latin American Countries and the Establishment of the Multilateral Trading System: The Havana Conference (1947–1948)." *Revista de Economía Política* 36, no. 2 (2016): 309–29.

Britton, John A. "Redefining Intervention: Mexico's Contribution to Anti-Americanism." In *Anti-Americanism in Latin America and the Caribbean*, edited by Alan McPherson, 37–60. New York: Berghahn Books, 2011.

Brown, Jonathan. *Oil and Revolution in Mexico*. Berkeley: University of California Press, 1993.

Brown, Jonathan, and Alan Knight, eds. *The Mexican Petroleum Industry in the Twentieth Century*. Austin: University of Texas Press, 1992.

Browne, Stephen. *United Nations Development Programme and System*. London: Routledge, 2012.

Buchenau, Jürgen. *In the Shadow of the Giant: The Making of Mexico's Central America Policy, 1876–1930*. Tuscaloosa: University of Alabama Press, 1996.

————. *The Last Caudillo: Álvaro Obregón and the Mexican Revolution.* Chichester, UK: Wiley-Blackwell, 2011.

————. *Plutarco Elías Calles and the Mexican Revolution.* Lanham, MD: Rowman & Littlefield, 2007.

Bull, Hedley. "The Revolt Against the West." In *The Expansion of International Society,* edited by Hedley Bull and Adam Watson, 217–28. Oxford: Oxford University Press, 1984.

Bulmer-Thomas, Victor. *The Economic History of Latin America Since Independence.* 3rd. ed. New York: Cambridge University Press, 2014.

Burke, Roland. "Competing for the Last Utopia? The NIEO, Human Rights, and the World Conference for the International Women's Year, Mexico City, June 1975." *Humanity: An International Journal of Human Rights, Humanitarianism, and Development* 6, no. 1 (2015): 47–61.

Butler, Michael Anthony. *Cautious Visionary: Cordell Hull and Trade Reform, 1933–1937.* Kent, OH: Kent State University Press, 1998.

Calhoun, Craig. "Explanation in Historical Sociology: Narrative, General Theory, and Historically Specific Theory." *American Journal of Sociology* 104, no. 3 (1998): 846–71.

Camp, Roderic Ai. "The Cabinet and the Técnico in Mexico and the United States." *Journal of Comparative Administration* 3, no. 2 (1971): 188–214.

Campos Álvarez Tostado, Ricardo. *El Fondo Monetario Internacional y la deuda externa mexicana en las administraciones públicas contemporáneas.* Hermosillo: Instituto Sonorense de Administración Pública, 2003.

Carbone, Sergio M., and Lorenzo Schiano di Pepe. "States, Fundamental Rights and Duties." In *Max Planck Encyclopedia of Public International Law.* Oxford: Oxford University Press, 2009.

Cárdenas, Enrique. *La hacienda pública y la política económica, 1929–1958.* México, D.F.: Colegio de México, 1994.

————. *La industrialización mexicana durante la gran depresión.* México, D.F.: Colegio de México, 1987.

————. *La política económica en México, 1950–1994.* México, D.F.: Colegio de México, 1996.

Cárdenas García, Nicolás. *La Reconstrucción del estado mexicano: Los años sonorenses, 1920–1935.* México, D.F.: Universidad Autónoma Metropolitana, Unidad Xochimilco, División de Ciencias Sociales y Humanidades, 1992.

Cardoso, Fernando Henrique, and Enzo Faletto. *Dependency and Development in Latin America.* Berkeley: University of California Press, 1979.

Carey, Elaine. *Plaza of Sacrifices: Gender, Power, and Terror in 1968 Mexico.* Albuquerque: University of New Mexico Press, 2005.

Carmona, Fernando. "Homenaje a Juan F. Noyola Vázquez." *Problemas del Desarrollo* 10, no. 39 (1979): 130–39.

Carr, Barry. *Marxism and Communism in Twentieth-Century Mexico.* Omaha: University of Nebraska Press, 1992.

Casey, Kevin M. *Saving International Capitalism during the Early Truman Presidency: The National Advisory Council on International Monetary and Financial Problems.* New York: Routledge, 2001.

Césaire, Aimé. *Discourse on Colonialism.* Translated by Joan Pinkham. New York: Monthly Review Press, [1950] 2000.

Chase-Dunn, Christopher, Bruce Lerro, Hiroko Inoue, and Alexis Álvarez. "Democratic Global Governance: Moving from Ideal to Reality." *International Journal of Sociology* 43, no. 2 (2013): 41–54.

Chorev, Nitsan. "Changing Global Norms through Reactive Diffusion: The Case of Intellectual Property Protection of AIDS Drugs." *American Sociological Review* 77, no. 5 (2012): 831–53.

Clavin, Patricia. "'The Fetishes of So-Called International Bankers': Central Bank Co-operation for the World Economic Conference, 1932–3," *Contemporary European History* 1, no. 3 (1992): 281–311.

———. *Securing the World Economy: The Reinvention of the League of Nations, 1920–1946.* New York: Oxford University Press, 2013.

Cline, H. F. *Mexico: Revolution to Evolution, 1940–1960.* New York: Oxford University Press, 1966.

Cohen, Benjamin J. *Advanced Introduction to International Political Economy.* Northampton, MA: Edward Elgar, 2014.

Comas, Xavier. *Los orígenes del BID: De unión monetaria a banco de desarrollo; La persistencia de un ideal: La integración económica continental.* Washington, DC: Asociación de Jubilados del Banco Interamericano de Desarrollo, 2000.

Commission on Global Governance. *Our Global Neighbourhood.* Oxford: Oxford University Press, 1995.

Contreras, José. *México 1940: Industrialización y crisis política; estado y sociedad civil en las elecciones presidenciales.* México, D.F.: Siglo XXI, 1992.

Cooper, Frederick, and Randall M. Packard, eds. *International Development and the Social Sciences: Essays on the History and Politics of Knowledge.* Berkeley: University of California Press, 1997.

Cooper, Frederick, Randall M. Packard, and Ann Laura Stoler, eds. *Tensions of Empire: Colonial Cultures in a Bourgeois World.* Berkeley: University of California Press, 1997.

Córdova, Arnaldo. *La formación del poder político en México.* México, D.F.: Ediciones Era, 1972.

Cox, Robert W. "The Crisis of World Order and the Problem of International Organization in the 1980s." *International Journal* 35, no. 2 (1980): 370–95.

———. *Production, Power, and World Order: Social Forces in the Making of History.* New York: Columbia University Press, 1987.

Craig, R. Bruce. *Treasonable Doubt: The Harry Dexter White Spy Case.* Lawrence: University Press of Kansas, 2004.

Cullather, Nick. "Development? It's History." *Diplomatic History* 24, no. 4 (2000): 641–53.

Cypher, James M. *State and Capital in Mexico: Development Policy Since 1940.* New York: Routledge, 2019.

Dallek, Robert. *Franklin D. Roosevelt and American Foreign Policy, 1932–1945.* New York: Oxford University Press, 1995.

Davis, Harold Eugene. "The History of Ideas in Latin America." *Latin American Research Review* 3, no. 4 (1968): 23–44.

Dell, Sidney. *The Inter-American Development Bank: A Study in Development Financing.* New York: Praeger, 1972.

Díaz-Bonilla, Eugenio, and Victoria del Campo. *A Long and Winding Road: The Creation of the Inter American Development Bank.* Washington, DC: Inter-American Development Bank, 2011.

Dormael, Armand van. *Bretton Woods: Birth of a Monetary System.* New York: Holmes & Meier, 1978.

Dosman, Edgar. *The Life and Times of Raúl Prebisch, 1901–1986.* Montreal: McGill-Queen's Press, 2008.

Drake, Paul, ed. *Money Doctors, Foreign Debts, and Economic Reforms in Latin America from the 1890s to the Present.* Wilmington, DE: Scholarly Resources, 1994.

Drinot, Paulo, and Alan Knight, eds. *The Great Depression in Latin America.* Durham, NC: Duke University Press, 2014.

Dwyer, John. *The Agrarian Dispute: The Expropriation of American-Owned Rural Land in Postrevolutionary Mexico.* Durham, NC: Duke University Press, 2009.

———. "Diplomatic Weapons of the Weak: Mexican Policymaking during the U.S.-Mexican Agrarian Dispute, 1934–1941." *Diplomatic History* 26, no. 3 (2002): 375–95.

Eckes, Alfred E., Jr. *A Search for Solvency: Bretton Woods and the International Monetary System, 1941–1971.* Austin: University of Texas Press, 1975.

Eichengreen, Barry. *Globalizing Capital: A History of the International Monetary System.* Princeton, NJ: Princeton University Press, 2009.

Eichengreen, Barry, and Peter H. Lindert. *The International Debt Crisis in Historical Perspective.* Cambridge, MA: MIT Press, 1992.

Eichengreen, Barry, and Jeffrey Sachs. "Competitive Devaluation and the Great Depression: A Theoretical Reassessment." *Economics Letters* 22 no. 1 (1986): 67–71.

Eley, Geoff. "No Need to Choose: History from Above, History from Below" (extended version of the Kaplan Memorial Lecture at the University of Pennsylvania), *Viewpoint,* June 27, 2014. www.viewpointmag.com/2014/06/27/no-need-to-choose-history-from-above-history-from-below/.

Emirbayer, Mustafa. "Manifesto for a Relational Sociology." *American Journal of Sociology* 103, no. 2 (1997): 281–317.

Epstein, Edward. "Business-Government Relations in Mexico: The Echeverria Challenge to the Existing Development Model." *Case Western Reserve Journal of International Law* 12, no. 3 (1980): 525–47.

Escobar, Arturo. *Encountering Development: The Making and Unmaking of the Third World.* Princeton, NJ: Princeton University Press, 1995.

Fabela, Isidro. *La política interior y exterior de Carranza.* México, D.F.: Editorial Jus, 1979.

———. *Las doctrinas Monroe y Drago*. México, D.F.: Escuela Nacional de Ciencias Políticas y Sociales, 1957.

Ferguson, James. *The Anti-Politics Machine: "Development," Depoliticization, and Bureaucratic Power in Lesotho*. Minneapolis: University of Minnesota Press, 1990.

FitzGerald, E. V. K. "The Financial Constraint on Relative Autonomy: The State and Capital Accumulation in Mexico, 1940–82." In *The State and Capital Accumulation in Latin America*, Vol. 1, *Brazil, Chile, Mexico*, edited by Christian Anglade and Carlos Fortin, 210–40. Pittsburgh: University of Pittsburgh Press, 1985.

Fonseca, Pedro Cezar Dutra and Ivan Colangelo Salomão. "Furtado vs. Prebisch: Una controversia latinoamericana." *Investigación Económica* 77, no. 306 (2018): 74–93.

Foster, Sheila R., and Daniel Bonilla. "Introduction: The Social Function of Property: A Comparative Perspective." *Fordham Law Review* 80, no. 3 (2011): 1003–15.

Franczak, Michael. "Human Rights and Basic Needs: Jimmy Carter's North-South Dialogue, 1977–81." *Cold War History* 18, no. 4 (2018): 447–64.

———. "Losing the Battle, Winning the War: Neoconservatives versus the New International Economic Order, 1974–82." *Diplomatic History* 43, no. 5 (2019): 867–89.

Friedman, Max Paul. "Fracas in Caracas: Latin American Diplomatic Resistance to United States Intervention in Guatemala in 1954." *Diplomacy & Statecraft* 21, no. 4 (2010): 669–89.

Friedman, Max Paul, and Tom Long. "Soft Balancing in the Americas: Latin American Opposition to US Intervention, 1898–1936." *International Security* 40, no. 1 (2015): 120–56.

Garavini, Giuliano. *After Empires: European Integration, Decolonization, and the Challenge from the Global South, 1957–1986*. Oxford: Oxford University Press, 2012.

———. "From Boumedienomics to Reaganomics: Algeria, OPEC, and the International Struggle for Economic Equality." *Humanity: An International Journal of Human Rights, Humanitarianism, and Development* 6, no. 1 (2015): 79–92.

Gardener, Lloyd. *Economic Aspects of New Deal Diplomacy*. Boston: Beacon Press, 1971.

Gardner, Richard N. *Sterling-Dollar Diplomacy: The Origins and the Prospects of Our International Economic Order*. New York: McGraw-Hill, 1969.

Garritsen de Vries, Margaret. *The International Monetary Fund 1972–1978: Cooperation on Trial*. Vol. 2, *Narrative and Analysis*. Washington, DC: International Monetary Fund, 1985.

Gauss, Susan M. *Made in Mexico: Regions, Nation, and the State in the Rise of Mexican Industrialism, 1920s–1940s*. University Park: Penn State University Press, 2010.

———. "The Politics of Economic Nationalism in Postrevolutionary Mexico." *History Compass* 4, no. 3 (2006): 567–77.

Gellman, Irwin. *Good Neighbor Diplomacy: United States Policies in Latin America 1933–1945*. Baltimore, MD: Johns Hopkins University Press, 1979.

Getachew, Adom. *Worldmaking after Empire: The Rise and Fall of Self-Determination*. Princeton, NJ: Princeton University Press, 2019.

Gettig, Eric. "Cuba, the United States, and the Uses of the Third World Project." In *Latin America and the Global Cold War*, edited by Thomas Field, Stella Krepp, and Vanni Pettinà, 241–73. Chapel Hill: University of North Carolina Press, 2020.

Gilderhus, Mark T. *Diplomacy and Revolution: U.S.-Mexican Relations under Wilson and Carranza*. Tucson: University of Arizona Press, 1977.

———. *Pan American Visions: Woodrow Wilson in the Western Hemisphere, 1913–1921*. Tucson: University of Arizona Press, 1986.

———. "Wilson, Carranza, and the Monroe Doctrine: A Question in Regional Organization." *Diplomatic History* 7, no. 2 (1983): 103–16.

Gillingham, Paul, and Benjamin Smith, eds. *Dictablanda: Politics, Work, and Culture in Mexico, 1938–1968*. Durham, NC: Duke University Press, 2014.

Gilly, Adolfo. *The Mexican Revolution*. London: New Left Books, 1983.

Gilman, Nils. "The New International Economic Order: A Reintroduction." *Humanity: An International Journal of Human Rights, Humanitarianism, and Development* 6, no. 1 (2015): 1–16.

Glenn, John. "Global Governance and the Democratic Deficit: Stifling the Voice of the South." *Third World Quarterly* 29, no. 2 (2008): 217–38.

Go, Julian, and George Lawson. "For a Global Historical Sociology." In *Global Historical Sociology*, edited by Julian Go and George Lawson, ix–xii. New York: Cambridge University Press, 2017.

Gobat, Michel. "The Invention of Latin America: A Transnational History of Anti-Imperialism, Democracy, and Race." *American Historical Review* 118, no. 5 (2013): 1345–75.

Gold, Joseph. "Mexico and the Development of the Practice of the International Monetary Fund." *World Development* 16, no. 10 (1988): 1127–42.

Goldstein, Walter. "Redistributing the World's Wealth: Cancun 'Summit' Discord." *Resources Policy* 8, no. 1 (1982): 25–40.

Gómez-Galvarriato, Aurora. "La política económica del nuevo régimen: Alberto J. Pani 1923–1927, 1931–1933." In *Los secretarios de Hacienda y sus proyectos (1821–1933)*, Vol. 2, edited by Leonor Ludlow, 381–412. México, D.F.: Universidad Nacional Autónoma de México Instituto de Investigaciones Históricas, 2002.

Gómez Villanueva, Augusto. *Nacionalismo revolucionario: Orígenes socioeconómicos de la doctrina internacional de la revolución mexicana*. México, D.F.: Cámara de Diputados, LX Legislatura, 2009.

González Marín, María Luisa. "México ante el Diálogo Norte-Sur." *Foro Internacional* 24, no. 3 (1984): 327–40.

Gorman, Daniel. *The Emergence of International Society in the 1920s*. New York: Cambridge University Press, 2012.

Goswami, Manu. *Producing India: From Colonial Economy to National Space*. Chicago: University of Chicago Press, 2010.

Gramsci, Antonio. *Selections from the Prison Notebooks of Antonio Gramsci.* Edited by Quintin Hoare and Geoffrey Nowell Smith. New York: International Publishers, 1971.

Grandin, Greg. *Empire's Workshop: Latin America, the United States, and the Rise of the New Imperialism.* New York: Metropolitan Books, 2006.

———. *The Last Colonial Massacre: Latin America in the Cold War.* Chicago: University of Chicago Press, 2004.

———. "The Liberal Traditions in the Americas: Rights, Sovereignty, and the Origins of Liberal Multilateralism." *American Historical Review* 117, no. 1 (2012): 68–91.

———. "Your Americanism and Mine: Americanism and Anti-Americanism in the Americas." *American Historical Review* 111, no. 4 (2006): 1042–66.

Gray, Kevin, and Barry K. Gills. "South–South Cooperation and the Rise of the Global South." *Third World Quarterly* 37, no. 4 (2016): 557–74.

Green, David. *The Containment of Latin America: A History of the Myths and Realities of the Good Neighbor Policy.* Chicago: Quadrangle Books, 1971.

Gunder Frank, Andre. "North-South and East-West Keynesian Paradoxes: Brandt Commission's Report." *Economic and Political Weekly* 15, no. 31 (1980): 1314–20.

Guilhot, Nicolas. "Imperial Realism: Post-War IR Theory and Decolonisation." *International History Review* 36, no. 4 (2014): 698–720.

Haber, Stephen H. *Industry and Underdevelopment: The Industrialization of Mexico, 1890–1940.* Stanford, CA: Stanford University Press, 1989.

Haber, Stephen H., Noel Maurer, and Armando Razo, eds. *The Politics of Property Rights: Political Instability, Credible Commitments, and Economic Growth in Mexico, 1876–1929.* New York: Cambridge University Press, 2003.

Hall, Linda B. *Oil, Banks, and Politics: The United States and Postrevolutionary Mexico, 1917–1924.* Austin: University of Texas Press, 1995.

Hamilton, Nora. *The Limits of State Autonomy: Post-Revolutionary Mexico.* Princeton, NJ: Princeton University Press, 1982.

Hansen, Lawrence Douglas Taylor. "The Origins of the Maquila Industry in Mexico." *Comercio Exterior* 53, no. 11 (2003): 1–16.

Hardt, Michael. "Porto Alegre: Today's Bandung?" *New Left Review* 14 (2002): 112–18.

Hart, John M. *Empire and Revolution: The Americans in Mexico since the Civil War.* Berkeley: University of California Press, 2002.

———. *Revolutionary Mexico: The Coming and Process of the Mexican Revolution.* Berkeley: University of California Press, 1987.

Haynes, Keith. "Orden y Progreso: The Revolutionary Ideology of Alberto J. Pani." In *Los intelectuales y el poder en Mexico,* edited by Roderic A. Camp, Charles A. Hale, and Josefina Zoraida Vázquez, 259–80. Los Angeles: UCLA Latin American Center Publications, University of California, Los Angeles, 1981.

———. "Order and Progress: The Revolutionary Ideology of Alberto J. Pani." PhD diss., Northern Illinois University, 1981.

Helleiner, Eric. "The Development Mandate of International Institutions: Where Did It Come From?" *Studies in Comparative International Development*, no. 44 (2009): 189–211.

———. "Economic Nationalism as a Challenge to Economic Liberalism? Lessons from the 19th Century." *International Studies Quarterly* 46, no. 3 (2002): 307–29.

———. *The Forgotten Foundations of Bretton Woods: International Development and the Making of the Postwar Order*. Ithaca, NY: Cornell University Press, 2014.

———. "The Mystery of the Missing Sovereign Debt Restructuring Mechanism." *Contributions to Political Economy* 27, no. 1 (2008): 91–113.

———. "Reinterpreting Bretton Woods: International Development and the Neglected Origins of Embedded Liberalism." *Development and Change* 37, no. 5 (2006): 943–67.

———. "Sun Yat-Sen as a Pioneer of International Development." *History of Political Economy* 50, no. S1 (December 1, 2018): 76–93.

Helleiner, Eric, and Antulio Rosales. "Peripheral Thoughts for International Political Economy: Latin American Ideational Innovation and the Diffusion of the Nineteenth Century Free Trade Doctrine." *International Studies Quarterly* 61, no. 4 (2017): 924–34.

Henderson, Peter V. N. *In the Absence of Don Porfirio: Francisco León de La Barra and the Mexican Revolution*. New York: Rowman & Littlefield, 2000.

Henning, C. Randall. "The Group of Twenty-Four: Two Decades of Monetary and Financial Cooperation among Developing Countries." In *International Monetary and Financial Issues for the 1990s: Research Papers for the Group of Twenty-Four*, vol. 1, edited by United Nations Conference on Trade and Development, 137–54. New York: United Nations, 1992.

Herrera Calderón, Fernando, and Adela Cedillo, eds. *Challenging Authoritarianism in Mexico: Revolutionary Struggles and the Dirty War, 1964–1982*. New York: Routledge, 2012.

Herrera León, Fabián. "Luis Sánchez Pontón, correspondiente en México de La Sociedad de Naciones (1933–1942)." *Revista Mexicana de Política Exterior*, no. 92 (2011): 127–47.

———. "México en la Conferencia Económica Mundial de Londres: El Acuerdo de la Plata de 1933." *América Latina en la Historia Económica: Revista de Investigación* 34 (2010): 209–34.

———. "México en la Sociedad de Naciones: Modernización y consolidación de una política exterior, 1931–1940." PhD diss., El Colegio de México, 2010.

———. "México y la Organización Internacional del Trabajo: Los orígenes de una relación, 1919–1931." *Foro Internacional* 51, no. 2 (2011): 336–55.

Hewson, Martin, and Timothy J. Sinclair, eds. *Approaches to Global Governance Theory*. Albany: State University of New York Press, 1999.

Hershberg, James G. "'High-Spirited Confusion': Brazil, the 1961 Belgrade Non-Aligned Conference, and the Limits of an 'Independent' Foreign Policy during the High Cold War." *Cold War History* 7, no. 3 (2007): 373–88.

Hilderbrand, Robert C. *Dumbarton Oaks: The Origins of the United Nations and the Search for Postwar Security*. Chapel Hill: University of North Carolina Press, 1990.

Hilton, Stanley E. "The United States, Brazil, and the Cold War, 1945–1960: End of the Special Relationship." *Journal of American History* 68, no. 3 (1981): 599–624.

Hopewell, Kristen. *Breaking the WTO: How Emerging Powers Disrupted the Neoliberal Project*. Stanford, CA: Stanford University Press, 2016.

Hudec, Robert E. *Developing Countries in the GATT Legal System*. New York: Cambridge University Press, [1987] 2010.

Hudes, Karen. "Towards a New International Economic Order." *Yale Journal of International Law* 2, no. 1 (1975): 88–181.

Immerwahr, Daniel. *Thinking Small: The United States and the Lure of Community Development*. Cambridge, MA: Harvard University Press, 2015.

Iriye, Akira. *Global Community: The Role of International Organizations in the Making of the Contemporary World*. Berkeley: University of California Press, 2002.

Irwin, Douglas A. "The Nixon Shock after Forty Years: The Import Surcharge Revisited." *World Trade Review* 12 (2013): 29–56.

Irwin, Douglas A., Petros C. Mavroidis, and Alan O. Sykes. *The Genesis of the GATT*. Cambridge, UK: Cambridge University Press, 2008.

James, Harold. *International Monetary Cooperation since Bretton Woods*. Washington, DC: International Monetary Fund; New York: Oxford University Press, 1996.

Jensen, Jill. "Negotiating a World Trade and Employment Charter: The United States, the ILO and the Collapse of the ITO Ideal." In *The ILO from Geneva to the Pacific Rim: West Meets East*, edited by J. Jensen and N. Lichtenstein, 83–109. London: Palgrave Macmillan, 2015.

Johnson, Walter. "On Agency," *Journal of Social History* 37, no. 1 (2003): 113–24.

Jones, Halbert. *The War Has Brought Peace to Mexico: World War II and the Consolidation of the Post-Revolutionary State*. Albuquerque: University of New Mexico Press, 2014.

Joseph, Gilbert M. "Mexico's 'Popular Revolution': Mobilization and Myth in Yucatan, 1910–1940." *Latin American Perspectives* 6, no. 3 (1979): 46–65.

———, ed. *Reclaiming the Political in Latin American History: Essays from the North*. Durham, NC: Duke University Press, 2001.

———. *Revolution from Without: Yucatan, Mexico, and the United States, 1880–1924*. New York: Cambridge University Press, 1982.

Joseph, Gilbert M., and Jürgen Buchenau. *Mexico's Once and Future Revolution: Social Upheaval and the Challenges of Rule since the Late Nineteenth Century*. Durham, NC: Duke University Press, 2013.

Joseph, Gilbert M., and Timothy J. Henderson, eds. *The Mexico Reader: History, Culture, Politics*. Durham, NC: Duke University Press, 2009.

Joseph, Gilbert M., Catherine LeGrand, and Ricardo Salvatore, eds. *Close Encounters of Empire: Writing the Cultural History of U.S.-Latin American Relations*. Durham, NC: Duke University Press, 1998.

Joseph, Gilbert M., and Daniel Nugent, eds. *Everyday Forms of State Formation: Revolution and the Negotiation of Rule in Modern Mexico*. Durham, NC: Duke University Press, 1994.

Jolly, Richard, Louis Emmerij, Dharam Ghai, and Frédéric Lapeyre. *UN Contributions to Development Thinking and Practice*. Bloomington: Indiana University Press, 2004.

Kaplan, Amy, and Donald E. Pease. *Cultures of United States Imperialism*. Durham, NC: Duke University Press, 1994.

Kapur, Devesh, John Lewis, and Richard Webb. *The World Bank: Its First Half Century*. Washington, DC: Brookings, 1997.

Katz, Friedrich. *The Secret War in Mexico: Europe, the United States, and the Mexican Revolution*. Chicago: University of Chicago Press, 1981.

Kedar, Claudia. "The World Bank–United States–Latin American Triangle: The Negotiations with Socialist Chile, 1970–1973." *International History Review* 39, no. 4 (2017): 667–90.

Keller, Renata. "A Foreign Policy for Domestic Consumption: Mexico's Lukewarm Defense of Castro, 1959–1969." *Latin American Research Review* 47, no. 2 (2012): 100–119.

———. *Mexico's Cold War: Cuba, the United States, and the Legacy of the Mexican Revolution*. New York: Cambridge University Press, 2015.

Kiddle, Amelia M. *Mexico's Relations with Latin America during the Cárdenas Era*. Albuquerque: University of New Mexico Press, 2016.

King, Robin Ann. "The Mexican Proposal for a Continent-Wide Debt Moratorium: Lessons from the 1930s, Contrasts with the 1980s." Texas Papers on Latin America, Institute of Latin American Studies, University of Texas at Austin, 1989.

Kirshner, Orin, and Edward M Bernstein, eds. *The Bretton Woods-GATT System: Retrospect and Prospect after Fifty Years*. Armonk, NY: M. E. Sharpe, 1996.

Knight, Alan. "The End of the Mexican Revolution?" In *Dictablanda: Politics, Work, and Culture in Mexico, 1938–1968*, edited by Paul Gillingham and Benjamin Smith, 47–69. Durham, NC: Duke University Press, 2014.

———. "The Ideology of the Mexican Revolution, 1910–40." *Estudios Interdisciplinarios de América Latina y el Caribe* 8, no. 1 (1997): 77–110.

———. *The Mexican Revolution: Counter-Revolution and Reconstruction*. Lincoln: University of Nebraska Press, 1990.

———. *U.S.-Mexican Relations, 1910–1940: An Interpretation*. La Jolla: Center for U.S.-Mexican Studies, University of California, San Diego, 1987.

Kramer, Paul A. "Power and Connection: Imperial Histories of the United States in the World." *American Historical Review* 116, no. 5 (2011): 1348–91.

Krasner, Stephen D. *Structural Conflict: The Third World against Global Liberalism*. Berkeley: University of California Press, 1985.

———. "Transforming International Regimes: What the Third World Wants and Why," *International Studies Quarterly* 25, no. 1 (1981): 119–48.

Krauze, Enrique. *Mexico, Biography of Power: A History of Modern Mexico, 1810–1996*. Translated by Hank Heifetz. New York: Harper Perennial, 1997.

Lajous, Alejandra. *Los orígenes del partido único en México*. México, D.F.: Universidad Nacional Autónoma de México, 1979.

Lajous, Roberta. *Historia mínima de las relaciones exteriores de México, 1821–2000*. México, D.F.: El Colegio de México, 2012.

———. *La política exterior del Porfiriato*. México, D.F.: El Colegio de México, 2010.

Lee, Christopher J., ed. *Making a World after Empire: The Bandung Moment and Its Political Afterlives*. Athens: Ohio University Press, 2010.

Loaeza, Soledad. "La política intervencionista de Manuel Ávila Camacho: El caso de Argentina en 1945." *Foro Internacional* 56, no. 4 (2016): 851–902.

Long, Tom. *Latin America Confronts the United States: Asymmetry and Influence*. New York: Cambridge University Press, 2015.

López-Maya, Margarita. "The Change in the Discourse of U.S.-Latin American Relations from the End of the Second World War to the Beginning of the Cold War." *Review of International Political Economy* 2, no. 1 (1995): 135–49.

López Portillo, José. "Las Naciones Unidas en la encrucijada." *Comercio Exterior* 32, no. 11 (November 1982): 1244.

López Villafañe, Víctor. *La formación del sistema político mexicano*. México, D.F.: Siglo XXI, 1999.

Lorenzini, Sara. *Global Development: A Cold War History*. Princeton, NJ: Princeton University Press, 2019.

Loveman, Brian. *No Higher Law: American Foreign Policy and the Western Hemisphere Since 1776*. Chapel Hill: University of North Carolina Press, 2010.

Ludlow, Leonor, and María Eugenia Romero Sotelo, eds. *Temas a debate moneda y banca en México 1884–1954*. México, D.F.: Universidad Nacional Autónoma de México Instituto de Investigaciones Históricas, 2006.

Lustig, Nora. *Mexico: The Remaking of an Economy*. Washington, DC: Brookings Institution Press, 2000.

Macekura, Stephen. *Of Limits and Growth: The Rise of Global Sustainable Development in the Twentieth Century*. New York: Cambridge University Press, 2015.

Manela, Erez. *The Wilsonian Moment: Self-Determination and the International Origins of Anticolonial Nationalism*. New York: Oxford University Press, 2007.

Marichal, Carlos. *A Century of Debt Crises in Latin America: From Independence to the Great Depression, 1820–1930*. Princeton, NJ: Princeton University Press, 1989.

———. "Deuda externa y política en México, 1946–2000." In *Una historia contemporánea de México: Transformaciones y permanencias*, Vol. 1, edited by Ilán Bizberg and Lorenzo Meyer, 451–91. México, D.F.: Océano, 2003.

———. *Nueva historia de las grandes crisis financieras: Una Perspectiva global, 1873–2008*. Buenos Aires, Argentina: Debate, 2010.

Marshall, Don D. "Gender Tropes and Colonial Discourses in the Turbulence of Global Finance." *Contemporary Politics* 15, no. 4 (2009): 413–27.

Mason, Edward S., and Robert E. Asher. *The World Bank since Bretton Woods: The Origins, Policies, Operations, and Impact of the International Bank for Reconstruction*. Washington, DC: Brookings, 1973.

Maurer, Noel. *The Power and the Money: The Mexican Financial System, 1876–1932.* Stanford, CA: Stanford University Press, 2002.

Maxfield, Sylvia. *Gatekeepers of Growth: The International Political Economy of Central Banking in Developing Countries.* Princeton, NJ: Princeton University Press, 1998.

———. *Governing Capital: International Finance and Mexican Politics.* Ithaca, NY: Cornell University Press, 1990.

———. "The Politics of Mexican Financial Policy." In *The Politics of Finance in Developing Countries,* edited by Stephan Haggard, Sylvia Maxfield, and Chung H. Lee, 230–58. Ithaca, NY: Cornell University Press, 1993.

Mazower, Mark. "The End of Eurocentrism." *Critical Inquiry* 40, no. 4 (2014): 300–301.

———. *Governing the World: The History of an Idea.* New York: Penguin Press, 2012.

———. *No Enchanted Palace: The End of Empire and the Ideological Origins of the United Nations.* Princeton, NJ: Princeton University Press, 2009.

McCaa, Robert. "Missing Millions: The Demographic Costs of the Mexican Revolution." *Mexican Studies/Estudios Mexicanos* 19, no. 2 (2003): 367–400.

McCormick, Thomas J. "Walking the Tightrope: Adolf A. Berle and America's Journey from Social to Global Capitalism, 1933–1945." In *Behind the Throne: Servants of Power to Imperial Presidents, 1898–1968,* edited by Thomas J. McCormick and Walter LaFeber, 126–55. Madison: University of Wisconsin Press, 1993.

McCoy, Alfred W., and Francisco A. Scarano, eds. *The Colonial Crucible: Empire in the Making of the Modern American State.* Madison: University of Wisconsin Press, 2009.

McMichael, Philip. *Development and Social Change: A Global Perspective.* Los Angeles: Sage Publications, 2012.

McPherson, Alan. *Anti-Americanism in Latin America and the Caribbean.* New York: Berghahn Books, 2011.

Meagher, Robert F. *An International Redistribution of Wealth and Power: A Study of the Charter of Economic Rights and Duties of States.* Elmsford, NY: Pergamon Press, 1979.

Mecham, J. Lloyd. *The United States and Inter-American Security, 1889–1960.* Austin: University of Texas Press, 1961.

Meyer, Lorenzo. *La marca del nacionalismo: México y el mundo, historia de sus relaciones exteriores.* Vol. 6. México, D.F.: El Colegio de México, 2010.

———. *Mexico and the United States in the Oil Controversy, 1917–1942.* Austin: University of Texas Press, 1977.

———. *México para los mexicanos: La Revolución y sus adversarios.* México, D.F.: Colegio de México, 2010.

Middlebrook, Kevin J. *The Paradox of Revolution: Labor, the State, and Authoritarianism in Mexico.* Baltimore, MD: Johns Hopkins University Press, 1995.

Mitchell, Timothy. "Economentality: How the Future Entered Government." *Critical Inquiry* 40, no. 4 (2014): 479–507.

Monticelli, Carlo. *Reforming Global Economic Governance: An Unsettled Order.* New York: Routledge, 2019.

Moreno, Julio. *Yankee Don't Go Home: Mexican Nationalism, American Business Culture, and the Shaping of Modern Mexico, 1920–1950.* Chapel Hill: University of North Carolina Press, 2003.

Moreno-Brid, Juan Carlos, and Jaime Ros. *Development and Growth in the Mexican Economy: A Historical Perspective.* New York: Oxford University Press, 2009.

Mortimer, Robert A. *The Third World Coalition in International Politics.* Boulder, CO: Westview Press, 1984.

Morton, Adam David. *Revolution and State in Modern Mexico: The Political Economy of Uneven Development.* Lanham, MD: Rowman & Littlefield, 2011.

Moyn, Samuel. *The Last Utopia: Human Rights in History.* Cambridge, MA: Belknap Press of Harvard University Press, 2010.

———. "Rights vs. Duties: Reclaiming Civic Balance." *Boston Review,* May 16, 2016. http://bostonreview.net/books-ideas/samuel-moyn-rights-duties.

———. "The Universal Declaration of Human Rights of 1948 in the History of Cosmopolitanism." *Critical Inquiry* 40, no. 4 (2014): 613–45.

Murphy, Craig. *International Organization and Industrial Change: Global Governance Since 1850.* New York: Oxford University Press, 1994.

Navarro, Aaron W. *Political Intelligence and the Creation of Modern Mexico, 1938–1954.* University Park: Penn State University Press, 2010.

Niblo, Stephen R. *Mexico in the 1940s: Modernity, Politics, and Corruption.* Wilmington, DE: Scholarly Resources, 1999.

———. *War, Diplomacy and Development: The United States and Mexico, 1938–1954.* Wilmington, DE: Scholarly Resources, 1995.

Niemeyer, E. Victor. *Revolution at Querétaro: The Mexican Constitutional Convention of 1916–1917.* Austin: University of Texas Press, 1974.

Nye, Joseph S., Jr. "Globalization's Democratic Deficit: How to Make International Institutions More Accountable." *Foreign Affairs* 80, no. 4 (2001): 2–6.

Ogle, Vanessa. "State Rights against Private Capital: The 'New International Economic Order' and the Struggle over Aid, Trade, and Foreign Investment, 1962–1981." *Humanity: An International Journal of Human Rights, Humanitarianism, and Development* 5, no. 2 (2014): 211–34.

Oliver, Robert W. *International Economic Co-operation and the World Bank.* New York: Homes & Meier, 1975.

Olsson, Tore C. *Agrarian Crossings: Reformers and the Remaking of the US and Mexican Countryside.* Princeton, NJ: Princeton University Press, 2017.

Olvera Serrano, Margarita. "La Institucionalización de la economía y la sociología como disciplinas modernas en México: Una Reconstrucción historiográfica a través de sus revistas especializadas (1928–1958)." PhD diss., Universidad Autónoma Metropolitana, 2011.

Padilla, Tanalís. *Rural Resistance in the Land of Zapata: The Jaramillista Movement and the Myth of the Pax Priísta, 1940–1962.* Durham, NC: Duke University Press, 2008.

Pahuja, Sundhya. *Decolonising International Law: Development, Economic Growth and the Politics of Universality*. New York: Cambridge University Press, 2011.

Palomino, Pablo. "On the Disadvantages of 'Global South' for Latin American Studies." *Journal of World Philosophies* 4, no. 2 (2019): 22–39.

Pani, Arturo. *Alberto J. Pani: Ensayo biográfico*. México, D.F.: Imprenta de Manuel Casas, 1961.

Pastor, Manuel, and Carol Wise. "The Origins and Sustainability of Mexico's Free Trade Policy." *International Organization* 48, no. 3 (1994): 459–89.

Pedersen, Susan. "Back to the League of Nations." *American Historical Review* 112, no. 4 (2007): 1091–1117.

———. *The Guardians: The League of Nations and the Crisis of Empire*. New York: Oxford University Press, 2015.

Pellicer de Brody, Olga. *México y el mundo: Cambios y continuidades*. México, D.F.: Miguel Ángel Porrúa, 2006.

———. "Tercermundismo del capitalismo mexicano: Ideología y realidad." *Cuadernos Políticos* 3 (1975): 52–59.

———. "Veinte años de política exterior mexicana, 1960–1980." *Foro Internacional* 21, no. 2 (1980): 149–60.

Pérez Caldentey, Esteban, and Matias Vernengo. *Ideas, Policies and Economic Development in the Americas*. New York: Routledge, 2007.

Pettinà, Vanni. "Adapting to the New World: Mexico's International Strategy of Economic Development at the Outset of the Cold War, 1946–1952." *Culture & History Digital Journal* 4, no. 1 (2015): e003.

———. "Global Horizons: Mexico, the Third World, and the Non-Aligned Movement at the Time of the 1961 Belgrade Conference." *International History Review* 38, no. 4 (2016): 741–64.

Phillips, Nicola, ed. *Globalizing International Political Economy*. New York: Palgrave Macmillan, 2005.

Pollard, Robert. *Economic Security and the Origins of the Cold War, 1945–1950*. New York: Columbia University Press, 1985.

Pollock, David, Daniel Kerner, and Joseph L. Love. "Raúl Prebisch on ECLAC's Achievements and Deficiencies: An Unpublished Interview." *CEPAL Review* 75 (2001): 9–22.

Poniatowska, Elena. *Massacre in Mexico*. New York: Viking Press, 1975.

Prashad, Vijay. *The Darker Nations: A People's History of the Third World*. New York: New Press, 2008.

Rabe, Stephen G. "Alliance for Progress." In *Oxford Research Encyclopedia for Latin American History*, March 2016. https://oxfordindex.oup.com/view/10.1093/acrefore/9780199366439.013.95.

———. "The Elusive Conference: United States Economic Relations with Latin America, 1945–1952." *Diplomatic History* 2, no. 3 (1978): 279–94.

Ramírez, Blanca Torres. *México y el mundo: Historia de sus relaciones exteriores*. 9 vols. México, D.F.: El Colegio de México, 2010.

Ramos, José Luis. "The Impact of the Mexican Revolution in InterAmerican Politics: U.S.–Mexican Relations and U.S. Foreign Policy at the Fifth Pan-American Conference of 1923." *Journal of Iberian and Latin American Research* 21, no. 1 (2015): 87–101.

Rath, Thomas G. *Myths of Demilitarization in Postrevolutionary Mexico, 1920–1960.* Chapel Hill: University of North Carolina Press, 2013.

Rees, David. *Harry Dexter White: A Study in Paradox.* New York: Coward, McCann & Geoghegan, 1973.

Richmond, Douglas W. *Venustiano Carranza's Nationalist Struggle, 1893–1920.* Lincoln: University of Nebraska Press, 1983.

Rist, Gilbert. *The History of Development: From Western Origins to Global Faith.* London: Zed Books, 2002.

Rock, David, ed. *Latin America in the 1940s: War and Postwar Transitions.* Berkeley: University of California Press, 1994.

Roos, Jerome E. *Why Not Default? The Political Economy of Sovereign Debt.* Princeton, NJ: Princeton University Press, 2019.

Roseberry, William. "Hegemony and the Language of Contention." In *Everyday Forms of State Formation: Revolution and the Negotiation of Rule in Modern Mexico,* edited by Gilbert M. Joseph and Daniel Nugent, 355–66. Durham, NC: Duke University Press, 1994.

Rosenberg, Emily S. *Financial Missionaries to the World: The Politics and Culture of Dollar Diplomacy, 1900–1930.* Cambridge, MA: Harvard University Press, 1999.

Salceda Olivares, Juan Manuel. "México y la V conferencia panamericana: Un Campo de batalla diplomática contra el intervencionismo norteamericano." *Tzintzun: Revista de Estudios Históricos,* no. 50 (2009): 61–104.

Saldaña-Portillo, María Josefina. *The Revolutionary Imagination in the Americas and the Age of Development.* Durham, NC: Duke University Press, 2003.

Sargent, Daniel J. "North/South: The United States Responds to the New International Economic Order." *Humanity: An International Journal of Human Rights, Humanitarianism, and Development* 6, no. 1 (2015): 201–16.

Scarfi, Juan Pablo. "In the Name of the Americas: The Pan-American Redefinition of the Monroe Doctrine and the Emerging Language of American International Law in the Western Hemisphere, 1898–1933." *Diplomatic History* 40, no. 2 (2016): 189–218.

Schuler, Friedrich E. *Mexico between Hitler and Roosevelt: Mexican Foreign Relations in the Age of Lázaro Cárdenas, 1934–1940.* Albuquerque: University of New Mexico Press, 1998.

———. *Secret Wars and Secret Policies in the Americas, 1842–1929.* Albuquerque: University of New Mexico Press, 2011.

Schwartz, Anna J. "From Obscurity to Notoriety: A Biography of the Exchange Stabilization Fund." *Journal of Money, Credit and Banking* 29, no. 2 (1997): 135–53.

Scott-Smith, Giles, and J. Simon Rofe, eds. *Global Perspectives on the Bretton Woods Conference and the Post-War World Order.* New York: Palgrave Macmillan, 2017.

Sepulveda, César. "El Sentido y el alcance de la Carta de Derechos y Deberes Económicos de los Estados." In *Estudios en honor del doctor Luis Recaséns Siches*, edited by Fausto E. Rodríguez García, 651–61. México, D.F.: Universidad Nacional Autónoma de México, 1980.

Servín, Elisa, Leticia Reina, and John Tutino, eds. *Cycles of Conflict, Centuries of Change: Crisis, Reform, and Revolution in Mexico*. Durham, NC: Duke University Press, 2007.

Sewell, Bevan. "A Perfect (Free-Market) World? Economics, the Eisenhower Administration, and the Soviet Economic Offensive in Latin America." *Diplomatic History* 32, no. 5 (2008): 841–68.

Sexton, Jay. *The Monroe Doctrine: Empire and Nation in Nineteenth-Century America*. New York: Hill and Wang, 2011.

Sheinin, David, ed. *Argentina and the United States at the Sixth Pan American Conference: Havana 1928*. London: Institute of Latin American Studies, University of London, 1991.

———. *Beyond the Ideal: Pan Americanism in Inter-American Affairs*. New York: Praeger, 2000.

Shilliam, Robert. "What the Haitian Revolution Might Tell Us about Development, Security, and the Politics of Race." *Comparative Studies in Society and History* 50, no. 3 (2008): 778–808.

Sikkink, Kathryn. "Latin American Countries as Norm Protagonists of the Idea of International Human Rights." *Global Governance* 20, no. 3 (2014), 389–404.

Silva Herzog, Jesús. *Imagen y obra escogida*. México, D.F.: Universidad Nacional Autónoma de México, 1989.

Simpson, Bradley. "Self-Determination and Decolonization." In *Oxford Handbook of the Ends of Empire*, edited by Martin Thomas and Andrew S. Thompson, 417–36. New York: Oxford University Press, 2018.

Singer, H. W. "The Terms of Trade Controversy and the Evolution of Soft Financing: Early Years in the UN." In *Pioneers in Development*, edited by Gerald M. Meier and Dudley Seers, 275–303. Oxford: Oxford University Press, 1984.

Skidelsky, Robert. "Resurrecting Creditor Adjustment." *Project Syndicate*, October 24, 2017.

Slobodian, Quinn. *Globalists: The End of Empire and the Birth of Neoliberalism*. Cambridge, MA: Harvard University Press, 2018.

Sluga, Glenda. *Internationalism in the Age of Nationalism*. Philadelphia: University of Pennsylvania Press, 2013.

Sluga, Glenda, and Patricia Clavin, eds. *Internationalisms: A Twentieth-Century History*. New York: Cambridge University Press, 2016.

Smith, Benjamin T. *Pistoleros and Popular Movements: The Politics of State Formation in Postrevolutionary Oaxaca*. Lincoln: University of Nebraska Press, 2009.

Smith, Neil. *American Empire: Roosevelt's Geographer and the Prelude to Globalization*. Berkeley: University of California Press, 2004.

Smith, Peter. "Mexico Since 1946." In *Cambridge History of Latin America*, Vol. 7, edited by Leslie Bethell, 83–157. New York: Cambridge University Press, 2008.

Smith, Robert Freeman. *The United States and Revolutionary Nationalism in Mexico, 1916–1932.* Chicago: University of Chicago Press, 1972.

Spenser, Daniela. *En combate: La vida de Lombardo Toledano.* México, D.F.: Penguin Random House Grupo Editorial México, 2018.

———. *The Impossible Triangle: Mexico, Soviet Russia, and the United States in the 1920s.* Durham, NC: Duke University Press, 1999.

Staples, Amy. *The Birth of Development: How the World Bank, Food and Agriculture Organization, and World Health Organization Changed the World, 1945–1965.* Kent, OH: Kent State University Press, 2006.

Stallings, Barbara. *Banker to the Third World: U.S. Portfolio Investment in Latin America, 1900–1986.* Berkeley: University of California Press, 1987.

Steffek, Jens. *Embedded Liberalism and Its Critics: Justifying Global Governance in the American Century.* New York: Palgrave Macmillan, 2006.

Steil, Benn. *The Battle of Bretton Woods: John Maynard Keynes, Harry Dexter White, and the Making of a New World Order.* Princeton, NJ: Princeton University Press, 2013.

———. "Red White." *Foreign Affairs* 92, no. 2 (2013): 141–51.

Stern, Steve. "Between Tragedy and Promise: The Politics of Writing Latin American History in the Late Twentieth Century." In *Reclaiming the Political in Latin American History: Essays from the North,* edited by Gilbert M. Joseph, 32–77. Durham, NC: Duke University Press, 2001.

Story, Dale. "Trade Politics in the Third World: A Case Study of the Mexican GATT Decision." *International Organization* 36 (1982): 767–94.

Suárez Dávila, Francisco. "Desarrollismo y ortodoxia monetaria (1927–1952): El debate entre dos visiones de política financiera mexicana." In *Temas a debate: Moneda y banca en México 1884–1954,* edited by María Eugenia Romero Sotelo and Leonor Ludlow, 281–358. México, D.F.: Universidad Nacional Autónoma de México, 2006.

Talesnick, Daniel. "Monumentality and Resignification: The UNCTAD III Building in Chile." In *Latin American Modern Architectures: Ambiguous Territories,* edited by Patricio del Real and Helen Gyger, 135–52. New York: Routledge, 2013.

Thompson, John K. *Inflation, Financial Markets and Economic Development: The Experience of Mexico.* Greenwich, CT: JAI Press, 1979.

Thornton, Christy. "A Mexican International Economic Order? Tracing the Hidden Roots of the Charter of Economic Rights and Duties of States." *Humanity: An International Journal of Human Rights, Humanitarianism, and Development* 9, no. 3 (2018): 389–421.

Tickner, Arlene. "Hearing Latin American Voices in International Relations Studies." *International Studies Perspectives* 4, no. 4 (November 1, 2003): 325–50.

Toniolo, Gianni. *Central Bank Cooperation at the Bank for International Settlements, 1930–1973.* New York: Cambridge University Press, 2005.

Tooze, Adam. *The Deluge: The Great War, America and the Remaking of the Global Order, 1916–1931.* New York: Viking, 2014.

Toye, John, and Richard Toye. *The UN and Global Political Economy: Trade, Finance, and Development*. Bloomington: Indiana University Press, 2004.

Toye, Richard. "Developing Multilateralism: The Havana Charter and the Fight for the International Trade Organization, 1947–1948." *International History Review* 25, no. 2 (2003): 282–305.

Turrent y Díaz, Eduardo. *México en Bretton Woods*. México, D.F.: Banco de México, 2009.

Tussie, Diana, and Pia Riggirozzi. "A Global Conversation: Rethinking IPE in Post-Hegemonic Scenarios." *Contexto Internacional* 37, no. 3 (2015): 1041–68.

Urzúa, Carlos M. "Five Decades of Relations between the World Bank and Mexico." In *The World Bank: Its First Half Century*, Vol. 2, *Perspectives*, edited by Devesh Kapur, John Prior Lewis, and Richard Charles Webb, 49–108. Washington, DC: Brookings Institution Press, 1997.

Vargas Escobar, Natalia. "Hacia una sociología histórica sobre los orígenes del tipo estatal de financiamiento al desarrollo, México 1932: El caso de Nacional Financiera." PhD diss., Colegio de México, 2013.

Vaughan, Mary K., and Stephen E Lewis, eds. *The Eagle and the Virgin: Nation and Cultural Revolution in Mexico, 1920–1940*. Durham, NC: Duke University Press, 2006.

Walker, Louise. *Waking from the Dream: Mexico's Middle Classes after 1968*. Stanford, CA: Stanford University Press, 2013.

Wallerstein, Immanuel. "The New World Disorder: If the States Collapse, Can the Nations Be United?" In *Between Sovereignty and Global Governance: The United Nations, the State and Civil Society*, edited by Albert J. Paolini, Anthony P. Jarvis, and Christian Reus-Smit, 171–85. London: Palgrave Macmillan UK, 1998.

Wasserman, Mark. *Persistent Oligarchs: Elites and Politics in Chihuahua, Mexico, 1910–1940*. Durham, NC: Duke University Press, 1993.

Weinstein, Barbara. "Developing Inequality." *American Historical Review* 113, no. 1 (2008): 1–18.

———. *For Social Peace in Brazil: Industrialists and the Remaking of the Working Class in São Paulo, 1920–1964*. Chapel Hill: University of North Carolina Press, 1996.

Wertheim, Stephen. "The League That Wasn't: American Designs for a Legalist-Sanctionist League of Nations and the Intellectual Origins of International Organization, 1914–1920." *Diplomatic History* 35, no. 5 (2011): 797–836.

Westad, Odd Arne. *The Global Cold War: Third World Interventions and the Making of Our Times*. New York: Cambridge University Press, 2005.

Whelan, Daniel J. "'Under the Aegis of Man': The Right to Development and the Origins of the New International Economic Order." *Humanity: An International Journal of Human Rights, Humanitarianism, and Development* 6, no. 1 (2015): 93–108.

Whiting, Van R. *The Political Economy of Foreign Investment in Mexico: Nationalism, Liberalism, and Constraints on Choice*. Baltimore, MD: Johns Hopkins University Press, 1992.

Wilkie James W., and Edna Monzón Wilkie. *Daniel Costo Villegas: Un protagonista de la etapa constructiva de la revolución mexicana*. México, D.F.: El Colegio de México, 2013.

Woods, Ngaire. *The Globalizers: The IMF, the World Bank, and Their Borrowers*. Ithaca, NY: Cornell University Press, 2006.

Wynne, William H. *State Insolvency and Foreign Bondholders: Selected Case Histories of Governmental Foreign Bond Defaults and Debt Readjustments*. New Haven, CT: Yale University Press, 1951.

Yankelevich, Pablo. "En la retaguardia de la revolución mexicana: Propaganda y propagandistas mexicanos en América Latina, 1914–1920." *Mexican Studies/ Estudios Mexicanos* 15, no. 1 (1999): 35–71.

———. *La revolución mexicana en América Latina: Intereses políticos e itinerarios intelectuales*. México, D.F.: Instituto de Investigaciones Dr. José María Luis Mora, 2003.

Young, Marilyn. "Ne Plus Ultra Imperialism." *Radical History Review*, no. 57 (1993): 33–37.

Zeiler, Thomas. *Free Trade, Free World: The Advent of GATT*. Chapel Hill: University of North Carolina Press, 1999.

Zinman, Ira B. "Nationalism as a Factor in Legislation Restricting Foreign Investment: Extractive Industries in Mexico." *Indiana Law Journal* 45, no. 4 (1970): 616–30.

Zolov, Eric. *The Last Good Neighbor: Mexico in the Global Sixties*. Durham, NC: Duke University Press, 2020.

Global South: defining, 207n1; global economic governance and, 4–6, 16, 207n1; international economic development and, 58; international financial institutions (IFIs) and, 16; political mobilization and, 11, 198; representation and, 1; world order and, 6–7. *See also* Latin America; North-South relations

Gómez, Rodrigo, 87–88, 146, 150, 157

González, Henry, 161–62

González Gálvez, Sergio, 175, 185

González Roa, Fernando, 44, 46, 59

Good Neighbor Policy, 38, 46, 113, 196

Gramsci, Antonio, 7

Great Britain: abandonment of gold standard, 42; Bretton Woods Conference and, 3, 80, 88–89, 97; currency stabilization and, 43; economic rules and, 54; gold parity value determination and, 92; ITO proposal and, 124; stabilization proposals and, 85, 91; trade negotiations with Argentina and Uruguay, 49. *See also* United Kingdom

Great Depression, 41–43, 45–46, 59

Group of 10 (G10), 160, 163

Group of 77 (G77), 151, 160, 162–63, 177, 191–92

Guatemala, 104, 116, 148–49

Guatemala conference (1939), 67–69

Guevara, Che, 149

Haberler, Gottfried, 185

Haiti, 35, 104, 152

Haldeman, H. R., 173

Hanson, Simon, 69–70

Harding, Warren G., 25–26, 196

Havana Charter, 142–43. *See also* International Trade Organization (ITO)

Havana Conference, 134–42. *See also* International Trade Organization (ITO)

Hay, Eduardo, 67

Hayek, Friedrich, 125

Heymann, Hans, 60

Hoover, Herbert, 46

Huerta, Victoriano, 40

Hughes, Charles Evans, 31–32, 36

Hull, Cordell: Dumbarton Oaks conference and, 103; free-trade proposal, 55–56; on government nonintervention, 54; Montevideo conference and, 51–52, 55–56; opposition to debt moratorium proposal, 50–51; renouncement of military intervention, 56; stabilization agreement and, 83

IAB. *See* Inter-American Bank (IAB)

IADB. *See* Inter-American Development Bank (IADB)

IA-ECOSOC. *See* Inter-American Economic and Social Council (IA-ECOSOC)

IFEAC. *See* Inter-American Financial and Economic Advisory Committee (IFEAC)

Independent Commission on International Development Issues, 192

India, 5, 44, 104, 125

industrialization: Ávila Camacho administration and, 81; Cárdenas administration and, 65; Echeverría administration and, 16; economic growth and, 81, 100, 164; import substitution, 78, 144, 146; international monopolies and, 116; international trade and, 68; ITO proposal and, 131, 139–40; Latin America and, 101, 122, 131; long-term development financing and, 102, 122; monetary policy and, 157; PRI and, 12; protective tariffs and, 138; public/private investment in, 101–2, 122–23; stabilization agreement and, 84; state intervention and, 100–102; underdeveloped countries and, 125–26, 139–40; urban, 81; US support for, 71, 101–2; Villaseñor and, 68

Ingersoll, Robert, 185

Inman, Samuel Guy, 26, 28, 34, 37

insurgent politics, 167–68

Inter-American Bank (IAB): development of, 58, 60–64; draft convention for, 72–74; Latin American advocacy for, 68–69, 73–74; Latin American skepticism over, 70; long-term development financing and, 72–73; Mexican

International Monetary Fund (IMF) (continued)
expropriation and, 161–62; US power and, 81; White and, 78–79
international political economy: economic relations and, 167–69; Global South actors in, 8; Mexico and, 2–3, 8, 14; US hegemony and, 4, 208n12
International Stabilization Fund, 84, 88
international trade: commodity prices and, 121; Economic Charter of the Americas and, 118; economic cooperation and, 87; imbalance in, 91, 107; impact on employment, 140; industrializing countries and, 68, 125–26; long-term development financing and, 72; regulation of, 121, 123; US partisan fight over, 129; US redefining of, 11
International Trade Organization (ITO): Belgian proposal and, 132; Calvo Doctrine and, 139; Chapultepec resolutions and, 126–27; Committee on Economic Development, 141–42; economic development and, 131–32, 138–39; GATT negotiations and, 124, 126, 130; Geneva meeting and, 126–27, 129–30, 136–40; Havana Conference and, 134–42; industrializing countries and, 125–26, 131, 139–40; influence of 1942 trade agreement on, 124; Mexican allies and, 130–32, 136–37; Mexican leadership and, 136–37; Mexican leftist opposition to, 133–34; Mexican proposals and, 122, 126–28, 131, 134, 138–42; Mexican representation and, 141; most-favored nation (MFN) principle and, 131–32; opposition of US capital, 142–43; protective tariffs and, 138; public opinion and, 128–30, 133–34; quantitative restrictions and, 138, 141; redistribution and, 137; reform agenda, 137–41; restraints on US, 142; tariff negotiations and, 131, 140–42; US-Great Britain discord, 132–33; US proposals for, 124–26, 134

ITO. See International Trade Organization (ITO)

jacobinos, 19
Japan, 160, 175, 179, 188

Kelley, Francis, 22
Kemmerer, Edwin, 61, 63
Keynes, John Maynard: Bretton Woods Conference and, 90; dismissal of Latin American delegates, 80; dismissal of Mexican advocacy, 12, 89; General Theory, 53; Mexican economic development proposal and, 96–97; scarce currency provisions and, 91; World Bank and, 79, 86
Kissinger, Henry: Echeverría Álvarez and, 173; on Latin American relations, 180, 250n79; support for Charter of Economic Rights, 178–80, 182, 184, 187; US-Mexican compromise and, 182–87; on US-Mexican relations, 182, 186–87, 191
Kubitschek, Juscelino, 153, 165

labor: Alemán Valdés administration and, 123; bracero program and, 100, 138; Constitution of 1917 and, 19, 41; Economic Charter of the Americas and, 114–16; ECOSOC and, 107; Havana Conference and, 134–35; impact of 1948 devaluation on, 157; opposition to Clayton Plan, 133–34; relations with the state, 65; support for industrialization and, 115–16
Lamont, Thomas, 40–41
Larrañaga, Pedro, 70
Latin America: anti-interventionism and, 208n13; Argentinian leadership and, 47; balance-of-payment and, 55–56, 59; Bretton Woods Conference and, 3, 6, 79–80, 88–89, 94–95; BRICS consortium and, 5; CECLA and, 160–63; Chapultepec Conference proposals, 116–18; Dávila plan and, 71–72; debt defaults and, 45, 49; economic development and, 58, 78; economic solidarity and, 8, 47, 56, 61, 100; economic

petroleum nationalization, 65–66, 83–84, 161

Pittman, Key, 44

Poindexter, Miles, 38

political sovereignty, 9, 168, 172

Prebisch, Raúl, 55, 87, 113, 154–55

PRI. *See* Partido Revolucionario Institucional (PRI)

property rights: constitutional provision on, 14, 19–20, 22–23, 53; Mexican revolution and, 40, 46; social function of, 53; US/British opposition to reforms, 20, 22–23, 26

Prudential Insurance Company, 147

Puig Casauranc, José Manuel: debt default proposal and, 39, 45–46, 48, 50–55; on economic predation of private capital, 52, 218n62; hemispheric balance and, 48–51; international finance proposal and, 39, 47–48, 52–55, 61–62, 91; monetary use of silver and, 39; Monroe Doctrine proposal, 48, 50–51; Roosevelt and, 51; on social relations of credit, 52–54; on terms of trade, 55–56; on trade imbalances, 91

Rabasa, Emilio: Charter development and, 174; promotion of Charter of Economic Rights, 179–80, 188; US-Mexican relationship and, 179, 181–84, 186, 189, 191

Reagan, Ronald, 174, 189, 192

redistribution: acquisitive power and, 136; of capital from North to South, 1, 10, 101, 188, 192, 194, 196; global economic governance for, 193–94; land and, 18, 20, 41; Latin American economies and, 64; Mexican advocacy for, 14–16, 39, 56, 145; Mexican representation and, 99

representation: CECLA and, 160–61; Charter of Economic Rights and Duties of States, 174, 188; Costa Rican proposal and, 29, 31–36; global economic governance and, 86, 93–95, 97–99, 164, 166, 193; Global South and, 1; IAB and, 58, 68; international order and, 104, 106, 111–12; ITO proposal and, 136, 141–42; Latin America and, 81; Mexican

advocacy for, 10, 14–16, 21, 37, 39, 145, 194; Pan-American Union and, 24–25; redistribution and, 14, 16, 99, 111; Santiago conference and, 27–30; sovereign equality and, 18, 24, 37, 194; SUNFED and, 155; Versailles talks and, 21–22

Reyes, Alfonso, 49–50

Reyes Heroles, Jesús, 198

Rio Economic Conference (1954), 152

Rivera, Diego, 134

Roa, Raúl, 163

Robles, Gonzalo, 130

Rockefeller, Nelson, 74, 77, 102, 110, 173

Rodríguez, Abelardo, 41

Rogers, William, 179

Roosevelt, Franklin D.: abandonment of gold standard, 42; on currency stabilization, 43; development of Ex-Im Bank, 65; Foreign Bondholders Council and, 50; Good Neighbor Policy, 46; IAB and, 74; international assistance and, 69; international trade and, 129; Latin American living standards and, 102; Pani and, 49; Puig Casauranc and, 51

Root, Elihu, 28

Rowe, Leo S., 27, 29, 31, 33

Ruiz Cortines, Adolfo, 146, 158–59

Ruiz Galindo, Antonio, 123, 135

Ruiz Moreno, Isidoro, 44

Saavedra Lamas, Carlos, 54–55

Sáenz, Josué, 140

Salinas, Carlos, 194

Sánchez Pontón, Luis, 45

Santa Cruz, Hernán, 156, 162

Santiago conference. *See* Inter-American Conference (1923, Santiago, Chile)

Santiago Draft (IADB), 152

Saulsbury, Willard, Jr., 32

Scali, John, 186

Schwebel, Stephen, 181, 183, 185–86

Secretaría de Hacienda y Crédito Público, 7. *See also* Mexican Ministry of Finance

Secretaría de Relaciónes Exteriores (SRE): foreign ownership and, 109; ITO proposal and, 126, 128, 130; Mexican economic thought and, 7; Montevideo conference and, 45, 49; NIEO and, 178;

United Nations Conference on Trade and Employment (1947). *See* Havana Conference

United Nations Development Program (UNDP), 151

United Nations Relief and Rehabilitation Administration (UNRRA), 105

United States: abandonment of gold standard, 42; critique of SUNFED, 155–56; currency stabilization and, 43; ECLA and IA-ECOSOC merger proposal, 153; global economic governance and, 11, 86–87, 93, 101; gold parity value determination and, 92; importance of Latin America to, 99; import surcharges and, 160; influence on Latin American, 24, 33, 35, 37–38, 112–13; internationalism and, 32; Latin American contention, 11, 23; Latin American finance capital and, 46, 65, 67, 69, 75; Mexican finance capital and, 84; Mexican silver and, 44, 66, 84; multilateral liberalism and, 2, 31, 38; nonrecognition of Obregón government, 25–30, 212n43; Panama conference, 66; Pan-American Union governance and, 30–35; renouncement of military intervention, 56; rise to power, 3–4, 7, 99. *See also* Mexican-US relationship

Universidad Nacional Autónoma de México (UNAM), 62, 154, 169

UN Universal Declaration of Human Rights, 120, 171

Uribe Echeverri, Carlos, 34

Urquidi, Víctor: on balance of payment problems, 91; Bretton Woods Conference and, 88; British dismissal of, 80; ECLA and, 153–55; economic development and, 95–97, 158–59; on exports to the US, 222n41; sovereign equality and, 92, 94; stance on stabilization proposal, 85–87, 91; on US economic power, 93

Uruguay: Costa Rican proposal and, 34, 36; debt defaults and, 45; European trade and, 49, 63; Geneva meeting and, 131; IADB and, 152; international order and, 104, 108; ITO proposal and, 139; stabilization proposals and, 49–50

US hegemony: Bretton Woods Conference and, 79; consensus and, 4, 7; international political economy and, 4, 38; Mexican influence on, 195–97; multilateralism and, 4, 15, 112, 162, 196; relations with weaker states, 4, 31, 208n8; subordinate state struggles and, 7; Third World efforts against, 177–78

US-Mexico Claims Commission, 46

US State Department: Bretton Woods Conference and, 80; Chapultepec Conference and, 108, 110, 112; Charter of Economic Rights and Duties of States and, 181; Costa Rican proposal and, 32; Dumbarton Oaks conference and, 103; Ex-Im Bank and, 65; free trade promotion and, 114; Havana Conference and, 135; IAB and, 66–67, 74; IADC and, 102; ITO proposal and, 124; Mexican crisis and, 222n39; Mexican economy and, 70; Montevideo conference and, 47; multilateralism and, 25; nonrecognition of Obregón government, 40; petroleum nationalization and, 83; surplus capital and, 78; trade negotiations and, 133, 140

US Treasury Department: Bretton Woods Conference and, 79, 89; dismissal of Latin American officials, 3; ESF and, 82; IAB and, 58, 66–67, 69–70, 75, 78; IFEAC and, 223n54; Latin American support and, 93; Mexican/Brazilian support and, 89; Mexican crisis and, 66, 222n39; peso devaluation and, 157; stabilization proposals and, 83, 87–88; White and, 79–80, 82–83

Vanderlip, Frank A., 60

Velasco Alvarado, Juan, 161, 163

Venezuela: on ECOSOC, 107; on exclusion of small nations in UN planning, 104; foreign trade expansion and, 71; international currency clearinghouse proposal, 59; Pan-American governance proposal and, 29, 34–35

Villa, Pancho, 18

Villaseñor, Eduardo: Banco de México and, 65, 93; Guatemala conference and,

Founded in 1893,
UNIVERSITY OF CALIFORNIA PRESS
publishes bold, progressive books and journals
on topics in the arts, humanities, social sciences,
and natural sciences—with a focus on social
justice issues—that inspire thought and action
among readers worldwide.

The UC PRESS FOUNDATION
raises funds to uphold the press's vital role
as an independent, nonprofit publisher, and
receives philanthropic support from a wide
range of individuals and institutions—and from
committed readers like you. To learn more, visit
ucpress.edu/supportus.